Defrosting the Cold War and Beyond

This volume tells the story of the Helsinki Process from the immediate post-war period through the signing of the Helsinki Final Act in 1975 to the collapse of the Soviet empire and up to the present day. Treating it as a single narrative in the search for a just and stable order in Europe adds significantly to the copious but mostly narrowly focused academic literature on the subject.

Divided into 26 chapters, it can also serve as a handy reference book for different phases of the story. Chapter 22 examines the continuing debate over whether the West is responsible for the breakdown of relations with Russia and why the Helsinki Process failed to avert it. Chapter 26 asks whether the remarkable multilateral diplomacy that produced the Final Act could be replicated in other troubled areas today. It then offers 12 lessons that may be drawn from that experience.

Defrosting the Cold War and Beyond: An Introduction to the Helsinki Process, 1954–2022 will help students and others understand the long arc of the Helsinki Process, its place in European history and its continuing relevance today. Drawing on the first-hand experience of the author and other sources, the book corrects common errors and identifies some of the key people involved.

Richard Davy graduated in Modern History from Magdalen College, Oxford University. After teaching in Italy and training in Edinburgh, he worked for nearly 30 years on *The Times* (London) as a foreign correspondent in Germany, Washington and Eastern Europe, and as Chief Foreign Leader Writer specialising in East–West relations. He covered much of the Prague Spring of 1968 and the long negotiations that produced the Helsinki Final Act of 1975. Later he was a leader writer for *The Independent*, a guest scholar at the Woodrow Wilson Center, Washington DC, an Associate Fellow of the Royal Institute of International Affairs, and a Senior Member of St Antony's College, Oxford University.

Routledge Studies in Modern History

Christianity, the Sovereign Subject, and Ethnic Nationalism in Colonial Korea: Specters of Western Metaphysics
Hannah Amaris Roh

Missionaries and the Colonial State
Radicalism and Governance in Rwanda and Burundi, 1900–1972
David Whitehouse

Jewish Self-Defense in South America
Facing Anti-Semitism with a Club in Hand
Raanan Rein

Journalists and Knowledge Practices
Histories of Observing the Everyday in the Newspaper Age
Edited by Hansjakob Ziemer

Reenactment Case Studies
Global Perspectives on Experiential History
Edited by Vanessa Agnew, Sabine Stach, and Juliane Tomann

Defrosting the Cold War and Beyond
An Introduction to the Helsinki Process, 1954–2022
Richard Davy

Narratives of Dictatorship in the Age of Revolution
Emotions, Power and Legitimacy in the Atlantic Space
Moisés Prieto

Political Power and Colonial Development in British Central Africa 1938–1960s
Alan H. Cousins

For more information about this series, please visit: https://www.routledge.com/Routledge-Research-in-Modern-History/book-series/MODHIST

Defrosting the Cold War and Beyond

An Introduction to the Helsinki Process, 1954–2022

Richard Davy

Routledge
Taylor & Francis Group
LONDON AND NEW YORK

First published 2023
by Routledge
4 Park Square, Milton Park, Abingdon, Oxon OX14 4RN

and by Routledge
605 Third Avenue, New York, NY 10158

Routledge is an imprint of the Taylor & Francis Group, an informa business

British Library Cataloguing-in-Publication Data
A catalogue record for this book is available from the British Library

ISBN: 978-0-367-70403-2 (hbk)
ISBN: 978-0-367-70405-6 (pbk)
ISBN: 978-1-003-14612-4 (ebk)

DOI: 10.4324/9781003146124

Typeset in Times New Roman
by SPi Technologies India Pvt Ltd (Straive)

To all the brave people who fought for human rights under communism and those who carry on the struggle today wherever skies darken.

Contents

Acknowledgements

I owe thanks to many people. First, to Kai Hebel, who urged me to write this book for his students and then contributed perceptive comments while writing his own book on the British contribution to the CSCE.[1] Special thanks for invaluable help with later chapters to Katya Andrusz, Alexandra Taylor, Matt Preston and Marcin Walecki; to Sir Brian Fall and George Walden for particularly illuminating interviews; Roy Allison for advice and the loan of files; Thomas Marsden for valuable research and translations; Laurien Crump for a stimulating exchange on the expansion of NATO; Rowan Hart for access to her Master's thesis on Putin and the OSCE; Rob Langham of Routledge for taking on the book; Nick Brock and Fleming Ambrose for copy-editing; and very special thanks to Juliet Field for huge help along the way, great comments, keeping me organised, expert spotting of typing errors, faulty footnotes and unclear phrases, and for then taking on the added burden of compiling the index. Others who contributed valuable advice, comments, information or general support (in alphabetical order): Archie Brown, Norman Davies, Rahel Freist-Held, Timothy Garton Ash, Audrey Glover, Andrei Kovalev, Magda Leichtova, Steve Levine, Margaret MacMillan, Adam Roberts, Hannah Roberts, Olga Smirnova, and Christian Strohal. Needless to say, the errors are all mine. I am also indebted to St Antony's College, Oxford University, for many stimulating years as a Senior Member. Last but far from least, my wife Regine, a Berliner who experienced the Cold War up close, and without whose unending patience and encouragement I would probably not have stayed the course.

Oxford, February 2022.

Note

1 Hebel, *Fathers of the Final Act*. Abingdon: Routledge (forthcoming).

Preface

I had two reasons for writing this book. The first was to clear up some common misconceptions about the Helsinki Final Act of 1975.[1] When I returned to London from reporting on its signing I was convinced that it represented a considerable diplomatic success for the West. Although it contained compromises, it was strongly weighted in favour of promoting change in Europe's frozen confrontation. I was therefore surprised to find that many commentators, mainly but not only in the United States, depicted it as endorsing the division of Europe and thus betraying the "captive nations"[2] of Central and Eastern Europe under Soviet rule, a betrayal mitigated only by supposedly hollow promises on human rights. This false interpretation has persisted in some quarters.

I first wrote a corrective in Chatham House's *The World Today*.[3] I then edited and partly wrote a book on European détente for Chatham House in which I took the opportunity to include another corrective.[4] The book was published in 1992 and well reviewed by Michael Cox in *Cold War History*. For many years, it was on the reading list for Oxford students of International Relations, but it made no visible impact on interpretations of the Helsinki story in mainstream writings on the Cold War. Eventually I felt that something more had to be done so I collected plentiful examples of error and published a strongly argued paper in *Cold War History* (9/1 Feb. 2009). This was widely cited and began to make an impact.

I was then urged to follow up with a book, so I started rather slowly on this one. It was partly written when Michael Cotey Morgan's book *The Final Act* appeared. He had come to see me in Oxford, read my article in *Cold War History*, and done his own extremely extensive and impressive research to come up with a brilliant in-depth account of the Final Act that reached the right interpretation of that document. Obviously my book overlaps with Morgan's in the middle section but it covers a longer period and is pitched at a more basic level for newcomers to the subject. It occasionally diverges a little from Morgan. For instance, I think he slightly underplays the vital role of Europe in negotiating the Final Act and slightly exaggerates the document's contribution to ending the Cold War. He has, however, achieved an excellent combination of deep research, vivid description and good writing, so I have no hesitation in strongly recommending his book to anyone looking for a fuller, deeper and richly contextualised study of the creation of the Final Act. But start with this book, of course!

Feeling that my mission had been accomplished, albeit by someone else, I was tempted to put my own draft aside, but I was then advised by Kai Hebel of the University of Leiden, who has extensive university teaching experience, that there was still a need for a readable introduction to the whole Helsinki Process over a longer period.

This brings me to my second reason for writing this book. The Helsinki Process is mostly treated as distant history belonging in the Cold War and its immediate aftermath, yet the organ that grew out of it, the Organization for Security and Co-operation in Europe (OSCE), is still alive today and working hard among its 57 members to promote democracy, human rights, and other elements of cooperative security. Its work has become all the more important now that many of its members, including especially Russia, are rejecting its values and joining the wider trend against liberal democracy. Hence the need for this longer narrative that redefines the Helsinki Process as a continuous search for a just and stable in Europe running from the 1950s to the present day.

Chapter 22 steps slightly aside to look at the ongoing debate over whether an opportunity was missed at the end of the Cold War to create a pan-European security system that included Russia, thereby, it is often alleged, sowing the seeds of Vladimir Putin's growing hostility today.

Chapter 26 discusses whether, as is often suggested, the lessons of Helsinki could be applied to other trouble spots around the globe.

I have referred as far as possible to published sources in the English language and websites that are easy for newcomers and non-specialist readers to find. For this reason my footnotes sometimes cite "quoted in…" rather than the original source. And instead of directing readers to British archives, I refer to the much more accessible bound and edited volumes in the series *Documents on British Policy Overseas*. Readers who wish to dig deeper into primary sources will find plentiful references in the books listed in the bibliography and referred to in the text.

I have allowed repetitions because some issues crop up repeatedly in different contexts and readers may wish to dip into individual chapters rather than read the whole narrative.

Richard Davy
Oxford, February 2022

Notes

1 OSCE, 1 August 1975, *Helsinki Final Act*, viewed 8 February 2022, https://www.osce.org/helsinki-final-act

2 As they were frequently, and accurately, called in the United States.

3 'Helsinki Scoreboard', *The World Today*, 32/8, 1 August 1976, pp. 279–281 published by the Royal Institute of International Affairs, London. Or https://www.jstor.org/stable/40394935, viewed 21 March 2022.

4 Davy, ed., *European Détente: a Reappraisal*. London: Sage Publications for the Royal Institute of International Affairs, 1992. Reprint 2014 by Fast-Print Publishing of Peterborough, England.

Abbreviations

ABM Treaty	Anti-Ballistic Missile treaty
CBMs	Confidence-Building Measures
CFE	Conventional Forces in Europe (treaty)
CiO	Chairman/Chairperson-in-Office
CIS	Commonwealth of Independent States
CSBMs	Confidence- and Security- Building Measures
CSCE	Conference on Security and Co-operation in Europe
CSTO	Collective Security Treaty Organization
EAEU	Eurasian Economic Union
ECE	Economic Commission for Europe
EDC	European Defence Community
HDIM	Human Dimension Implementation Meetings
IFOR	Implementation Force [of NATO]
INF	Intermediate-Range Nuclear Forces Treaty
MAD	Mutual Assured Destruction
MBFR	Mutual and Balanced Forces Reduction
MLF	Multilateral [Nuclear] Force
NATO	North Atlantic Treaty Organization
NNA	Neutrals and Non-Aligned [Countries]
NPT	[Nuclear] Non-Proliferation Treaty
ODIHR	Office for Democratic Institutions and Human Rights
OSCE	Organization for Security and Co-operation in Europe
PfP	Partnership for Peace
SALT	Strategic Arms Limitation Talks
SHDM	Supplementary Human Dimension Meeting
SMM	Special Monitoring Mission
SORT	Strategic Offensive Reductions Treaty

Introduction

What is the Helsinki Process?

In the high summer of 1975 an extraordinary event took place in Helsinki. The background did not look favourable. The Cold War still cast its pall over much of the world as communism and capitalism struggled for supremacy. Europe was still divided by an "Iron Curtain" of barbed wire and minefields which also divided Germany. Eastern Europe[1] still chafed under the rule of the Soviet Union. Across the city of Berlin ran a huge concrete wall guarded by East Germans with orders to kill their own people trying to escape. East and west of the border massive military forces confronted each other, backed by more than enough nuclear weapons to destroy life on Earth. Despite some progress towards détente the gulf between East and West remained deep and seemed likely to last.

Yet in Helsinki that summer leaders from both sides in the Cold War plus neutrals and non-aligned gathered for several days in the Finnish capital's spectacular Finlandia Hall. President Gerald Ford came from the United States, communist leader Leonid Brezhnev from the Soviet Union, and Prime Minister Pierre Trudeau from Canada. Joining them were heads of state or government or senior figures from all the states of East and West Europe except Albania. Among them were Chancellor Helmut Schmidt of West Germany, Communist leader Erich Honecker of East Germany, President Valéry Giscard d'Estaing of France, and Prime Minister Harold Wilson of Britain. Altogether 35 states were represented, including the tiniest: Monaco, Liechtenstein, San Marino and the Vatican.

After delivering lengthy speeches these leaders signed a very long and complex document which had cost their officials nearly three years of arduous negotiation. The document is called the Final Act of the Conference on Security and Co-operation in Europe (CSCE).

Very few people read the Helsinki Final Act at the time, and still fewer understood it or foresaw its long-term significance. Even now it is frequently misunderstood. Reactions at the time ranged across the spectrum. The Soviet Union hailed it as a triumph for Soviet diplomacy that would finally bring peace to Europe by endorsing the division of the continent. Some misguided people on both sides thought it ended the Cold War. More vocal were many angry critics in the West who alleged that it legitimized Soviet rule over the unhappy peoples of Eastern Europe and the Baltic states, thereby freezing in

DOI: 10.4324/9781003146124-1

place the unjust results of World War II. What, asked these critics, had we got in return? Just a lot of empty promises on human rights and freer movement that no one would take seriously.

The Russians were wrong, and so were the Western critics, most of whom later recanted. The Final Act did not endorse the division of Europe. On the contrary, although it was carefully balanced to acknowledge existing realities, it was essentially an agenda for change, a subversive document that had a profound impact on European history up to the end of the Cold War and beyond to the present day. Its texts on human rights were grasped eagerly by courageous individuals in Russia and Eastern Europe who challenged their governments to live up to the obligations contained in the document. Networks of activists spread across the continent and assembled vast dossiers on abuses of human rights in the Soviet sphere. Western governments and NGOs, mostly surprised by what they had unleashed, then presented this information at the stormy follow-up meetings to which they had agreed at Helsinki.

They could do this because the Final Act established the important principle that peace and security depend not just on relations between states but also on how governments treat their people. The signatories had therefore given themselves a licence to scrutinize each other's internal affairs and place them on the diplomatic agenda. This explicit link between security and respect for human rights was a new departure in international relations, introducing the concept of "human security".

The Final Act thus fostered the growth of civil societies behind the Iron Curtain, weakened the communist regimes of Eastern Europe, helped to enlighten Western opinion on the realities of life under communism, and eventually provided a framework of norms and institutions that Soviet leader Mikhail Gorbachev could invoke as he brought the Cold War to a largely peaceful end. In addition, by specifically allowing for the peaceful change of frontiers it kept open a door to the reunification of Germany 15 years later. That clause was strongly resisted by the East German regime, which rightly saw in it the prospect of its own political demise.

Nor was that the end of the story. Today the permanent body that eventually grew out of the Helsinki conference, the Organization for Security and Co-operation in Europe (OSCE), is still at work among its 57 members monitoring conflicts, observing elections and promoting democracy and human rights. Its critical reports on elections have contributed to toppling some governments and improving others. Its monitoring teams have shown great courage in areas of conflict such as eastern Ukraine. Its field missions in many countries work tirelessly to fulfil its mandates. Its work deserves more attention than it normally gets, especially now that some members have been retreating from the values to which they signed up at Helsinki and at subsequent meetings.

Note

1 Eastern Europe was a political not a geographical term in the Cold War, denoting the European countries under Soviet control.

Part I

Origins

1 Where did it come from?

The long trajectory of the Helsinki Process started amid the ruins of Europe after World War II. The continent was left divided between the communist east and the capitalist west. The division split Germany and the city of Berlin and allowed massive military forces to build up on each side. It was a situation that neither side could accept as safe or permanent but neither could change without war. Or so it seemed until the Helsinki Process came into view offering the possibility of peaceful change.

Europe had been devastated by war. By the time the fighting stopped in 1945 more than 36 million Europeans had died of war-related causes. Millions more were homeless; refugees were flooding in all directions; towns and cities had been flattened, roads and railways destroyed, and industry and agriculture severely damaged over a vast area from France to Russia.[1]

The Soviet Union had acquired a new empire stretching into the heart of Europe, giving it control of eastern Germany, Poland, Czechoslovakia, Hungary, Bulgaria and Romania. This area came to be known in the Cold War as Eastern Europe, although much it was in Central Europe. The Soviet Union had also regained control of the Baltic states: Latvia, Estonia and Lithuania. They had been absorbed by the Soviet Union in 1940, then occupied by the Nazis, then reclaimed by the Soviet Union during the war, in each case amid extreme suffering and many killings. Meanwhile Yugoslavia and Albania were taken over by their own communists with help from Britain; they then joined the Soviet bloc until Yugoslavia broke away in 1948 and Albania in 1956.

In February 1945, as the end of the war approached, the three wartime leaders who had been allies against Hitler met in Yalta on the Black Sea to decide on the fate of Europe. They were Soviet leader Josef Stalin, US President Franklin D. Roosevelt, and British Prime Minister Winston Churchill. The Yalta agreement is often reviled as the moment when the great powers divided Europe between themselves, but by that time Stalin's troops had already taken Poland and were deep into Germany, so Roosevelt and Churchill had limited choices. In effect they had to agree to the division of Europe roughly as defined by troops on the ground. An exception was Prague, which had not yet been liberated from the Nazis. When the Czechs rose up on 5 May, General Eisenhower's American forces had already crossed the

DOI: 10.4324/9781003146124-3

frontier and could have advanced to Prague to support the uprising. Churchill wrote to Eisenhower strongly urging him to move, foreseeing that otherwise Czechoslovakia would be taken into the Soviet orbit. Yet Eisenhower held back in order not to provoke Stalin, whose support he needed in the continuing war against Japan. The result was as Churchill had predicted: Czechoslovakia remained under Soviet control until 1989.

The fate of Poland was especially bitter because Britain had originally gone to war in response to Hitler's attack on Poland, and many Poles had fought bravely with the British. Now they were being delivered to communism, much against their will. Churchill remarked sadly to his secretary before going to Yalta "There is nothing I can do for Poland".[2]

Churchill was vigorously attacked at home but he saw no alternative since war against the Soviet Union was out of the question. He and President Roosevelt tried to mitigate their surrender of Poland and Eastern Europe by persuading Stalin to sign the "Declaration on Liberated Europe", which included a promise of free elections. When Vyacheslav Molotov, Stalin's Foreign Minister (see Chapter 2), queried this, Stalin replied "Do not worry. We will implement it in our own way later. The essence is in the correlation of forces".[3] He was right, and showed it by luring to Moscow 16 generals and democratic party leaders of the Polish underground, a branch of the exiled Polish government in London, which was Britain's formal ally. They were given written promises of safe conduct by a Soviet general, ostensibly to discuss forming a new provisional Polish government, but were then ambushed, kidnapped, tortured, put on trial and sentenced to prison, where one of them died. Unusually for that time, they were not sentenced to death, which may have had something to do with their being allies of Britain. The show trial—a travesty of justice—was watched by George Bolsover, then a British diplomat and later the Director of the School of Slavonic and East European Studies in London.

Then Stalin moved quickly to control his new empire. He had no plan except to ensure that Germany and Eastern Europe would never again pose a threat to the Soviet Union, and in particular that Poland would never again provide a transit route for German armies attacking the Soviet Union. Initially, he allowed some semblance of democracy in order to reassure his Western allies, from whom he still hoped to get help in rebuilding the Soviet Union and controlling Germany, but he was always determined to ensure that he remained in control. Thus, in the wake of Soviet troops came commissars and secret police whose job it was to consolidate Soviet control over Eastern Europe by the same ruthless methods that had been used to quell opposition in the Soviet Union after the revolution of 1917: a ubiquitous police presence, the destruction or infiltration of political parties, and eventually show trials, prison sentences, executions and the use or threat of Soviet tanks.[4] As he told the Yugoslav communist Milovan Djilas: "Everyone imposes his own system as far as his arm can reach. It cannot be otherwise".[5] Winston Churchill summed up the European situation in his famous speech in Fulton, Missouri, in 1946: "From Stettin in the Baltic to Trieste in the Adriatic, an iron curtain has descended across the continent".[6]

Germany remained a central issue throughout the Cold War up to and beyond the Helsinki talks. At first it was divided into occupation zones by the victorious forces, then into two states. No peace treaty could be signed because there was no all-German government with which to sign it and no agreement among the victorious allies on what its status should be. The German problem proved so intractable that a peace treaty was not signed until the country was reunited in 1990. In the meantime, a series of temporary arrangements gradually froze the division of Germany and Europe into seeming permanence. None provided the basis for a just and lasting peace. The Helsinki Process was part of the search for that elusive goal.

In July 1945, after Germany had surrendered, the wartime leaders met again, this time in Potsdam, just outside Berlin. By the end of the talks Stalin was the only one of the leaders who had also been at Yalta. Roosevelt had died and been replaced by Harry Truman, while Churchill departed in the midst of the talks to be replaced by Clement Attlee, the Labour politician who had won Britain's first post-war election, mystifying the Russians, who could not understand how such a great war leader could be rejected by his people.

At Potsdam, these leaders agreed on the "reduction or destruction of all [German] civilian heavy industry with war potential, such as ship building, machine production and chemical factories". Ten per cent of capacity in the Western zones judged "unnecessary for the German peace economy" was to be transferred to the Soviet Union within two years. The aim was to render Germany unable to rise again as a military power, reducing its economy to one of agriculture and light industry.[7]

In Washington this policy was promoted by Henry Morgenthau, an old friend of Roosevelt, who had appointed him Treasury Secretary although he had no background in economics. The "Morgenthau Plan" became official policy after Potsdam but was soon abandoned as it became obvious to the British and Americans that it was hugely costly and made no economic sense. Britain, for instance, was paying $80m a year to feed the starving Germans while extracting only $29m in reparations.[8]

Thus the tide turned fairly quickly in Washington. One adviser described the Morgenthau plan as "assembled by economic idiots".[9] Truman called Morgenthau a "blockhead"[10]and sacked him in July 1945, turning instead to saner heads in the State Department who could see that trying to "pastoralize" Germany would delay the recovery of Europe and encourage communists or fascists or both to exploit the unrest that was growing throughout the continent. Churchill described Europe in that period as "a rubble heap, a charnel house, a breeding ground of pestilence and hate".[11] John McCloy, US Assistant Secretary for War, reported after a trip to Europe in April 1945: "There is complete economic, social and political collapse going on in Central Europe, the extent of which is unparalleled in history."[12] Dean Acheson, then Undersecretary of State, told a Senate Committee that the situation in Europe "threatens the very foundations, the whole fabric of world organizations".[13]

Communist parties were growing throughout Europe because of disillusion with capitalism and admiration for the Soviet Union for its victory in the war. (At that time little was known in the West about the horrors of Stalin's rule.) In France, Italy and Finland communists were getting 20 per cent of the vote.[14] In Germany, communism had been imposed on the Soviet zone while fascism was far from dead throughout the whole of Germany. Washington feared that in this unstable situation Stalin would be able to take over Western Europe without firing a single shot. Then the whole productive potential of Western Europe would fall into his hands. At the same time pressure was growing in the United States to "bring the boys home", so it was assumed (wrongly, as it turned out) that Western Europe might soon need to stand on its own feet.

Against the objections of France and the Soviet Union, both of which had been invaded by Germany and therefore had particularly good reason to fear a German revival, the Americans and British decided that Europe must be helped. They saw that this could be achieved only by harnessing the huge industrial potential of Germany, particularly in coal, steel and machine-building. Stalin resisted these plans because he was obsessed by the suspicion that the Western allies would rearm Germany and help it to launch another attack on the Soviet Union.[15] His suspicions were completely baseless. The Western allies were as worried as he was about the potential threat from a resurgent Germany, but they believed that a weak and resentful Germany in a ravaged Europe would pose a greater danger than a restored Germany under Allied control. They recalled how Hitler had exploited German resentment against the harsh terms of the Versailles Treaty at the end of World War I.[16] They were also coming to realize that they needed West Germany as an ally in the looming confrontation with Stalin. France wavered but eventually went along with this policy.

In March 1947, after a particularly harsh winter in Europe, George Marshall, the American Secretary of State, travelled to Moscow to talk, first with Molotov and then with Stalin. They disagreed over the issue of reparations, each accusing the other (correctly) of reneging on the Potsdam agreement. Stalin had not sent the food and other goods westwards that were promised at Potsdam, and General Lucius Clay, the forceful US deputy military governor in Germany, had taken his own decision the previous year to stop dismantling German factories and to ban further reparations to Russia from the American zone. Stalin told Marshall that reparations were right and necessary, explaining that he had "no pity, sympathy or love" for the Germans. This was hardly surprising in view of what Germany had done to Russia (see Chapter 3), but it did not make for rational policies.[17]

Marshall did his best to find common ground but after six weeks of fruitless negotiation, first with Molotov and then with Stalin, he returned to Washington convinced that Stalin was waiting for conditions in Europe to worsen in the hope of exploiting the chaos. The Soviet Union was "doing everything possible to achieve a complete breakdown in Europe", he told an interviewer.[18] Stalin's aim was in fact to take over the whole of Germany in order to prevent further attacks on the Soviet Union. The first stage would be to consolidate his hold over his zone of occupation (later to become East Germany) and then to enlist the support of public opinion and left-wing forces in the West for a united neutral Germany that would in fact come under his control.[19] "All of Germany must be ours, that is, Soviet, communist", he had told Bulgarian and Yugoslav leaders in 1946.[20]

Marshall felt there was no time to waste, so he ordered his staff to prepare a plan for European recovery. This became the Marshall Plan, approved by Congress in 1948. It was a hugely imaginative project to lift impoverished Europe out of the ruins of the war with a big infusion of aid to be administered largely by the Europeans themselves but subject to US conditions. In order to avoid presenting the plan as anti-Soviet, Marshall offered it to the whole of Europe and the Soviet Union, explaining that its aim was solely to combat "hunger, poverty, desperation and chaos". He knew that Stalin would refuse because it would have meant opening Eastern Europe to Western market economies and foreign investment, in effect to capitalism.

Stalin at first thought he might get American aid without these conditions. In June 1947 he sent Molotov to Paris with an 89-strong delegation to join talks on the Marshall Plan. He also encouraged his new subject governments in Eastern Europe to participate. They agreed as they were all eager to get their hands on American money. However, Stalin's suspicions of American intentions were confirmed when he received information from a British diplomat in Washington, Donald Maclean, who was spying for the Soviet Union, to the effect that the Marshall Plan was intended to ensure American economic domination of Europe.[21] Stalin immediately cabled Molotov in Paris, who suddenly hardened his position and eventually withdrew his delegation from the talks. The East Europeans then reluctantly stayed away, though Czechoslovakia at first refused. However, Stalin angrily summoned a Czech delegation that happened to be in Moscow and told them firmly that participation in the Marshall Plan would endanger Czechoslovakia's political and economic sovereignty. That was a bit rich as he himself was busy destroying that sovereignty. The Czechs argued in vain. What Stalin meant, of course, was that participation in the scheme would challenge Soviet control of Eastern Europe. Thus he condemned Eastern Europe to years of backwardness while Western Europe forged ahead.

The Czechs were particularly devastated as they were very dependent on western trade. Jan Masaryk, their Foreign Minister, said afterwards: "I went to Moscow as the foreign minister of an independent sovereign state. I returned as a lackey of the Soviet Government".[22] On 10 March 1948 he jumped or was pushed to his death from a window of his ministry. The government announced that he had committed suicide, whereas most ordinary Czechs believe he was murdered. In 2004 Czech police agreed, but no conclusive evidence emerged.

The Marshall Plan was a great success in terms of reviving Western Europe, but it sealed the division of the continent. Stalin now decided that the potential for cooperation was finally at an end. He tightened his grip on Eastern

Europe and blockaded Berlin (see below). Some later commentators[23] have blamed the Marshall Plan for dividing Europe and helping to start the Cold War, but the conflict was already well under way by 1948, and the alternative would have been to leave western Germany festering in ruins, delaying its recovery and that of the rest of Europe. The argument that Europe would have recovered anyway[24] is contested by Benn Steil in his definitive book on the Marshall Plan, which also examines the debate over responsibility for starting the Cold War.[25]

As the Marshall Plan got under way, the British and Americans merged their zones of occupation, later carving out a small zone for a grumbling and very obstructive France, which had been defeated by the Nazis but was now included among the victors. In 1948, the three countries introduced into their zones a new currency, the Deutschmark, to end rampant inflation and corruption. That was the beginning of West Germany's rapid rise to prosperity that became known as the "economic miracle".

In 1949 the division of Germany was confirmed when the occupation zones on both sides were transformed into two separate states. The Soviet zone became communist East Germany, officially calling itself the German Democratic Republic (GDR), although in reality the regime was far from democratic. The West Germans called it the "Soviet zone" or the "so-called GDR" and successfully pressed their allies to refuse recognition for many years. The American, British and French zones became West Germany, a truly democratic state officially known as the Federal Republic of Germany. In both states, the occupying forces retained some rights and were legally responsible for the future of the whole country pending a peace treaty.

The Polish frontier

A particularly contentious issue that became central to the Helsinki talks was the new shape of Poland demanded by Stalin and provisionally accepted by the Western leaders at Yalta and later at Potsdam. They had agreed that Poland would be shifted about 200 miles to the west, acquiring 40,000 square miles of German territory and a new western frontier on the Oder–Neisse line. At the same time it would cede about 69,000 square miles of its eastern territories to the Soviet Union. As a result, Germany lost about a quarter of its former territory.

The leaders also agreed to massive transfers of populations, which today would be called ethnic cleansing. About 7 million ethnic Germans were driven out of the new Poland, about 2 million from Czechoslovakia and 3 million from other areas. The leaders stipulated that these moves should be conducted "in an orderly and humane manner", but they were not. Nearly half a million died and millions suffered in very brutal expulsions.

For many people these expulsions were just retribution for the deportations and devastation that the Nazis had inflicted on Europe, and on Poland in particular, but they left a running sore in West Germany's relations with its eastern neighbours. The 12 million or so ethnic Germans from the east who found themselves in the fragile new state of West Germany formed a powerful political lobby. They argued that technically Poland's new western territories were only "under Polish administration" pending a peace treaty, so they remained legally German and should therefore be restored in any final settlement, or at any rate held as a bargaining chip for the eventual reunification of Germany. In reality, the area was quickly integrated into Poland and re-populated, mostly by Poles displaced from the former eastern territories.

Defying this reality, many expellees in Germany nurtured fantasies of returning. Their claims stoked Polish fears, vigorously encouraged by the Soviet Union, that Germany would one day try to reclaim these lost lands. Poland's unpopular communist government maintained a steady drumbeat of anti-German propaganda in order to justify remaining under the protection of the Soviet Union. Not until Willy Brandt came to power in West Germany in 1969 (see Chapter 9) and accepted the new frontiers, which were then endorsed at Helsinki, was the threat largely removed. Brandt had thus taken away one of the essential props of the Polish regime. After that, Poles could legitimately ask why they should remain in the Soviet orbit, so they became more restless than ever.

Berlin

Another hot issue in the run-up to Helsinki, and also at the conference itself, was the status of divided Berlin, where the Western allies maintained in their sector a shiny island of capitalism in the midst of the drab GDR, supported by vulnerable road, rail and air links to West Germany. Only after the Quadripartite Agreement on the status of Berlin in 1971 could the Helsinki talks get under way, and even then Berlin remained a sticky issue, resolved only at nearly the last minute before the summit in 1975 (see Chapter 13 part I).

West Berlin was an embarrassment to the Russians and bitterly resented by the East German regime because it showed up the relative backwardness of their state. In military terms, West Berlin was indefensible. It was in the middle of East Germany, surrounded by 22 divisions of the Soviet Union's finest forces. Fortunately, no Soviet leader dared attack it for fear of sparking a nuclear war. In fact, if a third world war had broken out Berlin would probably have provided the spark, so delicate was its situation. Daniel Ellsberg quotes a cynical Pentagon colleague on US plans for meeting a Soviet attack on West Berlin: "We send in a series of increasingly larger probes. If they're all stopped, we fire a [nuclear] warning shot. If that doesn't work, we blow up the world".[26]

In June 1948 Stalin blockaded land routes to West Berlin in the hope of cutting its links with the West, but the Allies mounted an astonishing airlift to supply the city of more than two million people with food and fuel for more than a year,[27] transforming the West Berliners from defeated enemies into staunch allies of the West, grateful for protection. Stalin gave way in the end but friction continued until the 1971 agreement. In the meantime, in 1961 the East German regime had built a wall across the city to staunch the ever-growing exodus of their citizens. By that time about 3.5 million East Germans had fled to the West, so a wall had come to be a condition of survival for the deeply unpopular regime.

It was against this background of rising tension and fears of a resurgent Germany that the Soviet Union launched its campaign for a European security conference, leading eventually to Helsinki.

Notes

1 For graphic descriptions of post-war Europe see Tony Judt's epic work *Postwar* and Benn Steil's *The Marshall Plan: Dawn of the Cold War*.
2 Sir John Colville *Diaries* quoted by Martin Walker in *The Cold War*.
3 Quoted from Feliks Chuev, *Molotov remembers*, in different translations by, among others, Dobbs *Six Months in 1945*, 87, and Steil *The Marshall Plan*, 4.
4 See Applebaum, *Iron Curtain*.
5 Djilas, *Conversations with Stalin*, 114.
6 W. S. Churchill, 5 March1945, *Speech at Westminster College, Fulton, MO*, International Churchill Society, viewed 9 January 2022, https://winstonchurchill.org/resources/speeches/1946-1963-elder-statesman/the-sinews-of-peace/
7 Wikipedia, 2022, *The Potsdam Conference*, viewed 9 January 2022, https://en.wikipedia.org/wiki/Potsdam_Conference
8 Judt, *Postwar*, 123.
9 Lewis Douglas quoted in Steil, 90.
10 Steil, 9.
11 Steil, 15.
12 Leffler, *For the Soul of Mankind*, 58.
13 Leffler, 58.
14 Leffler, 59.
15 Zubok and Pleshakov, *Inside the Kremlin's Cold War*, 47–8.
16 Actually few reparations were paid, and Margaret MacMillan largely absolves the Versailles Treaty of responsibility for Hitler in *The War that Ended Peace*. See also Clay in Hanhimäki and Westad, *The Cold War*, 90.
17 Steil, 77.
18 Steil, 83.
19 Gaddis, *We Now Know*, 116, drawing on archival and other sources.
20 Djilas, 153.
21 Steil, 127.
22 Steil, 143.
23 Michael Cox and Caroline Kennedy-Pipe. 'The Tragedy of American Diplomacy? Rethinking the Marshall Plan', *Journal of Cold War Studies* 7/1, (Winter 2005), 97–134.
24 Notably in Alan Milward, *The Reconstruction of Western Europe 1945–1951*. London: Methuen, 1984.
25 See Note 1.
26 Daniel Ellsberg, *The Doomsday Machine*, 157.
27 The blockade lasted from 24 June 1948 to 12 May 1949 but the airlift was maintained until 30 September that year in case the blockade was reimposed.

2 Who started it?

Vyacheslav Molotov was an unlikely peacemaker. He was a dedicated Bolshevik who played a leading role in the Russian revolution of 1917. A brutal colleague of the Soviet leader Josef Stalin, he was instrumental in causing millions to starve to death during the forced collectivisation of agriculture in the Soviet Union. He survived the Great Terror of 1937–8 by helping Stalin direct it and signing countless death warrants with his own hand, sometimes adding "Give the dog a dog's death". Together, he and Stalin ordered nearly 40,000 people to be shot.[1] His signature was also on the 1939 pact with Hitler and on the infamous order to massacre 22,000 Polish officers in Katyn forest and other sites in 1940.[2] He remained unrepentant until his death in 1986. Winston Churchill said he resembled a robot, but was impressed by his diplomatic skills. John Foster Dulles, US Secretary of State, described him as "one of the shrewdest and wiliest diplomats of this century, or, indeed, of any century".[3] Kathleen Harriman, daughter of the US ambassador to Moscow, wrote that he had "a hellova sense of humor and nice twinkling eyes".[4]

Despite his appalling record, Molotov is generally credited with launching the Helsinki Process on its long and winding journey to the summit of 1975, and then beyond to an unexpected destination. This was not because he had undergone some kind of conversion. On the contrary, his beliefs and aims remained wholly consistent. He and Stalin were concerned above all else with the security of the Soviet Union, so they wanted a European settlement that would consolidate their country's wartime gains in Eastern Europe, neutralise Germany, and drive the Americans out of Europe. Neither they nor their successors achieved any of these aims. Instead, the Helsinki Process took Europe in the opposite direction, committing the Americans to Europe, weakening the Soviet hold over Eastern Europe, and eventually contributing to the mostly peaceful dissolution of the Soviet empire. That is the central paradox of the story.

Stalin sacked Molotov as Foreign Minister in 1949, having arrested his wife the previous year. Yet Molotov remained in the Politburo responsible for foreign affairs. After Stalin died in 1953 Molotov was reinstated as Foreign Minister and reunited with his wife, to whom he had been writing passionate love letters.[5]

DOI: 10.4324/9781003146124-4

In January 1954 he came to Berlin with a large delegation to attend a conference of foreign ministers of the Four Powers responsible for the future of defeated Germany. Joining him around the table were John Foster Dulles from the United States, Anthony Eden from Britain and Georges Bidault from France. There followed more than three weeks of negotiations that failed to decide on the future of Germany. In the course of the talks, Molotov proposed a European security conference intended to contain a neutral and disarmed Germany within a wider security system. His proposal remained on the table, changing shape as the years went by until—by then almost unrecognisable—it gave birth to the 35-nation Helsinki Conference of 1975. Even after that, Russia continued to press for a pan-European security structure that would give it a controlling voice in European security affairs (see Chapter 23). That thread runs right through the Helsinki Process.

Molotov's plan was not entirely new. Two years earlier, Stalin had sent the Western allies diplomatic Notes, drafted largely by Molotov from his position in the Politburo, also proposing a neutral united Germany from which occupation forces would withdraw.[6]

Much scholarly time has been devoted to debating whether the Western powers missed opportunities in this period for a European settlement around a united neutral Germany in cooperation with the Soviet Union, thereby avoiding the Cold War in Europe. That debate is beyond the scope of this book. In the opinion of this author, no such chance was missed because it would have been impossible at that time to bridge the gulf between the aims of the two sides. Apart from the fact that Stalin was not a person with whom genuine cooperation was possible over a longer term, his desire for a subjugated, de-industrialised, neutralised Germany was incompatible with the American and British view that the revival of West German industry was essential for the recovery of a devastated Europe.[7]

As a marginal comment on a complex debate, it is doubtful whether Stalin even wanted or expected his Notes to be accepted. Before sending the first one in March 1952 he sought assurance that it would be rejected from one of his top experts on Germany, Vladimir Semyonov.[8] It is likely that his main aim was to influence the West German election, due the following year, by tempting West German voters with the prospect of reuniting their country if they replaced Dr Adenauer's Christian Democrat government with a government of Social Democrats, who at that time were leaning towards neutrality. In April 1952, just after sending his Notes, he told a delegation of East German leaders: "Whatever proposals we make on the German question the Western powers won't agree with them and they won't withdraw from West Germany. To think that the Americans will compromise or accept the draft peace treaty would be a mistake.... They will draw West Germany into the Atlantic Pact".[9] And so they did.

This was consistent with the change in Stalin's earlier view. In 1946, according to Milovan Djilas, a leading Yugoslav communist until he broke with the regime, Stalin, buoyed by his success in the war, told a delegation of Bulgarians and Yugoslavs that "all of Germany must be ours, that is Soviet, Communist".[10]

He had been encouraged in these hopes by President Roosevelt, who had told him at the Tehran Conference in 1943 that US forces would withdraw from Europe within two years of the end of the war. By 1948 the Cold War had set in and President Truman had become determined to keep troops in Europe, so Stalin, ever the realist, became resigned to the continuing division of Germany. He told another Yugoslav/Bulgarian delegation, as he had told the East Germans, that "The West will make Western Germany their own, and we shall turn Eastern Germany into our own state".[11] Yet the Soviet Union continued for years to hope that European public opinion and isolationist pressures in the United States would eventually drive the Americans back across the Atlantic, meaning that the idea of a neutral Germany did not entirely disappear from the Soviet agenda until Mikhail Gorbachev became Soviet leader in 1985.[12]

When Molotov came to Berlin in 1954 with his proposal for a security conference, West Germany, still under the leadership of Dr Adenauer, was about to rearm and join an integrated European Defence Community (EDC). What actually happened was that the French Assembly refused to ratify the EDC, so the following year West Germany joined the North Atlantic Treaty Organization (NATO). That is what Stalin had been working to stop, and what Molotov was still trying to prevent when he presented the three other foreign ministers in Berlin with a "Draft General European Treaty on Collective Security in Europe". This was to be open to all European states including both German states until the establishment of a "united, pacific, democratic German State". Signatories would "undertake not to enter any coalition or alliance… which would contradict the purposes of the treaty". In other words, there was to be no West German membership of either the EDC or NATO.

Occupation forces would be withdrawn simultaneously from both parts of Germany, leaving only limited contingents to perform "protective functions", but they would have the right to move in their forces if there were a threat to the security of either part of Germany. A "permanent consultative political committee" and a "military consultative body" would be set up, to which the United States and China would be invited merely as observers, leaving the Soviet Union in a dominant position on the continent with a right to intervene in Germany. The declared aim would be to "assure the neutralisation of Germany". In order to achieve this the four powers were to take urgent steps to conclude the draft treaty presented by Molotov and "take the initiative of convening an appropriate conference of European States".[13]

This, then, was the first specific call for a European security conference. When it became clear that the United States was to be excluded from Molotov's collective security organisation and granted only observer status along with China, "We all laughed out loud", reported an American participant, "and the Russians were taken completely by surprise at our reaction. Molotov did a double take and finally managed a smile, but the Russian momentum was gone".[14]

Molotov's surprise was surprising because he was normally very well informed. Maybe it was just the laughter that surprised him. In any case,

Dulles dismissed Molotov's plan as "preposterous" and later told the American public that the Soviet aim was a communist-controlled Germany and a Soviet-controlled Europe from which the United States would be excluded, which was just about right.[15] Clearly the United States was not going to leave the Soviet Union with a huge strategic advantage in Europe. Nor was it going to be excluded from any new security arrangements. As for the idea of a united neutral Germany, this was much discussed in London and Washington[16] but eventually ruled out as too risky because it would leave a power vacuum in the middle of Europe that the Russians would quickly attempt to fill by the same ruthless methods they had employed to take control of Eastern Europe. As General Clay put it, responding to George Kennan, who had come round to proposing German neutrality: "The Russians would cheat, the French would panic, and the Germans would go communist, militarist or both".[17]

Rebuffed in Berlin, Molotov returned to Moscow, where a modified proposal was drawn up allowing the United States to participate in a system of pan-European collective security. Behind the scenes, Molotov envisaged that American participation would be temporary until the conclusion of a peace treaty, but he advised that this should not be stated openly because it would harm the struggle against the EDC.[18]

Reporting to his colleagues, he presented a very gloomy picture. He poured scorn on Western demands for free elections in Germany, pointing out that Hitler had come to power initially through free elections. The Americans, he said, were seeking greater power in Europe even though it meant restoring German militarism and "Hitlerism". A new West German army would have Hitlerite generals at its head (which turned out to be true) and would be aggressively revanchist (which turned out to be untrue). There was no doubt, he said, that Washington and Bonn (then the capital of West Germany) were preparing a new war. "It can mean nothing else".[19]

He was quite wrong. Nobody wanted war (see Chapter 3). The reality was that both sides feared a resurgent Germany, but they sought different solutions to the problem. As we have seen above, Stalin at first hoped that a neutral Germany would give him security because he thought he could control it in the same way as he controlled his new empire in Eastern Europe. Later, he accepted the reality of a divided Germany for the time being.

The Western answer to fears of a resurgent Germany was to draw West Germany into the warm but firm embrace of Western institutions, including NATO. Once safely bound into that organisation, West Germany would not be able to act independently. Hence the famous remark by Lord Ismay, first Secretary-General of NATO, that the purpose of the alliance was "to keep the Russians out, the Americans in and the Germans down".[20] Actually this was slightly misleading. The real aim was to build Germany up as a prosperous, peace-loving democracy, an aim that was eventually achieved beyond most expectations. The Russians could never bring themselves to believe that NATO was a defensive alliance designed in part to keep Germany from developing its own independent defence capability, even though their spies supplied them with copious inside information to that effect. That rooted belief in NATO as a threat to Russia persisted even after NATO changed its posture and greatly reduced its forces at the end of the Cold War (see Chapter 22). It has continued up to the present day, carefully nurtured and exploited by Russia's leader, Vladimir Putin.

After the fruitless conference of foreign ministers in Berlin the further response of the three Western powers to Molotov provided early insight into what would be a principal item on the Western agenda for the Helsinki talks twenty years later. At the Geneva summit in July1955 they put forward an item calling for "the development of human contacts between East and West". Subsequently, when their foreign ministers met in Geneva in October, they tabled a proposal with 17 items on the "freer exchange of information and ideas".[21] This was very close to the eventual wording of the Helsinki Final Act except that the Soviet Union refused to include in that document any reference to ideas, a curious position for a state that claimed to represent the greatest idea in human history, but revealing its deep insecurity in the face of Western influence (see Chapter 11).

Molotov's reply also remained the standard Soviet response for twenty years. He demanded respect for "sovereign rights and non-interference in internal affairs".[22] This demand was endlessly repeated throughout the Helsinki talks by Soviet negotiators, who tried in vain to insert it into the Helsinki Final Act. They had to make do instead with "non-intervention", meaning physical intervention, leaving the Final Act to legitimise mutual monitoring of, among other things, respect for human rights (see Chapter 13). The demand for "non-interference" was taken up again by Putin's Russia, which had become particularly resistant to anyone passing judgement on its rigged elections. This is in the long tradition of Russian sensitivity to any outside influences or activities that impinge on its realm. Needless to say, this sensitivity has never inhibited Moscow from interfering and intervening in other countries.

Soviet leaders correctly saw Western policy as intended to subvert their empire. It was a policy that ran right through the Cold War and occupied a central place in the Helsinki negotiations. In the early days it took the form of reckless talk in Washington of rolling back the Soviet empire and liberating the "captive nations" of Eastern Europe. After the US failed to prevent the Soviet Union from brutally crushing the Hungarian uprising of 1956 a lot of this rhetoric was dropped in favour of a more cautious policy of gradually building bridges to Eastern Europe.

The reappraisal included an examination of the role of Radio Free Europe (RFE), the American station in Munich, financed by the CIA, which broadcast to Eastern Europe in local languages. It was widely accused of having encouraged the doomed Hungarian fighters to expect US intervention. A subsequent inquiry showed this to be not quite true but a lot of blame still rested on the United States for giving strong moral support to the rising while having no plans to help it. Critics acknowledge that Washington was right to fear being dragged into war with Russia, but argue that RFE was irresponsible in egging on the rebels to make maximalist demands that could not be met within the Soviet orbit. It could have offered support and guidance to Imre Nagy, the reformist communist leader, later executed, who might have negotiated a compromise if he had had more understanding and support from both inside and outside his country—and better skills. Instead, Nagy was systematically vilified by RFE as he struggled with the situation. Soviet archives suggest that Nikita Khrushchev, the Soviet leader, might have been open to a compromise if one had been offered, especially as he was busy at the time trying to improve relations with the West. That, at any rate, is the view of Charles Gati, a former Hungarian journalist who became a distinguished professor and policy adviser in the United States, and who studied the 1956 archives many years after the events.[23]

Even as US policy became more cautious it remained in essence the same: to undermine Soviet rule in Eastern Europe by opening the area to Western influence, and if possible to induce change in the Soviet Union as well.

Dulles, the realist, acknowledged that "everyone wants to penetrate the Soviet Union but no one wants the Soviet Union to penetrate us".[24]

Thus the "bridge building" of the 1950s was a direct ancestor of the Helsinki commitment to increased contact between Eastern and Western Europe. General Dwight Eisenhower, US President from 1953 to 1961, was an ardent bridge builder. In January 1955 he called for more trade with Eastern Europe in order to draw those states away from Moscow. He wanted "evolutionary rather than revolutionary change".[25] In 1956, before the Hungarian revolt later that year, a US policy document (NSC 5607[26]) had called for "promoting within Russia evolution towards a regime which will abandon predatory policies, which will seek to promote the aspirations of the Russian people... and which will increasingly rest upon the consent of the governed rather than upon despotic police power". It concluded that "our foreign policies are necessarily defensive, so far as the use of force is concerned. But they can be offensive in terms of promoting a desire for greater individual freedom, well-being and security within the Soviet Union, and greater independence within the satellites".[27]

Even at that time, as throughout the Helsinki Process, there was dissent in Washington. Many members of Congress objected to any trade with the "Reds", so Eisenhower failed to get support for reducing export controls, but he persevered, and often found support in the State Department. Not for the first or last time, contradictory statements emerged from Washington, reflecting profound divisions on how to deal with the communist world. These continued throughout the Helsinki Process and up to the end of the Cold War.

The next president, John F. Kennedy, was also a bridge builder, as was his successor, Lyndon Johnson, who called for "bridges of increased trade, of ideas, of visitors, and of humanitarian aid... so that all of Europe may be joined in a shared society of freedom".[28] Eleven years later this vision was embodied in the Final Act of the Helsinki conference. The Soviet Union signed it but did not share the vision. It still feared the subversive intentions behind Western policies, but its need for trade and arms control and other aspects of détente gradually overrode its doubts. It reassured itself that it could control unrest in its empire. "We are masters in our own house", said Soviet Foreign minister Gromyko in 1975 as he tried to calm colleagues worried by the potentially subversive effects of the Helsinki Final Act (see Chapter 15).

This part of the story shows that the Helsinki Process had deep roots going back to the early days of the Cold War, when the West committed itself to the liberation of Eastern Europe while the Soviet Union was equally determined to retain control. Methods changed on both sides, but the aims remained constant. Right from the beginning, the road to Helsinki was paved with conflicting intentions.

Notes

1 Roberts, *Molotov*, 14.
2 Roberts, 77.
3 Roberts, 147.
4 Roberts, 69.
5 Dobbs, *Six Months in 1945*, 174.
6 Roberts, 127.
7 For a concise summary of the arguments, with references, see Ruggenthaler, 'The 1952 Stalin Note on German Unification: The Ongoing Debate' in *Journal of Cold War Studies*, 13/4, 172–212.
8 Gaddis *We Now Know*, 27.
9 Roberts, 128–9, and Hanhimäki and Westad, *The Cold War*, 103.
10 Djilas, *Conversations with Stalin*, 153.
11 Djilas, *Conversations with Stalin*, 153.
12 Steil, *The Marshall Plan*, 78.
13 For the full text see 'Soviet proposal for a General European Treaty on Collective Security in Europe, February 10, 1954', viewed 18 January 2022, http://digital.library.wisc.edu/1711.dl/History.BackgrndDocs, p.120.
14 Roberts, 145.
15 Roberts, 147.
16 Steil 326, Leffler, *For the Soul of Mankind*, 128–9, 143.
17 Steil, 327.
18 For a detailed account of the process by which these proposals evolved see Geoffrey Roberts, c2011, 'CWIHP e-Dossier No. 27', Wilson Center, Washington DC, viewed 9 January 2022, https://www.wilsoncenter.org/publication/molotovs-proposal-the-ussr-join-nato-march-1954
19 Leffler, 141.
20 Many references, including https://en.wikiquote.org/wiki/Hastings_Ismay
21 Kieninger, *Dynamic Détente*, 8.
22 Kieninger, 8.
23 *Gati, Failed Illusions: Moscow, Washington, Budapest and the 1956 Hungarian Revolt*. Stanford University Press (2006), 64.
24 Quoted in Kieninger, 8.
25 Kieninger, 7.
26 'NSC 5607: Statement of Policy on East–West Exchanges', in *Foreign Relations of the United States, 1955–1957, Soviet Union, Eastern Mediterranean*, XXIV, June 1956, Office of the Historian, viewed 9 January 2022, http://history.state.gov/historicaldocuments/frus1955-57v24/d104
27 Quoted in Kieninger, 8.
28 Kieninger, 28.

3 What were they afraid of?

Fear shaped the Cold War at least as much as each side's ambition to prevail over the other. We look first at Soviet fears and then at those on the Western side, all of which informed the Helsinki Process.

Soviet fears

Germany

It is impossible to understand the Soviet Union's proposals for a European security conference without appreciating its fear of Germany. This was relentlessly played up for propaganda purposes to justify tightening the regime's grip, but the fear itself lay deep in Russia's collective memory, going back to constant wars around its periphery, including Napoleon's march on Moscow in 1812, World War I, Western help for the anti-Bolshevik forces in Russia's civil war of 1917–22, and then the horrors of Hitler's invasion in 1941. The devastation wrought by that was beyond anything that could be imagined by a reasonably sane mind. It was not just a military conquest in the traditional sense but the start of a deliberate attempt to pillage the country and starve and subjugate the Russian people. They were to be humiliated and enslaved, reduced in number, and conscripted to work for Hitler's "master race". When they were not killed they were treated as sub-human, worked to death, tortured in prison camps and used (as the Germans also used the Jews) for medical experiments. In the initial phase of the war more than three million Russians died in German camps. By the end of the war the Soviet Union had lost a staggering 25 million or more people, with many more millions wounded. Large areas of the country had been devastated. Even while retreating in 1943–4, German soldiers vindictively obliterated 1,710 towns and 70,000 villages and systematically burned down hospitals, radio stations, schools and libraries.[1] Then they demolished Warsaw before retreating.

Against that horrific background, any Soviet leader would have regarded his principal task as preventing the rearmament of Germany. The fact that Stalin was paranoid and deeply imbued with the communist doctrine of inevitable conflict with capitalism merely exacerbated his suspicions. He frequently predicted that Germany would rearm and attack again: "The

DOI: 10.4324/9781003146124-5

Germans are a sturdy people… they will rise again…; in the future this [an attack] will probably, even certainly, occur".[2] He also believed that the capitalist powers were likely to go to war with each other, as Lenin had predicted, though his predictions were sometimes modified by hopes, to which Soviet leaders clung throughout the Cold War, that public opinion in the Western world could be mobilised in "peace campaigns" to thwart the designs of the capitalists.[3]

His successor, Nikita Khrushchev (see chapter 4), professed to be less afraid. According to Oleg Grinevsky, a former Soviet diplomat, "the idea of nuclear weapons in German hands frightened neither him nor the Soviet military, whose huge arsenal of nuclear missiles filled them with pride and conceit. But shaking up the West Europeans with the possible nuclear threat by the Federal Republic and trying to break up their alliance—that was something different. To achieve that Khrushchev was ready to unleash the most furious propaganda campaign".[4] But perhaps he was more afraid than he admitted because in reality, and probably unknown to Grinevsky and almost everyone else at that time, his arsenal was much smaller than he claimed. According to Ellsberg, in 1960–61 the Soviet Union had only four liquid-fuelled intercontinental missiles standing together in the open, an easy target as they would take hours to prepare for launch.[5]

This did not stop Khrushchev boasting that the Soviet Union was turning out rockets "like sausages". As recounted by Willy Brandt: "At a New Year reception in 1960, after consuming a good deal of vodka, he even 'divulged' to Western ambassadors that there were 50 rockets ready for France, 50 for Britain and 30 for West Germany. When the French Ambassador's wife inquired how many were set aside for the USA, the jovial Khrushchev replied that that was a military secret".[6]

Khrushchev made his fears clear to Norman Cousins, editor of the *Saturday Review*: "We could crush Germany in a few minutes. But what we fear is the ability of an armed Germany to commit the United States by its own actions. We fear the ability of Germany to start a world atomic war".[7]

Thus it is hardly surprising that anti-German propaganda fell on fertile ground in the Soviet Union. The next Soviet leader, Leonid Brezhnev, who succeeded Khrushchev in 1964 (see Chapter 5), appeared also to have genuine worries, although these were difficult to disentangle from propaganda. In a speech in 1965 on the twentieth anniversary of the end of the war, he said the West Germans yearned for revenge: "The aim of the political and military leaders of the German Federal Republic is to lay their hands on these [nuclear] weapons and with such backing to revise the results of World War II", meaning that they would take back the German territories lost to Poland.[8]

Although most West Germans were so traumatised by war that they had become almost pacifist, their politicians did not dare formally renounce their claim to the lost territories for fear of facing the wrath of their very vocal and well-organised expellees from those territories, so the claim was maintained until 1990, feeding the propaganda machines and to some extent the genuine fears of the Eastern bloc. In addition, some did indeed speak of acquiring nuclear weapons, notably Franz Joseph Strauss, leader of the CSU, the southern wing of the Christian Democrat Party.[9]

China

Germany was not Brezhnev's only worry, nor his only reason for pursuing a European security conference. On the Eastern frontiers of his huge country fear of war with China made him doubly anxious to secure his Western flank. Supposedly linked by a common dedication to Marxism, China and the Soviet Union had seldom had easy relations, especially since Khrushchev had denounced Stalin, who continued to be revered by Mao Zedong.[10] By the late 1960s relations were so bad that in 1969 armed clashes took place between Soviet and Chinese troops on their common border, provoking Moscow to make veiled threats of a pre-emptive nuclear strike against China, thereby stoking fears of a full-scale war. Relations were then not helped by China's constant attacks on Brezhnev's fervent promotion of the Helsinki conference, which it denounced as an "insecurity conference" that would lead to the "Finlandisation" of Western Europe, rendering it subservient to Moscow. In this they found common ground with the West German Christian Democrats, who also attacked the Helsinki conference. China ramped up tension by inviting Franz Josef Strauss, one of Helsinki's severest critics, to visit China in January 1975, where he was feted and granted the rare privilege of a meeting with Mao.[11]

Eastern Europe

Moscow had a third worry nearer home: Eastern Europe. A war prize bought at huge cost with the blood of Soviet soldiers, it was supposed to provide a barrier to any future attacks from the West as well as a launch pad for communism's inevitable spread into Western Europe. But Soviet rule was never accepted by most of the populations of Eastern Europe, so instability was a constant threat. Imposed largely by force with the help of local communists (see Chapter 1), it was an unusual empire in that some of the colonies, notably Czechoslovakia, were more advanced than the colonial power, which held back their economic development, suppressed their cultural life and cut them off from their natural economic, cultural and political relations with the rest of Europe. After the 1953 uprising in East Berlin there was another in Hungary in 1956, which was savagely put down by Soviet tanks. In the same year there was a revolt in Poznan, Poland, in which many died. In 1961 the East German regime, with Soviet backing, built a wall across the middle of Berlin to stop the massive exodus of its people to West Germany (see Chapter 1). In 1968 Soviet tanks were once again deployed, this time to crush a peaceful attempt to reform the communist system in Czechoslovakia (see Chapter 8). Later came further trouble in Poland, put down by force, and finally, in 1981, martial law imposed by the Polish regime itself with Soviet backing.

So one of the principal aims of the Soviet Union at Helsinki was to gain formal and final acceptance of its rule over Eastern Europe, hoping that the people of the area would become resigned to their fate and that the West would stop talking about liberation, give up supporting dissidents, and instead provide economic help to buy off discontent. As we shall see, Helsinki had the opposite effect. The West refused to endorse the status quo and increased its support for dissidents. It did proffer credits and technical help but largely in the vain hope that greater prosperity would encourage democratic reforms. Instead, Western credits were mostly used to avoid reform, thereby driving the area deeply into debt and giving the West more leverage.[12]

Western fears

The West feared a rearmed Soviet Union committed to world revolution, fear which grew as Stalin tightened his grip on Eastern Europe, blockaded Berlin in 1948, inflicted a communist coup on Prague in the same year, and supported the North Korean invasion of South Korea in 1950, sucking the United States and its allies into long and costly war. It was then that American rearmament started in earnest as communism appeared to be on the march everywhere, while the Soviet Union also embarked on heavy rearmament, each stoking the fears of the other.

Some in the West even feared that a rearmed Soviet Union would at some point embolden a reckless Soviet leader to push westwards. More common was the fear that an implied threat to do so could make Western Europe bend to his wishes, especially if the Americans decided to go home, which was always another fear. To the great annoyance of the Finns, this feared future for Europe was often described as "Finlandisation", meaning a posture of general subservience to Soviet power without actual occupation, for it was true that Finland did have to bend to the Soviet Union on some issues.

Germany

Germany appeared to pose two contradictory threats. On the one hand it might revive as a major power and get its hands on nuclear weapons. On the other hand the German people, traumatised by war, might turn to neutralism. In the post-war years, neutralism certainly seemed much more likely. Although Western Europe was, in Geir Lundestad's phrase, an American "empire by invitation",[13] in contrast to the Soviet empire imposed by force, it contained strong communist parties in France and Italy, while the West German Social Democratic Party favoured neutrality until 1959, when it came round to supporting NATO. Even after that, anti-American feeling sometimes welled up, particularly over nuclear weapons, since the Germans were well aware that they would be likely to become a devastated battlefield in the event of nuclear war. Thus, throughout the Cold War there were fears in Western capitals that West Germany and/or Western Europe would go "soft", especially on defence spending, allowing Soviet influence to spread westwards with the help of indigenous communist parties and left-wing movements. Nevertheless, when it came to elections, the majority of voters opted for the safety of American protection.

At the same time the old fear of a resurgent Germany did not entirely vanish. Apart from the noisy claims of the expellees mentioned above, some German politicians did discuss the possibility of gaining access to nuclear weapons in case the American commitment to Europe weakened, a possibility that always loomed in the background. West Germany had renounced nuclear weapons in the London Treaty of 1954, but this was not enough to reassure allies or adversaries. NATO was constantly preoccupied with the problem. Recent research has shown just how anxious the Americans were to keep nuclear weapons out of German hands. At one point President Kennedy said that the US might have to withdraw from Europe if West Germany acquired nuclear weapons.[14]

NATO's initial solution in the early 1960s was the Multilateral Nuclear Force (MLF), which was intended to give the West Germans a say in nuclear decision-making but no control. The idea was to educate them in the realities of nuclear warfare while forestalling nationalist pressures for possession of nuclear weapons. The Russians were not reassured, and nor were the French, the British and members of the US Congress, so the MLF was dropped in favour of a Nuclear Non-Proliferation Treaty (NPT). That also ran into West German opposition until Willy Brandt's government signed it in 1969.

Even then, Germany continued to worry the Western alliance right up to reunification in 1990, when new questions arose about a united Germany's place in Europe. President François Mitterrand of France pushed the German Chancellor, Helmut Kohl, into accepting a common European currency (the Euro) as a way of tying Germany into Europe.[15] Margaret Thatcher, the British Prime Minister, was deeply prejudiced against Germany and shamefully tried to persuade Gorbachev to prevent German reunification.[16] President Bush insisted that all of united Germany should be in NATO (see Chapter 22).

Notes

1 Service, *Stalin*, 482–3.
2 Roberts, *Stalin's Wars*, 236.
3 Roberts, *Molotov*, 148.
4 Oleg Grinevsky, *Tauwetter: Entspannung, Krisen und neue Eiszeit*, 36.
5 Ellsberg, *The Doomsday Machine*, 158–61.
6 Brandt, *My Life*, 188.
7 Quoted in Leffler, *For the Soul of Mankind*, 164.
8 Leffler, 225, 228.
9 Bernd Schaefer 'Europe must not become Greater Finland' in Wenger et al., *Origins of the European Security System*, 129.
10 Years later, after Mao's death, the new leadership was held back from denouncing Mao's crimes by memories of the shattering blow that Khrushchev had dealt to the morale of the Soviet Communist Party.

11 Schaefer, in Wenger et al., *Origins of the European Security System*, 132–4.
12 Garton Ash, *The Polish Revolution: Solidarity*, 255–6; Davy, *European Détente* 253–6. See also Davy, 'Policies for Eastern Europe' in Robert E. Hunter, *NATO, the Next Generation*.
13 Geir Lundestad, 'Empire by Invitation? The United States and Western Europe, 1945–1952' in *Journal of Peace Research*, 23/3 (September 1986).
14 US National Security Archives Briefing Book 617, 2 February 2018. See also Douglas Selvage, 'The Warsaw Pact and Nuclear Non-proliferation 1963–1965' Cold War International History Project, Working Paper #32, 2001.
15 Bozo, 'German Unification and European Integration' in Bozo et al., *Europe and the end of the Cold War*.
16 Brown, *The Human Factor*, 330–3.

Part II

Moving forward

4 Khrushchev, the accidental helper

The death of Stalin in 1953 left a gaping hole in the leadership of the Soviet Union. This was eventually filled by Nikita Khrushchev, who manoeuvred his way to the top, quickly disposing of Lavrenty Beria, Stalin's odious security chief, who was arrested, subjected to a brief trial, and then shot in the head as he pleaded for mercy. He had wanted the top job for himself but was much feared and hated by his colleagues.

Once in power, Khrushchev changed the scenery in four ways that helped to shape the Helsinki agenda. This is not to take a teleological approach; there was no automatic or deliberate progress towards Helsinki, just a series of developments that can be seen in retrospect to have smoothed the path.

First, Khrushchev started to open up to the world and move away from Stalin's reign of terror. He believed passionately in the future of communism but was also fascinated by the United States. Stalin had discouraged comparisons on the grounds that communism was simply a different system. Khrushchev had no such inhibitions. Under his leadership a new Party Programme[1] was published in 1961, forecasting that by 1970 the Soviet Union would overtake the United States in production per head of the population, and that by1980 "a communist society will in the main be built in the USSR",[2] when real income per head would have increased by more than 250 per cent. Archie Brown has described the document as a "remarkable combination of self-delusion, wishful thinking, and utopianism".[3]

In 1959 he had visited the great rival superpower and resolutely but unconvincingly pretended to be unimpressed. Later, meeting in 1963 with Norman Cousins, editor of *The Saturday Review*, he said:

> The workers in your society will bury the system… This is as certain as the rising sun… I have great admiration for the American people. Mark my words, when they become a socialist society they will have the finest socialist society in the world… What a wonderful thing it will be for them and for the world.[4]

Molotov had also said something similar after being hugely impressed when he visited San Francisco for the inauguration of the United Nations in 1945.[5]

DOI: 10.4324/9781003146124-7

But Khrushchev's outward show of confidence could not entirely hide his insecurity and his resentful envy of the capitalist world. He was small and round and reached a height of only 1.6 metres. Introduced in New York to the author of this book, who was some 30 cm taller, he stared up in silence for a while and then said rather bitterly, "Capitalists eat a lot of vitamins!"

The changes he brought to the Soviet Union went deep. The most dramatic was his devastating indictment of Stalin in a speech to a closed session of the 20th Congress of the Soviet Communist Party in 1956.[6] It was supposed to be secret but soon leaked out. Stalin had been raised to almost god-like status as the source of all wisdom and authority, his brutality widely excused as necessary in the struggle against enemies of communism. Khrushchev's attack was therefore equivalent to a Catholic saying that the Pope was not only fallible but criminal.

It was very risky because Khrushchev himself had been complicit in Stalin's crimes. Many of his colleagues were equally guilty but they were glad to leave behind the terrifying insecurities of the Stalin era, which had devastated the party apparatus. As Khrushchev pointed out, of the 139 people elected to the Central Committee in 1934, 70 per cent were shot between 1937 and 1938.[7] Yet the speech still provoked a major crisis in the communist movement at home and abroad, demoralising the faithful and infuriating the Chinese regime, which decided that it must never jeopardise its own authority by discrediting its own mass killer, Mao Zedong, even when radically departing from his policies in the 1980s. At the same time Khrushchev's speech had the positive effect of raising hopes among Russians who yearned for more freedom or believed that communism could be given a "human face", as the Czech reformers promised much later, in 1968 (see Chapter 8). Khrushchev's biographer, William Taubman, wrote that "he began the process that destroyed the Soviet regime".[8]

Thousands of political prisoners were released, lifting the pall of fear that had hung over the Soviet Union. The rate of housing construction doubled, allowing more people to move from shared apartments to single-family units, where they felt freer to criticise the regime. Controls were loosened on cultural and intellectual life, allowing new journals and films to appear. Aleksandr Tvardovsky, the poet who had been sacked as editor of *Novyi mir* (New World) in 1954, found himself reappointed after long conversations with Khrushchev. But battles over literature remained to be fought, particularly over Pasternak and Solzhenitsyn, both of whom were awarded the Nobel Prize. Not everything worked out as Khrushchev hoped. The World Youth Festival in 1957 was supposed to impress the world with Moscow's new openness, but as thousands of young people flooded in from around the world Soviet youths were even more impressed by Western popular culture, discovering a disturbing taste for "decadent" jazz and rock'n'roll.[9]

Memories of that period remained vivid among Russians who were young at the time, particularly in the intelligentsia. They became known as the "Khrushchev generation". Although suppressed during the grey regime of Leonid Brezhnev that followed, their hopes of change revived when Helsinki came into view with its promise of greater respect for human rights. Thus, there was a body of opinion inside and outside the party apparatus that yearned for meaningful détente with the West and hoped that Helsinki would bring it closer. Among them was Anatoly Kovalev, who later led the Soviet delegation through the Helsinki negotiations (see Chapter 12). He described these people as "renovationists" who were the "veterans and volunteers comprising the backbone of the Helsinki process".[10]

Secondly, Khrushchev changed the terms of the German question. At the Geneva summit meeting in July 1955 he had seemed to go along with the standard demand for a united neutral Germany as put forward by Molotov in London the previous year, and now by Prime Minister Nikolai Bulganin, with Molotov looking over his shoulder. But the Americans rightly detected differences among the Soviet delegates, suspecting that the Russians in fact feared German reunification because it would mean liquidating East Germany as a separate state.[11] This was exactly the point that Khrushchev had made in an unpublished speech to the Supreme Soviet in February of that year, but at that time he had not yet fully secured his position and he had to wait until June the following year to sack Molotov. In this speech he said: "To abandon socialism in the GDR, this means to abandon East Germany, to unite Germany and send it to the West... Will Germany be a neutral country in our current conditions? This is impossible. Either it will go with us or go against us".[12] Two years earlier, one of his accusations against Beria had been that he was planning to hand East Germany to the Americans.

Khrushchev was realistic enough to see that East Germany could be held only by force. The Soviet occupation was deeply unpopular. Soviet troops had engaged in mass rape of German women and then embarked on looting households and dismantling much of East German industry. Unsurprisingly, the communists lost heavily in the Berlin city elections of 1946, receiving only 19.8 per cent of the votes. The Russians had also imposed on their zone an extremely unpopular regime under Walter Ulbricht, a rigidly doctrinaire communist who managed to provoke an uprising of German workers in 1953, which was brutally put down by Soviet tanks. From then on the division of Germany was inevitable, even while Moscow preached reunification for largely propagandist purposes.[13]

This act of force by the Soviet Union contributed indirectly to the Helsinki Process by demonstrating to the West that it would have to come to terms with the existence of two Germanys for the foreseeable future. The lesson was repeated by the building of the Berlin Wall in 1961. Together these two lessons gave West Germany and the Western alliance a push down the long road towards recognising East Germany, which became a precondition for starting the Helsinki negotiations.

Khrushchev's third indirect contribution to the Helsinki Process was to abandon Stalin's belief in the inevitability of war. In its place he formally adopted Lenin's doctrine of "peaceful coexistence". Frequently misunderstood in the West as meaning acceptance of the status quo, it was clearly understood by Marxists as a doctrine requiring intense ideological struggle against capitalism to promote the spread of communism by peaceful means.

This doctrine became an issue in the Helsinki talks. The Soviet Union tried hard to include it in the Final Act and then continued to claim that it was included when in fact it had been excluded by stubborn Western diplomats. Undeterred, Brezhnev and other communist leaders made this presumably deliberate error in their speeches at Helsinki (see Chapter 14). Harold Wilson, the British Prime Minister, also used the phrase in his Helsinki speech, ignoring the pleas of a British official the night before, who tried to persuade him that he would be giving away a point that his diplomats had fought hard to win. But Wilson was a stubborn man who thought he knew better.

The reason for the sensitivity of this subject, and for the refusal of Western negotiators to include it in the Final Act, was that it would have defined Europe as an ideological battlefield between two systems and spheres of influence, allowing the Russians a free hand in theirs, whereas the Western framers of the Final Act wanted it to treat Europe as a whole, with rules such as non-intervention that would apply to all. This they achieved in the final text, thereby ruling out the so-called Brezhnev doctrine that the Soviet leader invented to defend his invasion of Czechoslovakia in 1968 (see Chapter 8 and Appendix C).

Despite the West's refusal to endorse "peaceful coexistence" as a doctrine, it was infinitely preferable to Stalin's belief in the inevitability of war. It re-defined the Cold War as a competition between systems, not an arms race but a race to produce the best model of society. In this Khrushchev closely mirrored George Kennan, the American diplomat in Moscow whose advice to his masters in Washington, set out in his famous "long telegram" of 1946,[14] was to concentrate on perfecting American society in order to prove its superiority while containing the Soviet Union until it mellowed or collapsed, as it eventually did. Kennan, of course, believed that Western capitalism would win a peaceful competition, while Khrushchev was equally confident that communism would win.

A surprising number of the people in the West believed Khrushchev at the time, both those on the left, who still saw in communism the promise of a just society, and those on the right, who feared that the appeal of communism would weaken or even destroy Western democracy. That is why some negotiators in the Helsinki process, particularly the British, saw it as one of their tasks to use the negotiations to drive home to Western opinion the denial of human rights in the Soviet empire (see the "lemon strategy" in Chapter 11). In other words, the Helsinki conference was to have an educative role in addition to its other dimensions. Incidentally, Dr Konrad Adenauer, Chancellor of West Germany from 1949 to 1963, was remarkably relaxed and far-sighted on this issue. Talking to a small group of British journalists in the late 1950s, he said: "Communism is simply unworkable. It will collapse in the end. We just have to wait".[15]

Khrushchev's paradoxical fourth legacy to Helsinki was to bring the world close to war on more than one occasion, thereby stimulating new thinking on how to preserve peace. He genuinely wanted peace in order to divert resources from the military to improve the lives of the Soviet people. He constantly grumbled about the costs of the arms race. When Marshal Malinovsky asked for more men and longer terms of service, Khrushchev replied angrily: "Has it ever occurred to you how many useful things are produced by young men during the third year they *don't* spend in the army?... We spend billions training needed specialists, and all you want to do is grab them away and make them goosestep".[16] Like most of his generation he had experienced the horrors of war and alluded to them frequently. He had been at the vicious battle of Stalingrad as a political commissar, and the memories never left him. He genuinely hoped for peace. Between 1955 and 1957 he defied Malinovsky and others like him by reducing Soviet troops by more than two million men, later announcing further reductions. The Soviet military complained that this was a "terrible blow to our defence capacity".[17] He also withdrew his forces from Finland, Manchuria and Austria, which he allowed to go neutral.

However, he became disillusioned by the negative responses of the West and turned to more combative policies that merely increased Western suspicions. Despite his belief in the inevitable victory of communism, he was not prepared to wait patiently for history to take its course. It was his job to push it forward, not only in the Third World, where he believed that former colonies would fall into his lap, but also in Europe. He took risks. He was profoundly irritated by the Western presence in Berlin and thought he could use its vulnerability to his advantage. In 1956 he told Western ambassadors: "Berlin is the testicle of the West. When I want the West to scream, I squeeze on Berlin".[18]

In 1958 he threatened to sign a peace treaty with the East German regime and give it control over access routes to Berlin. This would have been a dangerous move because it would have both deprived the Soviet Union of its own occupation rights in Berlin and granted East Germany the power to start a war. Khrushchev eventually backed down after reaching a fudged compromise with President Eisenhower during his visit to the United States in 1959.

His hopes of further peace moves stalled in 1960 after his forces shot down an American high-altitude U2 reconnaissance plane over his country, having failed at previous attempts. He was about to meet Eisenhower in Paris and expected the president to apologise for this intrusion into Soviet airspace. Instead, Eisenhower lied about the flight until Khrushchev triumphantly produced the pilot alive and well (later exchanged for a spy). Khrushchev felt humiliated by this new form of espionage. He hesitated before going to Paris and then pulled out of the meeting almost before it started, after venting his fury on the Western leaders and haranguing the foreign press. Then he took drives around the French countryside before returning home.[19]

In June 1961 he had an acrimonious meeting with President Kennedy in Vienna at which he again threatened to sign a peace treaty with East Germany, ending occupation rights, including Western access to West Berlin. He blustered and bullied and at one point said that if the United States wanted to start a war over Germany "let it begin now".[20] Kennedy was deeply shaken and moved up troops. Khrushchev was held back by his advisers, who knew that the Soviet Union was much weaker than he pretended (see Chapter 3).

Thus, in August 1961, Khrushchev settled instead for allowing Ulbricht to build a wall across the middle of Berlin to stem the massive outflow of people to the West: 100,000 had left in the first half of 1961, and in June alone almost 20,000. On one day alone, 9 August 1961, a few days before the wall was built, 1,926 people fled. By then about a fifth of the entire population of East Germany had gone, mainly through Berlin, and the number was rising. Closing this escape route had become a matter of survival for the East German regime, as Ulbricht told Khrushchev. If the border remained open, he warned "collapse is inevitable".[21] Meanwhile he badgered Khrushchev for huge amounts of aid. So the wall saved East Germany but it was also a humiliating demonstration of the failure of communism to win over its supposed beneficiaries.

The Western powers merely protested. There seemed to be nothing they could do short of breaking down the wall and thereby provoking direct conflict with the Soviet Union. As a result, it became clear to the Germans that, while the West was formally committed to the reunification of Germany, the current reality was that it was committed only to the defence of West Germany and West Berlin. This caused consternation in West Berlin and provoked fierce criticism of President Kennedy by Willy Brandt, then Governing Mayor of Berlin, but it accelerated thinking among Social Democrats in Berlin on how to unfreeze the situation in Germany. If Germany was not going to be reunited by the occupying powers, the Germans themselves would have to take the matter in hand. As Brandt told his House of Representatives, it would be foolish to "sit around for the Four Powers to do something about Germany. That way we'll go down the drain".[22]

His answer was to work by small steps towards reunification via modest attempts to ameliorate the human costs of the division. He started by negotiating an agreement with East Germany on passes for West Berliners to visit the East. For nearly two years he tried to negotiate at a low level in order to avoid recognising the East German regime but in the end he had to give in and negotiate directly, thereby granting the regime de facto recognition. The agreement was signed on 17 December 1963. East Berlin had expected 30,000 visitors but got 790,000.[23] This made Brandt hugely popular in Berlin but deeply suspect with the Federal Government in Bonn, which remained rigidly opposed to recognising East Germany.

The passes agreement was a turning point in that it exemplified what later became the new eastern policy (*Ostpolitik*) of the Social Democrats when they came to power in Bonn in 1969. It also opened the road to the Helsinki negotiations, which were in many respects a widescreen version of Brandt's *Ostpolitik*. In essence, the idea was to accept existing reality in order to change it, initially with practical steps to alleviate the humanitarian costs of the Cold War, then to gradually lower barriers between East and West Germany with the ultimate aim of reuniting the country in the distant future (see Chapter 9).

Thus the agreement pointed the way to the third section (known as Basket III) of the Helsinki Final Act, the section concerned with humanitarian issues, including freer movement of people and information. It meant granting East Germany a degree of recognition in return for more human traffic from West to East. This was a gamble that the West German government in Bonn was not yet ready to take as it was still fixated on denying recognition to East Germany. But Brandt had posed the question: if barriers could be lowered, which side would gain most?[24] The clear answer turned out to be the West, confirming one of the basic arguments in favour of détente, which was that lower barriers would allow influence to flow from West to East, rather than the other way round.

Meanwhile the wall did not entirely remove tension from Berlin. In October 1961 there was a dangerous confrontation between American and Russian tanks at the notorious Berlin crossing point, Checkpoint Charlie. Tension remained until the Quadripartite Agreement of 1971, which the West had made a condition of attending the Helsinki talks. That agreement, signed by the four occupying powers, confirmed Allied rights and responsibilities in Berlin, agreed measures for "unimpeded" traffic between West Berlin and West Germany, and facilitated easier visits by West Berliners to East Berlin. An odd feature of the agreement was that Berlin itself was not mentioned, only being referred to as "the relevant area", signifying agreement to disagree on the legal status of the city. Even then, there was more work to be done on Berlin before the Final Act could be signed (see Chapter 9).

Nor was Khrushchev's risky behaviour over. In October 1962 he brought the world to the brink of nuclear war by installing nuclear missiles in Cuba, only to withdraw them after a tense stand-off with President Kennedy. The shock was salutary for both men, who then reached out for safer relations. In a letter to Kennedy on 30 October 1962 Khrushchev pleaded for peace, though of course on his terms, which included closing foreign military bases "since military bases have lost now their importance", settling the German question (without specifying how), banning nuclear tests in the atmosphere, in outer space and under water, and eventually dissolving the military blocs.[25]

On 10 June 1963 Kennedy responded with a remarkable speech at the American University in Washington setting out a "strategy for peace" that foreshadowed the Helsinki Process in so far as it proposed accepting current realities as a starting point for change through "a series of concrete actions and effective agreements which are in the interest of all concerned".[26] By this time he had developed very close relations with Willy Brandt and largely shared his thinking, by-passing the disgruntled Christian Democrat Federal Government in Bonn.

Later in June Kennedy went to Berlin, where the population had been dismayed by his lack of reaction to the building of the wall. He gave an electrifying speech to a huge crowd in which he committed the United States to the defence of West Berlin with the famous words: "All free men, wherever they may live, are citizens of Berlin, and, therefore, as a free man, I take pride in the words '*Ich bin ein Berliner*'".[27] The crowd roared. Many young Berliners were deeply impressed by the contrast between this fresh young American president and their own stubborn old Chancellor, Dr Adenauer.[28] (Berliners later became annoyed by a rather silly joke that made the rounds alleging, wrongly, that Kennedy had claimed to be a particular type of doughnut known as a Berliner.)

Kennedy then gave a more measured speech at the Free University in West Berlin, endorsing almost point by point the policies that Brandt was pursuing in Berlin. Clearly aiming his remarks at the West German government in Bonn, he said that a policy of strength alone would not bring down the wall. It was necessary to face the reality of the situation and work for small steps.[29] Dr Adenauer listened stony-faced and refused to applaud.

In August 1963 Khrushchev and Kennedy agreed, after difficult negotiations, to ban nuclear tests in the atmosphere, space and under water. They also set up a "hot line" between their capitals for rapid communication in emergencies. This promising start was aborted when Kennedy was assassinated in November 1963, and Khrushchev was removed from power the following year by colleagues fed up with his "hare-brained" agricultural schemes, his disruption of the ordered life of the bureaucracy, and his reckless behaviour and subsequent humiliation in Cuba.

But both men had set up signposts to Helsinki by re-defining superpower relations and provoking the West Germans and later the rest of Western Europe to develop a specifically European concept of détente that diverged, as we shall see later, from that of the superpowers and formed the basis of the Helsinki agreement in 1975.

Notes

1 Khrushchev, 1961, *Report of the Central Committee of the Communist Party to the 22nd Congress of the CPSU*, viewed 14 January 2022, https://archive.org/details/RoadToCommunism22ndCongressCPSU/page/n5
2 Communist doctrine held that socialism was a stage on the route to communism.
3 Brown, *The Rise and Fall of Communism*, 255.
4 Quoted in Leffler, *For the Soul of Mankind*, 168–9.
5 Dobbs, *Six Months in 1945*, 179.
6 Khrushchev, 25 February 1956, 'Secret Speech "On the Cult of Personality and its Consequences", Delivered at the Twentieth Party Congress of the Communist Party of the Soviet Union', History and Public Policy Program Digital Archive, From the Congressional Record: Proceedings and Debates of the 84th Congress, 2nd Session (May 22, 1956-June 11, 1956), C11, Part 7 (June 4, 1956), pp. 9389–9403, viewed 14 January 2022, https://digitalarchive.wilsoncenter.org/document/115995.pdf?v=3c22b71b65bcbbe9fdfadead9419c995
7 Roberts, *Molotov*, 176.
8 Taubman, *Khrushchev*, xx.
9 Taubman, 383.
10 Quoted in Maresca, *Helsinki revisited*, 196.
11 1955, 'Memorandum of Discussion at the 256th Meeting of the National Security Council, Washington', US Dept. of State, viewed 14 January 2022, https://history.state.gov/historicaldocuments/frus1955-57v05/d259
12 Roberts, 156.

13 See Naimark, *The Russians in Germany*.
14 G. F. Kennan, 'Long Telegram 22 February, 1946', History and Public Policy Program Digital Archive, National Archives and Records Administration, Department of State Records (Record Group 59), Central Decimal File, 1945–1949, 861.00/2-2246; reprinted in US Department of State, ed., Foreign Relations of the United States, 1946, Volume VI, Eastern Europe; The Soviet Union (Washington, DC: United States Government Printing Office, 1969), 696–709, viewed 14 January 2022, http://digitalarchive.wilsoncenter.org/document/116178. See also his article signed "X" in *Foreign Affairs*, July 1947.
15 Author's recollection.
16 Taubman, 586.
17 Quoted in Mastny and Byrne, *A Cardboard Castle?*, 7.
18 Nikita Sergeevich Khrushchev, *Memoirs of Nikita Khrushchev: Volume 3: Statesman, 1953–1964*, 893.
19 For a vivid account of the aborted Paris trip see Taubman, *Khrushchev*, 459–71.
20 Taubman, 499.
21 Quoted in Zubok and Pleshakov, *Inside the Kremlin's Cold War*, 251.
22 Hofmann, *The Emergence of Détente in Europe*, 91.
23 Hofmann, 93.
24 Hofmann, 93.
25 Khrushchev, 1962, 'Letter to President Kennedy, 30 October', US Dept. of State, viewed 14 January 2022, https://history.state.gov/historicaldocuments/frus1961-63v06/d71
26 J F Kennedy, 1963, 'Commencement Address, American University, Washington DC, 10 June', JFK Library, viewed 14 January 2022, https://www.jfklibrary.org/archives/other-resources/john-f-kennedy-speeches/american-university-19630610
27 J F Kennedy, 1963, 'Remarks at the Rudolph Wilde Platz, Berlin, 26 June', JFK Library, viewed 14 January 2022, https://www.jfklibrary.org/archives/other-resources/john-f-kennedy-speeches/berlin-w-germany-rudolph-wilde-platz-19630626. And many other sources.
28 Author's wife was present as a student.
29 J F Kennedy, 1963, Remarks at the Free University of West Berlin, 26 June', JFK Library, viewed 14 January 2022, https://www.jfklibrary.org/asset-viewer/archives/JFKPOF/045/JFKPOF-045-028

5 Brezhnev, the deluded visionary

When Leonid Brezhnev succeeded Khrushchev as Soviet leader in 1964, he gradually became the driving force behind the Soviet campaign for a European security conference. He made it his personal mission, a grandiose project that he hoped would finally seal the post-war order in Europe at a spectacular summit conference where heads of state would sign the equivalent of a peace treaty. He would then, he assumed, be honoured as the man who had finally brought lasting peace to the war-torn continent—peace on his terms, of course. It was a measure of his almost delusional belief in the project that he expected to win the Nobel Peace Prize. He was very bitter when he did not.[1] As we shall see later, the laboriously negotiated text that he signed at Helsinki in 1975 was almost the opposite of what he had hoped for, and brought him little but trouble.

Born in 1906, he was a simple man of great vanity and ambition with little education who had worked his way quickly up through the party apparatus as older members fell victim to Stalin's purges. After the chaotic but hopeful reforms of Nikita Khrushchev he led the country into what many of his own countrymen labelled the "era of stagnation". He showed no interest in reforming the system despite its increasingly visible shortcomings. He was even tempted to rehabilitate Stalin but he held back when the probable repercussions were explained to him.[2] Economic and intellectual developments were stifled while huge resources were poured into the armed forces, partly against his will, according to him. He complained that when his Minister of Defence asked him for money he wondered "Should I give the military 140 billion or 156 billion roubles? And I do give them money, again and again—money that disappears into the funnel".[3] Thus, whether willingly or not, he presided over a massive military build-up that alarmed the West and contributed to Washington's rejection of détente in the years after the Helsinki agreement.

At the same time he became passionately devoted to détente. What did he mean by it? In public and sometimes in private he presented it in orthodox terms as a means of spreading communism by peaceful competition with the West. For instance, he said on 24 April 1967:

> The past few years have shown quite clearly that in conditions of slackened international tension the pointer of the political barometer [in

DOI: 10.4324/9781003146124-8

> bourgeois states] moves left...; the influence of Western European Communist parties is most directly correlated with the reduction in tension which has taken place in Europe.[4]

At a communist gathering in Prague in January 1972, buoyed up by the approach of the security conference, he said: "The historical moment has arrived when we can also increase our influence on the Western European countries through economic relations and thus reduce American influence, even if we cannot eliminate it completely".[5] One notices this mirroring of Western hopes that détente would reduce Soviet influence in Eastern Europe.

At another meeting in Prague in 1973 he said: "Trust me, comrades, by 1985, as a consequence of what we are now achieving with détente... we will be able to extend our will wherever we need to".[6]

In February 1976 he told the 25th Party Congress in Moscow:

> Détente does not in the slightest abolish, nor can it alter, the laws of the class struggle... We make no secret of the fact that we see détente as the way to create more favourable conditions for peaceful socialist and communist construction.[7]

Statements such as these were seized upon by opponents of détente in the West to show that détente was a Soviet plot to weaken the Western alliance. But did these statements represent his genuine views or were they just tactical expressions of orthodoxy to placate opponents in Moscow? Probably a bit of both. Certainly, the long-term aim of the Soviet Union remained to get the Americans out of Europe and promote the spread of communism. In the early stage of the Helsinki talks internal documents proposed three stages of détente, the third of which would look forward to the dissolution of the blocs in Europe and the creation of a European security system, with European forces for "conflict resolution". No mention of Americans.[8] The idea of a European security system to replace the blocs remained on the Soviet agenda and was eagerly pursued by Mikhail Gorbachev in the dying days of the Soviet Union, with the major difference that he envisaged American participation (see Chapter 19).

For Brezhnev, however, it was the immediate future of détente that mainly preoccupied him, and that was difficult enough. He had to fight for détente against sceptics within the Kremlin as well as trying to bring together his quarrelsome allies in the Warsaw Pact. He was not an absolute ruler, and nor was the Soviet system as monolithic as many Westerners thought at the time. Around him were a lot of crusty old communists, such as Mikhail Suslov, who were unwilling to give up revolutionary ideology as the main prop of the system.[9] As a result, the CSCE became "a highly contested topic inside the country, the subject of an acute political and ideological struggle invisible to an outsider".[10]

According to Vladislav Zubok, a distinguished Russian historian who moved to the West, there were no doves in Brezhnev's entourage. The majority of the Politburo remained ideologically orthodox even during détente:

> Militant attitudes reigned among the majority of Brezhnev's colleagues. To begin acting as a peacemaker in this milieu was extremely difficult and dangerous for one's career. Against all expectations Brezhnev succeeded in this endeavour.[11]

Some of his opponents had not given up Stalin's belief in a coming war with the United States. Among them was Alexander Shelepin, a hard-line member of the Politburo, who was quoted as saying "People must know the truth: a war with America is inevitable".[12] Even short of war, these hard-liners were afraid that their system would be subverted and weakened by more open contacts between the two systems and the friendlier face of the useful enemy. Maintaining the illusion that the Soviet Union was under constant threat from the West had always been a useful way of rallying support. Détente could strip away that illusion. It could also bring more exposure to the realities of Western life. Nikolai Polianski, a Soviet diplomat, wrote that

> Détente became necessary for economic reasons. But the Soviet ideologues understood perfectly the threat that détente posed: neither more nor less than a crumbling of the Soviet system. Contact with the material and spiritual riches of Western countries—the abundance of goods and freedom of information—would immediately reveal to the Soviet citizen his material and spiritual misery.[13]

The role of Yury Andropov, head of the KGB, was crucial but also ambiguous. On the one hand he gave considerable personal support to Anatoly Kovalev, head of the Soviet team at the CSCE negotiations (see Chapter 12), accepting the need to make concessions on humanitarian issues in the final phase of the talks. On the other hand, he warned constantly of the danger that détente would undermine controls in the Soviet Union by exposing the population to Western influence. The country, he said, was not ready for greater freedom of expression, and would not be for another ten or fifteen years, after substantial improvements in the economic situation. Meanwhile, the borders would be inviolable in the military sense "but in all other respects, as a result of the expansion of contacts, of the flow of information, they will become transparent".[14]

He therefore tightened controls quite brutally. In September 1972, the dissident network that had been publishing the clandestine *Chronicle of Current Events* was dismantled amid waves of arrests, while a particularly nasty form of repression was introduced when dissidents such as Vladimir Bukovsky (later released to the West) and General Petr Grigorenko found themselves imprisoned in psychiatric hospitals and subjected to punitive "treatment", provoking scandalised protests in the West. At the same time political prisoners were sent to more remote camps, while the official press stepped up its efforts to warn people against their fascination with Western music and dress.[15]

One of the reasons Brezhnev succeeded in pushing forward with détente against so much opposition was that he was able to call on help from a rising generation within the apparatus that wanted to overcome the sterile and expensive confrontation of the Cold War. They were better educated than the older generation, more open to Western ideas, and in many cases had had their hopes of reform raised by Khrushchev's denunciation of Stalin in 1956 and the thaw that followed (see Chapter 4). They were appalled when Soviet tanks were sent in to crush the "Prague Spring" in 1968 (see Chapter 8). They were now rising in the power structure, and were available in various state institutes to advise Brezhnev and draft speeches promoting détente. They were also to be found in the Foreign Ministry and the Foreign Trade Ministry and even within the otherwise hard-line International Department of the Central Committee, where Boris Ponomarev defended them against critics, saying: "These are educated people who know how to think and write. As a general rule, the hardliners don't know how to do either".[16]

Hence there was a mixture of tactics and belief in Brezhnev's approach to détente. He had to be careful to couch his defence of détente in orthodox revolutionary terms in order to reassure his powerful domestic critics. This was not entirely contrived: his thinking was conditioned by his deeply embedded belief in the ultimate triumph of communism. At the same time there are now many accounts of private meetings at which he spoke with great feeling and without reference to ideology on the need for peace in Europe, sometimes moved to tears. For instance, at a meeting in a dacha, preparing for his visit to France in 1973, he rejected the orthodox draft prepared by officials and spoke with deep emotion of the need for peace in Europe. As recounted by Yuri Dubinin, a key member of the Soviet delegation to the CSCE, who was present at the meeting,

> He started to discuss the scale and dramatic nature of European history, speaking of Europe as a continent on which civilisations of importance to the entire world had arisen, a place where empires had risen and fallen, through which tornados of violence and war had swept, a land that had witnessed massive movements of people. All this he combined with memories of World War II, recalling his own life experience and concluding, as always, with his sincere wish that at long last this war-torn Europe should be granted peace.[17]

In 1974, while driving President Gerald Ford around Vladivostok after negotiating the second agreement on strategic weapons (Salt II) he grabbed Ford's hand and began telling him how much his people had suffered in the war. "I do not want to inflict that on my people again", he said, as he continued to hold Ford's hand tightly for the rest of the drive.[18] So there was no doubt about his passionate desire for peace in Europe. It sprang from personal experience as well as ideology.

The trouble was that his concept of peace was not shared by the rest of Europe. For him, peace meant freezing the status quo by confirming Soviet hegemony over Eastern Europe and finally legalising the gains that had cost the Soviet Union so much blood in the war. Unfortunately for him, most

Europeans in East and West were not so ready to settle for the status quo. They chafed under the unnatural division of the continent, the economic backwardness of Eastern Europe, the suppression of human rights under Soviet rule, and the continuing dangerous confrontation between military blocs. They wanted change, and they wanted the Helsinki Process to push it forward. As we shall see, it did just that.

Notes

1 English, *Russia and the Idea of the West*, 302, n220.
2 Brown, *The Rise and Fall of Communism*, 400; Brandt. *My Life*, 183.
3 Leffler, *For the Soul of Mankind*, 256, and Zubok, *A Failed Empire*, Chapter 7.
4 *DBPO III/III*, 369.
5 This material is part of the Parallel History Project (PHP), held by the Technical University in Zürich (www.ethz.ch), and is normally available through their website; however online access was affected by IT problems at the time of going to press. The text here is quoted in Morgan, *The Final Act*, 154 and see his chapter 5 endnote number 51.
6 Quoted in Korey, *The Promises We Keep*, 131.
7 *Soviet News*, 2 March 1976, quoted in Davy, *European Détente*, 8.
8 Savranskaya in Bange and Niedhart, *Helsinki 1975, and the Transformation of Europe*, 178.
9 English, 154.
10 Yuri Kashlev, 'The CSCE in the Soviet Union's Politics' in *International Affairs* (Moscow), 11–12 (1995), 66–92.
11 Zubok, *A Failed Empire*, 204.
12 Zubok, 197.
13 Rey, 'The USSR and the Helsinki process, 1969–75: Optimism, doubt, or defiance?' in Wenger et al., *Origins of the European Security System*, 71.
14 Savranskaya in Bange and Niedhart, 181.
15 Rey in Wenger et al., 76–7.
16 Rey in Wenger et al., 74.
17 Dubinin, 2013, in *CSCE Testimonies, Causes and Consequences of the Helsinki Final Act 1972 –1989*, OSCE, viewed 20 January 2022, https://www.osce.org/files/f/documents/6/c/459244.pdf, p, 192.
18 Ford, *A Time to Heal*, 213.

6 1966: Dialogue of the deaf

From 1954 and through most of the 1960s Soviet proposals for a European security conference were largely propagandistic, aimed at driving a wedge between Europe and the United States. They usually proposed the dissolution of both military alliances, safe in the knowledge that the Warsaw Pact would still be held together by a web of bilateral agreements. This did not prevent disagreements arising among members of the Warsaw Pact, for it was not the united, obedient bloc that it sometimes seemed to outside observers during the Cold War, but a group of restless, disputatious and often reluctant allies, with their own interests to pursue within the tight confines of Soviet control.[1] While Romania, for instance, wanted to use a European security conference to gain more freedom of movement, Poland pulled in the opposite direction, seeking to hold the Pact together in a common line against West Germany to demand ratification of the post-war frontiers.[2]

In 1964 Adam Rapacki, the Polish Foreign Minister, jumped ahead of Moscow by calling for a European security conference in a speech to the United Nations. Poland had become worried that Moscow might reach its own deals with West Germany at the expense of Polish interests, largely for economic reasons but also to secure the Soviet Union's western flank as it began to fear war with China. Poland wanted to ensure that the Warsaw Pact would stick together to defend Poland's essential interest in having its new frontiers recognised as permanent. East Germany had the same interest in permanent frontiers, and nurtured the same fears of Soviet betrayal. These eventually proved justified when the Soviet Union agreed to a clause in the Helsinki Final Act allowing for the peaceful change of frontiers. Rapacki therefore had East German backing when he proposed that a European security conference should recognise the state of East Germany and Poland's frontiers, ban West German access to nuclear weapons, and (deviating from Moscow at that time) include the United States to guarantee frontiers. He conspicuously omitted any demand for dissolution of the military alliances. His proposal was rather coolly received by his allies, who nevertheless approved it in modified form, omitting his crucial reference to the participation of the United States and Canada.[3]

In July 1966, these fractious allies met in Bucharest, where they managed to cobble together an awkward compromise around a renewed joint call for a

DOI: 10.4324/9781003146124-9

security conference. It is worth quoting at some length to reveal the inner conflicts between hard and soft lines within the Warsaw Pact and the crude anti-American language that made it impossible for the West to agree to a conference at that stage.[4]

It opens with a history lecture blaming the Cold War on the United States and reactionary forces in Western Europe. Then it calls aggressively for Europeans to rally to the cause of peace in opposition to the United States. It continues, in the words of a rather clumsy official translation:

> The European peoples... can and must create in this part of the globe a climate of detente... Imperialist reactionary circles... are trying to foster tension, to poison the relations among European states. A direct peril to peace in Europe... is... the present policy of the United States... It is no doubt that the aim of the US policy in Europe has nothing in common with the vital interests of the European peoples... The US ruling circles would like to impose their will on their allies in Western Europe in order that Western Europe should become a tool of the US general policy... US aggressive circles, supported by the reactionary forces of Western Europe, are seeking, by means of the North Atlantic military bloc and of the military machine set up by it, to increasingly aggravate the division of Europe, to intensify the arms race...
>
> In the name of these aims, which are alien to the genuine interests of the European peoples' security, US troops are still maintained in Europe... The policy promoted by the USA in Europe in the post-war years is all the more dangerous for the European peoples as it is increasingly based on the coalition with the militaristic and revanchist forces in West Germany. These forces are directly impelling the USA towards promoting an even more dangerous line in Europe. This policy finds its expression in a kind of alliance which is taking shape between the US imperialists and the West German revenge-seekers... At present this policy is focused on the demand for nuclear weapons possession. In the German Federal Republic endeavours are intensified, overtly and secretly, for the establishment of a technico-scientific and industrial basis which, at a favourable moment, would serve for the production of its own A- and H-bombs.

Now on frontiers, which remained at the centre of the whole Helsinki Process:

> The question of frontiers in Europe has been finally and irreversibly settled... One of the main requisites of guaranteeing European security is the inviolability of the existing frontiers... The German people... should proceed from the existence of the two German states.

The confrontational tone then gives way to a slightly more differentiated approach in an attempt to accommodate other views, including Moscow's, but also those of Hungary and Czechoslovakia, which needed more trade with the West. János Kádár, the Hungarian leader, pointed out with typical dry realism that the economic benefits of normal relations with West Germany were in his country's state interest even if they were not in the interest of proletarian internationalism.[5]

Continuing to slightly soften its stance, the declaration acknowledges that not all is bad on the other side of the Iron Curtain. Although the efforts of the socialist countries for peace are "of decisive importance", it says,

> the efforts of the working class in Western Europe are concentrated with the full energy of its vanguard detachments, of the democratic progressive organizations, and of the peace movements, which express the opinion of the broadest masses of the working people… The influence of these people fighting for peace and security in Europe is getting more and more evident. (The Soviet Union always placed great hopes on the peace movements in Western Europe, particularly in the later phases of the Cold War, but it was invariably disappointed at elections when a majority of voters rejected their policies.)

Then, following Moscow's anti-American line, the declaration appeals to Europeans to unite against "outside" interference—meaning, of course, American interference, since Russia regarded itself as inside Europe: "The European states are in a position to solve their problems of the mutual relationship without interference from the outside". (In fact, of course, Soviet "interference" in Eastern Europe was far more intrusive and controlling than that of the Americans in Western Europe.)

Now, at last, a concession to Mr Kádár and others: "The European countries, linked by traditional trade relations, cannot but benefit by the development of their economic cooperation on mutually advantageous basis. The expansion of economic relations between the European states, the removal of the discriminations and barriers existing in this respect is an outstandingly important factor for rapprochement and for the establishment of an atmosphere of mutual confidence and understanding between peoples. The development of economic links between the European countries facilitates expanded trade with partners in other regions of the world. These links, together with a many-sided development of technico-scientific and cultural cooperation enabling the achievement of better mutual knowledge between peoples may, concomitantly with their development, become the material basis of European security and of strengthening peace the world over…; the European states and peoples have a common cause, namely the duty of preventing the violation of peace in Europe".

Next it moves on to proposing a new security system: "The real guarantee of the security and progress of each European country lies… in the establishment in Europe of an efficient security system based on relations of equality and mutual respect among all the states of the Continent… The radical way to this would be concomitant abolition of existing military alliances… If, however, the North Atlantic Pact member states are not yet ready to go over to the complete abolition of the two military groups, the signatory states to this Declaration consider as rational that an agreement should already be reached on the liquidation of the military organizations, both of the North Atlantic Pact and of the Warsaw Pact".

Then it calls for partial measures "such as the dismantling of foreign military bases, the withdrawal of all troops from the territories of other states,… reduction… of the armed forces of both German states…, creation of denuclearized zones…, discontinuing flights of foreign aircraft with nuclear bombs over the territories of Europe states…, excluding the possibility of West Germany getting access to nuclear weapons under any form, directly or indirectly, and acknowledgement of the actually existing frontiers between the European states, frontiers established after the most devastating of wars in mankind's history, inclusive of the Polish frontier on the Oder and Neisse [rivers] and of the frontiers between the two German states".

The declaration then attempts to woo West German opinion by departing from the usual position, taken earlier in this document, that the division of Germany must be permanent: "As to the unification of both German states, the path towards the realization of this goal passes through the lessening of tension, gradual rapprochement between the two sovereign Germans states, [and]… agreement on disarmament in Germany and in Europe… In the condition of achieving Germany's unification, such a united German state will be a truly peace-loving and democratic state".

And now to the security conference: "Of great positive significance would be the convening of a general European conference for the discussion of the questions related to ensuring security in Europe…; [it] could contribute to the formation in Europe of a system of collective security and would be a great event in the history of contemporary Europe".

Grudgingly, the declaration grants towards the end that "it is in the competence of each country to choose whether to participate", thereby leaving the door slightly open to the United States. But then it tacks back again: "The states represented at the meeting turn to all *European* [author's emphasis] governments and nations".

Needless to say, most of the demands in the Declaration, notably for the withdrawal of all troops from the territories of other states, were regarded by the Western powers as completely unrealistic. Privately, Moscow must have agreed because it knew perfectly well that its hold over Eastern Europe, especially East Germany, could be sustained only by the presence or threat of very substantial Soviet forces, but it saw propaganda value in seeming ready to leave if the Americans left Western Europe. Had that actually happened, American forces would have been left on the other side of the Atlantic while Soviet forces would have been poised on the frontiers of Europe. Predictably, the Bucharest Declaration did little, if anything to bring closer Mr Brezhnev's dream of a European security conference.

Notes

1 See Crump, *The Warsaw Pact Reconsidered.*
2 Selvage 'The Warsaw Pact and the European Security Conference, 1964–69: Sovereignty, Hegemony, and the German Question' in Wenger et al., *Origins of the European Security System*, 85–106.
3 Crump, 163.
4 See *Soviet News*, 12 July 1966, 'The Warsaw Pact Declaration', in *Survival*, 8/9, pp. 289–293, viewed 25 January 2022, https://www.tandfonline.com/doi/pdf/10.1080/00396336608440674.
5 Mastny, *The Warsaw Pact*, 148.

7 1967: Détente, but what was it?

By the 1960s each side had come up against limits to its ambitions in Europe. The Soviet Union had failed to stop the rearmament of West Germany, the integration of Europe and the formation of NATO. Nor had it driven the Americans out of Europe, or even out of Berlin. Meanwhile the Americans had failed to liberate Eastern Europe despite their rhetorical promises. They had stood by while Soviet tanks crushed risings in Berlin in 1953 and Hungary in 1956. In August 1961 they had found themselves unable to stop the communist regime building a concrete wall across the middle of Berlin. In 1968, as we shall see in the next chapter, they could not prevent a Soviet-led invasion of Czechoslovakia.

Thus, the division of Europe was becoming a fact of life, not accepted but requiring new thinking. Both alliances became restive as threats appeared to diminish.

On the Eastern side the fragile unity of the Warsaw Pact achieved at Bucharest in 1966 (see Chapter 6) soon cracked. In January 1967 Romania caused consternation by opening diplomatic relations with West Germany. This provoked an angry Polish regime to gather East Germany and the Soviet Union in support of what became known as the "Warsaw Package". This bound members of the Warsaw Pact to refuse relations with West Germany until that state accepted existing borders (meaning primarily Poland's), recognised the state of East Germany, and renounced nuclear weapons (a constant worry on both sides of the Iron Curtain).[1]

At the same time Romanian leaders were resisting a Soviet plan for a division of labour in Eastern Europe that would have consigned their country to a largely agricultural role, so they defied Moscow by embarking on their own industrialisation. They also cultivated relations with China, and refused to join the rest of the Warsaw Pact in the invasion of Czechoslovakia in 1968 (see Chapter 8).

Meanwhile Poland was also asserting itself, demanding more say in the Warsaw Pact in order to allay its worries that Moscow might reach a deal with West Germany without insisting on prior recognition of the new frontiers.[2]

On the Western side, President de Gaulle withdrew France from the integrated military structure of NATO in 1966 and expelled American and Canadian troops. He then set off for Moscow in pursuit of his own vision of

DOI: 10.4324/9781003146124-10

a European answer to the Cold War. It came to nothing but unsettled NATO and aroused false hopes in Moscow of splitting the Western alliance.

In the same year the West German Social Democrats entered a coalition government with the Christian Democrats. The new government, with Willy Brandt as Foreign Minister, began cautiously abandoning the "Hallstein Doctrine", which had bound previous governments to refuse to recognise any state except the Soviet Union that recognised East Germany (see Chapter 9). As a first step it opened relations with Romania, as mentioned above, only to find Poland and East Germany blocking further progress.

These new uncertainties unsettled NATO, so it decided that in order to hold the alliance together it must redefine its purpose and reassure a restive public that it was pursing peace as well as military security. It asked Pierre Harmel, Belgium's Foreign Minister, to write a report on the future tasks of the alliance. He drew up four reports and put them together in a summary that became known as the Harmel Report, a key document in the history of the alliance. Its main point was to propose a two-track policy combining military preparedness with political dialogue. It stated that "military security and a policy of détente are not contradictory but complementary". In other words, combine confrontation with engagement and commit to détente, emphatically together with the United States as the essential guarantor of European security.

It continued with words that later formed the basis of NATO's approach to the Helsinki talks, clearly signalling that NATO would not ratify the status quo:

> But no final and stable settlement in Europe is possible without a solution of the German question which lies at the heart of present tensions in Europe. Any such settlement must end the unnatural barriers between Eastern and Western Europe, which are most clearly and cruelly manifested in the division of Germany.
>
> Accordingly the Allies are resolved to direct their energies to this purpose by realistic measures designed to further a détente in East–West relations. The relaxation of tensions is not the final goal but is part of a long-term process to promote better relations and to foster a European settlement. The ultimate political purpose of the Alliance is to achieve a just and lasting peaceful order in Europe accompanied by appropriate security guarantees.[3]

Harmel's report was unanimously adopted by NATO defence ministers in December 1967.

The report had the full support of US President Johnson, who had given a speech on 7 October the previous year that took exactly the same approach as Willy Brandt, by calling for Europe and Germany to be reunited by means of peaceful engagement intended eventually to win the consent of the Soviet Union.[4]

Now that détente had become official NATO policy, what was it exactly? Derived from the French term for releasing a bowstring or unstringing a bow, it signified relaxing tension by seeking areas of common ground and better communication without ending the adversarial relationship or accepting the status quo. It did not arrive suddenly in 1967 but grew gradually over many years through a series of false starts, as both sides tried to control the dangerous and costly confrontation in which they found themselves after the war.[5]

By the time NATO gave its stamp of approval, détente was acquiring a set of concepts but it remained fundamentally ambiguous, often misunderstood, and the subject of bitter debates. Was it aimed at stability or change, conciliation or subversion? The answer was: actually a bit of all these. Hence the confusion.

For Leonid Brezhnev, as we have seen, it meant freezing the status quo in Europe while still hoping to weaken the Western alliance and expand Soviet influence in Europe and the Third World. For Western Europe it meant doing business with obnoxious regimes, and thereby possibly making them stronger, while at the same hoping in the long run to weaken them through closer contacts at all levels. For East European regimes it meant gaining technology, trade and credits while risking exposure to the dangerous appeal of Western ideas and consumer goods. For most European people on both sides of the Iron Curtain it brought hopes of ameliorating and eventually overcoming the division of the continent.

For the purposes of the Helsinki story it is important to distinguish between superpower détente and European détente. At the superpower or global level between the Soviet Union and the United States détente was primarily an attempt to regulate the arms race and avoid stumbling into war. Brezhnev believed that nuclear parity had created a new correlation of forces that entitled him to sit proudly at the top table with the Americans. President Nixon, who succeeded Johnson in 1969, and Henry Kissinger, his Security Advisor and later Secretary of State, were prepared to grant him that much legitimacy. They treated him as leader of a rival superpower rather than as the ideological foe that obsessed many Americans, including Nixon in his earlier days. Kissinger hoped to enmesh the Soviet Union in a web of agreements that would give it incentives to moderate its external behaviour. As Kissinger put it, “By acquiring a stake in this network of relationships with the West the Soviet Union may become more conscious of what it would lose by a return to confrontation”.[6]

Although these efforts did chalk up some credits, they suffered from a fundamental misunderstanding. While Kissinger expected to restrain the Soviet Union, it nearly doubled its armed forces between 1965 and 1985, as well as continuing to support revolutionary movements in the Third World, not always willingly but because it could not be seen to let down regimes or movements that proclaimed themselves socialist, such as in Cuba, Angola, Ethiopia and, eventually, Afghanistan. Critics of détente in the United States and, to a lesser extent, in Europe, therefore condemned détente as a failure, a Soviet trick to lull the West into dropping its guard. In their view, the Soviet Union was so irredeemably dedicated to world conquest that almost any agreement with it would be to the disadvantage of the West. They believed that the bracing air of confrontation was needed to maintain political control, stiffen the sinews of Western public opinion, support defence budgets and bind their respective alliances together. Their counterparts in Moscow agreed. As described in Chapter 5, Brezhnev had to face many opponents of détente within his own circles who preferred confrontation as the glue that held their own country and their empire together.

European détente was different and much more successful. While Kissinger believed that détente must not be tied to basic changes in the internal behaviour of the Soviet and East European regimes,[7] internal changes were exactly what the West Europeans wanted, as did the oppressed people of Eastern Europe. The division of the continent was not only dangerous and oppressive but an historical anomaly, an artificial separation of two parts that for centuries had shared a common cultural and economic identity, even when riven by wars.

Thus, in the short-hand language of those days, Nixon and Kissinger preferred stability to justice in Europe, whereas Europeans believed that there could be no true security or fundamental stability without justice for both parts of Europe, which meant having governments that represented their people. Those two contrasting concepts of security—consent or coercion—divided not only East and West but also initially Europe from the United States and the White House from the State Department, which showed much more understanding for the European desire to continue the bridge building of previous administrations. The fundamental question was whether peace could be secure if based on the denial of human rights to Eastern Europe. The answer embodied in the Helsinki Final Act was "no".

The arguments that raged over détente were often depicted as between hawks and doves. A better categorisation would be confronters and engagers because the engagers were not always doves in the usual sense. There were indeed some true doves in Western Europe who supported détente because they either sympathised with communism or believed that the danger of nuclear war was so great that we would be "better red than dead", as one of their slogans put it. Or they urged unilateral disarmament because they believed that the Soviet Union was driven primarily by fear and would therefore become benign if not threatened. Some even saw the two superpowers as morally equivalent and dreamed of seeing them withdraw from Europe as both alliances dissolved, as proposed by the Soviet Union. This was despite the fact that Western Europe, although under American protection, was ruled by democratically elected governments whereas Eastern Europe was ruled by unelected governments controlled by the Soviet Union.[8]

None of these views gained much traction among the Western governments that drove the Helsinki agenda. They were far from being doves or appeasers, as alleged by their critics. Perhaps they could be better described as hawks in doves' feathers because they were hawkish in their aims but dovelike in their methods. They believed that peaceful engagement would gradually erode Soviet power in Eastern Europe. They were ready to accept existing realities for the time being but only in order to create better conditions for the spread of Western values eastward, leading eventually to the liberation of Eastern Europe, the departure of Soviet troops, and the reunification of Germany. In other words, "change through rapprochement", as Willy Brandt put it when defining his Eastern policy, as Foreign Minister and then Chancellor of West Germany (see Chapter 9). This was to be achieved at Helsinki by negotiating for human rights and the freer movement of goods, people and information between the two parts of Europe. In that sense the détente pursued by Western Europe was quite aggressive, and was often seen as such by Moscow.

Soviet aims were almost a mirror image. As we have seen in Chapter 5, Brezhnev's immediate aim in Europe was to cement the status quo, but he never ceased to declare that the ultimate aim of détente was to improve conditions for the spread of socialism by peaceful means. Of course, he had to say that to reassure his critics, but he was still deeply imbued with an ideological view of the world in which the victory of communism was inevitable in the long run, so he could never wholly abandon his hopes that European détente would soften and split the West, reduce political support for Western defence budgets, and eventually cause the Americans to retreat across the Atlantic.

Thus the question that faced both sides was which would gain most if barriers were lowered in Europe. Western critics of détente feared (and Brezhnev hoped) that détente would allow Soviet influence to creep westward, helped by communist parties and left-wing opinion in Western Europe. These critics believed that Western Europe was going soft, and that if there was to be more open competition between the two sides the rules were rigged because the Soviet Union was able to control the movement of people and information on its side while enjoying open access to the free press, communist parties and other political sympathisers on the other side. The result, these critics predicted, would be the gradual spread of Soviet influence westward. President Nixon shared these fears, and was deeply sceptical of the value of a security conference. Talking with British Prime Minister Harold Wilson, he said he feared it would produce no tangible results, only "an appearance of détente and euphoria".[9]

The pessimism that gripped some Western commentators was quite extraordinary, especially in retrospect. For instance, Leo Labedz, editor of *Survey*, an excellent journal on Soviet and East European studies, had this to say: "When I look at the state of Western Europe I am struck… by the question whether Western Europe is at all in a position to survive. Such is the measure of our failure".[10] Or Richard Pipes, a distinguished professor of Russian history: "Weariness and disillusionment with war and politics and the pursuit of material wealth… have… sapped the political will of Europe".[11] Even the British worried that Europe could become infected by "détente fever", leading to the "Finlandisation" of Western Europe.

The West German Christian Democrats were particularly vocal critics of détente while in opposition because they thought that détente meant accepting the division of Germany and the permanent loss to Poland of their former eastern lands. They turned out to be right about the lost lands but wrong in assuming that détente would mean renouncing the reunification of Germany, which was, as it turned out, in fact facilitated by détente. They found themselves in uneasy alliance with communist China in denouncing what the Chinese regime called the Helsinki "insecurity conference". A few days before the Final Act was signed in 1975 they even went so far as to introduce a motion in parliament calling on the government not to sign, a move much regretted later by Helmut Kohl, who became German Chancellor in 1982 and continued, in essence, the policies of Brandt that he and his colleagues had criticised so vigorously in opposition.

Debates in the West were especially contentious over trading with the Soviet bloc. Would it strengthen or weaken the adversary? Sir Alec Douglas-Home, British Prime Minister 1963–64 and Foreign Minister for the second time in 1970–74 (during the Helsinki negotiations), summed up the issue by asking whether a fat communist would be less dangerous than a thin communist. He decided that a fat communist would be less dangerous because he (or she, presumably, though not admitted in those days) would become more dependent on the West, more infected by Western ideas, and more interested in consumer goods than ideology. He turned out to be largely right, except that East European communists never became truly fat.

The contrary view was that it was madness to help the adversary become stronger. Soviet aims, said critics, had not changed since Lenin wrote in 1922: "They [the Western powers] will supply us with the materials and technology which we lack, and will restore our military industry, which we need for our future victorious attacks upon our suppliers. In other words, they will work hard in order to prepare their own suicide".[12]

As it turned out, Western trade and generous credits to Eastern Europe were largely used by the regimes to buy off trouble and avoid reforms rather than to increase productivity, so debts piled up and dependence on the West increased, together with the cost to the Soviet Union of propping them up. The gross debt to the West of the six East European states and Yugoslavia rose from $9 billion in 1970 to $84 billion by 1980.[13]

This gave the West useful leverage. For instance, Timothy Garton Ash asks why the Polish leader Edouard Gierek tolerated the ferment of independent activity in the mid-1970s. One reason was détente, he writes: "By 1977 Gierek was already in desperate financial straits, while the 'Helsinki process' was in full swing and the Carter administration made the most explicit 'linkage' between the economic and human rights components of détente". That, he suggests, was a likely reason why a number of opposition activists who were arrested in 1977 were suddenly released before trial.[14]

East Germany was also in dire straits. The true state of its economy was concealed by hopelessly unreal statistics which appeared to make it the most economically successful state in Eastern Europe, much admired by some leftists in the West. The delusion became apparent only after reunification with West Germany in 1990. A report for the World Bank by Professor Jan Prybyla described the shock experienced by a West German Volkswagen executive on a visit to the East German factory that produced the tiny Trabant cars. He discovered that the plant was actually subtracting value from inputs. "What was not fully understood at the time", he wrote, "was that East Germany's whole economy was value-subtracting and cost-unconscious". Thus, in 1989 a deluded Hans Modrow, the last communist head of the GDR, put the East German economy's net worth at 1.5 trillion West German marks (DM). After reunification, the heads of the privatisation agency Treuhand steadily reduced their estimates to zero and then even to minus DM 300 billion.[15] By the time of its collapse, East Germany was, by any definition, bankrupt. When Egon Krenz, its leader briefly in 1989, went to Moscow to plead for loans of around DM 12 billion, Gorbachev was "speechless" on learning of East Germany's dire situation.[16]

Altogether, Western critics of détente overestimated the strength and appeal of the Soviet Union, and underestimated the crisis building up in Eastern Europe, where the failings of its political systems and falling growth were becoming more obvious by the day.[17] Disillusion pervaded the area at all levels, increasing the restless desire of the populations to restore their ancient links with Western Europe. Confronters in the West believed that the answer was to increase pressure in the hope of provoking collapse. Engagers did not believe that would work. The Soviet Union, they argued, was not ready to release its hard-won territory in Eastern Europe. Under pressure, it would merely tighten controls, regardless of hardship, so it was best to work for slow evolution. They cited Aesop's fable in which the wind and the sun compete to make a man remove his coat. The wind blows as hard as it can but the man merely pulls his coat tighter. When the sun's turn comes it shines warmly until the man removes his coat. Détente would be that sun.[18]

To the promoters of Helsinki, it seemed obvious that if barriers could be lowered Western influence would flow eastward. They were proved right. The greatly superior wealth and soft power of Western Europe proved infinitely more attractive to the East than was the influence of the Soviet Union in the West, particularly as the Helsinki process helped to educate Western opinion in the realities of life under communism.

Joseph Nye has described soft power as "the ability to get what you want through attraction rather than coercion or payments. It arises from the attractiveness of a country's culture, political ideals, and policies".[19] Melvyn Leffler, one of the most distinguished American historians of the Cold War, has also acknowledged the role it played in the Cold War: "Not long ago, few of us [historians of the Cold War] would have focused on Coke, and Reeboks, on jazz and rock, on Sesame Street and Donald Duck, but we now know that their appeal perhaps counted for more than the Pershing missiles and the neutron bombs that seemed to dominate the diplomacy of the 1970s".[20] He might also have mentioned the British group the Beatles, who had a huge underground following in the Soviet Union and Eastern Europe, where fans found ways of recording them on discarded X-ray plates.

Soviet leaders were acutely aware of the magnetic attraction of the West, which is why they so strongly resisted the Western agenda for freer movement at Helsinki, and lectured their own people with increasingly anxious intensity on the need for ideological vigilance against Western influence. They could see that engagement was in many ways more threatening than confrontation because the Soviet Union could defend itself more easily against the armed forces of NATO than against the insidious influence of the richer, freer and more successful West, which was spreading among the elites in Moscow and the people of Eastern Europe, especially the young. As Brezhnev told the Polish party congress in 1968: "In the new conditions the imperialists… seek weak links in the socialist front, follow a course of ideological subversion,… sow discord to drive wedges,… seek to isolate one or another socialist state so as to seize them later by the throat".[21]

Erich Honecker, the East German leader, felt particularly vulnerable on the front line against West Germany, so he announced the policy of *Abgrenzung* (demarcation or delimitation) in a vain attempt to shield his state from Western influence. He told his party congress in June 1971 that "a process of *Abgrenzung* rather than rapprochement is objectively taking place between the socialist GDR and imperialist FRG".[22] In reality, the opposite was happening as contacts increased. At the same time the regime's attempts to counteract Western influence by increasing surveillance made the regime even more unpopular.

The European stage, therefore, seemed to be set for a gradual shift of emphasis from hard to soft power. Each side feared more exposure to the other while hoping to subvert it. Détente was thus ambiguous. On the one hand, it seemed to promote stability by requiring a certain level of agreement and cooperation between the two sides. On the other hand, it threatened stability by lowering the threat perceptions that held both alliances together. By promoting contacts between peoples it also stimulated pressures for change, especially in Eastern Europe.

Despite these conflicting hopes and fears, both sides found themselves moving cautiously towards a European security conference. While the Warsaw Pact wrestled with its internal conflicts, as we saw in the previous chapter, NATO was also trying to find a common position. Clearly, it could not agree to a security conference on the terms of the Bucharest declaration (Chapter 6) but it gradually worked through its own disagreements until, at a ministerial meeting in Reykjavik in June 1968, it achieved a cautious response to the Warsaw Pact. Without committing members to attend, it set out initial conditions, among them that the United States and Canada must participate, and that negotiations should first start on mutual and balanced force reductions (MBFR) in Europe (see Chapter 10 for more on MBFR): "Ministers concluded that the intensified examination and review, within the Alliance, of suitable policies to achieve a just and stable order in Europe, to overcome the division of Germany and to foster European security had proved of great value and should continue. This task will be part of a process of active and constant preparation for the time when fruitful discussions of these complex questions may be possible bilaterally or multilaterally between Eastern and Western nations".[23]

The time of "fruitful discussions" arrived slowly after much arguing within and between the alliances, and not before the whole project received a severe setback when Soviet-led forces invaded Czechoslovakia in August 1968, shattering Western hopes that détente would encourage the Soviet Union to allow gradual liberalisation in Eastern Europe. We look at this in the next chapter.

Notes

1 Selvage, 'The Warsaw Pact and the European Security Conference, 1964–69: Sovereignty, Hegemony, and the German Question' in Wenger et. al., *Origins of the European Security System.*
2 Morgan, *The Final Act*, 27–32.
3 NATO, December 1967, 'The Harmel Report', viewed 11 January 2022, https://www.nato.int/cps/en/natohq/official_texts_26700.htm?sel. See also Hanhimäki and Westad, *The Cold War*, 495–7.
4 Quoted in Kieninger, *Dynamic Détente*, 49.
5 Melvyn Leffler has analysed these false starts in his illuminating book *For the Soul of Mankind.*
6 Statement to the Senate Foreign Relations Committee quoted in Davy, ed., *European Détente*, 6.
7 Statement to the Senate Foreign Relations Committee, 19 September, 1974, *Department of State Bulletin* 71, 14 October 1974, 505.
8 Peter Bender quoted in Rupnik, *The Other Europe*, 58.
9 Quoted in Kieninger, *Dynamic Détente*, 161.
10 Urban, *Détente*, 295–297.
11 Urban, 193.
12 Quoted in Urban, 338.
13 Paul Marer, 'Economies and trade of Eastern Europe' in Griffith ed., *Central and Eastern Europe: The Opening Curtain?*.
14 Garton Ash, *The Polish Revolution*, 21–2, quoted in Davy, ed., *European Détente*, 255–6.
15 Jan S. Prybyla, 'The price of German unification', in *Transition* (Prague), 75–6, May–June 1996. World Bank Policy Research Department, Washington DC.
16 Lévesque, *The Enigma of 1989*, 158.
17 Lévesque, 158, and Davy, 'Eastern Europe: New Policies for Old' in *Washington Quarterly*, Spring 1984.
18 Sir William Hayter in Urban, *Détente*, 27.
19 Nye, *Soft Power*, p. x.
20 Leffler, 'Bringing it together: the parts and the whole' in Westad, ed., *Reviewing the Cold War*, 46.
21 Quoted in Davy, ed., *European Détente*, 244.
22 Quoted by Kasper in Davy, ed., *European Détente*, 152.
23 North Atlantic Council, June 1968, *Final Communiqué*, NATO, viewed 11 January 2022, https://www.nato.int/docu/comm/49-95/c680624a.htm

8 1968: Dubček, martyred by the "Brezhnev Doctrine"

Alexander Dubček was a mild and friendly man from Slovakia, a dedicated, idealistic communist devoted to the Soviet Union, where he had grown up and attended school and party college. As party leader in the Slovak part of Czechoslovakia he had the reputation for being more humane and tolerant than most communist leaders of that time but he was in other respects safely orthodox. Or so it seemed.

On 5 January 1968, after stormy party meetings, he was elected leader of the Communist Party of Czechoslovakia (in effect, ruler of the country), to replace the dully oppressive regime of Antonin Novotny. By the spring he was somewhat bewildered to find himself riding a huge wave of popularity such as no communist leader in Eastern Europe had ever come near to experiencing—or would experience thereafter. In August of the same year he was equally bewildered to find his country invaded by his revered friends from Moscow and Eastern Europe,[1] who sent their tanks into Prague to arrest him and his close colleagues and ship them out of the country.[2]

The crushing of the so-called "Prague Spring" had two important effects on the Helsinki Process. First, it aborted an experiment that would have shown whether it was possible for East European states to evolve peacefully into something resembling social democracy while remaining loyal to the Soviet alliance. Had that unlikely scenario proved possible, the history of Europe and the Cold War would have taken a very different path. As it was, the invasion demonstrated the harsh limits of Soviet tolerance, largely crushing hopes that European communism could be reformed or that the systems of East and West could converge, which was a popular illusion in some quarters. When the Helsinki talks got under way four years later, the best that seemed possible in the immediate future was modest incremental improvements in human rights and a gradual lowering of barriers between East and West, although the seemingly distant dream of reuniting Europe and Germany remained. By the time Mikhail Gorbachev became Soviet leader in 1985 and tried to bring his own version of the Prague Spring to the Soviet Union and Eastern Europe (in 1989 he formally condemned the invasion), it was too late. The idea of reformed communism had been killed. The Soviet Union descended into chaos, while in Eastern Europe the failures

DOI: 10.4324/9781003146124-11

of the system and hatred of Russia combined to make most people eager only to escape the Soviet orbit and join the democracies of Western Europe.

The second effect of the invasion on the Helsinki Process was to make the "Brezhnev Doctrine" a central issue in negotiating the Final Act. That was the name given to the excuse for the invasion invented by Leonid Brezhnev, the Soviet leader. He claimed that the need to "save socialism" took precedence over respect for Czechoslovak sovereignty. The West became determined to exclude that notion from the Final Act in the hope of discouraging further such Soviet interventions. More of that later and in Appendix C.

Dubček thus enters the Helsinki story as a victim, but he was much more than that. The Prague Spring that flowered under his leadership gave the Czechoslovak people a few heady months of freedom. It shook and divided the entire communist world and fascinated the rest, shaping the environment in which the Helsinki talks unfolded.[3]

What made the Soviet invasion particularly bitter for Dubček and the other leaders of the Prague Spring was that they were not in fact aiming to abandon socialism or leave the Warsaw Pact. They regarded themselves as loyal communists who were simply trying to make the system more humane and efficient while remaining within the alliance. Some of them even thought they were doing the communist world a favour by offering a more efficient and humane model: "socialism with a human face".

Initially, they had not been pushed by public opinion. There had been no popular uprising or street protests. Until the spring of 1968 the country was superficially at peace under a grey cloud of resignation, ruled by Antonin Novotny and a generation of unqualified bureaucrats who had been promoted after the communist takeover in 1948 for their working-class credentials and ideological loyalty rather than for ability, which they mostly conspicuously lacked.[4]

Frustration had, however, been building up for a long time, especially among rising generations impatient with the unfulfilled promises of the ruling ideology and the Novotny regime's failure to come to terms with the crimes of the Stalin era. It was first articulated by writers at a stormy meeting of the Writers' Union in 1967,[5] but it had festered for years among a few exceptional senior members of the party, who had been keen communists in their youth but had seen their dream turn into a nightmare of oppression and stultifying inefficiency. Among the leading figures was Zdeněk Mlynář, who helped draft a new "Action Programme" for Dubček that aimed to introduce limited elements of democracy and market economics. He had been a student in Moscow, where he became friendly with the future leader of the Soviet Union, Mikhail Gorbachev. Both men had privately criticised the system under which they lived. In retirement, they met to discuss the failure of their attempts to reform it. A record of their melancholy conversation was published in a book.[6]

Almost the first move by the Dubček leadership in 1968 was to abolish censorship. Their aim was to stimulate open discussion and allow checks on the misuse of power that the monolithic Soviet system had failed to provide.

The censors, who were placed in every publishing house, found they had no instructions, so, in mid-March, responding to the spirit of the time, they took their own initiative and voted to abolish censorship. But they still had to come to work, so they did so and spent their time making tea and toast and playing cards before wandering along to the nearest wine bar.[7] Such was the almost surreal atmosphere in the early days of the Prague Spring as the old constraints fell away.

Initially, the people of Czechoslovakia were sceptical of Dubček's programme. They thought it was just another in a long line of false promises. Many workers also worried that the introduction of market values would end the relatively comfortable life they enjoyed under the planned economy. As they used to say, "We pretend to work and they pretend to pay us". But soon enthusiasm began to sweep the country as people realised that real change was arriving. Admittedly, it was not the full parliamentary democracy that most of them wanted but it did represent something far better than the oppressive mediocrity that had ruled them for twenty years. The result was an explosion of free speech and writing, as if the lid had blown off a pressure cooker. Excited discussions broke out at street corners and in newspapers, hitherto mostly unread but now sold out almost as soon as they appeared. The new leaders exposed themselves for the first time to sharp questioning at huge public meetings. The brutal rigged show trials of the 1950s could now be openly discussed as the heavy burden of fear was lifted. A journalist on the party newspaper told this author that he had not previously realised how unpopular the regime had been because his neighbours were too scared to tell him.

All this was wholly beyond the comprehension of Moscow's leaders, who regarded control of the media as essential to the exercise of political control. Their alarm was fed by misleading reports from their agents in Prague that described the reforms as "counter-revolutionary" and forecast the overthrow of the communist system. They seemed very wrong at the time, and clearly wrote with malign intentions, but, looking further ahead, they may have had a point. Although Brezhnev was wrong to accuse Dubček and his colleagues of counter-revolution, he was not entirely wrong to fear that the Prague experiment might have led eventually to the communists losing control and thus destabilising the whole Soviet empire. In 1989 Dubček himself rather surprisingly admitted in an interview that the Prague Spring would have led to a pluralist multi-party society, which was exactly what Brezhnev feared—and what the Czechs wanted.[8]

Moscow therefore became particularly worried when the Czech experiment began to raise hopes of change in other parts of Eastern Europe and even in the Soviet Union, where many of the young were infected, and "liberal intellectuals were transfixed by the experiment under way in Prague", which they hoped would bring change to their own country.[9] In the summer of 1968 even some members of the Soviet Central Committee sent private messages of encouragement to friends in the party apparatus in Prague, while their official press was attacking Dubček.[10] In Warsaw in

March 1968 some of the students demonstrating on other issues shouted "Dubček! Dubček!"[11]

Brezhnev himself had been reluctant to invade. During the crisis he was observed to be shaken and pale. He became so distressed that he relied for the rest of his life on sleeping pills or tranquillisers.[12] Dubček had been his protégé and he knew him well. In a telephone conversation on 8 August 1968, less than two weeks before the invasion, he pleaded with Dubček to curb the reformers and, in particular, the media. He simply could not understand why Dubček lacked the power to do so. "Sasha", he says in a transcript, "over the past two to three days the newspapers I mentioned have been doggedly continuing to occupy themselves with the publication of defamatory ravings about the Soviet Union and the other fraternal countries… I thought that I was dealing with the leader of the chief party organ, the organ that has complete power… Don't you see that I'm talking with you as a friend, and that I wish only the best for you?… The rightists have planted their agents everywhere, literally everywhere".

Dubček pleaded for more time, saying that the situation was complex, but he had become weary and discouraged: "I would just as soon go where it would be pleasant to work. I don't set great store by this post…, I'm running out of steam; I'm thinking of giving up this work".[13]

In the end Brezhnev felt he had no choice. He had been under heavy pressure from his own circle and from the nervous regimes in both East Germany and Poland, who feared political infection from Prague, so he calculated, probably rightly, that he would not survive if he failed to invade.

Thus, on the night of 20–21 August 1968, Soviet forces, with some token support from the other members of the Warsaw Pact (except Romania), rolled into Prague, had Dubček and his colleagues arrested, and flew them off to Moscow. The invaders had been misled by their informers in Prague to believe that Dubček did not have wide support, so they were surprised to encounter massive peaceful resistance by the Czechs, who took down or changed signposts, refused food and water to the invading forces, climbed on the tanks to argue with the confused crews, and cleverly ran wires to a clandestine radio station in the basement of the official radio station while the upper floors were occupied by the Russians.

This underground station, together with provincial radio stations and some army equipment, kept the people and the rest of the world informed. They more or less ran the country for the first week of the invasion while Dubček and his colleagues were held in Moscow. Listeners could hear regular updates and advice on how to resist the Russians without violence. For instance, on 23 August the call went out to stop or delay a Russian train carrying equipment for jamming radio transmissions. The train found itself held up in a station, then stopped on the main line when the electricity appeared to fail, and finally immobilised on a branch line.[14] Party members also managed to bring forward the special party congress that had been called for 8 September to endorse Dubček's programme. The Russians had planned to stop it because it would have consolidated the reforms and brought more progressives into party jobs. They failed when the congress was convened secretly in a factory, with amazing skill and speed, on 22 August. All the members except one voted to support Dubček.[15]

Eventually, the Russians found they were unable to install the puppet government that their mendacious informers had told them would find support. The candidates for that government lost their nerve, and President Svoboda refused to back them, so Dubček and his colleagues were returned to Prague after signing a humiliating document in which they promised, in effect, to cancel much of the Prague Spring and control the media to "serve the cause of socialism fully".[16] All but one of the group, the courageous František Kriegel, signed in the hope that they could still rescue something of the reforms. Dubček at first refused to sign but then, heavily sedated, gave in, and delivered a tearful speech on his return to Prague. His close friend and colleague, Josef Smrkovský, appeared on a balcony in the Old Town Square to plead with the assembled crowd. "Should we", he asked, with dramatic gestures, "have bared our breasts to the bayonets? Instead, we did our best to save what we could".[17] Dubcek and his colleagues were then allowed to remain nominally in power until April 1969, when Gustáv Husák took over and imposed "normalisation"—meaning, of course, the Soviet version of "normal", which ensured that the reforms were stopped.

An estimated 300,000 fled the demoralised country. About half a million people resigned or were expelled from the party. Intellectuals who refused to approve the invasion were given menial jobs such as cleaning windows or minding boilers. One of those boiler-minders was Jiří Dienstbier, a bright young journalist who, following a spell in prison, became Foreign Minister of democratic Czechoslovakia after the collapse of the Soviet Union. Timothy Garton Ash has described the situation in darkly comic terms: "That window cleaner over there: his thesis was on Wittgenstein. Ask your waiter about Kafka: before his trial he lectured on *The Trial*. Yes, the night watchman is reading Aristotle. Your coal will be delivered by an ordained priest of the Czech brethren. Kiss the milkman's ring: he is your bishop".[18]

Gloom settled over Czechoslovakia as people digested the loss of the intoxicating freedoms they had enjoyed over the summer, the humiliation of being invaded, and the crushing of their spirits as they were forced to pretend loyalty to the new regime. Many wept openly in the streets. Surveillance returned. In the Alcron hotel, frequented by Western journalists, the hidden microphones in the rooms that had been switched off in the summer were now re-activated, as this author was warned by a receptionist, with tears streaming down her face.

The crushing of the Prague Spring was a blow not only to the Czechs but also to those in the East and the West who had hoped that détente would promote liberalisation in Eastern Europe. It showed that Moscow was not prepared to allow any significant reform in its empire. Among communists in Western Europe, mainly in France and Italy, deep splits opened up between those loyal to Moscow and others who saw the need for a more democratic form of communism, which came to be known as Eurocommunism.

In Eastern Europe dissidents began re-thinking their tactics, as we shall see in Chapter 15.

In the Soviet Union a few brave dissidents protested in public and were punished very harshly. Many more did so out of the public eye. According to a report by the Czech ambassador in Moscow, some 800 party cells out of a total of 60,000 expressed their disapproval, in an astonishing show of courage.[19] Members of the intelligentsia were devastated by this blow to their own hopes of reform. They expressed shame at being "part of a barbarian country that had clubbed its enlightened neighbour".[20] They had hoped that the Czechoslovak example would inspire reforms in the Soviet Union. Frustrated, they then attached those hopes to the Helsinki Process, swallowing their dislike of Brezhnev to support his campaign for a European security conference. Among them was the man who later became head of the Soviet delegation to the Helsinki negotiations, Anatoly Kovalev (see Chapter 12).

The Brezhnev Doctrine and the Helsinki Final Act[21]

While the effects of the Prague Spring and its suppression rippled out in many directions it also had one very specific effect on the Helsinki conference, as we indicated at the start of this chapter: it made Western negotiators determined to exclude the "Brezhnev Doctrine" from the text of the Final Act.[22] Throughout his campaign for the conference Brezhnev had declared that its main aim should be to endorse the permanence and inviolability of European frontiers and the principles of sovereignty and non-interference. This was in line with the Warsaw Pact of 1955, which included among its provisions "respect for the independence and sovereignty of states". The *Great Soviet Encyclopaedia* in 1956 even stated that any violation of sovereignty was illegal. Yet Brezhnev's invasion of Czechoslovakia was a massive breach of that country's sovereignty and about as blatant an illegal interference in its internal affairs as could be imagined. How was he to explain the apparent contradiction between his actions and the principles, not only of international law but of the Warsaw Pact, as constantly reiterated in his campaign for a European security conference?

He had plenty of explaining to do. The essence of his argument was that the need to protect socialism took precedence over respect for sovereignty. In other words, his pious words on frontiers, sovereignty and non-interference were now to be understood as applying only to East–West relations, and not to his own relations with the countries of Eastern Europe. Put another way, the Soviet Union could do what it liked in Eastern Europe to "save socialism".

This position had already long been implicit in the Soviet doctrine of "peaceful coexistence" between East and West, which rested on recognition of spheres of interest. It had been brutally asserted by his predecessor, who sent Soviet tanks into Hungary in 1956 to put down a "counter-revolution". The Hungarian uprising was very different from the Prague Spring. It turned into a bloody struggle against the government, with many dead, leading eventually to a declaration of neutrality after Soviet tanks had gone into action. The leaders of the Prague Spring thought they had learned the lessons of Hungary. Their experiment was wholly peaceful and popular, an attempt to reform the system rather than to overthrow the government or abandon communism. There was no public disorder, and no secret policemen were hanged from lamp posts, as they had been in Hungary.

Brezhnev therefore had to redefine the limits of Soviet tolerance. He made them explicit on 3 August 1968 at a meeting in Bratislava with representatives of Eastern Europe, whom he warned that the Soviet Union would not allow any East European country to reject socialism (as defined by him). After the invasion, in the face of widespread criticism, he felt obliged to lay out his justification more fully in a long rambling speech to the Polish Workers' Party on 13 November, which became the basic text of the Brezhnev Doctrine.[23]

This doctrine therefore became shorthand for Moscow's claim to a free hand in Eastern Europe. During the Helsinki negotiations, Soviet negotiators tried repeatedly to get this claim included in the Final Act in various guises. For instance, they wanted the "Declaration on Principles Guiding Relations between Participating States" to apply only to relations between states with different social systems, that is between East and West, not between Moscow and its colonies in Eastern Europe. The Western negotiators resisted resolutely from the start and were ultimately successful. The Brezhnev Doctrine found no place in the Final Act, which grants no special rights to the Soviet Union in Eastern Europe. The Principles, it says, apply to "relations with all other participating states, irrespective of their political, economic or social systems". Thus, any further Soviet interventions in Eastern Europe would breach solemn undertakings signed by the Soviet leader himself.

Epilogue

When the Soviet empire collapsed in 1969 Dubček returned to Prague from his menial job with the Forestry Department in Slovakia (at least he had not been shot). He was greeted by huge cheers as a revered figure from the past but the people were no longer interested in any version of communism. They wanted democracy on the West European model. Dubček was given the honourable job of Chairman of the Federal Parliament. He proposed Václav Havel, the dissident playwright recently out of prison, as President.[24]

Shortly before that, Dubček had been awarded the Sakharov Prize by the European Parliament. Andrei Sakharov, a distinguished Soviet scientist who had himself been persecuted and exiled, welcomed the award. "The [Prague] Spring", he wrote, "brought hope; it encouraged me to work on my Reflections. August destroyed my illusions and spurred my public activity. The same was true for many of my friends. The handful of Soviet dissidents drew from the Prague Spring the strength they needed to carry on a tough battle for many years".[25]

Dubček died on 7 November 1992, aged 70, as a result of injuries sustained in a car crash.

Notes

1 Romania refused to participate.
2 For a collection of eye-witness accounts of the invasion see Robert Littell, ed. *The Czech Black Book*.
3 For a scholarly analysis of the Prague Spring see Kieran Williams, *The Prague Spring and its Aftermath*. See also Gordon Skilling, *Czechoslovakia's Interrupted Revolution*.
4 Williams, 5–6.
5 Some of the speeches in translation together with other documents from Prague Spring are in Oxley, Pravda and Ritchie, *Czechoslovakia, the Party and the People*.
6 Mikhail Gorbachev and Zdeněk Mlynář, *Conversations with Gorbachev on Perestroika, the Prague Spring and the Crossroads of Socialism*.
7 Shawcross, *Dubček*, 125.
8 Shawcross, 228.
9 English; *Russia and the Idea of the West*; 110.
10 Recounted to the author in summer 1968 by the late Dr Milan Hübl, Rector of the Party college and a member of the Czechoslovak Central Committee, during furtive night walks through the streets of Prague. Hübl was later imprisoned by the Husak regime.
11 Heard by the author on a brief visit to Warsaw before being expelled and returning to Prague.
12 Zubok, *A Failed Empire*, 208.
13 Transcript of Brezhnev's Telephone Conversation with Dubcek, 13 August 1968, viewed 1 February 2022, https://sites.fas.harvard.edu/~hpcws/translation.htm
14 Roberts and Windsor, *Czechoslovakia 1968*, 120.
15 Jiri Pelikan, ed., *The Secret Vysočany Congress*.
16 Full text in Tigrid, *Why Dubcek Fell*, 210.
17 An approximate rendering from the memory of the author, who was present.
18 Garton Ash, *The Uses of Adversity* 56–7.
19 Tigrid, 97.
20 English, 111.
21 Ouimet, *The Rise and Fall of the Brezhnev Doctrine in Soviet Foreign Policy*. (Chapel Hill and London: The University of North Carolina Press, 2003), 67.
22 *DBPO III/II*, 7.
23 The full text from *Pravda*, translated by Novosti, the Soviet press agency, can be found in the Fordham University Internet Modern History Sourcebook: https://sourcebooks.fordham.edu/mod/1968brezhnev.asp, viewed 21 March 2022.
24 Shawcross, 224.
25 Shawcross 226.

9 1969–74: Willy Brandt, the realistic idealist

Willy Brandt removed one of the principal blocks on the road to Helsinki: West Germany's refusal to recognise East Germany and the post-war frontiers of Poland. We met him in Chapter 4 as Governing Mayor of West Berlin and then Foreign Minister of West Germany in coalition with the Christian Democrats. In 1969 he won the national election in his own right and became Chancellor of West Germany in coalition with the Free Democrats. He thus became able to launch his new eastern policy (*Ostpolitik*) under the slogan "Change through rapprochement" (*Wandlung durch Annäherung*).This later became the guiding principle of West European efforts in the Helsinki negotiations, where the underlying aim was to induce change in Eastern Europe through closer contacts with Western Europe.

For Brandt, this meant breaking with established West German policy by provisionally accepting the post-war frontiers and recognising East Germany as a separate state (though not its people as a separate nation), and in general building trust with Moscow and his eastern neighbours. Until then West German governments had insisted that there would be no true détente without the reunification of Germany. Brandt reversed this, arguing that there could be no reunification without a prior process of détente.

Brandt was a surprising figure to reach the top in generally conservative West Germany. Born in 1913 as Herbert Frahm to an unwed salesgirl in Lübeck, he grew up to be an active socialist. He risked his life opposing Hitler and eventually fled to Scandinavia, where he spent most of the war years before returning to Germany in Norwegian uniform as Willy Brandt. He then reclaimed his German nationality and entered politics as a Social Democrat, rising quickly to become Governing Mayor of West Berlin in 1957, then Foreign Minister of West Germany in 1967, and Chancellor of the Federal Republic of [West] Germany in October 1969. His energy and fresh face led many to compare him with US president John F. Kennedy, with whom he established close relations while Governing Mayor of Berlin. This often meant by-passing the disgruntled Dr Konrad Adenauer, Chancellor of the federal government in the then capital, Bonn.

His motivation was not purely political. He felt deep moral concern for the terrible suffering that Hitler's Germany had inflicted on Europe, and on Poland in particular. On a visit to Warsaw in April 1970 he fell to his knees at

DOI: 10.4324/9781003146124-12

the monument to the Warsaw ghetto uprising of 1943, when many thousands of Jews were killed or deported to death camps. The photo of that moment went around the world as one of most memorable images of the Cold War, a gesture of contrition for Germany's appalling crimes. Many West Germans criticised him for debasing himself. In his memoir he defended his action in words that still resonate with deep feeling: "From the bottom of the abyss of German history, under the burden of millions of victims of murder, I did what human beings do when speech fails them".[1]

Like many turning points in history, Brandt's *Ostpolitik* had long antecedents. He and his colleagues, notably Egon Bahr, had been thinking hard about the whole German question since the building of the Berlin Wall in 1961, and even before that. They had come to the conclusion that isolating East Germany was bringing no gains and certainly not helping the people of East Germany. Nor was there any benefit in maintaining claims to territories that had been lost to Poland after the war. These claims merely exacerbated Polish fears of Germany and drove Poland deeper into dependence on Soviet protection. Brandt and Bahr began to speak out more openly after President Kennedy's ground-breaking speeches on his "strategy of peace" in Washington and Berlin in 1963 (see Chapter 4).

Only a few weeks later Egon Bahr set out the new thinking in his now-famous (or, for his opponents, infamous) speech at the Protestant Academy in Tutzing, Bavaria. Speaking after Brandt, and citing Kennedy, he uttered what at that time were political heresies in West Germany, provoking huge controversy. He said that the Germany question could be solved only by engaging with the Soviet Union. He went on to argue that tension between the two parts of Germany only strengthened the East German regime and deepened the division of the country. Therefore trade and credits should be increased. Material improvements in East Germany were in the interest of West Germany because they would help to relax tension and reduce popular discontent that might otherwise lead to "uncontrolled developments". What was needed was a "narrow path of relief for the people in such homeopathic doses that no danger of a revolutionary turn develops". By gradually reducing the regime's "quite justified" fears, the loosening of the frontiers might become practicable because the risk to the regime would be bearable. Bahr then summed up this policy in the phrase mentioned above: "Change through rapprochement".[2]

On another occasion in a private meeting Bahr said: "We do not differ about Soviet intentions to retain control in Eastern Europe. We hope to put an end to this, but the problem is how to do it". His answer was to "disengage the Soviets from Eastern Europe step by step… by beginning projects that link Eastern and Western Europe in ways the Soviets don't consider dangerous".[3] He and Brandt hoped that gradual relaxation would reduce Soviet fears of Germany and expose Eastern Europe to Western influence, eventually opening a road to the unification of Europe and Germany. He added rather naively that this should not be discussed in public. In fact, of course, the Russians knew exactly what he was up to. Rightly assessing the subversive intent behind Brandt's smile, East Germany's Foreign Minister, Otto Winzer, called Bahr's Tutzing speech "aggression in felt slippers".[4]

As it turned out, history took a much faster road to the reunification of Germany and Europe than Bahr had expected; it came in October 1990, less than a year after the Berlin Wall had opened on 9 November 1989. But Brandt can claim much of the credit because his *Ostpolitik* had weakened the East German regime through intensified contacts, and built trust with the Soviet Union by accepting the post-war frontiers. This enabled Mikhail Gorbachev, the reformist Soviet leader, to risk allowing the regime to collapse rather than sending in tanks to support it. Although West Germany did not formally and legally renounce the former German territories that were now in Poland, Brandt's political acceptance of the Oder–Neisse frontier and the existence of East Germany were sufficient at the time to unblock his relations with the East.

The main blockage had been the so-called Hallstein Doctrine (see Chapter 7), named after a Foreign Ministry official and announced by Chancellor Adenauer in September 1955. It ruled that diplomatic relations could not be opened with any country that recognised East Germany except the Soviet Union, which was exempted because it was one of the four victorious powers responsible for the future of Germany, pending a peace treaty. This exemption enabled Dr Adenauer to go to Moscow in the same month and open relations, winning the repatriation of 15,000 prisoners of war and civilians. As we have seen, the Social Democrats had long been thinking beyond that doctrine, while the Christian Democrats remained stubbornly bound to it until January1967, when they found themselves in coalition with the Social Democrats. Then they agreed to risk one small breach in the doctrine by opening diplomatic relations with Romania, which was regarded as a maverick within the Soviet camp. The other members of the Warsaw Pact, mobilised by Poland, then rallied reluctantly behind East Germany to insist that it must be recognised before any other member could open an embassy in Bonn.

The Christian Democrats were unable to take that further painful step, so it was left to Brandt. As soon as he could form his own government in 1969 he moved quickly to sign treaties with the Soviet Union (August 1970), Poland (December 1970) and Czechoslovakia (December 1973), accepting the post-war borders while still making it clear that West Germany could commit only itself, not a future united Germany. In 1972, he took the bold step of recognising East Germany as a separate state but within a single nation, which annoyed the East German regime because it meant that when its citizens escaped they were automatically accepted as full citizens of West Germany. The new relationship was enshrined in an agreement known as the Basic Treaty, which provided for agreements on a range of issues, including travel, trade, culture and sports, and the exchange of missions below full diplomatic level. This fell short of the full diplomatic relations sought by the East German regime but was markedly better than no recognition at all.

The contentious claim to eventual reunification was asserted by means of an attached West German "Letter on German Unity" that was accepted but not endorsed by the East German regime, a wonderfully obscure compromise that turned out to be insufficient to satisfy the drafters of the Helsinki Final Act. In the letter the West German government stated that "this Treaty does not conflict with the political aim of the Federal Republic of Germany to work for a state of peace in Europe in which the German nation will regain its unity through free self-determination". We will see how the Helsinki Final Act improved on that.

Brandt's *Ostpolitik* opened a wholly new phase in European diplomacy, allowing West Germany and its allies, and other countries, to develop relations with East Germany and the rest of Eastern Europe, but he ran into bitter criticism from the Christian Democrats. They accused him of surrendering German territory and getting nothing in return, thereby, they said, merely strengthening the communist adversary. In April 1972, amid bitter arguments, Brandt lost his majority in parliament when he was deserted not only by some of his Free Democrat coalition partners but even by members of his own party. The Christian Democrats called a parliamentary "constructive vote of no-confidence". On paper, they could expect 250 votes, enough to win by one vote and put their own man, Rainer Barzel, in power as Chancellor. They were surprised to receive only 247, so Brandt survived. There were rumours of East German influence, later confirmed by Markus Wolf (if he is to be believed), who was then the chief of the East German foreign intelligence service. In his memoir he writes that his service secretly paid Julius Steiner, a Christian Democrat, 50,000 marks to abstain.[5] Another member was rumoured to have been blackmailed by the East Germans. A parliamentary investigation at the time found nothing.

By such methods and by such a small margin was history made. Yet, later that year, Brandt won overwhelming endorsement for his policies with a decisive victory in the federal elections. When the Christian Democrats returned to power in 1982 they eagerly pursued the policies they had condemned in opposition. Meanwhile, in July 1975, they had voted against the Helsinki Final Act. Chancellor Kohl later described that as the one foreign policy mistake of his early political career.[6]

Brandt's *Ostpolitik* also worried Washington, where it revived familiar fears that West Germany would detach itself from the Western alliance and drift eastward into neutrality. Strenuous diplomatic efforts by Brandt and Bahr largely allayed those fears. There is an almost comic account by Kissinger of Bahr's visit to the White House in October 1969 when, in order to deceive the State Department, which Kissinger routinely tried to exclude from his diplomacy, Bahr left the White House by the front door after talks that included the State Department and then re-entered through the basement for private talks with Kissinger, thereby establishing a back channel between the two men which by-passed the State Department.[7]

The East German regime was glad to end its isolation and increase trade with West Germany but feared the potentially destabilising effects of more contacts with the West. Its response was to announce a policy of *Abgrenzung* (demarcation, or fencing off) to protect its population from ideological infection from the West. The result was counter-productive. As surveillance increased, the regime became even more unpopular. In any case, *Abgrenzung* largely failed as travel between the two parts of Germany increased, and practically everyone in East Germany became able to watch West German television, which in earlier years had been a crime. Now they could say: "We spend our days in the GDR but our evenings [mentally] in the West".

Nor was another preventive measure any more successful. East Germany's 1968 constitution committed the state to gradual rapprochement between the two German states "until their reunification on the basis of democracy and socialism". By 1974 this looked dangerously close to Brandt's concept and too far from the Soviet Union's determination to cement the status quo, so the text was modified to affirm that East Germany was "for ever and irrevocably" allied with the Soviet Union.[8]

Thus, Brandt brought Europe to a critical new departure. Without his acceptance of the post-war frontiers (albeit provisional), and without the trust that he started to build with his eastern neighbours, it is difficult to imagine that any Soviet government could have accepted the reunification of Germany only 18 years later. Nor is it likely that the Helsinki summit could have taken place in 1975 as that required Western recognition of East Germany. The road to that extraordinary event now looked open, although the rest of the journey still proved far from easy.

Notes

1 Brandt, *My life*, 200.
2 Garton Ash, *In Europe's Name*, 65–6.
3 Kieninger, *Dynamic Détente*, 163.
4 Garton Ash, 188.
5 Wolf, *Man Without a Face*, 172.
6 Quoted from Kohl's Memoir by Schaefer in Wenger et al., *Origins of the European Security System*, 136.
7 Kissinger, *The White House Years*, 411.
8 Garton Ash, 189.

10 1969: Now they are talking

The Soviet-led invasion of Czechoslovakia in August 1968 appeared at first to damage the prospects for a security conference. The Soviet Union had marched into a wholly peaceful country in the middle of Europe, breaking most of the principles that a security conference was supposed to establish, including respect for sovereignty, non-interference and non-use of force. Moreover, by crushing an attempt to reform communism it set back Western hopes that détente would encourage liberalisation in Eastern Europe.

Yet, after a pause, the actual effect of the invasion was to encourage both sides to seek new ways forward. Willy Brandt, now leading West Germany, removed the principal roadblocks to a European security conference by signing treaties with his Eastern neighbours (see Chapter 9). At the same time the Warsaw Pact wanted to repair the damage done by the invasion. Gradually, therefore, a more constructive dialogue got under way. Here, in brief, is how it went.

March 1969: Warsaw Pact in Budapest

The Warsaw Pact's tone became more conciliatory. At a meeting in Budapest it called again for an "all-European" security conference but with fewer preconditions and without directly attacking the United States or West Germany. It said it wanted to strengthen economic, political and cultural relations "on the basis of respect for the equality, independence and sovereignty of countries... [and] the inviolability of existing borders",[1] conveniently forgetting that it had just violated Czechoslovakia's borders. It called on West Germany to give up its claim to represent Germans in both German states, to renounce atomic weapons, and to declare West Berlin to be not part of West Germany.

However, it could not resist an indirect attack on the United States: "Forces are continuing to work in Europe which do not want to contribute to the development of Europe by solving disputed questions and arranging peaceful agreements but are instead deploying more divisions and rockets". It is worth repeating here that the Soviet Union was engaged in a steady build-up of military forces in Europe throughout the time it was preaching détente.

DOI: 10.4324/9781003146124-13

10 April 1969: NATO ministers in Washington DC

NATO still could not accept Soviet conditions but was anxious not to appear wholly negative, so it proposed to explore "which concrete issues best lend themselves to fruitful negotiation and an early resolution". Consequently, they instructed the Council to "draft a list of these issues and to study how a useful process of negotiation could best be initiated, in due course, and to draw up a report for the next meeting of ministers".[2]

5 May 1969: Finland offers to host

Finland wrote to every state in Europe, plus the United States and Canada, offering to host the proposed security conference. Wily President Kekkonen saw this as an opportunity to safeguard his country's neutrality, which was often under threat from the neighbouring Soviet Union. He had constantly rejected Soviet demands that he recognise East Germany, preferring instead to maintain consular relations with both Germanys. This put him in a good position to invite both sides in the Cold War, as well as fellow neutrals and non-aligned.

4–5 December 1969: NATO ministers in Brussels

NATO could now agree on cautious approval for a security conference provided it was carefully prepared and likely to produce concrete results. In a Declaration the ministers said that "Peace and Security in Europe must rest upon universal respect for the principles of sovereign equality, political independence and the territorial integrity of each European state; the right of its peoples to shape their own destinies; the peaceful settlement of disputes; non-intervention in the internal affairs of any state by any other state, whatever their political or social system; and the renunciation of the use or the threat of force against any state". The penultimate point was to rule out the Brezhnev Doctrine, which would have justified invading other countries to "save socialism". The alert reader will have noticed a marked similarity between Eastern and Western texts on sovereignty and territorial integrity. The ministers comment, with perhaps a flicker of dry humour: "Past experience has shown that there is, as yet, no common interpretation of these principles".

The Declaration then introduced a formula that became central to the Western agenda throughout the subsequent negotiations. It called for "freer movement of people, ideas and information between the countries of East and West".[3] Although, as we have seen in Chapter 2, similar words had been used as early as 1955, and had remained in the vocabulary of bridge builders ever since, the phrase was first proposed specifically for a European security conference by the Belgian delegation at a meeting of the Inter-Parliamentary Union before the NATO meeting.[4] On stubborn Western insistence it eventually found its way into the Helsinki Final Act in 1975 except that "ideas" had to be dropped in the face of adamant Soviet objections (see Chapter 11).

A key passage in the NATO declaration came at the end: "The Ministers affirmed that, in considering all constructive possibilities, including a general conference or conferences, they will wish to assure that any such meeting should not serve to ratify the present division of Europe and should be the result of a common effort among all interested countries to tackle the problems which separate them".[5]

In view of NATO's constant reassertions at this early stage and throughout the CSCE negotiations that it would not ratify the post-war division of Europe—a position it successfully maintained to the end—it remains astonishing that so many misguided critics accused it of doing just that when the Final Act was signed. Some historians still perpetuate that error (see Chapter 15).

US departments of State and Defense instructed the US ambassador to NATO, Robert Ellsworth, that the American aim at the security conference would be the gradual establishment of more normal and constructive cooperation between East and West in Europe, and to break down obstacles against free movement of people, information and ideas.[6]

26–27 May 1970: NATO ministers in Rome

NATO still refused to go along with the Soviet desire for a quick declaratory conference, insisting, as in April 1969, that it should deal with concrete issues. The Allies "remain willing to negotiate, in a suitable forum, those concrete issues whose resolution would enhance the security of Europe". It repeated its earlier insistence that "peace must rest upon universal respect of the sovereign equality, political independence and territorial integrity of each European State, regardless of its political or social system and for the right of its peoples to shape their own destinies, free of the threat of external intervention, coercion or constraint". In other words, no "Brezhnev Doctrine" but also, if the words "coercion or constraint" are taken seriously, no Soviet rule over Eastern Europe, a maximalist demand with which to open a negotiation.

Noting the good news that West Germany was in talks with the Soviet Union, Poland and East Germany, that the Four Powers were negotiating on Berlin, and that talks on arms control were also continuing, they said that, provided progress was recorded in these talks (a vital proviso), they "would be ready to enter into multilateral contacts with all interested governments" to "explore when it will be possible to convene a conference, or a series of conferences, on European security and cooperation". The ministers suggest that the conference could consider ways of ensuring closer cooperation on cultural, economic and scientific matters, and on the environment. They then reaffirm that "the freer movement of people, ideas and information is an essential element for the development of such co-operation".[7]

June 1970: Warsaw Pact, Budapest

The Warsaw Pact took a significant step forward by formally accepting the participation of the United States and Canada. Now that Brezhnev's long-cherished conference seemed at last to be within reach, it was time to drop propaganda in favour of pragmatism. But it also insisted on recognition of East Germany which Brandt delivered in reduced and conditional form in 1972, accepting East Germany as a separate state but not the East German people as a separate nationality.

Autumn 1970: US insists on freer movement

The US State Department asked West Europeans to make specific proposals on freer movement and instructed its mission at NATO to emphasise that "freer movement between East and West of people, ideas and information would tend to increase pressure for liberalisation upon Warsaw Pact regimes and thereby dilute ideological rigidities of present policies".[8]

Thus, the agenda for Helsinki, and indeed the shape of the Final Act, were already becoming clear.

23 October 1970: the Davignon report

During this period human rights found their way onto the Western agenda. Western Europe had been trying to define its own identity, especially in response to the military coup in Greece in 1967. In 1969 Etienne Davignon, political director of the Belgian Foreign Ministry, suggested bringing together the six members of the European Community (Belgium, France, West Germany, Italy, the Netherlands, Luxembourg) to agree on a common foreign policy based on democratic values. The result was the Davignon Report, which said that this common policy must correspond to Europe's traditions and that a united Europe "must be founded on a common patrimony of respect for liberty and human rights". Although aimed initially at the Greek military junta that was in power at the time, the commitment to human rights as a pillar of Europe's identity could scarcely be ignored when drawing up an agenda for the CSCE. This pillar was reinforced on 14 December 1973, when the nine members of the European Community signed the Copenhagen Document on the European Identity 1973 stating that democracy, the rule of law, social justice and respect for human rights were "fundamental elements of the European identity".[9]

In November 1971 a West German working paper on the agenda for the CSCE introduced "in a nonchalant manner" a specific reference to human rights.[10] Although not yet mentioned by NATO, and dismissed by Kissinger, respect for human rights became an essential Western demand that was eventually included in the first section of the Final Act as one of the most resonant and controversial of the ten principles guiding relations between states. Together with the provisions for freer movement and other humanitarian measures in the third section, it represents what came to be called the human dimension of the CSCE.

April 1971: US State Department on liberalization

Meanwhile, the State Department had told NATO members that "the long-range objective is to encourage the liberalization of Warsaw Pact regimes (principally the Soviet) in the expectation that this would help overcome the unnatural division of Europe and the tensions which it endangers [presumably 'engenders']".[11] In another statement that looked naive at the time but today looks far-sighted, it suggested that "the possibility of significant liberalisation in the Soviet Union should not be ruled out altogether". Later, Nixon tried to rein in the State Department but in the meantime it was allowed to press forward its agenda for freer movement between East and West Europe.[12]

The State Department worked partly by stealth while Kissinger and Nixon were preoccupied with superpower diplomacy, so it was able to an extent to evade their outright hostility.[13] Nixon was quoted as saying that nobody expected anything to come from a security conference: it was just talk.[14] In October 1970 he told Gromyko that he would like to determine the results of a security conference bilaterally with the Soviet Union, a suggestion that was doubtless music to Gromyko's ears until he discovered much later, to his chagrin, that Washington could not control its West European allies.[15] Kissinger particularly wanted to keep the State Department out of preparations for a planned summit conference with Brezhnev and Nixon in Moscow in 1972. He saw to it that Secretary of State Rogers was humiliated when they reached the Soviet capital. Rogers fought back and successfully defended his department's role in preparing for the Helsinki conference.[16]

May 1971: MBFR, Brezhnev in Tbilisi

There was, however, another hurdle to surmount, namely the Western desire, particularly strong in Washington, to discuss mutual and balanced force reductions in Europe (MBFR). At that point the Russians appeared to believe that talks on MBFR could follow the security conference, so they resisted Western insistence on making the start of these talks a precondition of agreeing to the security conference. They were in any case very reluctant to cut their forces in Europe, which were vastly greater than those of NATO.

MBFR talks were perceived—quite wrongly as it turned out—as more important than the CSCE because they aimed to reduce forces on the ground rather than issue cloudy political declarations, from which critics expected nothing useful. In addition, the American administration was trying to ward off congressional pressure to draw down US forces in Europe, so a negotiated balance, if successful, would seem to meet those pressures.

At first, the State Department believed MBFR could be included in security conference but it gradually dropped the idea in the face of opposition from Nixon and Kissinger. MBFR concerned only NATO members and included too many tricky issues, so involving neutral and non-aligned states in talks on arms control would be too complicated, they argued. Moscow was also anxious to avoid arms talks getting in the way of the security conference. Nixon became determined to keep control of MBFR, especially as he realised that he would not be able to control the security conference, with its unruly European participants. He therefore made his consent to the CSCE conditional on Soviet agreement to start talks on MBFR separately from the CSCE, overriding objections from the State Department.[17] In 1970 The Pentagon had already made its support for the freer movement item on NATO's agenda contingent on removing MBFR from the agenda of the security conference, so the two negotiations were separated.

Brezhnev dragged his feet on MBFR, waiting for Bonn's eastern treaties and the Berlin agreement to be ratified. But then he dropped a bombshell. In a speech in Tbilisi on 13 May 1971, just as the US Senate was about to debate a motion by Senator Mansfield to reduce US forces in Europe, he came out in favour of starting talks on MBFR, effectively killing the Mansfield Amendment, which had previously been expected to pass. It made no sense to reduce forces unilaterally when there was a chance of mutual reductions.[18]

Kissinger has denied any connection between the vote and Brezhnev's speech,[19] but Garthoff argues convincingly that the timing of the speech was deliberate because Soviet leaders were concerned that a sudden massive withdrawal of American troops would bring instability to Europe that might lead to a more integrated European defence, with West Germany acquiring nuclear weapons (a constant nightmare that haunted both sides).[20] In other words, despite his propaganda, Brezhnev accepted that the United States could, for the time being at any rate, contribute to security in Europe by containing Germany. He may also have worried that the crumbling of NATO would start a process of erosion in the Warsaw Pact, so it seemed better to cling to the status quo and hope that superpower relations could be nurtured sufficiently to allow some element of joint management to keep the restless Europeans in order.

1 December 1971: Rogers speaks out

US Secretary of State William Rogers told Overseas Writers in Washington that the aim of a security conference should be dynamic; to encourage freer movement of people, ideas and information: "We would firmly oppose any attempt to use it to perpetuate the political and social division of Europe. We would see the conference not as a ratification of the existing division but as a step on the long road to a new situation—a situation in which the causes of tension are fewer, contacts are greater, and the continent could once more be thought of as Europe rather than as two parts".[21]

3 December 1971: Agreement on Berlin

One roadblock on the way to the conference was removed when the Four Powers reached agreement on the status of Berlin. The Soviet Union accepted responsibility for Western access to Berlin, depriving East Germany of power to interfere. Because of still-unresolved views on the status of Berlin the city was not actually mentioned, being merely referred to as the "relevant area".

9–10 December 1971: NATO ministers in Brussels

NATO members were now ready to start preparations for a conference. They emphasised again the vital point that the conference "should not serve to perpetuate the post-war division of Europe but rather should contribute to reconciliation and cooperation… by reducing the barriers that still exist… The Conference should address in a concrete manner the underlying causes of tension in Europe and the basic principles which should govern relations among states irrespective of political and social systems". Thus, NATO was already putting itself on a collision course with Soviet attempts to cement the status quo.[22]

January 1972: Warsaw Pact in Prague

The Warsaw Pact responded with a declaration emphasising seven "fundamental principles of European security": inviolability of borders, non-use of force, peaceful coexistence, good neighbourly relations and cooperation in the interest of peace, mutually advantageous contacts among states [N.B. not "people", as demanded by NATO], disarmament, and support for the United Nations. It was clear, however, that the Soviet Union still envisaged these principles applying only to East–West relations, not to its own relations with Eastern Europe, which should remain subject to the Brezhnev Doctrine.

22–30 May 1972: Nixon and Brezhnev in Moscow

Nixon and Kissinger in Moscow agreed with Brezhnev that the conference should be convened "without undue delay", thereby undercutting the European view that it should not be convened until there was a guarantee that it would negotiate issues of real substance and not just issue cloudy generalities, as the Russians wanted.

Kissinger also rather casually encouraged the US president to sign a misguided document, largely drafted by the Soviet Union, called "Basic Principles of Relations". This endorsed the Soviet agenda for cementing the status quo, and included an empty promise of "non-interference" and a similarly unrealistic undertaking not to seek unilateral advantage at the expense of the other. Inevitably, both sides continued to seek unilateral advantage. Indeed, Kissinger soon succeeded in driving the Russians out of Egypt.

The document also contained a commitment to "peaceful coexistence", a seemingly harmless Soviet doctrine according to which capitalism and communism could co-exist without war while continuing the ideological struggle. As mentioned in Chapter 4, this had replaced Stalin's belief in the inevitability of war. West Europeans steadfastly refused to include "peaceful coexistence" in the Helsinki Final Act because it would have meant accepting the Soviet view that the principles of behaviour applied only to East–West relations, thereby endorsing the Brezhnev Doctrine and granting the Soviet Union a free hand in Eastern Europe.

There was no mention in this Moscow document of freer movement or human rights. It merely urged getting the security conference on the road and out of the way as soon as possible. It thus highlighted the difference between largely static détente envisaged by the two superpowers and the more dynamic concept promoted by the Europeans and the US State Department.

30–31 May 1972: NATO in Bonn

With the green light from the Moscow summit, NATO managed to paper over cracks in the alliance and declared itself ready to enter multilateral preparations for a conference in Helsinki. NATO's limited aim at this stage was simply to establish whether enough common ground existed to allow a reasonable expectation of success if a full conference were called.[23]

October 1972: A last-minute hitch

One issue still stood in the way. The West Germans were still opposing a reference to "freer movement" as too provocative. They knew that the communist regime in East Germany depended for its survival on preventing a renewal of the exodus of its population that had been taking place before it built the Berlin Wall in 1961. The French diplomat Jacques Andréani therefore drafted a series of mandates for committees referring to "human contacts" instead of freer movement. This wording survived into the Final Act as one of the headings under "humanitarian and other fields", but the text still strongly committed signatories "to facilitate freer movement and contacts, individually and collectively, either privately or officially, among persons, institutions and organisations".

9 November 1972: Finland invites

Finland, after extensive consultations, formally invited 33 states to join it in multilateral preparatory talks at Dipoli, just outside Helsinki. (Albania refused to join; Monaco joined the process on 25 June 1973 in time to take part in the main negotiations.) Significantly, the invitation was sent out the day after the two Germanys reached agreement on their relationship. Finland was therefore well placed to be the impartial host, with its own Secretary of State for Foreign Affairs, Richard Tötterman, in the chair.

Responding to Finland's invitation, governments now started to assemble their delegations for the preparatory talks.

Notes

1 Mastny and Byrne, *A Cardboard Castle?*, 330.
2 North Atlantic Council, 10–11 April 1969, 'Final Communiqué', NATO, viewed 6 February 2022, https://www.nato.int/cps/en/natohq/official_texts_26754.htm?selectedLocale=en. Quoting paragraph 5. [For readers of the printed book: to avoid keying in long URLs for NATO documents in this chapter, search online for the document title, or visit the NATO website (https://www.nato.int/) and search keywords there.]
3 North Atlantic Council, 4–5 December 1969, 'Declaration of the North Atlantic Council', NATO, viewed 22 January 2022, https://www.nato.int/docu/comm/49-95/c691204b.htm or https://www.nato.int/cps/en/natolive/official_texts_26760.htm. Quoting paragraphs 2 and 11.
4 Thomas, *The Helsinki Effect*, 41.
5 North Atlantic Council, 4–5 December 1969, 'Declaration of the North Atlantic Council', NATO, viewed 22 January 2022, https://www.nato.int/docu/comm/49-95/c691204b.htm or https://www.nato.int/cps/en/natolive/official_texts_26760.htm. Quoting paragraph 15.
6 Kieninger, *Dynamic Détente*, 210, note 16.
7 North Atlantic Council, 3–4 December 1970, 'Final Communiqué', NATO, viewed 6 February 2022, https://www.nato.int/cps/en/natolive/official_texts_26793.htm. Quoting paragraph 13.
8 Kieninger, 193.
9 Quoted in Thomas, *The Helsinki Effect*, 80. See also Möckli, *European Foreign Policy during the Cold War*.
10 Hakkarainen, *A State of Peace in Europe*, 166.
11 Kieninger, 198.
12 Kieninger, 201.
13 Kieninger, 164.
14 Kieninger, 192.
15 Kieninger, 192.
16 Kieninger, 203–4.
17 Kieninger 204–7.
18 Reported in Kissinger, 'Memorandum From the President's Assistant for National Security Affairs (Kissinger) to President Nixon', 15 May 1971, in *Foreign Relations of the United States*, 1969–1976, XLI, viewed 28 January 2022, https://history.state.gov/historicaldocuments/frus1969-76v41/d66. A summary of Brezhnev's speech appeared in the *New York Times* on 15 May 1971.
19 Kissinger, *The White House Years*, 947.
20 Garthoff, *Détente and Confrontation*, 133.
21 Kieninger, 203.
22 North Atlantic Council, 9–10 December 1971, 'Final Communiqué', NATO, viewed 15 January 2022, https://www.nato.int/docu/comm/49-95/c711209a.htm. Quoting paragraph 12.
23 North Atlantic Council, 30–31 May 1972, 'Final Communiqué', NATO, viewed 7 January 2022, https://www.nato.int/cps/en/natohq/official_texts_26844.htm?selectedLocale=en

Part III

Heading for the summit

11 Dipoli 1972–3

Together at last

On 22 November 1972, in the freezing gloom of a Scandinavian winter, with a bitter wind blowing off the sea, diplomats and other officials of 34 countries (Monaco joined later) converged on a warm modern building belonging to the student union of Helsinki's University of Technology in Dipoli, just outside Helsinki, for what were officially called the Multilateral Preparatory Talks (MPT). Among the facilities was a "sexy bar", which suggested a degree of intimacy among the delegates that nobody expected at that stage, although, as it turned out, quite a lot of informal negotiation was conducted there. Few of the officials knew what to expect, except that there was already a deep gulf between East and West on the basic purpose of the talks.

NATO, however, was well prepared with a steering brief based on a British draft that set out three main aims for the West:

- Reduce barriers in Europe, especially by promoting freer movement of persons, information and ideas.
- Agree on military confidence-building measures (CBMs).
- Rule out the "Brezhnev Doctrine"[1]

(see Chapter 8 and Appendix C)

The Soviet side was clear that it was looking for an early commitment to a summit conference in order to fulfil Brezhnev's dream of finally sealing the division of Europe. The Western side, despite its many differences, was equally clear that it could not accept that division as permanent. Its purpose in coming to Dipoli was simply to find out whether a full security conference was feasible and worthwhile.

In this unpromising situation, could there be any real understanding between the two? Could there even be a security conference? Pessimists said no, and damned the whole enterprise. Others thought it would be largely pointless, or merely a forum for Soviet propaganda, or, at worst, an endorsement of the division of Europe. These critics were eventually proved wrong.

Many accounts of the Helsinki Process ignore the Dipoli talks on the assumption that they were what they were supposed to be: just exploratory talks to see if there was sufficient common ground for a full security conference. That is indeed how they were initially approached by the participating

DOI: 10.4324/9781003146124-15

states. They had even been described as a "tea party" at which ambassadors to Helsinki would meet to discuss an agenda for the conference.

Reality turned out to be very different. Many of the ambassadors dropped out at an early stage as they lacked the time and expertise to deal with the fine detail of subjects that ranged across the whole agenda of divided Europe, from the status of frontiers to marriage and families, from agricultural research to conditions for journalists.[2] Responsibility for the conference therefore fell largely on officials from the capitals of the states involved, many of whom had been working together for a long time on preparations for the talks and were deeply immersed in the detail. This applied particularly to the nine members of the European Community, who became known as The Nine.

Very soon Dipoli became a substantive conference that negotiated most of the key points that appeared in the Helsinki Final Act nearly three years later. This can be seen by comparing the Final Act with the so-called Blue Book that emerged from the Dipoli talks.[3] The reason for the similarity was that Western officials at Dipoli were determined to withhold agreement to a full conference until they had achieved an agenda that would force the Soviet Union to engage with NATO's proposals for opening up contacts between East and West. As a result, the talks dragged on for almost seven months while delegations wrangled over detailed terms of reference.

The unfortunate Soviet delegation was under enormous pressure from Brezhnev to achieve a quick declaratory conference embodying his vision of a peaceful Europe. For him the key issue was to declare the frontiers of Europe immutable and establish the principle of "non-interference", a demand that revealed the Soviet Union's deep sense of insecurity.

When the Soviet delegation realised how difficult it was going to be to achieve these aims, in particular immutable frontiers, they displayed "signs of panic", according to a British report.[4] The West Germans were not going to give up their claim to unification with East Germany. The Irish also wanted national unity, and Spain would not renounce Gibraltar. At the same time many idealistic Europeans hoped that integration would eventually remove all frontiers within Europe, so immutable frontiers were never going to be accepted by the West. Nor were they going to agree to "non-interference" if it meant, for instance, giving up broadcasts in local languages to the Soviet bloc. These enjoyed large audiences and were a key element in projecting the West's "soft power" to the communist world.

The Soviet side was not helped by the actions of one of its team, Valerian Zorin, who became extremely unpopular. Edouard Brunner, the head of the Swiss delegation, described him years later as "an anxious, sneaky character who was rather dangerous to my mind".[5] George Walden, of the British delegation, reported from Dipoli that Zorin was known among Western delegates as "The Poisoned Dwarf", having obviously been sent to oversee work of interest to the KGB. "Needless to say", wrote Walden, "the interest of the KGB as well as of the Soviet Government as a whole would have been better protected if Zorin had stayed at home. His abrasive style exercised a unifying effect on the West, who also gained from his clumsy negotiating tactics".[6] Elsewhere Brian Fall has described how Zorin "made a speech of such unrelenting Stalinist bloody-mindedness that solidarity among delegations of the Nine and NATO, and the sympathy of key neutrals, was restored without the need for premature drafting concessions".[7]

Thus, the officials who gathered in Dipoli for the opening session faced a daunting task. Never before in the Cold War had there been a conference of such size and complexity facing such a multitude of conflicting interests and ideas.

The United States delegation had to cope with mixed signals from the White House and the State Department, so it tried to avoid getting instructions. The White House was preoccupied with the Watergate scandal[8] and the Vietnam War (1955–1975). The mood was demoralised and pessimistic. The prevailing view was that the Dipoli talks were unimportant, even pointless, except as a bargaining chip to secure Soviet concessions on Berlin and the start of separate talks on mutual and balanced force reductions in Europe (MBFR). Dr Henry Kissinger, at that time US National Security Advisor, was reported as telling Mr Gaston Thorn, Foreign Minister of Luxembourg, that the Europeans were being "thoroughly unhelpful… [and] should let the Russians, as sponsors, have what they wanted, a short snappy conference with little substance".[9]

The State Department was more understanding and willing to leave matters largely to the Europeans. Its head of delegation at Dipoli was George Vest, an immensely experienced and sensible diplomat with whom relations were easy and informal, often conducted over a drink in his hotel room. He excused his boss by saying that Dr Kissinger had given little deep thought to the CSCE, which was true. Vest was much respected, unlike, in particular, one member of the delegation, "an extremely tiresome man who came up from the [US] embassy in Moscow and, based on reading some *Pravda*, would tell us that we had gone as far as we could and that the Soviets could not possibly give another millimetre. He was invariably proved wrong".[10]

Although relations among officials of the nine members of the European Community were close, this did not mean that they agreed on everything, nor that they agreed with all NATO's members or with Washington, so coordinating a Western position was not easy. There were also plentiful differences among members of the Warsaw Pact, even though the Soviet Union normally had the last word.[11] Then there were the neutrals and the non-aligned, who generally aligned with the West but had their own ideas and priorities to promote, and did so very effectively.[12]

Thus, the whole Helsinki Process at this stage and through later stages involved multiple negotiations taking place simultaneously between East and West, within the Warsaw Pact, within the European Community, between it and the United States, sometimes in Washington between the White House and the State Department, and in some Western capitals between or within government departments. It was a complex multi-layered political operation that eventually produced a surprisingly coherent result.

The nine members of the European Community worked mainly through a consultative body known as European Political Cooperation (EPC), run by the political directors of the members' foreign ministries. This had been set up following the Davignon Report of 1970[13] to shape a common European foreign policy. The CSCE was its first test, which it passed with great success—a success that it was largely unable to replicate in subsequent years. Although Britain, Ireland and Denmark did not join the European Community until January 1973, their officials were brought informally into the EPC before that in order to work on a common West European approach to the CSCE negotiations. Gradually, the Nine became "the key driving force behind the expanding notion of security that resulted in the recognition of human rights as a principle of international relations".[14] NATO took a step back, not only because Kissinger hated the whole enterprise (he even expressed a desire to kill the Davignon Report[15]) and did not think human rights was a proper subject for international diplomacy but also because three members of NATO—Spain, Portugal and Greece—were at that time ruled by undemocratic regimes that were not interested in human rights.

Initially, the Nine were far from united. The Germans were almost entirely concerned with the German question and were anxious not to demand too much, for fear of getting nothing. They believed that change would follow automatically from détente and that too much pressure could be counter-productive.[16]

The French were more ambitious. In 1970 their president, Georges Pompidou, tried to convince Nixon that freedom was contagious and that contacts with the Soviets and their satellites would increase pressures to shake off the yoke of a totalitarian system. He said he hoped to weaken the Soviet grip on Eastern Europe by spreading the "virus of liberty".[17]

But he was also cautious, urging Brandt not to use too much vigour in trying to undermine Soviet dominance in Eastern Europe. His Foreign Minister, Maurice Schumann, spoke privately of hoping to roll back Soviet influence in Eastern Europe.[18] Nixon remained unconvinced, fearing that the West Europeans might want to loosen their ties to the United States.[19]

The Dutch were frank about wanting to get the Soviet Union out of Eastern Europe, but tougher in private than in public.[20]

Italian officials were somewhat sceptical of the value of the conference, but détente was favoured by their public opinion, the Roman Catholic Church, industrialists and a large communist party, so the government loyally, if sometimes erratically, supported NATO positions.[21]

The British were initially very sceptical of the whole project. They feared that it would tempt people to believe that the Cold War was over and succumb to "détente euphoria".[22] This would weaken support for defence budgets and the NATO alliance. The ever-present fear in London was that creeping Soviet influence would lead to the "Finlandisation" of Western Europe, meaning subservience without actual occupation.

Nevertheless, even cautious British diplomats could envisage change in Eastern Europe. In a far-sighted internal report dated 12 February 1974 they wrote that "the association of the East European states with the Soviet Union seems to us unnatural and in the long run unstable... We believe that Western Europe can play a role by showing sympathy and patience, against the day when events may weaken the Soviet grip upon Eastern Europe".[23]

The British were also anxious to prove themselves good Europeans and avoid isolation as they were just joining the European Community, so they came round to seeing that there could be potential advantages, even if the results turned out to be meagre. After a cautious start, they made a very substantial contribution to the negotiations.[24] Their delegation was driven mainly by very bright young diplomats, much to the annoyance of the Russians, who sent officials of ambassadorial rank to signal the importance they attached to the talks. Brian Fall, Deputy Head of the British delegation, was in his mid-thirties. (He later rose to become ambassador to Russia.) George Walden (mentioned above) was even younger.

The responsibility carried on these young shoulders is illustrated by the unusual double role described by Fall: "Between sessions we would be back in capitals.... At the end of session in Helsinki I would draft a telegram for the Ambassador, Anthony Elliot, reporting on the main points of the session and pinpointing where we would need instructions for the next one. Then I would be back at my desk in [London], drafting an answer to the telegram from Helsinki. An interesting way of running a conference".[25] (Jacques Andréani, of the French delegation to the Geneva talks, also drafted his own instructions. See Chapter 12.)

The British were particularly unpopular with Moscow at that time because they had recently expelled 105 Soviet officials from London. At first, the Soviet delegation at Dipoli tried to ignore the British and do their business with the French, Germans and Americans, but, as Fall wrote later, "the Russians came to recognise that the British needed to be regarded and worked with as one of the key interlocutors on the western side".[26] The change was signalled by an invitation to a bilateral lunch at the Soviet embassy.

This did not soften the British approach. Walden argued for a particularly tough line: "In our aim to secure genuine improvements in reducing barriers within Europe and 'generally to spread the contagion of liberty' we should not shrink from asserting western beliefs in the freedom of movement, information and cultural contacts".[27] Later he explained what Kai Hebel[28] has called the "lemon strategy", a "win–win" approach to the conference: either the Soviet Union would in fact grant some modest concessions on freer movement or its repressive nature would be exposed to the supposedly softening British public. Therefore, wrote Walden, "we must squeeze the Russian lemon very hard to demonstrate to public opinion how little juice there is in *détente à la russe*".[29]

Many of the neutrals and non-aligned had their own agendas but they gradually found themselves working together. They played constructive roles as mediators while mostly supporting Western positions on human rights and the need to lower barriers in Europe.[30] Franz Ceska, of the Austrian delegation, was remarkably far-sighted, writing in his reports from 1973 onwards that the

West had the power to impose conditions that could promote evolution leading to the fall of communism: "Everybody thought I was crazy".[31]

The first significant battle was over the consensus rule, pressed particularly hard by Romania and Yugoslavia. Both were determined that smaller countries would not be outvoted by larger powers. This caused endless delays and disputes, and was occasionally challenged by the Russians, but it had the very big advantages of preventing the superpowers overruling the rest and giving the smaller powers an incentive to engage constructively in the talks. The essential difference between unanimity and consensus was that unanimity would have required a positive vote by every participant, whereas consensus meant, in the words of paragraph 69 of the Blue Book,[32] "the absence of any objection expressed by a representative and submitted by him as constituting an obstacle to the taking of the decision in question". This meant that a state could merely withhold objections and even make negative interpretative statements while still going along with a decision. With consensus settled, there remained lengthy wrangles over the structures of committees and working groups and whether chairmen should automatically rotate.

The most fundamental issue was whether the agenda for the CSCE should contain detailed and binding terms of reference, as the Western side demanded, or only the general declaratory outlines sought by the Soviet Union, which also wanted everyone to commit to starting and finishing dates for the main conference and to a final summit meeting where heads of state or government would put their signatures to the results. That would be the climax that Brezhnev dreamed of.

Western members stubbornly argued that no date could be fixed for starting the CSCE without detailed agreement on terms of reference. Nor could any commitment be made to its ending, still less to a summit conference, until the conference achieved acceptable results. This put the West in a strong bargaining position but caused the preparatory talks to last much longer than expected, as the Soviet delegates tried vainly to defend their position.

Not every point was won by the West. NATO had to drop the reference to the freer movement of "ideas" that had been on the NATO agenda since December 1969. It never reappeared, although many historians still write as if it were in the Final Act.[33] The Eastern side was adamant. Although the Soviet Union claimed to be the custodian of the greatest idea in human history, holding the key to its "scientific laws", at Dipoli its negotiators were absolute in their refusal to legitimise the movement of ideas from West to East. This was despite the Soviet Union unashamedly promoting its own ideas in the West by financing communist parties, communist newspapers, front organisations and peace movements. It was never concerned by double standards. The movement of ideas was to be in one direction only, from East to West, as history marched towards the inevitable victory of communism.

A British report from Dipoli[34] described the tussle over this issue during negotiations on Western proposals for the freer flow of information between East and West. The East Germans had wanted to impose qualifications on information. "They then offered to drop restrictive language about 'peace, intellectual values and good neighbourly relations' if we would drop the references to the 'flow' of information and, more importantly, of 'ideas'... [They] maintained their insistence that 'ideas' must be either heavily qualified by specific references to promoting 'peace and good neighbourliness' or dropped altogether... It gradually became clear to us that... it would be impossible to secure from them a formula on 'ideas' which would imply clearly that it was the dissemination of ideas rather than 'their peace-loving nature' which promoted security". Eventually, the Western negotiators agreed to drop 'ideas' in return for a satisfactory text instructing the committee to "prepare proposals to facilitate the freer and wider dissemination of information of all kinds".

Rather surprisingly the Soviets accepted "of all kinds", having frequently railed against alleged threats from pornography or demanded that only information serving peace should be allowed. The leader of the East German delegation, Siegfried Bock, appeared to be preparing to resist this phrase, as his country was particularly exposed to information from West Germany, but the Russians eventually waved it through, leaving Bock high and dry.

That was not the end of the story. Just as this phrase was about to be registered, Brian Fall noticed his colleague having a serious disagreement with John Campbell, the Irish representative. It turned out that Campbell was threatening to block consensus, explaining that the Irish had a problem with information on birth control getting into [Roman Catholic] Ireland. He had not consulted Dublin because he knew he would get into trouble. Instead, he was expecting something to drop off this rather heavy sentence under Soviet pressure. Fall continues the story with a joke: "It was the only time that I have ever in my diplomatic career witnessed an act of God because exactly at the time that the Anglo-Irish dispute was at its worst, in came the Vatican representative, Silvestrini, wearing wonderful robes. He swept into the room, jumped the speakers' order (because the Vatican regarded that as their historic right), and reminded us of a Holy See proposal for the freer distribution of religious information, which we had all forgotten about... It had been tabled at Stage 2, right at the beginning. And he said that, having seen this admirable text now in front of the plenary, he was more than happy to withdraw this particular proposal because it was so obviously covered". Sighs of relief all round.[35]

The Soviet concession on this point was seen as a clear sign of their impatience to end the talks because they could probably have modified the text if they had tried harder. It also showed how important it had been to agree that the text should not be a legal document because otherwise Western lawyers would have gone over it objecting to information "of all kinds" and trying to exclude pornography, libel, "hate mail" and suchlike, or inserting escape clauses relating to national security, as in United Nations Covenants on Civil and Political Rights. The Soviets would have been happy with that. A political declaration could do without qualifications because it was essentially a declaration of intent, not a legally binding commitment. Thus, the Final

Act says that the participating states "make it their aim to facilitate the freer and wider dissemination of information of all kinds". In other words, it sets no absolute standards that could be measured in a legal document, merely a promise to improve, but a promise backed by the signatures of 35 leaders at Helsinki.

On 8 June 1973, after nearly seven months of argument, the Multilateral Preparatory Talks (MPT) reached agreement on procedures and terms of reference for the main conference. By the end, the West had largely prevailed. Detailed terms of reference were set out in the Blue Book.[36] They were grouped in four "baskets" that came later to define the Final Act. The term was coined at Dipoli by the Swiss as a means of grouping related subjects in a way that did not accord priority to any one of them.

Basket I was about security and contained 10 principles to guide relations between participating states (later to become the Decalogue of the Final Act). Frontiers were declared inviolable, not immutable. Human rights were to be respected. Proposals were to be drawn up for military confidence-building measures, such as prior notification of major military manoeuvres and exchange of observers. These were designed to create greater transparency and deter surprise attacks. The Brezhnev doctrine was excluded by stating that the principles to guide relations between states, including respect for sovereignty, must be observed by each signatory "in its relations with all other participating States, irrespective of their political, economic or social systems". Hence there were to be no special rights for the Soviet Union in Eastern Europe. In other words, this was not a code of conduct for East–West relations but one that applied to all participating states in their relations with each other, including relations between the Soviet Union and its subject states in Eastern Europe.

Basket II instructed the relevant committee to draw up recommendations for increased cooperation in the fields of economics, science and technology and environment. There was not much controversy here except over commercial information and the difficulty of reconciling the practices of planned systems with those of free market economies.

Basket III was particularly uncomfortable for the Soviet side. It required many months to negotiate at Dipoli, and even more when the conference proper got going in Geneva. It instructed the relevant committee to "prepare proposals to facilitate freer movement and contacts, individually or collectively, privately or officially, among persons, institutions and organisations of the participating states". The Soviet Union had resisted strongly because it wanted all movements and contacts to be controlled by governments.

Basket IV told the committee to "consider, on the basis of the progress made at the Conference, such measures as may be required to give effect to the decision of the Conference". In other words, the conference was to be followed up with meetings to check on implementation. The Russians had originally been keen on follow-up meetings because it expected them to form the basis of a European security structure that would give them a say in pan-European affairs. For the same reason the West disliked the idea. When it became clear that the meetings would be about holding members to account for their implementation of the accords the positions were reversed. (For accounts of these meetings see Chapters 16–19.)

The security conference, it was decided, would take place in three stages:

Stage I: Foreign ministers would meet in Helsinki on 3 July 1973 to start the conference by endorsing the Blue Book and deciding on a date for Stage II.

Stage II: Specialised committees and sub-committees would meet in Geneva to prepare drafts of declarations, recommendations, resolutions or any other final documents. A Co-ordinating Committee would submit to participating governments recommendations regarding the organisation of the third stage.

Stage III: would be held in Helsinki and adopt a final document "in the light of the recommendations drawn up by the Co-ordinating Committee".

This fell far short of the commitment the Russians wanted. It meant that Brezhnev's coveted summit conference would not take place unless everyone was satisfied with the work of the committees, and unless the results were sufficiently weighty in Western eyes to merit attendance by heads of state or government. The Soviet Union was therefore under notice that the conference would have to produce real substance. Generalised declarations would not be enough to bring world leaders to Helsinki.

Stage I duly opened as planned in Helsinki on 3 July 1973, when foreign ministers gave speeches and endorsed the Blue Book. They had agreed to move Stage II to Geneva, mainly because it was more conveniently located, well set-up with infrastructure for a major conference, and somewhat less vulnerable to Soviet surveillance. (A West German diplomat said that his telephone calls from Helsinki to Bonn, then the capital of West Germany, were routed through Moscow and East Berlin.[37]) Two more years of intense negotiation then followed before it became possible to agree on holding Stage III in Helsinki. The delay was caused largely by the Soviet team trying to claw back and re-negotiate many of the points it had lost at Dipoli.

Notes

1 *DBPO III/II*, 73.
2 *DBPO III/II*, 140.
3 See both documents in Maresca, *To Helsinki*, Appendix I, or see www.osce.org/helsinki-final-act> and <www.osce.org/eventg/mc_1973
4 *DBPO III/II*, 144.
5 E Brunner, 2013, *CSCE Testimonies, Causes and Consequences of the Helsinki Final Act 1972–1989*, OSCE, 97, viewed 20 January 2022, https://www.osce.org/files/f/documents/6/c/459244.pdf
6 *DBPO III/II*, 144n.
7 Brian Fall 23 January 2017, 'Recollections of Sir Brian Fall' in Manning, *British Diplomatic Oral History Programme*, viewed 5 January 2022, https://www.chu.cam.ac.uk/media/uploads/files/Fall.pdf, p. 27.

8 President Nixon had to resign in 1974 after two years of trying to cover up a break-in at the Democratic Party offices.
9 *DBPO III/II*, 103.
10 Author's conversation with a British official who wished to remain anonymous.
11 See Crump, *The Warsaw Pact Reconsidered*; also Selvage 'The Warsaw Pact and the European Security Conference, 1964–69: Sovereignty, Hegemony, and the German Question' in Wenger et al., *Origins of the European Security System.*
12 For more on the NNA see Chapter 12 and Thomas Fischer, *Neutral Power in the CSCE.*
13 Published by Étienne Davignon of the Belgian Foreign Office in 1970. See CVCE 2013, *Davignon report (Luxembourg, 27 October 1970)*, viewed 5 January 2022, https://www.cvce.eu/content/publication/1999/4/22/4176efc3-c734-41e5-bb90-d34c4d17bbb5/publishable_en.pdf
14 Daniel Möckli, 'The EC Nine, the CSCE and the changing pattern of European security' in Wenger et al., *Origins of the European Security System.* See also Möckli, *European Foreign Policy during the Cold War.*
15 Suri, 'Henry Kissinger and the Reconceptualization of European Security, 1969–75' in Wenger et al., *Origins of the European Security System*, 56.
16 Garton Ash, *In Europe's Name*, and Petri Hakkarainen, A State of Peace in Europe.
17 Möckli, 'The EC Nine', 148. Nicolas Badalassi, 'Neither Too Much, Nor Too Little: France, the USSR and the Helsinki CSCE', in *Cold War History*, 18/1 (2018), 1–17.
18 *DBPO III/II*, 41.
19 Kieninger, *Dynamic Détente*, 195.
20 Baudet '"It Was Cold War and We Wanted to Win": Human Rights, "Détente", and the CSCE', in Wenger et al., *Origins of the European Security System*, 186. Crump et al., 'Firm, but inconspicuous. The Netherlands and the Conference on Security and Co-operation in Europe (1973–1983)', in Dutch, 'Nederland en de Conferentie over Veiligheid en Samenwerking in Europa (1973–1983)' in *Tijdschrift voor Geschiedenis*, 132/2 (Sept 2019), 257–79; useful English abstract, viewed 5 January 2022, at https://www.aup-online.com/content/journals/10.5117/TVGESCH2019.2.006.CRUM
21 Marta Dassu, 'An Italian View' in Davy, *European Détente.* Angela Romano, From Détente in Europe to European Détente, *How the West Shaped the Helsinki CSCE.*
22 Williams, 'Britain, Détente and the Conference on Security and Cooperation in Europe', in Dyson, European Détente: Case Studies of the Politics of East–West Relations, 221–36.
23 *DBPO III/III*, 257.
24 Hebel, *Fathers of the Final Act: Britain, Détente and the CSCE, 1954–1975.* Abingdon: Routledge (forthcoming).
25 British Diplomatic Oral History Programme, Churchill Archives Centre, Cambridge, 157, Sir Brian Fall p. 26; see https://www.chu.cam.ac.uk/archives/collections/bdohp/#F, viewed 20 January 2022.
26 Sir Brian Fall in R Smith ed., *Preparing for Helsinki: The CSCE Multilateral Preparatory Talks*, London: Foreign and Commonwealth Office, 2020. Also available online at https://issuu.com/fcohistorians/docs/preparing_for_helsinki_with_cover, viewed 3 February 2022.
27 *DBPO III/II*, 51.
28 Hebel, 'Propaganda Tools and Idealistic Goals: Britain and the Cold War Politics of Human Rights in the CSCE, 1972–1973', in Mariager et al., *Human Rights during the Cold War*, 113–35.
29 *DBPO III/II*, 121.
30 See Thomas Fischer, *Neutral Power in the CSCE.*

31 F Ceska, in 'The CSCE/OSCE Experience: A Model for Today's World?', The Austrian Foreign Ministry, 2007, viewed 6 January 2022, http://docplayer.net/155861262-The-csce-osce-experience-a-model-for-today-s-world.html
32 *DBPO III/II*, 144.
33 For instance, Maresca *To Helsinki*, 222, and Rey 'The USSR and the Helsinki Process, 1969–75: Optimism, Doubt, or Defiance?', in Wenger et al., *Origins*, 78.
34 British National Archives: Draft Report MPT FCO 28/2167. Available in print since 2020. Published by the Foreign and Commonwealth Office, London. ISBN 9798674658627.
35 Author's interview with Sir Brian Fall, Richmond, 15 March 2010. See note 26.
36 See Note 3.
37 Maresca, *To Helsinki*, 14.

12 1973: Setting up base camp in Geneva

On 18 September 1973 delegates from 35 countries assembled in Geneva to embark on what became nearly two years of arduous negotiation. The Russians arrived with a huge delegation that varied between 60 and 100 as the talks progressed (or, more often, did not). This was their show, and they threw a huge amount of resources at it, including senior officials. They expected to finish by Christmas in time to hold the grand summit that Brezhnev dreamed of early the following year. The Russian delegation were told in Moscow: "Off you go; it'll be at the utmost a matter of two or three months. Why would you need your wives to come?"[1] The head of the Finnish delegation, Jaako Iloniemi, was more realistic. Rightly foreseeing a long haul, he got permission to bring his horse to Geneva.

Maresca offers a vivid description of the opening with a rather surprising preponderance of national stereotypes:

> For the first few days, television cameras focused on the self-conscious diplomats who entered the building: gesticulating Italians, ruddy-faced Irishmen, a phalanx of smiling handshaking Russians, Vatican priests in round collars, oddly clothed East Germans, elegant Spaniards, and slouching, casual Americans. Considerable numbers of journalists of all nationalities mingled with the delegates in the lobby, trying to understand what was taking place, if anything.... Since it was difficult at first to know the faces of all the delegates, suggestions by journalists were sometimes considered along with national proposals and may even, in a few cases, have helped things along... An air of frantic negotiation filled the rooms and corridors... The contingent of journalists present on the first day dwindled rapidly and within a week had all but disappeared. Making sense of what was happening was not easy.[2]

When the journalists left, most of the press coverage ended or was sharply reduced. The conference largely disappeared from public view until the summit conference began to loom up in the summer of 1975. This turned out to be an advantage in so far as governments were not pressed for quick results and therefore left their officials to labour in relative peace on the vital finer points of drafting. On the other hand, when the Final Act emerged, many

DOI: 10.4324/9781003146124-16

people, particularly in the United States, had little or no understanding of what it was about. That is part of the explanation for extremely misleading press coverage that followed the final conclusions.

It may be useful to look at some of the individuals involved, partly as a reminder that these negotiations were not conducted by diplomatic robots but by human beings and partly to emphasise that some of these individuals made their mark on the result.

The Soviet Union

Among the most important delegates was Anatoly Kovalev, head of the Soviet delegation. He was a deputy Foreign Minister and thus a fairly senior figure. He had good reason to fear that his career was at stake. In effect, he was being asked to achieve the impossible: final endorsement of the division of Europe, which the Western nations were determined to refuse. As he wrote later, "We all understood the weight of the responsibility that lay upon us. The international legalisation[3] of the principle of immutability of borders had to be the main and most understandable result of a future conference in Helsinki for the Soviet people".[4] As we shall see later, he failed, but not without a long struggle and an act of considerable courage at the end.

He seemed a surprising choice because he spoke neither English nor French and had little international experience, but he was known in Moscow as one of the supporters of détente who could therefore be relied upon to do his best for Brezhnev against the many hard-line sceptics who surrounded the Soviet leader.

Born in 1923, Kovalev was from the (relatively) younger generation of the Soviet apparatus, many of whom were frustrated by the stagnation of the Brezhnev era, and had been restless even before that. In his memoir, published after the end of the Cold War, he wrote "Already in the 1940s, a group of people with unorthodox views about the surrounding world began to grow and take shape in our country…, a 'breed of reformers'… not time-servers but 'renovationists'. They are people of different professions, nationalities and ages who arrived at similar conclusions… These people are the veterans and volunteers comprising the backbone of the Helsinki process".[5] They hoped that détente would not only open up contacts with the West but also induce change within the Soviet Union. This gave him a private personal stake in the negotiations that clearly added to his stress because his wishes conflicted with the positions he had to take.

The pressures for change among people like Kovalev were largely concealed at the time behind the stubborn dogmatism of the more visible members of the Soviet elite and the media they controlled, but they provided a body of support for the Helsinki Process and later for the reformist efforts of Mikhail Gorbachev. Western observers were often deceived into regarding the Soviet system as a tightly controlled monolith run by deeply indoctrinated believers. Vladislav Zubok has described the steady loss of faith in communist ideology among the Soviet intelligentsia.[6] The distinguished Oxford scholar Archie

Brown was an exception among Western scholars in writing about the diversity of opinion that was growing within the party apparatus as Mikhail Gorbachev rose through its ranks to become leader in 1985: "The Communist Party of the Soviet Union (CPSU) in the post-Stalin years was by no means the monolithically united body which its propagandists like to pretend"—and which, adds Brown, some Western propagandists liked to promote.[7] After the system collapsed, scholars such as Robert English[8] and Marie-Pierre Rey[9] drew aside the curtain to reveal the full extent of diversity and dissatisfaction among the elites to which Kovalev refers, while acknowledging the dominant power of the old guard.

Kovalev was a very heavy smoker and clearly under a great deal of strain, especially towards the end. Michael Alexander of the British delegation described him as "a slightly puzzling figure… less able and authoritative than one might have expected… His idea of tactics for most of the Conference seemed to be to alternate flattery with threats while remaining unyielding on points of substance… He showed little flexibility and imagination, preferring, if he could, either to concede the Western demand or to hold out for his original position rather than to haggle his way towards a compromise".[10] He was occasionally rude and noticeably short-tempered.

Maresca describes him as "normally completely poker-faced… But when he lost patience or felt that had been tricked or deceived, a dark look would come across his brow and he was capable of pouring forth criticism with cold fury. He was also capable of labyrinthine conspiratorial plots".[11] Later Maresca befriended him and his son and helped arrange for the translation of his memoir, a rather moving example of former adversaries bonding after an intense shared experience.[12]

Behind the hard face that Kovalev presented at the negotiating table he struggled with passions that he released in writing poetry, which emerged later. When things were going well his poetry was ecstatic: "Sing, swans!… Give yourself up to the heights… the time for free songs has arrived. Sing, people are listening". When things went badly he fell into black despair: "Command grief to be quiet… Teach me… not to fear despair. A chasm to the left, a chasm to the right, one in front and one behind. Twisting blindly I dislocate my joints… Help me to mend these wounds".[13]

By the end, having given away too much in the eyes of his critics in Moscow, he had fallen out of favour, particularly with Mikhail Suslov, a powerful member of the Politburo, who ensured that he was conspicuously not decorated for his role in the CSCE negotiations. Nor did he receive the promotion that would otherwise have been his due. This was one of many signs of Soviet dissatisfaction with the outcome. His career revived when Gorbachev sought him out in 1990 and sent him to Oslo to receive the Nobel Peace Prize on his behalf.

In the meantime he had been instrumental in saving the dissident writer Alexander Solzhenitsyn from prison, demonstrating how the Soviet Union was willing to bend its internal rules to save the talks. In 1974 the Soviet Politburo had decided to put Solzhenitsyn on trial but it first sent a leading member, Alexander Shelepin, to Geneva to check if Kovalev would approve. Kovalev would not. He told Shelepin that it would derail the negotiations, so Solzhenitsyn was put on a plane to West Germany.[14]

Under Kovalev were two officials of ambassador rank.

Yuri Dubinin, born in 1930, was extremely intelligent and fluent in French, having served in Paris, where he became an expert on French wines and food. He made no secret of his enjoyment of the good things in life. As Michael Alexander described him, "His clothes were evidently bought in France or Switzerland and he devoted a good deal of attention to his appearances (*sic*), which at times verged on the fashionable... However, he finds it possible and convenient to combine genuine social ease and savoir faire with very hard-line views. For all his suavity, he was more ruthless than his immediate colleagues and correspondingly more widely mistrusted. His negotiating posture was always inflexible and the mailed fist was never far beneath the table... In private he could be impressively rude". Given the tough job of negotiating Basket III, he was a master at trying to drive wedges between Western delegates. He was also the only member of the Soviet delegation who sometimes gave the impression that he would not be unduly bothered if the Conference failed. He seemed to have a rather low opinion of Kovalev, making little attempt to conceal his boredom when Kovalev was speaking.[15]

Maresca writes that Dubinin "was capable of sticking to a point indefinitely, with considerable disdain and even rudeness toward his negotiating partners. Provoked, he would fly into a rage of belittling and insulting language. He seems not only to disagree with, but actually to despise, many of the principles of a free society for which the West was seeking recognition"[16]—and the fruits of which, it might be added, he clearly enjoyed in Paris and Geneva.

Lev Mendelyevich, born in 1918, spoke good English and was more flexible and sure of himself than were his colleagues, being more willing to engage in impromptu debates. Having served at the United Nations and at Dipoli (see Chapter 11), he had far more relevant experience than either of his colleagues, a fact that he did not attempt to conceal. He was extremely fat but uninterested in the finer points of cooking and much given to negotiating in his shirtsleeves, usually with a belt, occasionally with braces. "His appetite for negotiation and his stamina were alike remarkable. He is also extremely vain", reported Alexander, who also noticed that "rivalry between Dubinin and Mendelyevich was overt and intense... Dubinin, who was wont to roll his eyes and study the ceiling when Mendelyevich was speaking, used to refer in scathing terms to the 'orators' in Basket I".[17]

Sergei Kondrashev was the KGB representative and therefore not under the same discipline as the others. "Far more frequently than any of the others... he floated ideas. Almost as frequently they led nowhere".[18] Dubinin said of his colleague much later: "Of course, he always expressed the views of the KGB, which was perfectly natural, so we never had any internal disagreements".[19] After all, who would dare disagree with the KGB?

Soviet negotiating tactics were closely observed by Western delegates. Being under time pressure, the Russians and their allies tried at first to push ahead with generalities and belittle efforts to discuss specifics. Often they would try to play off one delegation against another, or a senior against a junior within a particularly awkward delegation. They could also use intimidation, heaping abuse on some delegates and threatening to ruin their careers.

Another tactic was to hint that if the West gave way on some issue of importance to the Soviet side, concessions would follow on other issues. They never did. Sometimes they tried to reach a private agreement with a single Western delegation, often the French, only to find the rest refusing to go along with it, provoking exasperation all round. Frequently they tried to by-pass the negotiators and reach higher up the line to foreign ministers or government leaders, many of whom were out of touch with the small but vital details of the negotiations. They made particular efforts to cultivate the Americans at all levels, hoping Washington would exert pressure on its pesky European allies. This tactic invariably failed as European solidarity proved remarkably strong. Russians clearly had difficulty understanding that Washington did not control Western Europe in the same way that they (mostly) controlled Eastern Europe.

The Soviet delegates were avid collectors of speeches and documents by Western leaders, which they often used against delegates in Geneva. As Maresca remarks, "There is nothing more embarrassing than to make a point in negotiation and to have your Soviet opponent quote from a speech by your foreign minister that seems to take the opposite line".[20]

Translations were the subject of an almost daily "war of attrition", in the words of a British expert translator, Tony Bishop.[21] The Russians would agree to an English or French text and then translate it into Russian in a way that weakened or changed the meaning, thereby trying to recoup points they had lost in negotiation.

Michael Alexander reinforced this comment: "Even with agreements that had been struck, there was a final opening for sharp practice which the Soviet delegation never overlooked: the rendering into Russian… There was a tendency for the Russians to produce a thoroughly self-serving translation of a text agreed in English or French; to feign astonishment and anger when this was queried; and then to resist all but minor changes in the hope that Western delegations would become bored and would move on to other things. Almost the last serious negotiation in Basket III related to a major mistranslation in the Russian version of a text agreed in English more than a year previously".[22]

Similar complaints were heard at the second follow-up meeting in Madrid (see Chapter 17). Nor was this a new problem. When negotiating the United Nations Charter in San Francisco in 1945, the British had to fly out the great philosopher Isaiah Berlin, a Russian expert, to check the translation, which he found to be thoroughly misleading. The Russians resisted change, claiming that Russian schoolchildren were already learning the proposed text by heart.

It was too late to make changes, they said. But they were eventually forced to concede.[23]

Alexander summed up a long reflective paper on negotiating with the Russians: "In short, the best way to deal with the Russians seemed to be to treat them as though they were exactly the same as everyone else, while bearing in mind that they were not".[24] Maresca also has a thoughtful section on negotiating with the Russians.[25]

The Nine

On the Western side the nine members of the European Community (later the European Union) overcame their differences sufficiently to become "a key driving force in making the Soviet Union subscribe to an expanding notion of security, with Moscow eventually acknowledging human rights as a principle of international relations, and the security of individuals as a complement to the security of states".[26]

Among key figures was Jacques Andréani, head of the French delegation: "A chain-smoking Frenchman with a Corsican background, [he] was one of the intellectual lights of the CSCE. He was perpetually dishevelled, in rumpled tweeds, and conveyed the aura of a junior professor in a Left Bank café. But his understanding of the Conference was among the most perceptive of any of the delegates".[27] He described later how he would send his proposals to Paris on Fridays and then travel to his desk in Paris, from where, on Mondays, he would send a telegram to Geneva approving his own proposals: "Looking back, it was a rather peculiar system".[28] Later he wrote an excellent book about the conference.[29] (Brian Fall played a similar double role in the Dipoli negotiations, see Chapter 11.)

Max van der Stoel was the Foreign Minister of the Netherlands during the negotiation of the Final Act, when he played a valuable role in stiffening the resolve of the European Nine to insist on including strong commitments to human rights. Born in 1924, his experiences during the brutal Nazi occupation of the Netherlands during World War II shaped his dedication to human rights and fundamental freedoms, which he pursued throughout his career. From 1993 to 2001 he occupied and developed the new post of High Commissioner on National Minorities for the successor organisation to the CSCE, the Organization for Security and Co-operation in Europe (OSCE). In 2013 a foundation for the promotion of democracy, development and dialogue was created in his name. In 2014, a new park in Prague was named after him in recognition of his support for dissidents under communism.

In the final phase of the negotiations a pivotal role was played by Michael Alexander, head of the political section in the British team. He conceived the "global solution" that unblocked the talks (see Chapter 13).[30] He had a varied background, having won a silver medal in fencing at the Rome Olympics in 1960, learnt Russian during his National Service, studied at Cambridge University, and then spent two years at Yale and Berkeley before entering the diplomatic service in 1962. In Geneva his fine brain served the conference well.

Neutrals and Non-aligned

They had started as a disparate group with different hopes and interests but gradually developed a degree of cohesion as they found common ground in mostly supporting Western positions. Often they played a valuable role as intermediaries and proposers of compromises, relishing their chance to influence East–West relations at a time when Europe was dominated by two rigid blocs.[31]

They also demonstrated that personalities really do count in negotiations such as these. A prime example was Edouard Brunner, deputy head of the Swiss delegation. Having served in the Swiss embassy in Warsaw he was familiar with conditions in Eastern Europe and fully understood the importance of Basket III. He frequently acted as an intermediary. He was "a brilliant innovator and indefatigable maneuverer (*sic*) who was constantly probing for devices to advance the Conference's work".[32] Fischer mentions "the agile and urbane Brunner, who navigated like a fish in the sea in the multilateral talks, engaging with all sides".[33]

Jaako Iloniemi, head of the Finnish delegation, had a proprietary interest in the conference because Finland had issued the initial invitations to Helsinki and hosted the opening meeting. Iloniemi was "one of the most intelligent and understanding of all the delegation heads... an unprepossessing, totally bald man with a dry, sometimes caustic sense of humor... one of the handful of diplomats who not only understood the CSCE but also made it work".[34]

He was put in a difficult position in June 1974 when he was pressured by his president to put forward a proposal that so obviously favoured the Soviet position that he knew it would have no chance of being accepted by the West. Almost thirty years later it emerged from United States archives that the proposal had been cooked up the previous month by Kissinger and Gromyko in Cyprus, with Kissinger largely accepting the Soviet draft. This was a rare case of Finland being used rather than taking its own initiatives. However, the negotiations that followed helped break a deadlock, opening the way to a further round of negotiations, so in the end the neutrals and the non-aligned could rightfully claim credit for an important contribution to the negotiations.[35]

The United States

As we saw in the previous chapter, officials of the US State Department had played a constructive role in NATO's early preparations for the conference, supporting the European desire to bring down barriers between Eastern and Western Europe. At Geneva, as at Dipoli, they had mostly withdrawn to a less active role in order to avoid conflict with Dr Kissinger, who was Security Advisor to President Nixon and then took over the State Department in September 1973. He was hostile to the whole enterprise. He saw it as interfering with his bilateral relations with Moscow, and as unrealistic in aiming to promote internal changes in the Soviet sphere.

Kissinger is on record as having made many derisory remarks about the Helsinki Process. He called it "multilateral diplomacy run amok".[36] He told a British diplomat that he had never wanted the conference and that it could do harm.[37] On another occasion he is said to have regarded it as "a positive obstacle to developing Soviet–American cooperation".[38] At one difficult moment in the negotiations he remarked in exasperation: "They can write it in Swahili for all I care".[39] Talking privately to Gromyko, he mocked the negotiations. A British official reported that Dr Kissinger did not understand "the genuinely idealistic element in the European approach".[40]

Kissinger knew that in the long term it was in the Western interest to loosen Moscow's grip on Eastern Europe but he did not believe there was any immediate prospect of doing so, or of inducing internal change in the Soviet sphere, so he seemed ready to accept the status quo for the foreseeable future.[41] His boss took the same view. President Nixon told the Russian people in a broadcast that he believed in "the right of each nation to chart its own course, to choose its own system, to go its own way, without interference from other nations".[42] He conveniently forgot that the nations of Eastern Europe were denied all those choices.

Kissinger failed to foresee or fully comprehend the pressures for change that were building up in Eastern Europe[43] and that eventually prevailed when Mikhail Gorbachev removed the threat of force in 1988. Nor did he at first appreciate the moral and political implications of appearing to accept the Soviet Union's oppressive and unpopular rule over Eastern Europe. His focus at the time was on bilateral relations with Moscow. The CSCE was an irritating distraction, as was European concern for human rights.

After the US defeat in Vietnam in 1975, and as the Soviet Union continued to make gains in the Third World, US opinion began to harden against détente, so Kissinger adjusted to the new atmosphere and began to acknowledge human rights. He told newspaper editors: "We must give up the illusion that foreign policy can choose between morality and pragmatism. America cannot be true to itself unless it upholds humane values and the dignity of the individual".[44] Observers reacted with scepticism, but Jeremi Suri has pointed out that Kissinger, throughout his career, had written and spoken of the importance of foreign policy serving moral, humanitarian ends. He believed, however, that these could not be achieved without first creating an environment of peace and security.[45]

The US delegation in Geneva partly solved its Kissinger problem by, as far as possible, avoiding getting written instructions from Washington. As Maresca tells it, "the officials concerned were afraid that if they attempted to put instructions in writing, Kissinger would not agree to a strong US position. The central core of the delegation knew this and rarely asked for instructions".[46]

The talks dragged on for nearly two years, increasingly bogged down in wrangles over fine points of language that fewer and fewer people understood but which in fact involved important issues of principle. At the same time the various groupings had to resolve differences between and within their own governments at the same time as negotiating with the other side across the East–West divide. This was no tidy confrontation between East and West.

The next chapter looks at the negotiations in two parts.

Notes

1 Yuri Dubinin, 2013 in *CSCE Testimonies, Causes and Consequences of the Helsinki Final Act 1972–1989*, OSCE, viewed 20 January 2022, https://www.osce.org/files/f/documents/6/c/459244.pdf, p. 198.
2 Maresca, *To Helsinki*, 48.
3 The Final Act was not a legal document but a political declaration.
4 Kovalev, Anatoly, *Azbuka diplomatii*, Moscow 1993, 184. Translated for the author by Thomas Marsden.
5 Quoted in Maresca, *Helsinki revisited*, 196, from *Transition* (Prague), 30 June 1995.
6 Zubok, *A Failed Empire*, 336–44.
7 Brown, *The Gorbachev Factor*, 21. For more on "within-system reformers" see Brown, *Seven Years that Changed the World*, 157–89.
8 See English, *Russia and the Idea of the West*.
9 Rey, 'The USSR and the Helsinki Process, 1969–75' in Wenger et al., *Origins of the European Security System*.
10 Alexander, *Managing the Cold War*, 68.
11 Maresca, *To Helsinki*, 96.
12 Maresca, *Helsinki Revisited*, 192–6.
13 Kovalev, *Azbuka Diplomatii*, tr. Marsden.
14 Maresca, *Helsinki Revisited*, 193. A slightly different account is given by Zubok, 235–7.
15 Alexander, 69–70.
16 Maresca, *To Helsinki*, 124.
17 Alexander, 70–6.
18 Alexander, 72.
19 Yuri Dubinin, 2013, in *CSCE Testimonies, Causes and Consequences of the Helsinki Final Act 1972–1989*, OSCE, viewed 20 January 2022, https://www.osce.org/files/f/documents/6/c/459244.pdf, p.197.
20 Maresca, *To Helsinki*, 61.
21 Kandiah and Staerck, 2006, *The Helsinki Negotiations: the Accords and their Impact* Institute of Contemporary British History, viewed on 14 December 2021, https://www.kcl.ac.uk/sspp/assets/icbh-witness/helsinki.pdf
22 Alexander, 96.
23 Michael Ignatieff, *Isaiah Berlin, A Life*, 133.
24 Alexander, 100.
25 Maresca, *To Helsinki*, 55–63.
26 Möckli, *European Foreign Policy during the Cold War*, 99.
27 Maresca, *To Helsinki*, 188.
28 Andréani, 2013, in *CSCE Testimonies, Causes and Consequences of the Helsinki Final Act 1972–1989*, OSCE, viewed 20 January 2022, https://www.osce.org/files/f/documents/6/c/459244.pdf, p 74.
29 Andréani, Jacques, *Le Piège: Helsinki et la Chute du Communisme*.
30 For a full account see Hebel, *Fathers of the Final Act*, chapter 9 (forthcoming).
31 See Fischer, *Neutral Power in the CSCE*.
32 Maresca, *To Helsinki*, 127.
33 Fischer, 333.
34 Maresca, *To Helsinki*, 126.

35 For a full account of this remarkable episode see Fischer, 278–93.
36 Kissinger, *Years of Renewal*, 642.
37 *DBPO III/II*, 50.
38 *DBPO III/II*, 323.
39 Hanhimäki '"They can write it in Swahili": Kissinger, the Soviets, and the Helsinki Accords, 1973–1975' in *Journal of Transatlantic Studies*, 1/1 (Spring 2003), 37–58.
40 *DBPO III/II*, 325.
41 Whether Kissinger truly accepted Soviet domination of Eastern Europe is a complex question, very hot at the time, examined in detail by Douglas Selvage, 'Transforming the Soviet Sphere of Influence? US–Soviet Détente and Eastern Europe, 1969–1976' in *Diplomatic History* 33/4, September 2009.
42 Maresca, *To Helsinki*, 12.
43 Davy, 'Policies for Eastern Europe' in Hunter, *NATO: The Next Generation*.
44 Maresca, *To Helsinki*, 121.
45 Suri, 'Henry Kissinger and the Reconceptualization of European Security, 1969–75' in Wenger et al., *Origins of the European Security System*, 61n.
46 Maresca, *To Helsinki*, 44.

13 Geneva 1973–5

The long climb to the summit

As this vast assembly came together in Geneva, with all its conflicting interests and idiosyncratic individuals, it faced a formidable task. There was fundamental disagreement between the two sides. The Soviet Union wanted to settle the post-war division of Europe and consolidate its empire in Eastern Europe. Western governments wanted to ameliorate and eventually overcome the division of Europe by promoting human rights and freer movement of people, information and trade. The Russians saw this, correctly, as an attempt to subvert their empire. The West Europeans, supported by many members of the US State Department but not by Kissinger, argued that true security in Europe could not be based indefinitely on the suppression of the peoples of Eastern Europe. Among the "red lines" with which they approached the talks was a determination to avoid agreeing to anything that would confirm the division of Europe or suggest Western acceptance of the "Brezhnev Doctrine".[1] In other words, the Soviet Union was to be allowed no special rights in Eastern Europe.

The Russians tried to take back the concessions they had made at Dipoli and renegotiate many issues from scratch. The Western side largely held firm, insisting on the agenda laid out in the Blue Book (see Chapter 11). Time was on their side because Brezhnev's deep personal commitment to the conference made failure almost unthinkable for his team.

We now look at the main issues in the four sections that had come to be known as Baskets into which proposals had been grouped.

Basket I: Questions relating to security in Europe

This contains ten "Principles Guiding Relations between Participating States" plus a section on military Confidence-Building Measures (CBMs). We select the main issues.

Frontiers

Frontiers were the most important issue for the Russians. They wanted the Principles to include a clear declaration that Europe's frontiers were immutable. This was because they saw their East European empire as essential to their

DOI: 10.4324/9781003146124-17

security, a bulwark to block the invasion routes used by Hitler and Napoleon. Frontiers were also a deeply emotional issue because this empire had been won with the blood of huge numbers of Soviet soldiers in World War II. There was an ideological dimension, too: the empire had to demonstrate that communism was on the march westwards. Socialism must never be seen to retreat.

The Poles also had a strong interest in immutable frontiers because their new western frontier along the Oder–Neisse demarcated the lands they had gained from Germany after the war. Since the West Germans were still maintaining a formal claim to those lands, which amounted to about a quarter of Germany's former territory, the Poles needed guarantees that the frontier would not be changed.

For both Germanys the frontier between them was also a central issue, albeit for opposite reasons. The East German leaders knew their state could not survive without that frontier. They were proved correct when their state vanished in 1990. The West Germans also felt strongly about that frontier because they were pledged to remove it in order to reunite the country. Hence their insistence on keeping open the possibility of change. Their government also dared not formally renounce the lands lost to Poland because a powerful political lobby of ethnic Germans expelled from Eastern Europe kept alive the wholly unrealistic dream of recovering them.

The Western powers also had to refuse immutable frontiers because they were committed in public to the reunification of Germany, although privately fearing it. The prospect seemed conveniently remote at the time, but there was no way they could formally agree to the permanent division of Germany without losing the trust of the West Germans, who had become essential allies in NATO. Another factor that crept into the fringes of the debate was that keen proponents of European unity hoped one day to remove all frontiers in Europe, so they too wanted to keep open the option of change.[2]

Frontiers were also important for the Baltic states: Latvia, Lithuania and Estonia. What they wanted was to restore their old frontiers. In 1939 they had been the victims of a carve-up by Hitler and Stalin, who signed secret protocols dividing Poland between them and agreeing to the Baltic states being taken over by the Soviet Union. They were soon conquered by the Nazis and then re-occupied and again absorbed into the Soviet Union, which regarded them as important strategic assets. Both occupations involved horrific killings, arrests and deportations, especially among the educated classes, who were feared by communists and Nazis alike. The United States and its allies had always refused to recognise the Soviet absorption of the Baltics, insisting on regarding them as separate states. Any American government that wavered on that point would face the wrath of a sizeable diaspora in the United States that was already hostile to the whole Helsinki project.

At Geneva the West Germans were the main driving force behind the Western stance on frontiers. They made it clear that they would refuse to sign any document that did not leave open the possibility of reunification. The issue had been fudged in their 1970 treaty with Moscow. In that document the two parties undertook "to respect without restriction the territorial integrity of all States in Europe within their present frontiers". They also declared that they had no territorial claims and that they "regard today and shall in future regard the frontiers of all States in Europe as inviolable". West Germany's claim to reunification was then asserted in a covering letter from its Foreign Minister, Walter Scheel, in which he stated that the treaty "does not conflict with the political objective of the Federal Republic of Germany to work for a state of peace in Europe in which the German nation will recover its unity in free self-determination".

That contradictory arrangement, by which only one side asserted Germany's right to self-determination, would not do for a multilateral agreement. Something better and clearer had to be achieved to keep open the road to German unity.

There was also another fudge in the 1970 treaty that worried the Russians and their allies. While the treaty clearly affirmed the inviolability of existing frontiers and renounced territorial claims, the West German government sent notes that carefully reserved the rights of the Four Powers in Germany pending a peace treaty, thereby keeping open the question of its frontiers. It also added that "the Federal Government… can act only in the name of the Federal Republic of Germany". Clearly, it could not commit a future government of a reunified Germany. This left open the possibility that a united Germany might one day reopen the question of Poland's western frontier, as indeed it did in 1989, when reunification loomed up as an immediate possibility. Chancellor Helmut Kohl, beset by pressure from the lobby of expellees, dithered shamefully until, under pressure from Washington and Paris, he belatedly allowed his foreign minister to sign the border treaty of November 1990 with Poland recognising the Oder–Neisse frontier under international law, thereby putting that issue to rest.

Negotiating these frontier issues in Geneva in 1973–5, the Western side tried to have the inviolability of frontiers included in the same Principle as provision for peaceful change, making it clear that inviolability did not mean permanence. The Russians tried to resist any mention of peaceful change but then, realising that they were asking the impossible, took half a step back and demanded that the two principles be separated in the hope that inviolability could be interpreted as immutability.[3]

After much wrangling, Spain, apparently at the instigation of the Russians,[4] proposed a "floating" text that could be inserted later saying that frontiers could be changed "only" in accordance with international law. Then the West Germans had second thoughts, fearing that this might rule out change because international law makes no specific provision for changing frontiers. At this point Kissinger engaged himself by negotiating a compromise directly with the Soviet Union, not because he had been converted to the value of the CSCE but because he hoped to unblock the negotiations.

The result was a slightly ambiguous but just satisfactory text that read: "Frontiers can be changed, in accordance with international law, by peaceful means and by agreement". The word "only" had disappeared and international law was placed between two parenthetical commas. Kissinger later remarked that the talks had become so abstruse that they depended on the placement of a comma.[5]

This text then took a conspicuous place in Principle I, while inviolability went down to Principle III: "The participating states regard as inviolable all one another's frontiers as well as the frontiers of all States in Europe and therefore they will refrain now and in the future from assaulting those frontiers". This made it clear that inviolability ruled out change by force but not peaceful change. The East German leaders were furious because the admission of peaceful change presaged the annihilation of their state. They thought the Soviet Union had sold them down the river, which was largely true, but there was no alternative in the face of adamant West German insistence on the right of peaceful change.

Even that compromise was not quite the end of the story. The Russians then managed to regain some ground by mistranslating "inviolable" into the Russian word for immutable, *nerushimost*, much to the annoyance of the British and others. Eventually, the British were persuaded to go along with it for the sake of allied unity, reassured by the fact that the principle of peaceful change was preserved in all languages in Principle I. That did not prevent the Russians later claiming that inviolable meant immutable.

Thus, contrary to many accounts, the Final Act did not change the status of Europe's frontiers. The most contentious ones, including Poland's western frontier, had already been recognised in treaties with West Germany in 1970–72 (see Chapter 9). Others had long been accepted in the course of normal diplomatic relations. The Final Act merely added formal multilateral endorsement while preserving Allied rights in Germany pending a peace treaty. It slightly weakened the status of the frontiers by introducing the novel principle of peaceful change.

The result was summed up by Harold S. Russell, who was principal US negotiator for Basket I: "It is the author's view, as well as that of all the Western negotiators, that the USSR failed in large part to achieve the kind of language it originally sought and that the document does not depart materially from previous international arrangements on frontiers and does nothing to recognize existing frontiers in Europe… During the course of these negotiations the Soviet representatives grudgingly gave ground inch by inch until in the final analysis they were willing to accept language which departs substantially from their initial draft and omits virtually all of its essential elements".

He then added drily, referring to very misleading American press coverage: "What the USSR may have failed to achieve at Geneva, it almost totally recouped at Helsinki through the North American press".[6]

Berlin

The precarious status of West Berlin had been an issue throughout the Cold War (see Chapter 1). A shining island of prosperous capitalism in the midst of drab East Germany, it depended on vulnerable road, rail and air links with

West Germany that ran across East Germany. It was surrounded by huge Russian armies that made it indefensible in military terms, but it was protected by the still valid rights of the four victorious occupying Powers. They had initially divided Berlin into four sectors until the three Western sectors were merged into one. Soviet leaders from Stalin onwards, together with the leaders of East Germany, had wanted to sever its supply lines from West Germany but were held back by the fear of provoking nuclear war with the United States.

As the CSCE approached, NATO used Soviet desire for the conference as a lever to settle the city's status, making this a condition of taking part. After difficult negotiations the Quadripartite Agreement was signed in 1971 but not ratified until early 1972. It confirmed the rights and responsibilities of the four victorious Powers for the whole of Berlin and Germany pending a peace treaty. Most importantly, it established that traffic between West Germany and West Berlin would be unimpeded. By confirming Soviet responsibility for unimpeded access, it deprived the East German regime of the leverage it had enjoyed to cause trouble by holding up traffic on the transit routes—trouble that could have started a war. At the same time the Agreement contained provision for West Berliners to visit East Berlin while East Berliners could visit West Germany, including West Berlin, for family reasons, so East–West travel increased fast. Curiously, the word "Berlin" did not appear in the Agreement because the status of the city was still disputed. The agreement referred instead to "the relevant area". It largely brought to an end the friction that had been the cause of so many crises and confrontations. The Russians had now become more interested in stability.

A problem remained for the Western negotiators at Geneva, which was to find a form of words that recognised Allied rights in Berlin and Germany without giving the Soviet Union special rights in East Germany and the rest of Eastern Europe, thereby endorsing the Brezhnev Doctrine. Agreement on this thorny issue was not reached until almost the last minute after an all-night session in July 1975. Placed in Principle X, the crucial part of this rather obscure text reads: "The participating States, paying due regard to the principles above and, in particular, to the first sentence of the tenth principle, 'Fulfilment in good faith of obligations under international law', note that the present Declaration does not affect their rights and obligations, nor the corresponding treaties and other agreements and arrangements".

"Non-intervention"

This was the next big issue. The Russians pressed hard for a clause that would rule out "interference", which they wished to define as including a range of peaceful activities, such as "hostile propaganda" and Western broadcasts in the languages of Eastern Europe and the Soviet Union. They were particularly annoyed by Radio Free Europe and Radio Liberty. Based in Munich and financed by the CIA, these stations were immensely popular in Eastern Europe and the Soviet Union, acting as domestic stations in exile by providing the news and comment that were not available in the tightly controlled communist media. All attempts to close them failed.

Eventually the Russians had to settle reluctantly for a text in Principle VI that says that the participating States "will refrain from any intervention, direct or indirect, individual or collective, in the internal or external affairs falling within the domestic jurisdiction of another participating State, regardless of their mutual relations. They will accordingly refrain from any form of armed intervention or threat of such intervention..., [and] any other act of military or of political, economic or other coercion".

This made it clear that "intervention" referred only to physical intervention, but that did not prevent the Russians continuing to claim that Principle VI ruled out non-physical "interference". Their stance revealed their profound fear of Western influence penetrating their empire. As we saw in Chapter 11, they resolutely refused to include in the Final Act any reference to the freer movement of ideas, which had been on the original NATO agenda but was dropped at Dipoli. They also fought long and hard but in vain for a declaration that governments should be held responsible for the content of media on their territory, a demand that no Western government could accept. Long after the conference, and indeed beyond the end of the Cold War, they continued to claim wrongly that the Final Act permitted curbs on peaceful activities, such as mutual monitoring of elections and compliance with the Final Act (see Chapter 24), whereas in fact it rules out only physical intervention.

Meanwhile they had no inhibitions about "interfering" in the West by funding communist parties and communist newspapers in Western Europe, broadcasting in West European languages, and even allowing East Germany to give sanctuary to members of the so-called Red Army Faction, a murderous terrorist group active in West Germany.[7] In Geneva they consistently refused to answer a British question about whether their draft principle on non-interference ruled out their giving material support to the Communist Party of Great Britain.[8]

Political status quo and the Brezhnev Doctrine

Commentators often lump together the territorial and political status quo, alleging that both were confirmed at Helsinki (see Chapter 15). It is important to distinguish between the two. The territorial status quo was about frontiers, the political status quo about political arrangements within those frontiers, meaning, in this context, the nature and practices of the regimes of Eastern Europe under Soviet control. The two issues came together in Western efforts to discourage the Soviet Union from invading its neighbours, as it had done in Hungary in 1956 and Czechoslovakia in 1968. Agreement on inviolable frontiers should have been enough to secure this point but there remained two problems. First, under the Brezhnev Doctrine (see Chapter 8 and Appendix C) the Soviet Union claimed the right to intervene to "defend socialism". Secondly, the Soviet Union initially insisted that the Principles in

Basket I, including inviolable frontiers, should apply only to relations between "states with different social systems". Had this been accepted it would have confirmed the Brezhnev Doctrine and given the Soviet Union a free hand in Eastern Europe. Eventually its team in Geneva were pressed into agreeing that the Principles should apply to relations "with all other participating states, irrespective of their political, economic or social systems".

This vital point meant quite clearly that the Final Act was not a code of conduct between East and West but one that applied to relations between all participating states. Thus the Soviet Union was obliged to respect the sovereignty of its allies. This was quietly welcomed by some East European regimes, notably that of Poland. Although they ultimately depended on Soviet protection, and collapsed when that was withdrawn in 1988, they were still not keen on being invaded.

The Brezhnev Doctrine was further excluded by the very strong language of Principle IV on the inviolability of frontiers, which pledges members to "refrain from any action inconsistent with the purposes and principles of the Charter of the United Nations against the territorial integrity, political independence or unity of any participating state…, [and] from making each other's territory the object of military occupation… No such occupation or acquisition will be recognised as legal". This final phrase was intended in particular to deny recognition to the Soviet Union's absorption of the Baltic States (as mentioned above).

Surprisingly, in the context of those times, Principle I states that participating states "also have the right to belong or not to belong to international organizations, to be or not to be a party to bilateral or multilateral treaties, including the right to be or not to be a party to treaties of alliance; they also have the right to neutrality". In addition, Principle VIII says that "all peoples [NB: not states] always have the right, in full freedom, to determine when and as they wish, their internal and external political status, without external interference".

This text embodies another defeat for the Soviet Union, which tried hard to confine the right of self-determination to colonial situations. These passages from Principles I and VIII seemed merely declaratory at the time, since there was no chance that the Soviet Union would allow its allies to leave the Warsaw Pact, but the words now look prophetic because they were invoked when the Warsaw Pact did in fact break up in 1991. For instance, they were quoted by James Baker, US Secretary of State, when persuading Gorbachev to agree to a united Germany joining NATO (see Chapter 22).

Human rights

Any suggestion that the Final Act legitimised the political status quo, meaning primarily the imposition of communist rule on the states of Eastern Europe, is not sustainable. It called for radical changes in the practices of those states, notably in regard to human rights, inclusion of which in the Final Act was resisted by the Soviet team (and Dr Kissinger) on the grounds that they were not a proper subject for international relations. One of the key achievements of the Western negotiators was to overcome this resistance and establish that the internal affairs of each country were the legitimate concern of others and relevant to the security of Europe.

The idea of putting human rights on the agenda was first proposed by France in 1969, then by West Germany in November 1971, and accepted by NATO in 1972.[9] The real push came from the nine members of the European Community "The Nine"), which Britain was just joining. The Davignon Report of 1970 (see Chapter 11) had stated that a "united Europe must be founded upon the common heritage of respect for the liberty and the rights of men". Since the Final Act was to be a pan-European security document it must, in the view of the Nine, reflect values essential to the European identity.[10] NATO went along with this but was less enthusiastic because it had among its members Spain, Portugal and Greece, which were then ruled by dictators who had no interest in human rights.

The key text on human rights is in Basket I of the Final Act, where we find the remarkable Principle VII. It states that "participating states will respect human rights and fundamental freedoms, including the freedom of thought, conscience, religion or belief… They will promote and encourage the effective exercise of civil, political, economic and social, cultural and other rights and freedoms, all of which derive from the inherent dignity of the human person and are essential for his free and full development". The Principle then goes on to say that such respect "is an essential factor for the peace, justice and well-being necessary to ensure the development of friendly relations and cooperation among themselves as among all states". Also endorsed in Principle VII is "the right of the individual to know and act upon his rights and duties in this field".

The importance of this Principle was fourfold: it asserted that human rights derive from the inherent dignity of the human person and are not just privileges granted by governments; it provided a text that the people of the Soviet bloc could—and did—legitimately invoke against their own governments; it placed human rights clearly on the agenda of international relations, thereby legitimising Western scrutiny of human rights in the Soviet sphere; and it established the essential link between security and respect for human rights. It said, in effect, that security in Europe must be based on the consent of the people. To put it another way, reversing Kissinger's priorities, there could be no stability without justice. Thus it also emphasised the Western view, which prevailed throughout the Final Act, that détente was not a state of affairs that had been achieved by signature of the Final Act but a process that depended on implementation of that document. This important point is also emphasised in the preamble to Basket I, which states that implementation of the results of the CSCE will be "a major contribution" to making détente a continuing process. Persistent Soviet attempts to have détente described as "irreversible" were dismissed by the British as "nonsense" because that would have removed the essential element of conditionality from the Final Act.[11]

One of the many tactics used by the Soviet team to weaken or qualify the wording on human rights was to invoke the International Covenant on Civil and Political Rights (1966), which includes exceptions relating to matters such as "public safety, order, health or morals" (Article 18). These exceptions, normal in a legal document but open to abuse in a political document, were music to Soviet ears, which may be why the Soviet Union hurriedly ratified the Covenant in October 1973. It was also one of the reasons for deciding that the Final Act was not a treaty or legal document but a political declaration. Initially, the Soviet team wanted the Final Act to state that implementation of Principle VII should be "in accordance with" the Covenant so as to include the exceptions. When that attempt failed they also tried in vain to write the exceptions into the text itself. After much haggling a fuzzy form of words was agreed that makes a subsidiary reference to the "obligations" of the Covenant, among other documents, so the exceptions largely disappear from view.

Even after admitting human rights to the text the Soviet team fought a rearguard battle to establish a hierarchy of Principles so that respect for human rights would be subordinate to principles of sovereignty and non-intervention. Here, too, they had to give way and allow all the Principles to be twice declared "of primary significance"—in the preamble to Basket I and the text of Principle X—so none could be quoted to qualify another.

It was primarily the texts on human rights in Principle VII and on freer movement of people and information in Basket III that the people of the Soviet Union and Eastern Europe invoked against their governments almost as soon as the document was signed (see Chapter 15).

Confidence-Building Measures (CBMs)

A European security agreement without a military dimension would have been less than convincing. But what shape should it take? The unwieldy CSCE, with its large contingent of neutrals and non-aligned, was clearly not the place for serious talks on reducing troops and hardware, so the task was allocated to separate talks in Vienna between members of the two military alliances. These were known as the talks on Mutual and Balanced Force Reductions (MBFR). They were expected to be much more important than the CSCE because they would reach binding agreements on arms, whereas the CSCE would produce only political declarations. As it turned out, the MBFR talks got nowhere while the CSCE altered the history of Europe.

Looking for a military element that seemed appropriate for the CSCE, NATO reached for ideas it had discussed in 1969 for mutual notification of military manoeuvres and exchange of observers. Their aim was to reduce anxiety and the risk of miscalculation on both sides, in particular by preventing routine military exercises from being seen as preparations for attack. Thus the principle of transparency, which ran through all aspects of the CSCE, would be extended to the military sphere.

There was resistance on both sides. The Russians argued that even these measures would distract from frontier issues and provide opportunities for Western espionage. Kissinger said that reconnaissance satellites already provided all the information needed, and anyway discussing military matters in the CSCE would distract from the MBFR talks. Nevertheless, after lengthy wrangles an agreement emerged to give 21 days' notice of military manoeuvres involving more than 25,000 troops within a specified area and to invite observers from participating states. Notification of military movements remained voluntary. (For details see the text of the Final Act.[12]) Anatoly Kovalev, head of the Soviet delegation, had to struggle hard with the Soviet military to get their reluctant consent.

Basket II: Cooperation in the field of economics, of science and technology and of the environment

For the Soviet Union and Eastern Europe, one of the main benefits they expected from détente in general and the Helsinki Process in particular was more access to Western trade and technology. They badly needed to modernise their generally backward and slowing economies, and they wanted consumer goods to buy off rising discontent. In 1969 their proposed agenda for a security conference included only two items: security (meaning mainly frontiers) and economic, technical and scientific cooperation. Behind the Western push for more trade with Eastern Europe was the belief or hope that it would help to loosen political controls and expose the area to Western influence.

This second item became Basket II under the rather clumsy heading at the top of this section. It was less obviously controversial than the other two but not without its own problems. Western businessmen could not easily work within the centrally controlled economies of Eastern Europe and the Soviet Union. They found themselves in the hands of government officials who were often reluctant to put them in contact with end users, and were anyway tightly controlled from the centre. Statistics were often secret or wildly wrong—or both, having been falsified from the bottom up, so that even the governments of those countries had no clear picture of reality. Credits that were intended for productive use were often diverted to buying consumer goods or equipment that was not used. Even when credits were invested in making products that were supposed to earn Western currency these often turned out to be of such a low standard that they could not compete in Western markets except at dumping prices.

As a result of these and other problems, some countries, notably Poland and East Germany, ran up huge debts to the West that they could not service or repay. The total gross debt of the six East European countries plus Yugoslavia rose from $9 billion in 1970 to $80 billion in 1980, much of it accounted for by Poland, Hungary and East Germany.[13] Constant requests by Eastern Europe to be granted Most Favoured Nation (MFN) status were rebuffed because there was no way of negotiating true reciprocity between the centrally controlled economies of the East and the free markets of the West, as would have been required under MFN rules.

This question of reciprocity held up the talks until almost the last minute but not before the human element intruded. The Russians invited a member of the French delegation to their mission and kept him up all night negotiating on this issue. He went to bed at 6 a.m. without informing his ambassador of what had been agreed. When other delegations met and learned of his secret negotiations, they were so angry that his text was never tabled.[14]

Another problem for Basket II was that it was fuzzy around the edges. Like the other baskets it consisted of declarations of intent by governments but implementation could involve any number of other bodies, such as individual ministries, institutes, enterprises, banks, the European Community (not yet recognised by the Eastern bloc), and the Economic Commission for Europe, a United Nations regional organisation based in Geneva that was set up to promote pan-European trade. (It was eventually given a formal role in the follow-up to the conference under paragraph 1c of Basket IV in the Final Act.)

To add further complications, the subject matter of Basket II overlapped with that of other baskets. For example, its mandate to promote cooperation in science and technology overlapped with Basket III's responsibility for education. Tourism as an industry overlapped with provision for freer movement of people and information in Basket III, as did the interest of Western businessmen in freer access to people and information and easier access to visas.

The negotiators battled through these complexities to produce a long section of the Final Act. After declaring a commitment to increasing trade as a contribution to peace, this section contains promises to improve contacts between sellers and users of products and services, to promote publication and dissemination of economic and commercial information at regular intervals, to promote industrial cooperation, harmonise standards, remove obstacles to cooperation in science and technology, cooperate in agricultural research and environmental protection, develop transport, promote tourism, and collaborate on the problems of migrant labour.

How much effect these pious promises had is difficult to judge. They assumed a lot of compatibility between the systems that did not exist in areas such as statistics and standards. East–West trade certainly grew very rapidly in the 1970s as détente evolved, propelled by the massive credits already mentioned,[15] but it was driven by many factors other than the commitments made in Basket II. These, however, provided some encouragement, a framework, and modest impetus for reluctant changes in the habits of some communist countries.

Basket III: Cooperation in humanitarian and other fields

This section was the subject of long and intensely difficult negotiations. Basket III had required "761 official negotiating sessions, and many more thousands of hours of work behind the scenes"[16] Contrary to many accounts it does not mention human rights as such (it refers briefly to matters such as family rights or migrant workers' rights) but it can be seen as a detailed programme for implementing the rights set out in Basket I, so it is sometimes subsumed with Principle VII under the general heading "the human dimension".

Soviet officials had originally wanted a brief mention of economic and cultural cooperation in one section. Later they tried to get Basket III separated entirely from the Final Act so that it could be downgraded. By the end they had agreed with extreme reluctance to include this long section, covering 17 pages in the British version. It sets out an extensive list of detailed commitments requiring substantial changes in Soviet and East European practices. Among many undertakings, signatories "make it their aim… to facilitate freer movement and contacts, individually and collectively, whether privately or officially…, [to] favourably consider applications for travel…, [and] facilitate the freer and wider dissemination of information of all kinds".

In these texts lie many hard-fought Western victories, including in particular references to individual travel and contacts, which the Soviet team resisted strongly because they held that all contacts and information should be under government control. They also disliked the dissemination of information "of all kinds". They often invoked the dangers of pornography and "hate speech" when their real fear was of a much broader spectrum of Western influence. As we saw in Chapter 11, the West had to make some compromises, such as dropping the reference to "ideas", which had appeared in early Western drafts, but overall the embattled Soviet negotiators lost on most points.

Their next tactic was to qualify or undermine practically everything in Basket III, particularly where it referred to information or to the role of individuals. Andrei Gromyko, Soviet Foreign Minister, told his French counterpart that "the bottom of Basket III must be cut away so that all the splendid things the West insisted on putting into it could fall through".[17] His team tried to do this by introducing qualifying clauses or preambles that would have made all contacts and exchanges subordinate to selected principles which they hoped to include in Basket I, such as "non-interference" or respect for the "sovereignty, laws and customs" or "cultural foundations" of participating states. They also wanted the flow of information to be restricted to the specific purpose of fostering peace and good relations. These infinitely flexible formulae would have enabled them to reject any contacts or information that did not, in their eyes, respect their "customs" or contribute to peace.

The battle over the Russians' desire for a restrictive preamble to Basket III, or a series of "mini-preambles" to different sections, sometimes divided the West. When Brezhnev visited Paris in early December 1974 the French secretly agreed to a mini-preamble for the human contacts section of Basket III. In Geneva, the Austrian chairman of that committee disliked the text but was persuaded to table it because the French told him "repeatedly and mendaciously", according to the British, that the Nine wished him to do so. But the Nine had not even seen the text, so their reaction was extremely cool. The Russians were also not happy when they found that the French could not deliver. "French tactics and the failure to reach agreement have led to a good deal of resentment and mistrust", reported David Hildyard, head of the British mission.[18] But he also praised the French: "They have had a large, able and articulate delegation, and they can be clear thinking and effective operators".[19]

We can divert briefly for an entertaining look at what Hildyard wrote about other delegations in his dispatches, illustrating some of the tensions that arose behind the scenes: "The West Germans are not good interlocuteurs (*sic*)..., they have not kept their allies fully informed of their thinking, and as they so often play their own game as well as change their minds frequently, they are seldom if ever in a position to bring along their partners...; [they] can be secretive and unreliable".

The Italians are "erratic, suddenly changing their minds". The Danes are "feeble", the Belgians "touchy and anxious to score personal successes (everyone suffers a little from this, I fear)". The Canadians are "particularly helpful". As for the Soviet side, "I have been impressed by the increasing willingness of the East Europeans to allow their differences with the Soviet Union to emerge publically (*sic*), and indeed what appear to be their hopes of building on their experiences during the Conference to press for a growing measure of consideration and thus for independence of view in the future. This movement could well eventually prove one of the most satisfactory results of the Conference".[20] The British singled out Dr Siegfried Bock, head of the East German delegation, for special praise, reporting that he "displayed an irrepressible intelligence and sophistication".[21]

Americans, who were more distant from the negotiations, remained sceptical of all the effort to put human rights into the texts. "Nearly everyone saw Basket III, on human rights [wrong Basket], as hortatory window dressing, a paper exercise of no consequence", wrote Robert Gates later.[22] Not true. Although Western participants embarked on the long haul with a very wide range of intentions, hopes and interests, the story of the negotiations reveals the remarkable tenacity with which the nine members of the European Community, with important support from neutrals and non-aligned, pressed for strong texts on human rights, contacts, travel, information, and family reunification. At one point, when some European backbones were sagging under the stress, Mr van der Stoel, Foreign Minister of the Netherlands, reminded his fellow ministers that only recently in Copenhagen they had signed a document stating that respect for human rights was a fundamental element of the European identity.[23] They could not immediately renege on that, he urged. Nor did they.

Basket IV: Follow-up

This Basket, often forgotten, contains the important obligation to publish and disseminate the text of the Final Act and make it known "as widely as possible". This was a gift to members of the opposition in the Soviet Union and Eastern Europe, who were astonished and delighted when they opened their newspapers to read what their governments had signed up to. Local party bureaucrats were equally astonished but not at all delighted. One can understand their distress when, for instance, 100,000 East Germans quickly applied for exit visas, most of them citing the Final Act. [24]

Even worse for the Soviet Union was the obligation to attend a series of follow-up conferences at which the performance of signatories would be monitored. It had initially favoured creating a follow-up body as an embryonic European system that would have given the Soviet Union a say in security matters over the whole continent, preferably without the United States. This was resisted by NATO delegations, which insisted that follow-up should be about implementing the Final Act. The Soviet negotiators gradually lost interest as they realised that they would be held to account for their violations of the Final Act, so the balance shifted as the West came to favour follow-up while Soviet enthusiasm cooled, but it was too late to drop the issue, so follow-up meetings duly followed in Belgrade (1977–8), Madrid (1980–83) and Vienna (1986–7), causing the Soviet Union acute discomfort (see Chapters 16–19).

The final stretch

By the spring of 1975 tension was building up in Geneva. During wrangles over frontiers the Russians had hinted that if the West made concessions on that issue they would reciprocate with more flexibility on Basket III. This turned out to be untrue. Having pocketed the agreement on frontiers they dug in their heels over Basket III and remained deeply resistant to Western demands for the freer movement of people and information, which they saw as major threats to their system. They seemed to think they could wear down the Western delegates, some of whom were becoming weary and impatient, wanting to get back to their families. However, Western governments could not sign a final agreement unless it contained clear provision for lowering barriers between Eastern and Western Europe, so, despite some wobbles, they stood firm.

The Russians became increasingly desperate as they were under pressure from Brezhnev to finish the conference in time for an early summit meeting. His health was failing, and he wanted to present his triumph to the 25th Soviet Party Congress due in early March the following year. On 8 March 1975 he wrote to several heads of Western governments, proposing that the final stage of the conference should open in Helsinki on 30 June. The Western governments replied that they could not agree to a date until agreement had been reached on outstanding issues. The Russian delegation became increasingly desperate but still refused concessions on Basket III. Among particularly thorny issues was the Western refusal to accept that governments should be held responsible for the content of information, an impossible demand to put to a democracy. In addition, the Americans had become increasingly tough on working conditions for journalists, doubtless thinking ahead to press coverage of the final agreement.

In this deadlocked situation a British diplomat, Michael Alexander (see Chapter 12), proposed a "global solution".[25] The Western delegations would agree on a package containing some concessions but also essential Western demands, mainly around information and human contacts. This would be presented to the Russians as a whole. If they accepted it, even with some minor amendments, open to negotiation, the conference could move forward. If they rejected it, the Western side would go back to negotiating each subject separately, thereby causing the conference to drag on into the autumn. Alexander reasoned that the Russians were now under such severe pressure to meet Brezhnev's deadline that they would accept. Other Western delegates were initially unenthusiastic. Even the British Foreign Office was cool. The Dutch, always the hard-liners, were particularly critical, but the Belgians and the Italians were also difficult. Nevertheless, agreement was eventually reached and the package was handed to Dubinin on 15 May. He did not like it at all.

Help then came from Kissinger, who met Gromyko in Vienna on 19–20 May. Kissinger had been tempted to reach a bilateral deal with the Russians but had been warned by Arthur Hartman, Assistant Secretary of State for European Affairs, that this would be deeply resented by the Europeans.[26] Hartman had also briefed him in detail, mainly on the basis of British notes, so he was therefore able to confront Gromyko with a surprising level of expertise; in the past he had joked with Gromyko about his ignorance of the details. To him, as we have seen, the CSCE was a misguided enterprise and not worth his close attention. However, American domestic opinion had been hardening against détente, so he had come to realise that he must engage more fully in order to avoid a weak outcome. Gromyko was thrown off-balance. He tried in vain to negotiate individual texts but Kissinger insisted on the global package and made it clear that there was no more give in the Western position.

On 21 May the Soviet delegation in Geneva proposed almost 50 changes to the package, provoking speculation that their response had been prepared before the Kissinger–Gromyko meeting. Dubinin became personally abusive, accusing the Western negotiators of "trickery". Maresca suspected (rightly as it turned out) that there were divisions within the Soviet delegation.

On 22 May the NATO caucus decided unanimously that the list of changes was too long. The next day Kovalev asked for an immediate meeting with Albert Sherer, head of the American delegation. He made a final attempt to soften the Western position, becoming extremely agitated. He spent three hours threatening Sherer and Maresca with the political implications of prolonging the conference. He said that the global initiative was not a compromise but an ultimatum, as indeed it was, even while allowing some room for flexibility. So there matters stood until 28 May, when a dramatic episode changed the whole situation. The French ambassador, Gerard André, had invited for lunch the representatives of the four powers responsible for Germany. They were supposed to discuss quadripartite rights in Germany but there were no new developments on that subject, so conversation turned to Basket III. "Kovalev was nervous and sullen, smoking even more than usual and apparently reluctant to speak".[27]

Suddenly Kovalev was called away to take a phone call. When he returned he talked to Dubinin in agitated tones. Then one of his officials arrived with a note. The Soviet group withdrew into a corner for a huddled conversation. When Kovalev returned to the table he spoke in tones of "triumph and spiteful anger" before listing concessions that the Soviet delegation was prepared to make.[28] These included key passages on freer movement, an undertaking not to expel journalists in legitimate pursuit of their profession, a paragraph accepting that governments would not be held responsible for radio broadcasts, and an undertaking to settle outstanding problems on family reunification. In other words, he had given way.

Light on this episode was shed years later by Kovalev in his memoirs "As the Geneva negotiations drew to a close it became obvious to me that without making concessions on several concrete issues in the section on information and contacts, a consensus as a whole on the final document would not be reached. But these were complicated issues requiring unusual changes in our existing practices and those of other Warsaw Pact countries—ideas that required the green light from Moscow. Before making a final decision I asked my wife to walk alone with me along the Geneva river. I told her that I planned to send Moscow a proposal that carried the risk of serious career difficulties that would also affect the situation of our family. Was she prepared for that? 'I am prepared,' she answered. And she added, 'I consider it our duty.'[29]

"Late in the evening the members of the delegation met in my office…; [their] reaction indicated that they were not psychologically or politically prepared for such a drastic change in several of the positions that they had maintained right up to that evening with such firmness and skill. They were also concerned that Moscow would not understand us. For the first time during the entire Geneva stage, the opinion of the head of the delegation did not find support from even one of the delegation members… Dubinin and Kondrashev [the KGB representative] spoke most definitively against my idea. Ending the discussion, I said I would submit to Moscow only my personal ideas and not the ideas of the delegation. Then, in front of my colleagues, I signed a telegram. In less than 24 hours I received a telegram from Moscow [expressing] agreement to all my suggestions".

The concessions related to family reunions, somewhat easier travel, exchange of information, increasing the import of foreign newspapers and improvements in the working conditions of journalists, including granting them multiple entry and exit visas, a big concession as the need to apply for each visit gave the authorities a useful instrument of control over foreign journalists. As Kovalev wrote in the above account, "These were not minor technical details". He was right about that, and also about the damage to his career. As mentioned in Chapter 12, he was conspicuously not decorated for his efforts and was denied the promotion that would otherwise have been his due.

So the West won most of the vital points: Brezhnev Doctrine excluded, frontiers open to change, human rights to be respected, freer movement of people and information of all kinds, reunification of families, publication of the text, and—very important, as it turned out—review meetings at which the member states would be held to account for their implementation or non-implementation of the Final Act.

Why did the Soviet negotiators give so much ground on these and many other points? Because they found that otherwise they would not get the summit conference to which Brezhnev had so misguidedly committed himself. An additional factor was that Kovalev himself had personal sympathies with the Western case, while in Moscow his bosses partly persuaded themselves that the texts on sovereignty would give them more protection than turned out to be the case. All this gave the Western negotiators far more leverage than they had expected at the outset. Time was on their side, and they used it well to put pressure on the other side.

There were still some further moments of drama. At the last minute, when everything else had been agreed, Malta attempted to hold the conference to ransom by demanding an absurd text to exclude foreign warships from the Mediterranean. Obviously, the Americans would never accept that, and nor would the Russians. Dom Mintoff, the Maltese premier, could not be reached. Tempers flared. Kovalev threatened to tear down the building with his bare hands, while Jaako Iloniemi of Finland reportedly only just managed to restrain himself from hitting the Maltese ambassador, Joseph Kingswell.[30] Eventually Kingswell quietly gave away his reserve position, dropping this pointless demand. Mintoff was furious and sacked him not only from the Foreign Ministry but altogether from the civil service, a harsh and very unjust punishment for a man who had saved the conference at the cost of his own career.[31]

Finally, late on the night of 20 July 1975, the Turkish, Greek and Cypriot delegates decided to have another of their familiar rows, but everyone was tired and no one wanted to listen, so Yuri Dubinin, who was in the chair at the time, brought down the gavel at 3 a.m., finally ending nearly three years of negotiation. All the journalists but one had long left the lobby, not expecting any progress. As Dubinin described the scene later: "A crumpled figure appeared at the far end of the foyer, rubbing his eyes… It was our Geneva correspondent from the TASS news agency. The most tenacious reporter in the world… What a guy!" At first Moscow was sceptical because there were no other sources but the reporter was later decorated.[32]

As exhausted delegates staggered out into the dawn of 21 July, the deputy head of the Polish delegation, Jerzy Nowak, said to Michael Alexander that when the text of the Final Act was distributed to provincial party secretaries they would phone the leadership in Warsaw and say "You people must have been mad to agree to our signing this thing".[33]

Notes

1 *DBPO III/II*, 7, note 17, and in Appendix III.
2 Möckli, 'The EC Nine, the CSCE, and the changing pattern of European security', in Wenger et al., *Origins of the European Security System*, 157.

3 *DBPO III/II*, 319.
4 Dubinin in *CSCE Testimonies, Causes and Consequences of the Helsinki Final Act 1972–1989*, OSCE, viewed 20 January 2022, https://www.osce.org/files/f/documents/6/c/459244.pdf, pp. 200–204.
5 Quoted in Maresca, *To Helsinki*, 116.
6 Russell, 'The Helsinki Declaration: Brobdingnag or Lilliput', in *The American Journal of International Law*, 70/2, (April 1976), 253–7.
7 Wolf, *Man without a Face*, 308–11.
8 *DBPO III/II*, 212.
9 Morgan, *The Final Act*, 126–8.
10 Gates, *From the Shadows*, 86.
11 British National Archives, FCO 41/1766. See also Russell, 260.
12 https://www.osce.org/helsinki-final-act
13 Richard Portes 'Debt and the Banks: East Europe's Debt to the West: Interdependence is a Two-Way Street', in *Foreign Affairs* 22/4 (July 1977).
14 *DBPO III/II*, 446.
15 Between Eastern Europe and the OECD countries trade rose by 34 per cent in 1973, a further 43 per cent in 1974, and 15 per cent more in 1975. East European imports grew much faster than their exports, so East European hard-currency balance-of-trade deficits nearly doubled each year from 1972 through 1975, rising from $2.2 billion in 1972 to $12 billion in 1975. See Portes.
16 Thomas, *The Helsinki Effect*, 86.
17 *DBPO III/II*, 320–21.
18 *DBPO III/II*, 364.
19 *DBPO III/II*, 365.
20 *DBPO III/II* 365–6.
21 *DBPO III/II*, 143.
22 Gates, *From the Shadows*, 86.
23 The Nine Foreign Ministers, 2013, *Declaration on European Identity, (Copenhagen, 14 December 1973)*, CVCE, viewed on 22 January 2022, https://www.cvce.eu/content/publication/1999/1/1/02798dc9-9c69-4b7d-b2c9-f03a8db7da32/publishable_en.pdf. Incident related in Thomas, *The Helsinki Effect*, 80.
24 Thomas, *The Helsinki Effect*, 109.
25 Alexander, *Managing the Cold War*, 47–51; also in *British Diplomatic Oral History Programme*, viewed 22 January 2022, https://www.chu.cam.ac.uk/media/uploads/files/Alexander.pdf, p. 15. For a full account of the global solution see Hebel, *Fathers of the Final Act*, chapter 9.
26 Maresca, *To Helsinki*, 149.
27 Maresca, 150.
28 Maresca, 151.
29 Quoted by Maresca in *Helsinki Revisited*, 194, from *Transition*, 30 June 1995. In 1974 Kovalev was accused by a KGB agent of high treason. Brunner, Testimonies, 111.
30 *DBPO III/II*, 436.
31 Dubinin in *CSCE Testimonies, Causes and Consequences of the Helsinki Final Act 1972–1989*, OSCE, viewed 20 January 2022, https://www.osce.org/files/f/documents/6/c/459244.pdf, pp. 203–4.
32 Dubinin,*Testimonies*, p. 210.
33 Alexander, *Managing the Cold War*, 64; confirmed with slight corrections by Nowak in a telephone conversation with the author on 21 November 2007; see also in *British Diplomatic Oral History Programme*, viewed 22 January 2022, https://www.chu.cam.ac.uk/media/uploads/files/Alexander.pdf, p. 17.

14 1975: Views from the summit

The summit was finally reached in late July 1975. Helsinki filled up as 35 heads of state and government arrived with their numerous officials, staff and bodyguards, more than a thousand journalists, and a massive security presence provided by the efficient Finnish government. After several days of speeches, the Final Act was signed on 1 August 1975. The sun shone through the long warm days of a northern summer, in sharp contrast to the freezing darkness in which the talks had started nearly three years earlier. Everyone professed to be happy. Toasts were drunk and meals taken long into the night as journalists tried to make sense of it all.

Watching the vast event, this author wondered whether it would turn out to be a significant moment in history or an insubstantial pageant that would fade away and "leave not a rack behind".[1] Clearly, the Soviet Union had achieved a major triumph by bringing about the summit conference for which it had been pressing for nearly twenty years, but it had saddled itself with a raft of unwelcome commitments that it had bitterly resisted and had no intention of honouring.

The question, therefore, was whether the potential for change embodied in the Final Act would be realised or stifled by a recalcitrant Soviet Union. As it turned out, the Helsinki Process changed the terms of the Cold War, helped unfreeze the division of Europe, and remains a lasting factor in European history.

Leonid Brezhnev, its main sponsor, had seen his dream come true, but it became a nightmare as dissidents seized on the Final Act to challenge the fundamentals of the Soviet system. As we have seen, it was almost the opposite of what he had wanted. Instead of endorsing the status quo it presented an agenda for change. Instead of legitimising the Soviet sphere of interest it legitimised Western intrusion into it. Instead of making frontiers immutable it specifically affirmed the principle of peaceful change. Instead of being a one-off declaration it initiated a continuing process of review that became acutely embarrassing for the Soviet Union until Mikhail Gorbachev became its leader in 1985.

So why did Brezhnev sign? Because he had staked his prestige on this conference and no one dared stop him, while some of those around him did not want to stop him because they hoped the document would bring changes

DOI: 10.4324/9781003146124-18

to the Soviet Union. Perhaps, as some have suggested, he had not read the text properly. He was known to have been addicted to tranquillisers ever since his invasion of Czechoslovakia in 1968, which had caused him deep distress. He was certainly in bad health when he came to Helsinki but to this witness he seemed to read his speech with only occasional signs of difficulty, and his signature on the Final Act looked reasonably firm. However, we learned only much later that he did not appear at the Politburo for weeks or even months afterwards, so he was clearly unwell, and the summit had taken its toll.[2] Thus, we have an almost sad picture of Brezhnev reaching what he hoped would be the summit of his achievements as the man of destiny who had finally brought peace to war-torn Europe affixing his signature to a document that brought him no glory and only trouble.

The speeches at the summit reflected the ambiguities and compromises in the document by presenting idiosyncratic mixes of selective interpretations, misinterpretations, pure ignorance, and calculated attempts to recapture ground lost during the negotiations.[3] Brezhnev himself offered an uneasy blend of triumphalism, revisionism and caution.[4] Unaware—or maybe unwilling to accept—how little public interest his grand project had generated in the West, and how sceptical were many in Eastern Europe, he made the grandiose and wholly false claim that "millions upon millions of people" were aware of the special nature of the conference, while those who had lived through the horrors of the Second World War "realise with utmost clarity the historical significance of the conference". Its results, he said, soaring into a world of his own imagination, "are linked with expectations and hopes never before engendered by any other collective action in the period following the well-known joint allied post-war decisions... The soil of Europe was drenched plentifully with blood in the years of the two world wars. Leading politicians and statesmen... have assembled in Helsinki so as to contribute by joint effort to transform Europe into a continent which would suffer no further military calamity. The right to peace must be guaranteed for all the peoples of Europe".

He then tried to recover ground lost in the negotiations by claiming that the Final Act had placed relations on the "fundamental principles... of peaceful coexistence which were fought for with such conviction and dedication by the founder of the Soviet State, Vladimir Ilyich Lenin, and which are being fought for by our people even today".

As we have seen, the Western negotiators managed to exclude "peaceful coexistence" from the Final Act because it was a communist doctrine requiring intensified ideological struggle with the capitalist world, whereas the Final Act recognises no ideological confrontation in Europe. Its ten Principles apply to relations between all participating states, including those between the Soviet Union and its colonies in Eastern Europe. In other words, Brezhnev was implicitly re-affirming the "Brezhnev Doctrine" by claiming special rights in Eastern Europe.[5]

He then turned to the long battles over information, where the Soviet Union had exhibited extreme sensitivity: "It is no secret that information media can serve the purposes of peace and confidence; they can also spread throughout the world the poison of discord between countries and peoples. We should like to hope that the results of the Conference will serve as correct guidelines for co-operation in these areas as well". In fact, as we have seen, the Final Act endorses "the freer and wider dissemination of information of all kinds".

He also tried to reintroduce the principle of "non-interference" for which his delegation had fought for so long in vain, claiming that "it is only the people of each given State and no-one else, who have the sovereign right to resolve their internal affairs and establish their internal laws". That right was, of course, conspicuously denied to the subject peoples of Eastern Europe by the Soviet Union. Moreover, the Final Act rules out only physical intervention, and makes it clear that respect for human rights is an essential ingredient of security in Europe and therefore the concern of all the participating states.

Near the end, however, a more modest note of realism crept in, doubtless drafted by Kovalev: "The outcome of the prolonged negotiations is such that there are neither victors nor vanquished, neither winners nor losers. It has been a victory of reason. Everyone has won". Actually, of course, the West had won most of the vital points, but he could hardly be expected to admit that.

President Gerald Ford, in a wisely restrained speech,[6] emphasised the need for implementation: "The American people, like the people of Europe, know well that mere assertions of good will, passing changes in the political mood of governments, laudable declarations of principles are not enough. But if we proceed with care, with commitment to real progress, there is now an opportunity to turn our peoples' hopes into realities...; much more remains to be done before we prematurely congratulate ourselves...; peace is not a piece of paper.... But lasting peace is at least possible today because we have learned from the experiences of the last 30 years that peace is a process requiring mutual restraint and practical arrangements... This Conference is a part of that process—a challenge, not a conclusion... Détente is an evolutionary process, not a static condition. Many formidable challenges yet remain... The goals we are stating today are the yardstick by which our performance will be measured.

"The people of all Europe and, I assure you, the people of North America, are thoroughly tired of having their hopes raised and then shattered by empty words and unfulfilled pledges. We had better say what we mean and mean what we say, or we will have the anger of our citizens to answer... Our peoples will be watching and measuring our progress. They will ask how these noble sentiments are being translated into actions that bring about a more secure and just order in the daily lives of each of our nations and its citizens".

He then launched into a ringing endorsement of human rights: "The documents produced here...affirm the most fundamental human rights: liberty of thought, conscience, and faith; the exercise of civil and political rights; the rights of minorities. They call for a freer flow of information, ideas, and people; greater scope for the press, cultural and educational exchange, family reunification, the right to travel and to marriage between nationals of different states; and for the protection of the priceless heritage of our diverse cultures". (Obviously no one had told his speechwriter that the freer movement of "ideas" had to be dropped at the preparatory talks in the face of Soviet intransigence (see Chapter 11).)

He went on to claim the universality of American values: "The founders of my country did not merely say that all Americans should have these rights but all men everywhere should have these rights. And these principles have guided the United States of America throughout its two centuries of nationhood. They have given hope to millions in Europe and on every continent".

He then made an important affirmation of the commitment of the United States to European security, a clear rebuff to Soviet efforts to drive the Americans out of Europe: "I believe, and my countrymen believe, in the interdependence of Europe and North America—indeed in the interdependence of the entire family of man… There is not a single people represented here whose blood does not flow in the veins of Americans and whose culture and traditions have not enriched the heritage which we Americans prize so highly…; my presence here symbolizes my country's vital interest in Europe's future. Our future is bound with yours. Our economic well-being, as well as our security, is linked increasingly with yours. The distance of geography is bridged by our common heritage and our common destiny. The United States, therefore, intends to participate fully in the affairs of Europe and in turning the results of this Conference into a living reality".

Then a pledge to the peoples of Eastern Europe: "The principles on which this Conference has agreed are a part of the great heritage of European civilization, which we all hold in trust for all mankind. To my country, they are not clichés or empty phrases. We take this work and these words very seriously. We will spare no effort to ease tensions and to solve problems between us. But it is important that you recognize the deep devotion of the American people and their Government to human rights and fundamental freedoms and thus to the pledges that this Conference has made regarding the freer movement of people, ideas [wrong again!], information".

Finally: "History will judge this Conference not by what we say here today, but by what we do tomorrow—not by the promises we make, but by the promises we keep".

This resonant conclusion was adopted by William Korey as the title of his book on the follow-up to the conference.[7]

British Prime Minister Harold Wilson made himself look foolish by using the phrase "peaceful coexistence" despite strenuous efforts to dissuade him by a horrified British official the night before. He was a stubborn man and thought he knew better. He also referred to the "spirit of live and let live" which may have been literally true but indicated more tolerance of the status quo than was justified or embodied in the Final Act. However, he partly redeemed himself with a bit of earthy common sense and a sharp dig at the current practices of the Soviet Union that largely contradicted his acceptance of the status quo elsewhere in this speech: "This Conference…will be judged by how that spirit is reflected in the lives of ordinary families, by such issues as the reunification of families, the marriages of citizens of different states, the greater possibilities of travel, by professional exchanges of all kinds, and by better working conditions for our journalists and businessmen. Détente means little if it is not reflected in the daily lives of our peoples. And there is no reason why, in 1975, Europeans should not be allowed to marry whom they want, hear and read what they want, travel abroad when and where they want, meet whom they want. And to deny that proposition is a sign not of strength but of weakness".

Helmut Schmidt, Chancellor of West Germany, ever the pragmatic realist, avoided the grandiose claims of Brezhnev: "The German Federal Republic and the citizens of my country fully appreciate the results of this Conference while viewing them quite dispassionately. Decades of confrontation are not replaced overnight by an era of co-operation. And it is not enough to give a single impetus to the process of détente; it requires the steady action of all of us so as to progress continuously… There remain fundamental differences between East and West in their ideological, political and economic systems… It would be wrong, given the present state of relations between East and West, to set immediate expectations too high…; the progress of détente depends very largely on how far we are going to translate these principles into realities… We have all to work very hard to translate these principles into realities".

Then to one of the main issues for West Germany: "Frontiers are inviolable; but one must be able to change them by peaceful means and by agreement. It remains our aim to work for a state of peace in Europe in which the German nation will regain its unity through free self-determination. In accordance with Principle I of the Conference concerning possible changes of frontiers through peaceful means and by agreement, this is an extremely important principle and it is also important in relation to the declared aim of the nine European countries of the European community which is going to lead us into a European union".

Then to contacts between peoples, with very much in mind the barriers between the two parts of Germany: "A great deal has been said by participants in the Conference about the need for human contacts, exchange of information and co-operation in the field of culture and education. The results so far achieved cannot be fully satisfactory to those European States in which freedom of movement and the free flow of ideas are taken for granted and are the source of the rich diversity of ideas and the prosperity of these countries.

"For the present people must content themselves with what is possible today in view of the diversity of the systems and the mistrust which still exists. But it is the earnest desire of mankind that the remaining restrictions be abolished… Confidence is built upon encounter.

"The citizens of all our countries have already witnessed many international conferences and they sometimes feel sceptical about them. Only substantial progress in their relations with their European fellow-citizens will convince them that these documents are not just an ingenious piece of diplomacy but a challenge to act, a challenge which no one can ignore in the future without detriment to himself. In signing these documents, therefore, we assume a grave responsibility to translate our words into deeds. What is at stake here is the credibility of every Head of State or government in the East and the West".

Erich Honecker, leader of communist East Germany, shamelessly misrepresented the Final Act, reflecting his own dissatisfaction with the result:

"It is for the first time on our continent that with the documents of this Conference what may be called a code for the application of the principles of peaceful co-existence between States with different social systems [wrong, as we have seen] has been agreed under international law [no!]. In view of the lessons of history and the immediate requirements of European politics, respect for, and recognition of, the principle of the inviolability of frontiers is the decisive point". He made no mention of the principle of peaceful change because that would mean—as in the end it did mean—the political annihilation of his state.

President Giscard d'Estaing of France used the opportunity to stress his country's usual grudging attitude towards the role of the United States in Europe: "The purpose of the Conference, as well as of the Final Act, is security in Europe. In Europe: it means that this Conference brings together first of all Europeans, and that it has to do in the first place with Europe. Needless to say, Europe is concerned by the balance of forces between the superpowers. But this is not the place to discuss it. The crux of the matter is to ascertain what Europeans can do among themselves in order to set up the conditions for greater security".

He particularly welcomed the fact that the CSCE had brought together 35 states on an equal footing "able to speak with their own voice, whether big or small, whether member or not of an Alliance... That all the principal leaders of Europe are meeting here, becoming acquainted, talking things over cordially and considering their problems is a vital, new and unprecedented fact".

Continuing to play down the role of the superpowers, he went on: "I know that reference has been made in this connexion to the Congress of Vienna [1814–15], but the situations are very different. For example, some time ago I examined the table of the Congress of Vienna which had been preserved by Talleyrand in a chateau in the French countryside. It is a very small table around which those sitting in the front row of our assembly could barely take places...; only four countries spoke there and at the end of the Congress a fifth, our country. All the others were invited to be silent".

The Polish leader, Edouard Gierek, spoke movingly of Poland's profound desire for peace after the appalling suffering of his people, who had been occupied and fought over by Nazis and Russians: "The cause of peace is one most dearly held by the people of Poland… The two world wars swept across our land. Thirty years ago we welcomed peace amidst more than six million graves, amid ruined cities and ravaged villages".

Pierre Graber, President of Switzerland, reflected the sober realism that his diplomats had demonstrated in their indefatigable and skilful efforts to find compromises during the negotiations. The results of the CSCE, he said, meant "both little and a lot… Little, if viewed isolated and as the endpoint of a long and difficult exercise. A lot, if they stand for a sign and promise of an actual new era of international relations".

President Kekkonen of Finland, the country which had done so much to pave the way and host the conference, was cautious. He called the Final Act "a serious attempt to lay foundations on which we and the coming generations can build a world better than the one we have to live in". In other words, the verdict would ultimately depend on future actions, not on the words of the document.

Notes

1 Shakespeare, *The Tempest*, Act 4, scene 1.
2 Zubok, *A Failed Empire*, 246.
3 Most of the texts of the speeches can be found at www.osce.org or from the embassies of the speaker's state. Alternatively, some are available from the OSCE Secretariat, náměsti Pod Kaštany 2, 160 00 Prague, Czech Republic.
4 L. Brezhnev, 'Address to the third stage of the Conference on Security and Co-operation in Europe', Helsinki, 30 July – 1 August 1975, viewed 4 February 2022, https://www.osce.org/files/f/documents/f/f/16089.pdf
5 See chapter 8 for the origin of this idea.
6 G Ford, 'Address to Final Helsinki Session', 2 August 1975, viewed 4 February 2022, https://www.nytimes.com/1975/08/02/archives/text-of-president-fords-address-to-final-helsinki-session.html
7 Korey, *The Promises We Keep*.

15 Coming down to earth[1]

As the 35 signatories came down from rarefied air of the summit and returned to their capitals they had to face the troubled atmosphere that still surrounded the Final Act. In public, the Soviet Union hailed the document as a triumph for Soviet diplomacy, frequently misquoting it to suggest that it rendered the frontiers immutable, endorsed the division of Europe, and ruled out "interference". But there were ructions behind the scenes. Zubok reports that when the draft Final Act reached the Politburo before it went for signature, "ideological conservatives there expressed outrage and dismay. Would the Soviet Union be open to subversion and interference from outside?"[2] A vivid account by Anatoly Dobrynin describes them as stunned: "As the opening day drew closer, the Politburo engaged in heated debates over the documents Brezhnev was to sign… Many in the Politburo (Podgorny, Suslov, Kosygin, and Andropov) had grave doubts about assuming international commitments that could open the way to foreign interference in our political life".[3]

Another account of the Kremlin's reaction comes from Svetlana Savranskaya's research into the Kremlin archives. She describes opposition from Suslov and Ponomarev, and criticism from Andropov.[4] Eventually Gromyko calmed them down by saying that he had reached an understanding with Kissinger that neither side should interfere with the other's domestic affairs, whatever the Final Act said. Moreover, "we remain the masters in our own house".[5]

Since Gromyko's people had conducted the negotiations he had to defend their performance as best he could, but, given their very strong resistance to the Western agenda over a long period, he cannot have been entirely happy with the outcome. Certainly, one of his men in Geneva, Yuri Dubinin, who was responsible for negotiating Basket III, conveyed the impression to both Western and Eastern delegates that he would not be unduly bothered if the conference failed.[6]

In the light of these accounts it is tempting to imagine that, at roughly the same time as the *Wall Street Journal* was advising President Ford "Jerry, don't go", Andropov and others would have liked to say, if they had dared, "Leonid, don't go". Much later Nikolai Leonov, Head of the Foreign Intelligence Department of the KGB, wrote that "the Soviet Union lost on all the points…; the only true result of the Helsinki agreement for the USSR was

DOI: 10.4324/9781003146124-19

the expansive growth in human rights movements in all the socialist countries, which eventually undermined the regimes and directly contributed to their collapse".[7]

Among the regimes of Eastern Europe, reactions were mixed but there was no lack of awareness that the Final Act could bring trouble. Adam Daniel Rotfeld, who was on the Polish team, confirmed later that there were "strong reservations" in Moscow, while the most negative responses came from the regimes of East Germany, Czechoslovakia and Romania. In Poland, members of the security services accused the Polish delegation in Geneva of being "national traitors", while party dogmatists criticised the "unbalanced commitments" in the Final Act and the lack of a principled approach to ideology, which, they warned, offered the opposition in Poland "a kind of international legitimisation and quasi-legal protection". On the other hand, the Polish leader, Edward Gierek, was pleased by further confirmation of his frontier with Germany, while both he and János Kádár, the Hungarian leader, welcomed what they saw as legitimation for modernisation, foreign contacts, and, above, all trade, with perhaps some protection from the Brezhnev Doctrine.[8]

Erich Honecker, the East German leader, enjoyed strutting the diplomatic stage in Helsinki after so many years of isolation. He confused his advisers by fretting over whether to wear a light or dark suit at the ceremony (he finally chose light). Behind the scenes in East Berlin there was much unhappiness about the openings for more East–West contacts in Basket III and more especially the provision in Basket I for peaceful change of frontiers, which left the German question open. Moscow was felt to have given away too much. An angry Politburo meeting was cut short by Honecker.[9] As two East German authors wrote later, "the document in its essentials contained the handwriting of the West".[10]

Dr Siegfried Bock, who led the East German delegation, saw the Final Act as a victory on points for the West, despite some successes for the East. The Soviets had weakened their negotiating position by committing themselves to a quick summit. "It was very painful for us that this sentence [on peaceful change] was in Principle I… We felt it as a provocation". The concession was forced on East Berlin by Moscow. When Hermann Axen, Party Secretary for Foreign Affairs, learned that Bock, under Soviet pressure in Geneva, was accepting the principle of peaceful change of frontiers, he was "completely hysterical" and went to Honecker complaining that "Bock is selling out the Republic!" But Bock had no choice. He describes Gromyko's haughty attitude to his East German allies as "I am Moscow; who are you?"[11] Bock, a very able diplomat, fell into disfavour and was sent as ambassador to Romania.

The Czechoslovak regime revealed its nervousness in a party document put together in months of work after the summit.[12] Systematically misinterpreting the Final Act, and invoking the principles of "peaceful coexistence", it called for "a more offensive assertion of… our interests" while not allowing the capitalist states to misuse the Final Act to intervene in others' internal affairs. On Basket III "[we will] proceed aggressively in every direction wherever there are conditions to do so". The Final Act, it says, sets clear criteria for cooperation while respecting the principles of non-interference [no, it refers to non-intervention] and a respect for the laws, traditions and customs of every state [a formula rejected at an early stage in the negotiations]. On information, the party is to "strive for conditions that would allow us to act aggressively towards the West and place maximum limitation on ideological penetration by the West... We will select Western press titles least harmful by their content... We will systematically train persons being sent abroad within the framework of cultural, scientific, scholarly and medical contacts with foreign countries... We [will] give them specific state propaganda assignments... We will assume that in today's world divided according to class, the implacable struggle between socialism and capitalism goes on". It ends with a call for more effective promotion of socialist ideas in the West. Similarly, an internal East German document welcomed the possibilities opened up by the Final Act for "offensive penetration of the capitalist lands".[13] So much for "non-interference".

Then on the Western side a very strange thing happened. Large sections of the American press and academia, and some of the British press, failed to read or understand the text and largely accepted the Soviet Union's false interpretation. There was a barrage of criticism wrongly accusing Western governments and President Ford of selling out Eastern Europe and the Baltic states by recognising the division of Europe and the Soviet empire. Some commentators later said it cost Ford the coming election.[14] Yet all of these objections derived from a complete misunderstanding of the text of the Final Act.

The widely believed charge that the Final Act endorsed the status quo was a serious one. If true, it would have meant that the Western powers finally accepted Soviet rule over the unwilling peoples of Eastern Europe, thereby reneging on the Yalta Agreement of 1945, which promised free elections, and on numerous commitments to the reunification of Germany. In other words, it would have been a massive betrayal of the people of Eastern Europe and everything that the Western alliance claimed to stand for. It would truly have amounted to a shameful act of appeasement.

Yet many supposedly well-informed people made just that allegation at the time. Much of the misrepresentation was politically motivated but it also reflected a simple failure to read the Final Act. What, for instance, possessed William Buckley Jr. to call the Final Act a treaty and to assert that it "gave the Soviet Union what it had wanted for so long, namely *de jure* recognition of the post-war frontiers"?[15] Even a hasty reading of the text would have shown him that nothing in the Final Act is "*de jure*" because it is not a treaty or any other form of legal instrument. It is a political declaration. The negotiators gave close attention to this issue and carefully included a passage stating that the Final Act is "not eligible for registration under Article 102 of the Charter of the United Nations" (which requires treaties to be registered).

Then there was Professor Richard Pipes, a distinguished expert on Russian history, who wrote that Helsinki "legitimised Russia's conquests of the rest of eastern Europe".[16] This was totally untrue, as was Professor Seweryn Bialer's almost casual assertion that "Soviet rule over its empire was legitimised internationally at Helsinki in 1975".[17] *Time* followed the same false trail: "At the Helsinki Conference... Brezhnev obtained long-sought legitimisation of Soviet rule over its empire".[18] Ronald Reagan proposed that "all Americans should be against it".[19] George Ball called it "a defeat for the West".[20] And so on, with similar, though fewer, critical voices in Europe.

President Ford, who signed for the United States, was shocked and surprised. He rightly regarded the Final Act as a success. In his memoirs he wrote: "The well-meaning ethnic groups in this country simply didn't understand our accomplishment. This was not a failure in substance. It was a failure in public relations, and I will have to accept a large share of the blame".[21] He recounts how some members of his White House staff were defensive in their comments to the press, suggesting that the Final Act was "another Kissinger deal that was forced down the President's throat".[22] They were doubly wrong—about the Final Act itself and also about Kissinger, who had been hostile to the whole enterprise.

Why so many people got it wrong is still not explained, except in part by the fact that the State Department and the White House gave very inadequate briefings to the press. The long negotiations had been almost invisible, or, when visible, were derided as meaningless, echoing Kissinger. After the signature of the Final Act, US officials were told to put it away and forget it, as if it were in some way shameful or anyway "yesterday's news".[23]

Nor did errors cease. For instance, Tony Judt, in his epic masterpiece *Postwar*, wrote that "Brezhnev and his colleagues could not have wished for more... The political divisions of post-war Europe [were] now officially and publicly accepted and the sovereignty and territorial integrity of the GDR [East Germany] and other satellite regimes officially conceded".[24] In fact, as we have seen, Brezhnev hoped for a lot more, and the political divisions of post-war Europe were not accepted, nor was the full sovereignty of East Germany conceded.

Other commentators also concurred with this erroneous conclusion. Melvyn Leffler, in his fascinating book *For the Soul of Mankind*, wrote that "Western countries agreed to accept the territorial and political status quo in Eastern Europe".[25] Philip Bobbitt, in *The Shield of Achilles*, similarly described the Final Act as effectively ratifying the Soviet sphere of influence over Eastern Europe.[26] John Lewis Gaddis wrote in *The Cold War* that "a fundamental premise of [détente] was that the West would not seek to alter the internal character of Marxist-Leninist regimes".[27] This is what Kissinger told Brezhnev but it was emphatically not what Europeans intended from détente. They certainly hoped that détente would help gradually alter the character of the Marxist-Leninist regimes. Zbigniew Brzezinski, at a conference in Warsaw in 2009 discussing Helsinki in the context of the 25th anniversary of the Polish free trade union Solidarity, referred to "a bargain in which the status quo would be guaranteed... for some nominal acknowledgement of the importance of human rights. Human rights for the status quo—that was the devil's bargain that was being negotiated in the first half of the 1970s".[28] Quite wrong.

Errors also spread in Europe. In 1990 the distinguished sociologist Ralf Dahrendorf wrote of "the Brezhnevian monstrosity of the Helsinki Agreement to leave everything in Europe exactly as it was with mutual guarantees of the status quo".[29] A useful book on the 1977 Belgrade review conference is sprinkled with casual assertions to the effect that the Final Act endorsed the status quo.[30] Many more examples could be found.

A partial explanation for these false readings of the Final Act is that the mood in the United States at that time was particularly pessimistic. The negotiations coincided with the Watergate scandal, humiliating defeat in Vietnam and Soviet advances in Africa, which fed the widespread impression that détente was not restraining the Soviet Union. Détente had acquired a bad name, and indeed Ford had stopped using the word, so Helsinki was thoughtlessly packaged under the label of a failed policy, making no distinction between the superpower détente of Nixon and Kissinger, which had limited results, and the very successful dynamic détente pursued by Europeans. In that atmosphere people found it difficult to believe that a diplomatic victory for the West could come out of a conference promoted by the Soviet Union.

Soon after Helsinki, however, the truth began slowly to dawn as very courageous dissidents and even ordinary people in the Soviet Union and Eastern Europe, who had been initially very sceptical, having accepted the Soviet interpretation of the Final Act, read the texts for themselves. Stunned and excited by discovering what their governments had signed up to, they adopted the texts to press for more rights. Although all signatories had undertaken to publish the full text of the Final Act and "disseminate it and make it known as widely as possible" there was general surprise that the Soviet Union and its allies at first complied more conscientiously than Western states, confident that their misinterpretation of the document would prevail. The Soviet Union published more than 20 million copies in its two main Russian-language newspapers and more in the national languages of its minorities.[31] East European regimes initially followed suit. But then it became clear that other more accurate interpretations were spreading, particularly on human rights, so copies started to be withdrawn. In Poland, 500 copies were published but removed from circulation. In Czechoslovakia, thousands of copies were published but never distributed.[32]

It was too late. The more explosive parts of the text had already been noticed by people who actually read the text rather than the misleading accounts in the official press. In the first year more than 100,000 East Germans (roughly one per cent of the population) applied to leave East Germany, most quoting the Final Act on travel and family reunification.[33] A traveller in a Bulgarian bus encountered an old man with a crumpled copy of the Final Act in his pocket which he believed would get him a visit to his brother in the West.[34] In Moscow, dissidents who had been struggling for years seized on the document to form a monitoring group that became known as the Moscow Helsinki Watch Group. It was proposed by dissident scientist Yuri Orlov, who aimed to inform both the Soviet population and the West of violations of civil and human rights in the Soviet Union in the hope that Western leaders would put pressure on the Soviet regime. As one of the founders, Anatoly Shcharansky, wrote later: "There were Zionists and monarchists, Russians and Ukrainians and Byelorussians, and even Eurocommunists, I'd say, people of absolutely different views. There were those who wanted to leave, like myself and Vitaly Rubin, and those who were concerned about the situation in Soviet prisons and camps, and those who were concerned mainly about religious freedoms. But all of us were united by the Helsinki group".[35]

Although the group was quickly told by the KGB that it was illegal, this did not stop it collecting information from around the country and transmitting it to the West. News of the group spread fast, helped by Western radio stations broadcasting in Russian. Orlov described receiving two or three visitors a day from many different parts of the country, including religious believers from the Caucasus and workers from the Baltic republics.[36]

Washington began to wake up to the true potency of the Final Act after 19 members of Congress embarked on a tour of Eastern Europe and the Soviet Union. They started sceptical but gradually became aware of how much the Helsinki texts meant behind the Iron Curtain. One member of the group, Millicent Fenwick, became a surprising key figure in what followed. A stately grandmother of 64, always wearing a string of pearls, she had been a writer on *Vogue* for 14 years and then a local politician in New Jersey concerned with civil rights, gender discrimination, child abuse, migrant workers and consumer protection. She brought these interests to Washington when she was elected to the House of Representatives in 1974.[37]

In Moscow on this trip she met Orlov and had what she described as "heartbreaking meetings in small shabby flats and hotel rooms… hearing the cries of all these desperate people".[38] She returned to Washington determined to act, and introduced a bill to set up a Commission to monitor compliance with the Final Act. Kissinger resisted strongly because it impinged on his responsibility for foreign affairs; in any case, he did not believe in interfering in the internal affairs of the Soviet empire. But Fenwick pushed it through. The Commission, chaired by Dante Fascell, became a hugely influential clearing house for information on human rights abuses in the Soviet bloc, maintaining a close relationship with the Moscow group and others. Information on individual cases flooded in, as well as underground writings which the Commission translated and forwarded to other states and interest groups. "It played a critical role, connecting different activists and policymakers across interests and national lines".[39]

It also played a key role after Jimmy Carter was elected President in 1976 and decided to make human rights a central element in his foreign policy. Members and staff of the Commission were appointed to the US delegation to the 1977 Belgrade conference mandated to review implementation of the Helsinki Final Act. Their influence was confirmed by the fierce attacks they attracted from Moscow for their "slanderous activities against the Socialist countries under the hypocritical pretext of monitoring observance of the Helsinki Accords".[40]

Soon monitoring groups spread in the East and the West, including Ukraine, Lithuania, Georgia and Armenia. In Poland, the Workers' Defence Committee (KOR), formed in 1976 to assist workers arrested in the protests of that year, evolved into a wider movement with contacts in Czechoslovakia, Hungary and the Soviet Union. In 1980 it grew further into the Solidarity movement, nominally a trade union but in fact bringing together a remarkable coalition of workers, peasants, priests, intellectuals and even many party members, and citing Helsinki in its documents.[41] Meanwhile in Czechoslovakia a relatively small group produced Charter 77, which called on the regime to comply with the Helsinki Final Act.[42] People who signed lost their jobs or were denied university education for their children. One father brought his children together and asked them if he should sign, even if it meant that they could not go to university. Unanimously, they told him to sign.[43]

The churches also started to invoke the Final Act. These included both the Evangelical Church in East Germany[44] and the Catholic Church in Poland, where Cardinal Wojtyla (later Pope John Paul II) spoke in terms of human dignity and human rights.[45]

There developed what was called the "boomerang effect" as dissidents sent information to the West, where Western governments and monitoring groups took up cases, which were then broadcast in local languages back to the communist countries by Western radio stations such as Radio Free Europe, Radio Liberty, the BBC's foreign language services, and Deutsche Welle.[46]

The result was a proliferation of underground literature, meetings and seminars in private homes, known as "Flying Universities", some addressed by academics from the West. By mid-1976 US and European foreign ministries were being flooded with documentation of human rights violations submitted by non-governmental organisations in East and West.[47]

As NATO began to take the subject more seriously, its communiqués began to strike a new note. In May 1976, having previously avoided a confrontational tone, it emphasised the importance of "full implementation of all parts of the Helsinki Final Act by all signatories, so that its benefits may be felt not only in relations between states but also in the lives of individuals". While it recognised some progress in human contacts and the working conditions of journalists it also expressed concern about the "sustained growth in the Warsaw Pact countries' military power…beyond levels apparently justified for defensive purposes".[48]

It should be emphasised here that dissidents in the Soviet Union and much of its empire had been active long before the Final Act was signed. From the 1950s, *samizdat* writings had circulated in the Soviet Union in the form of typescripts. Boris Pasternak's novel *Dr Zhivago*, for example, was first published in *samizdat* in 1957, laboriously typed with carbon copies and distributed by hand. Some writers were imprisoned, notably Yuri Daniel and Andrei Sinyavski, a record of whose trial in 1965 was documented and published in *samizdat*. In Eastern Europe, particularly in Poland and Czechoslovakia, underground writings circulated among the intelligentsia, both political commentaries and works of fiction or poetry that the censors banned because they contained barely concealed political messages.

What the Final Act did was provide a focus and encouragement for these writers and activists. It opened new channels for their contacts with the West and gave them an address to write to and a claim to legality since their governments had signed a document pledging respect for human rights and the "freer and wider dissemination of information of all kinds". It also established the principle of mutual monitoring of compliance, although the Russians never intended to comply.[49]

All this also contributed not only to pressure for human rights from inside and outside the Soviet empire but also to serious thinking among some of the leading opposition figures in Eastern Europe, particularly Adam Michnik and Jacek Kuroń in Poland, and Václav Havel in Czechoslovakia. Their discussions and writings did a lot to shape the activities and tactics of the opposition and prepare them for influential positions when communism collapsed. Michnik then became a leading newspaper editor, Kuroń became Minister for Labour, and Václav Havel became President of Czechoslovakia.

Early inspiration came from Leszek Kołakowski, a distinguished philosopher at Warsaw University until he was driven to flee to the West in 1968. At one point he had compared the idea of reformed communism to "fried snowballs". In an influential essay "On Hope and Hopelessness",[50] he argued that Poles should organise themselves outside the structure of the party-state in a way that would gradually expand the areas of self-determination. In the end the structures of the party-state might become just facades, a "Potemkin village"[51] for the eyes of the "Tsars" in Moscow, while Polish society would be re-formed in an increasingly open, democratic and pluralist way.

His thinking was taken up by Michnik, Kuroń and others. Essentially, they were saying this: We cannot use force to overthrow the system because we would be crushed, and in any case we have learnt from history that the means by which power is acquired often determines the way it is then exercised. Nor can we any longer expect reforms to emanate from within the party. Either these reforms are crushed, as they were in Prague in 1968, or they run into the sand, as in Poland, or they are very limited, as in Hungary. So we must set up a parallel civil society in which we can try to "live in truth" (Havel's phrase). Or, as Kuroń said: "Don't burn down the party headquarters; set up your own". When the Polish regime began to crumble in 1989 they guided the Solidarity movement into what they called a "self-limiting revolution" and went initially into coalition with the communists, soon winning a landslide victory in the election of 1989.

All this opposition activity in the Soviet Union and its empire gradually focussed on the Belgrade follow-up meeting due in 1977, which was mandated, among other things, to monitor implementation of the Final Act. As the meeting approached, dissidents sent to the West an increasing flow of information on violations of the Final Act, thus adding to pressure on

Western governments, particularly that of the United States, to take up both individual cases and general issues. This is the subject of the next chapter.

Notes

1 This chapter contains passages from the author's paper 'Helsinki Myths', published in *Cold War History*, 9/1, February 2009.
2 Zubok, *A Failed Empire*, 237.
3 Dobrynin, *In Confidence*, 346.
4 Svetlana Savranskaya, 'Unintended consequences' in Bange and Niedhart, *Helsinki 1975 and the Transformation of Europe*, 181–2.
5 Zubok, 237.
6 Alexander, *Managing the Cold War*, 70.
7 Quoted in Savranskaya, 188.
8 Adam D. Rotfeld, email to the author, 6 April 2007.
9 Author's telephone conversation with Peter Steglich of the East German delegation, 8 May 2008.
10 Steglich and Leuschner, *KSZE, Fossil oder Hoffnung?*, 42–50.
11 Siegfried Bock, interview with the author, Berlin 11 June 2008. See also Rostagni ed., *The Helsinki Process*, 54.
12 Mastny and Byrne, *A Cardboard Castle?*, 397–401.
13 Rostagni, *The Helsinki Process*, 192.
14 Snyder, 'Jerry, don't go: Domestic Opposition to the 1975 Helsinki Final Act' in *Journal of American Studies*, 144/1 (February 2010).
15 *Foreign Affairs*, Spring 1980, 779, 783 (bound edition).
16 Pipes, *Soviet Strategy in Europe*, 42.
17 Bialer, 'The Political System', in Byrnes *After Brezhnev: Sources of Soviet Conduct in the 1980s* (1983) 7.
18 *Time*, November 1982.
19 Quoted in Garthoff, *Détente and Confrontation* ,478.
20 *Newsweek* (international edition), 11 August 1975.
21 Ford, *A Time to Heal*, 297.
22 Ford, 292–3.
23 Quoted in Thomas, *The Helsinki Effect*, 126.
24 Judt, *Postwar*, 501–2.
25 Leffler, *For the Soul of Mankind*, 249.
26 Bobbitt, *The Shield of Achilles*, 60.
27 Gaddis, *The Cold War*, 187.
28 Brzezinski, 'Human Rights in Foreign Policy', in *25 Years, From Solidarnosc to Freedom, International Conference Warsaw-Gdansk August 29–31,2005*, Warsaw: The Solidarity Center Foundation (2005), 24.
29 Dahrendorf, *Reflections*, 113–14.
30 Andrén and Birnbaum, *Belgrade and Beyond.*
31 Snyder, *Human Rights Activism*, 55.
32 Thomas, 98.
33 Thomas, 109, and Garton Ash, *The Polish Revolution: Solidarity*, 335.
34 Sir Reginald Hibbert anecdote at Chatham House.
35 Snyder, 59.
36 Snyder, 62.
37 Snyder, 42.
38 Snyder, 41.
39 Snyder, 50.
40 Snyder, 52.
41 Garton Ash, *The Polish Revolution: Solidarity*.

42 Havel, *Disturbing the Peace*. 125.
43 Told to the author in 1977.
44 Thomas, 101–2.
45 Thomas, 104–5.
46 See Puddington, *Broadcasting Freedom: The Cold War Triumph of Radio Free Europe and Radio Liberty*.
47 Thomas, 130.
48 NATO, 20–21 May 1976, 'Final Communiqué', § 3, viewed 20 February 2022, https://www.nato.int/cps/fr/natohq/official_texts_26953.htm?selectedLocale=en
49 Snyder, 40.
50 First published in June 1971 in *Kultura*, the influential Polish émigré magazine published in Paris, and then in English translation in *Survey* (London) summer 1971.
51 Fake villages created by Grigory Potemkin, lover of the Russian Empress Catherine II, to impress her during her trip to the Crimea in 1787.

Part IV

Follow-up

16 Belgrade 1977–8

Human rights and wrongs

Human rights exploded into prominence at the stormy Belgrade meeting in 1977. This was the first of the follow-up meetings agreed in the Final Act. Although it ended in acrimonious deadlock and was dubbed a failure by some critics, it turned out to have deep and lasting effects.

The meeting was given two tasks: to review implementation of the Final Act and to discuss proposals for improving security, cooperation and détente in Europe.

The Russians knew they would face intense criticism for their failure to implement the Final Act's commitments on human rights and freer movement, so they tried hard to limit or dilute the review of implementation and instead focus on new proposals. They also wanted to predetermine a closing date. They failed on all counts and were duly roasted by the Americans.

The roles of Europe and the United States were now reversed. At Geneva, the West Europeans had pressed for strong text on human rights while the Americans were held back under instructions from Kissinger, who believed that human rights had no place in international relations.

By 1977 Jimmy Carter, a peanut farmer from the south, had been elected US president and had chosen as his Security Advisor Zbigniew Brzezinski, a combative academic of Polish origin. Under the influence of Brzezinski, but driven also by his own strong moral sense, Carter decided to put human rights in the forefront of US foreign policy, using the CSCE to highlight the issue. This marked a sharp reversal. He had been very critical of the CSCE in the early part of his campaign, having succumbed to the erroneous belief that it approved the Soviet takeover of Eastern Europe. Now, urged on by Brzezinski, he found it electorally useful to criticise Soviet failure to implement the Final Act.

The Belgrade meeting gave Carter a platform. At first, he left preparations for the meeting largely in the hands of Albert W. Sherer, the cautious, experienced diplomat who had led the US delegation at Geneva and was deeply versed in all aspects of the CSCE. In September, however, to the consternation of the State Department, Carter appointed Arthur Goldberg to lead the delegation with ambassadorial rank, reducing the unhappy Sherer to his deputy.

Goldberg was a brilliant, brash personality who had had a long career as a trade union lawyer before President John Kennedy appointed him Secretary

DOI: 10.4324/9781003146124-21

of Labor and then to the Supreme Court. President Johnson later persuaded him to leave the Supreme Court and serve as US ambassador to the United Nations, where he frequently clashed with the Soviet representatives. The Soviet Foreign Ministry described him privately (and accurately) as a "dangerous, powerful opponent, a polemicist inclined to aggravating situations, to sharp fights".[1]

Setting off to Belgrade he was instructed by the President to "aggressively pursue the subject of human rights".[2] He carried out this instruction with gusto. When anyone objected, as many did, even within his own delegation, he cited his personal mandate from the President. He rocked the boat so badly that Europeans and members of the State Department became worried that the whole Helsinki Process would sink. For them, détente was a fragile craft that could easily capsize. They feared that ructions at Belgrade would harm other areas of détente, such as arms control or, in the case of West Germany, easier travel and trade with East Germany. In an unpublished essay, a member of the State Department accused the Helsinki Commission of having little interest in or sympathy with the broader policy concerns of European governments.[3] Europeans also felt that the United States was too fixated on Soviet dissidents, neglecting the fundamental purpose of the CSCE, which was to open up contacts between Eastern and Western Europe. In the end, none of these fears proved justified.

What particularly annoyed the Russians—and worried the US State Department—was Goldberg's deliberate courting of publicity. From the start he broke with diplomatic precedent by including many non-diplomats in his delegation. As well as members of the Helsinki Commission, he appointed its staff director, Spencer Oliver, to be third in rank as counsellor of the delegation. Oliver worked closely with Goldberg on human rights cases. Altogether nine staff members of the Helsinki Commission were included and provided invaluable help.

More surprising still, Goldberg brought along a "citizens' delegation" to raise the public profile of the proceedings. It included a representative of the labour movement, a Roman Catholic priest, an Inuit, a black woman lawyer, a Polish-American political science professor, a college president and others.[4] He even included his wife, whose memoir remains a rich source on the tensions within the American delegation and also between Goldberg and the Europeans.[5]

He arrived with vast files of individual cases prepared for him largely by the Helsinki Commission. The approach of the meeting had galvanised activity among Helsinki monitoring groups in both West and East. The Moscow Helsinki Group produced 26 documents and drafted 195 reports, statements and letters aimed at the Belgrade meeting. In Czechoslovakia, Charter 77 published 150 books and many periodicals as well as distributing 1,000 *samizdat* materials in order to inform politicians, delegates and the public of cases of repression.[6]

In the West there had also been a proliferation of monitoring groups, as we saw in the previous chapter. At one point Goldberg mentioned "over 100 groups in my country freely exercising their monitoring rights. I have met with them before and will meet with them next week in Washington. Some may praise—some may criticize—but it is basic to our constitutional conception that all public officials are servants of the people and not their masters".[7]

The most dramatic intervention was by Andrei Sakharov, the distinguished Soviet nuclear scientist, who, as the meeting was opening, sent a strong letter to delegates asserting that there was "an inseparable bond between international security and an open society". He challenged the West to defend the "noble and vitally important principles of free movement, free exchange of information and freedom of conscience".[8]

An initial problem for Goldberg was that it had been the custom at earlier meetings of the CSCE (and at the United Nations) to avoid mentioning specific names and cases when discussing human rights so as not to offend other countries. During the preparatory meetings at Belgrade it was accepted that this custom would be retained, but Goldberg chafed, arguing that there could be no real review of implementation without mentioning individual cases. He told a NATO meeting before the conference that he would ensure the press was fully briefed, with names, after meetings. In the early days that turned out to be his way of getting around the restriction, to the great annoyance of the Russians.

He was careful in his first speech on 6 October.[9] "Our task", he said, "is part of a great and ancient enterprise: the search for security, the advancement of cooperation in Europe". Pointing out that the Final Act formalised the tie between the freedom and welfare of nations and the freedom and welfare of individual citizens, he went on: "Let me affirm in the most positive terms the wholehearted commitment of the United States to the pursuit of détente. Let me also state our considered view that a deepening of détente, a healing of the divisions in Europe, a relaxation of tensions in Europe, cannot be divorced from progress in humanitarian matters and human rights".

He then mentioned cases but no names. He referred to an ill and aged husband denied, after long years of separation, the company of his nearly blind wife and their daughter. Immediately after the meeting his Press Officer gave journalists the names of the people involved and the page references in the Helsinki Commission's report.[10] After that he was constantly badgered by American reporters to mention names. On 14 October he received a bipartisan letter signed by 127 members of the House of Representatives and 16 Senators, calling attention to Moscow's repressive campaign against the Helsinki Watch Group. The letter demanded that Soviet violations of the Final Act be vigorously raised lest the credibility and effectiveness of the Helsinki accord be undermined. The letter urged the US delegation to "press this point in as forceful a manner possible in closed as well as open session".[11]

Goldberg responded gradually. On 18 October he suddenly appeared at a session of the working group on Basket III and read from an article in the French communist newspaper *L'Humanité*, which complained that the

Czechoslovak government was barring its reporter from covering the Prague trial of four supporters of Charter 77.[12] The Czechoslovak and Soviet representatives were not amused by his citing of a communist source and objected strongly, alleging that he was interfering in the internal affairs of Czechoslovakia. Soon afterwards Hungary and East Germany joined in.

The next step came on 19 October, when Guy Coriden, a State Department official who was attached to the Helsinki Commission, offered examples of American journalists in the Soviet Union who had been expelled or detained. He named George Krimsky as well as Robert Toth, who had been interrogated by the police regarding his contacts with the Helsinki Watch Group. Then Coriden mentioned Yosef Begun, a Soviet cultural leader fired from his job.[13] The taboo on mentioning names was now being steadily eroded.

For a while Goldberg continued to avoid names but became increasingly specific. In a statement on 1 November, he said: "We understand the Final Act to mean that any delegation is free and indeed obligated to discuss shortcomings of any signatory in any area covered by the Final Act and to call attention of this Conference to action taken against individuals who dedicate themselves to a peaceful struggle for human rights. In the Soviet Union and Czechoslovakia, for example, authorities this year have brought criminal charges against men and women whose principal offense, in the view of the United States, has been their public effort to promote the aims of the Final Act. I assure these delegations that it is not in a confrontational spirit but in the spirit of full review, from which my country is not exempt, that we allude to these facts… Equally disturbing is the harassment of others who subscribe to the Final Act by governments putting people under house arrest, expelling one from his apartment, depriving others of drivers' licenses or jobs. Denial of job opportunities is particularly striking in countries that place great emphasis on the 'right to work'".[14]

As domestic pressure built up, so did Goldberg's frustration. He could be found stalking the corridors complaining to journalists that he was being muzzled. Stopping this author on a staircase he said "What's with you Europeans? I thought you were in favour of human rights". Eventually he broke free. In a plenary session on 9 November he referred by name to American journalists who had been refused visas to Czechoslovakia, or who had been offered them only on the impossible condition that they not contact dissidents. They were Murray Seeger of the *Los Angeles Times*, who had been refused a visa to Czechoslovakia, and Eric Bourne of the *Christian Science Monitor*, who was told he could not have a visa unless he promised not to contact dissidents, a condition he could not accept.[15] Also mentioned were two American journalists who had been expelled from Czechoslovakia: Paul Hofmann of the *New York Times* and Leslie Collitt of NBC.

Then he trod fearlessly into direct confrontation with the Soviet Union by raising the treatment of Orlov, Ginzburg and Shcharansky, three Soviet citizens who had been arrested for trying to monitor implementation of the Final Act. The wives of the first two had managed to get through a telephone call to alert the US delegation to their arrest.[16] Calling in support the statement of the Swedish Prime Minister at the Helsinki summit, who said that "frank criticism must be allowed in the face of phenomena such as the oppression of dissidents, torture and racial discrimination", Goldberg went on: "It is in this spirit that we raise the cases of Orlov, Shcharansky, and Ginzburg in the Soviet Union, and we raise them by way of illustration because they have been seeking to monitor the implementation of the Final Act in the Soviet Union... It is clear that the Final Act endorses such peaceful activities, and persons engaged in them should be free from harassment, arrest and imprisonment... I simply don't understand why it is said that it is not appropriate to raise such matters here. A full, specific and candid review of the human rights and other provisions of the Final Act is the business of this Conference. I continue in the hope that such a dialogue will take place".

The standard Soviet response,[17] often repeated, was that he was interfering in the internal affairs of other states, allegedly in violation of Principle VI of the Final Act. Goldberg was surprised to find that the State Department had not prepared a brief on this important point, so, as a good lawyer, he did his own homework and came back with a measured response. He pointed out that Principle VI clearly referred to "armed intervention or threat of such intervention" and to "subversive or other activities directed towards the violent overthrow of the regime of another participating State". It did not rule out mutual criticism of internal affairs. Moreover, Principle X states that "when exercising their sovereign rights, including the right to determine their own laws and regulations, they [the states] will conform with their legal obligations under international laws; they will furthermore pay due regard to and implement the provisions in the Final Act". Goldberg then broadened his argument to point out that "we are all subject to broad international legal obligations concerning human rights, and, in plain language, a state's fulfilment of its international legal obligations is not exclusively its own business".

Accused of disrupting détente, he quoted from Principle VII, which states that respect for human rights "is an essential factor for the peace, justice and well-being necessary to ensure the development of friendly relations and cooperation among themselves as among all States". The United States, he said, endorsed this connection between respect for human rights and peace and friendly relations. In other words, the affairs of one are the affairs of all when it comes to implementing the Final Act, so mutual criticism is entirely within the letter and spirit of that document.

At one point the exasperated leader of the Soviet delegation, Yuli Vorontsov, struck back with a catalogue of US failings, including racism, unemployment, and failure to ratify the International Covenants on Human Rights. Goldberg, who had been in favour of ratification, welcomed these accusations as evidence that the Russians now accepted discussion of the internal affairs of other states. In fact, Goldberg always took care to acknowledge the shortcomings of the United States, challenging the Soviet side to be equally self-critical. On one occasion he commented: "It is interesting to note that the distinguished representatives of the Soviet Union and Czechoslovakia quoted American sources, our press, congressional reports, comments by labor leaders and others, in what they regarded to be criticisms of our policy. This illustrates a crucial point—that everyone in our country is free to criticize our deficiencies without being subject to harassment, arrest, and imprisonment for doing so".

He could also point out that the United States had made some efforts to improve its performance, notably by removing restrictions on travel abroad by American citizens and relaxing requirements for entry visas so that visitors to the United States "will not be excluded because of political affiliations or belief except in the rarest instances".

The Russians became very abusive at times, accusing Goldberg of "political hypocrisy" and a "crude, provocative and pseudo-juridical" approach, although in fact, as one can see from re-reading Goldberg's speeches today, they were remarkably measured, balanced and well argued, especially on legal issues. Doubtless the Russians were frustrated to find that his legal arguments were unanswerable, so they resorted to bluster. Several times they threatened to go home if Goldberg's attacks continued, but Goldberg calculated correctly that they had invested so much prestige in the Helsinki project, claiming it as a triumph for Soviet diplomacy, that collapse would have been seen as a major setback, even if it was blamed on the West.

After a long Christmas break, Vorontsov returned to Belgrade with his own draft of what the Soviet Union wanted as a concluding document. It did not mention human rights or Principle VII, nor did it contain any reference to the review of implementation or lack of compliance. It did not even mention CBMs. However, it contained the very important commitment to a further follow-up meeting in Madrid in 1980. Until then, the Soviet delegation had refused to agree on this point, insisting that there could be no follow-up unless the United States stopped attacking the Soviet Union on human rights. Clearly, Moscow had now decided to ride out the attacks in order to save the Helsinki Process.

Eventually, compromise wording was agreed that skirted the most difficult issues. It reported that there had been a thorough exchange of views, which itself contributed towards the aims of the CSCE, although "different views were expressed as to the degree of implementation of the Final Act reached so far". It also agreed on a Swiss proposal for a meeting of experts on the peaceful settlement of disputes, a Scientific Forum to start in Bonn on 20 June 1978, and a meeting in Malta on the Mediterranean.[18]

So, was Goldberg right to rock the boat so vigorously? In retrospect, he had little choice, given his instructions from Carter, the pressure that was building up in Washington and among dissidents in the Soviet bloc, and Soviet refusal to discuss the harsh treatment of its people who were trying to monitor compliance with the Final Act. It is true, however, that American perceptions of the Final Act became distorted as attention became focussed almost entirely on Soviet dissidents. American newspapers began referring to the "Helsinki Human Rights Declaration" as if the Final Act had no other content. The Soviet Union was right to plead for a more balanced view covering all the Baskets. The meeting was also wrong to focus so much on the Soviet Union when the Final Act was primarily about security and cooperation in Europe.

It is, however, difficult to argue that a more diplomatic approach would have achieved more. The Soviet side kept talking about new proposals but all they offered were proposals that they knew to be non-starters. One such was an agreement not to use nuclear weapons first in Europe. Given their huge preponderance of conventional weapons in Europe they knew that NATO had to rely on the threat of a nuclear response to an attack, so their proposal was purely for propaganda. Another proposal was that neither NATO nor the Warsaw Pact would accept new members. This was aimed primarily at Spain, which had recently become a parliamentary democracy and entered discussions with NATO on possible membership. There was no way that an application by a democratic Spain could be bargained away at Belgrade, and the Russians must have known this. A third was their old proposal to dissolve the military blocs, which would destroy NATO but leave the Warsaw Pact effectively in being because it was held together by a network of bilateral agreements.

Thus, there was nothing that the West could realistically offer that would have persuaded the Russians to make more concessions on travel, information or other aspects of human rights, given their resistance to such concessions at the Geneva negotiations. So the Western delegates had little to bargain with. At Geneva they had been able to use Brezhnev's desire for a summit conference to extract concessions. That card had been played.

However, Belgrade still had several important achievements to its credit:

- Agreement on a further follow-up meeting established the principle that the CSCE was a continuing process of value to both sides. That helped it survive through the difficult meeting in Madrid two years later and the temporary collapse of superpower détente in the 1980s. Had the Helsinki process ended at Belgrade the West would have lost all leverage over the wide range of issues covered by the Final Act, including human rights.
- Belgrade "broke the silence barrier on human rights", as Congressman Dante Fascell, chairman of the Helsinki Commission, later wrote.[19] The barrier was never restored. Naming specific cases of persecution became increasingly common. In Belgrade only three Soviet dissidents were named. At the Madrid meeting, as we shall see in the next chapter, the number rose into the hundreds.
- Publicity brought funding for monitoring groups in the West and great encouragement for activists in the East. Dissidents were frequently asked if publicity merely provoked retribution by the authorities, and whether they would prefer quiet diplomacy on their behalf. Invariably they opted for publicity, explaining that this boosted their morale, especially when they were in prison, and also made the authorities somewhat more careful in their treatment of prisoners.
- Relentless pressure for human rights started the slow process by which the Russians began to realise that they could not push the issue off the agenda

of international relations. For a long time Soviet officials referred dismissively to "so-called human rights" and regarded Western concerns as purely propagandistic. They would complain about "interference" or, like Vorontsov in Belgrade, talk about social rights, such as full employment, free education, free medical care. Gromyko, the Soviet foreign minister, had told his underlings not to bother him with such "absurd" matters as individual cases, so he was genuinely baffled when President Carter raised the case of the very prominent dissident Anatoly Shcharansky during a meeting at the White House in 1977. He had never even heard of him. In the car afterwards he asked his ambassador, Anatoly Dobrynin, to tell him about Shcharansky.[20] Gradually, this attitude changed as more individual cases were discussed in the Politburo.

- Publicity for violations of human rights in the Soviet Union and Eastern Europe raised public awareness in the West and helped change the attitudes of some left-leaning Western intellectuals in and outside the communist parties of France and Italy, which became more critical of the Soviet Union.
- One concrete result of the Belgrade meeting was the formation of the US Helsinki Watch Committee. This was partly Goldberg's doing. Speaking before the Helsinki Commission, he said it was an anomaly that, while in the Soviet Union, Czechoslovakia and Poland private individuals had organised private groups to press for human rights, this had not happened in the United States. He therefore called for a private organisation to supplement the work of the Helsinki Commission. After discussions involving Goldberg, McGeorge Bundy (President of the Ford Foundation), the Association of American publishers, and human rights activists, the US Helsinki Watch Committee was set up in February 1979 with a grant from the Ford Foundation. Its purpose was to monitor domestic and international compliance with the human rights provisions of the Helsinki Final Act and to provide moral support for the activities of the beleaguered Helsinki monitors in the Soviet bloc. It also aimed to shape the approach of the United States and West European governments to the Madrid follow-up meeting due to start in 1980. It established a reputation for providing reliable information about human rights abuses within the Soviet bloc and came to play a particularly important role in persuading the Reagan administration not to withdraw from the CSCE.[21]

What Belgrade did not achieve was much improvement in the treatment of dissidents. Before the meeting some small concessions were made. The emigration of Soviet Jews increased (more than 2000 left in March 1978) and Bulgaria and Czechoslovakia resolved some cases of divided families. But these moves, although important for the individuals concerned, were little more than cosmetic in the broader context.[22] Shcharansky, Orlov and Ginzburg were imprisoned before the meeting. In Czechoslovakia, Vaclav Havel was given a suspended sentence in 1977 and then sentenced to four and a half years in 1979. Sakharov was arrested in January 1980 for opposing the Soviet invasion of Afghanistan.

This did not discourage activists, however; they continued to collect information, send it to the West, and set up transnational networks. As Snyder writes, "Belgrade motivated existing monitoring groups to continue their work and to strengthen the Helsinki network's transnational links. In the years that followed, Sakharov and others relentlessly sent missives to the West seeking to publicize the fate of human rights activists. At the same time human rights activists in the Soviet Union, Czechoslovakia and Poland all increased their contacts with one another". In August 1978, for instance, there was an important meeting of Polish and Czech activists on the mountain border between their two countries.[23] All this activity vastly intensified the flow of information on human rights abuses. Monitors in the Soviet Union and Eastern Europe were encouraged to assemble dossiers that they knew would reach not only NGOs in the West but also governments, which would then raise cases both privately and in more formal negotiations with the perpetrators. The information would then be reported back in their own languages to the Soviet Union and Eastern Europe by Radio Free Europe, Radio Liberty and other stations broadcasting from the West.

But what about linkage? Did Goldberg damage the wider framework of détente, as feared by the State Department and the Europeans? He himself later argued that "naming persecuted human rights activists and the countries responsible for their repression did not necessarily prejudice basic negotiations between the United States and the Soviet Union with respect to disarmament".[24] He was partly right. Carter's aggressive campaign on human rights certainly contributed to the decline in Soviet–American relations but it was not a major factor. It did not stop Carter and Brezhnev signing the SALT II arms control agreement in Vienna in June 1979. What stopped ratification of that agreement by the US Senate was the Soviet invasion of Afghanistan in December of that year, coming on top of mounting American disappointment with détente as a whole.

Soviet records now show that when the Politburo discussed invading Afghanistan in the spring of 1979 one of the factors that held it back was concern about the likely effect on relations with the West. When the embattled communist regime in Kabul appealed to Moscow again for help in December 1979, the détente boat had already partly sunk and Salt II was still unratified, so there was less to lose. However, it would be difficult to show that this was a critical factor in Moscow's decision to invade. The situation in Kabul had deteriorated by this time and Moscow feared losing its grip and seeing the regime tilt towards the United States. The small group in Moscow that made the decision persuaded themselves that forcibly installing a new government would solve the situation within a few weeks.[25] As it turned out, their troops remained embroiled in a bitter war for ten years. Nobody could reasonably blame Carter for that unless one imagines a rather unlikely scenario in which some kind of a Soviet–American agreement on Afghanistan averted a Soviet invasion.

A verdict on the Belgrade meeting therefore depends on what could have been reasonably expected. Its instructions were to review implementation and discuss proposals for improving security and cooperation. It found that the Russians did not want to discuss implementation in any meaningful way, and that the new proposals on offer were mostly either unimportant or unrealistic. As we have seen above, however, it can claim success in other respects, particularly in the agreement to continue the Helsinki Process.

Notes

1 Snyder *Human Rights Activism and the End of the Cold War*, 105.
2 Snyder, 103.
3 Korey, *The Promises We Keep*, 68.
4 Korey, 73.
5 Dorothy Goldberg, *A Private View of a Public Life*.
6 Snyder, 96.
7 All the US statements at the Belgrade conference can be found at https://www.csce.gov/sites/helsinkicommission.house.gov/files/Belgrade%20CSCE%20Meeting,%20U.S.%20Statements%201977.pdf. Viewed on 17 February 2022.
8 Korey, 61, from *International Herald Tribune* (Paris), 6 October 1977.
9 Full text in Andrén and Birnbaum, *Belgrade and Beyond*, 101–14. Or see note 7.
10 Mrs Michelson on page 82 of the report. See note 7.
11 Korey, 62.
12 Korey 82.
13 Korey, 83.
14 Snyder, 105.
15 The author of this book was also offered a visa on the same impossible condition.
16 Korey, 87–8.
17 Text of Vorontsov's opening statement in Andrén and Birnbaum, *Belgrade and Beyond*, 115–24.
18 Text of Goldberg's opening statement in Andrén and Birnbaum, *Belgrade and Beyond*, 161–3. Or see note 7.
19 Snyder, 110.
20 Dobrynin, *In Confidence*, 399–400.
21 Snyder, 115–34.
22 Snyder, 106.
23 Snyder, 112.
24 Snyder, 109.
25 Rodric Braithwaite, *Afgantsy, the Russians in Afghanistan 1979–89*, 81.

17 Madrid 1980–83

The stress test

As the second follow-up meeting opened in Madrid on 11 November 1980, the outlook was even worse than at the start of the Belgrade meeting in 1977, which had nearly brought down the Helsinki Process. Failure still looked possible. The Russians knew they could not expect to improve on the deal they got at Helsinki in 1975, unsatisfactory though it was from their point of view, so why, some of them must have thought, should they go to Madrid merely to listen to more criticisms of their internal affairs? At the same time American opinion had become increasingly hostile to détente. Critics of the Helsinki Process were pointing out that the Soviet Union was not honouring its side of the bargain by respecting human rights, so what was in it for the United States?

Then, on 4 November, Ronald Reagan was elected President of the United States. He had been a relentless opponent of the Helsinki Process, having fallen victim, like so many, to the erroneous belief that it endorsed Soviet rule over Eastern Europe and the Baltic states. He was therefore under pressure to be consistent and withdraw. Many assumed that he would do so. Yet, after much hesitation, he was persuaded that the texts on human rights in the Final Act offered a useful stick with which to beat the Russians, so he stayed with the process.

Nor did the Russians leave, despite several threats to do so. Madrid struggled on for nearly three years, often narrowly avoiding collapse. By the end, everyone had found some value in it, or had peered over the brink of failure and decided that the alternative was worse. So the Helsinki Process survived its most severe stress test and established itself as a lasting feature of the political landscape.

As the meeting opened, activists poured into Madrid. In the words of William Korey: "The Spanish capital had become a magnet for dissidents and democratic activists from every part of Eastern Europe, along with their human rights champions and advocates in the West…, the stage for grand human rights theater". Spouses and relatives of Soviet prisoners of conscience and refuseniks mingled with representatives of Western NGOs in rallies, demonstrations, press conferences and mini review sessions. Displays and leaflets, films and posters, books and recordings were everywhere. Reporters also arrived from almost every Western European country and

DOI: 10.4324/9781003146124-22

many Eastern European countries. The US Helsinki Watch leased office space and distributed huge amounts of information. At the same time in Marseilles a huge international gathering called on Western governments to insist on freer movement of people, including family reunions, in accordance with the terms of the Final Act. Pressure was particularly strong on behalf of those individuals and groups within the Soviet bloc who had been persecuted for trying to monitor the implementation—or, more accurately, the non-implementation—of the Final Act.[1]

Thus, the Soviet Union was again in the hot seat, and the seat was now even hotter than it had been in Belgrade. NATO was now much more united and eager to raise individual cases of persecution. During the course of the Madrid meeting 14 delegations cited 123 people who were suffering human rights abuses, while the United States alone named 119.[2] Gone were the disagreements of Belgrade, and European accusations that the US delegation was rocking the détente boat. By this point the boat had already sunk, or it was at any rate low in the water. In Washington the very term détente had become unmentionable, even before the arrival of Ronald Reagan. It was widely seen as a Soviet trick to lull the West into a sense of false security while the Soviet Union pursued its expansionist aims unhindered. In Washington's eyes, the final blow to détente had come in December 1979 with the Soviet Union's invasion of Afghanistan. This was taken by the West as a signal that Moscow had decided on an even more expansionist policy and was pushing south to the Persian Gulf. Western condemnation was immediate and almost unanimous.

In fact, as Soviet documents revealed much later, Western perceptions were completely mistaken. The invasion was, in fact, a defensive move by very reluctant Soviet leaders to prop up a crumbling and unpopular communist regime in Kabul which it feared was flirting with the United States. Earlier, in April of that year, the Kremlin had rejected pleas for help. One of the reasons raised in Kremlin discussions was the fear that military intervention would damage détente. By December the situation in Afghanistan had worsened and East–West relations had deteriorated to such an extent that Soviet leaders calculated they had little to lose.

Further darkening the scene, NATO decided (coincidentally on the same day as the Soviet invasion) to respond to Soviet deployment of powerful new SS-20 medium-range missiles in the European area. It took what became known as the "two-track" decision, the essence of which was that NATO would install new Pershing II and cruise missiles in Western Europe in 1983 unless the Soviet Union agreed to limit or remove its equivalent weapons. Much later, after Mikhail Gorbachev had become leader of the Soviet Union, successful negotiations did in fact lead to the INF Treaty of 1987 eliminating intermediate and short-range missiles in Europe, but at the time of the NATO decision in 1979 the Soviet Union refused to negotiate; it placed high hopes on protests that swept across Western Europe, aided in some cases by Soviet and East European agents. But these were not enough to stop the deployments, which went ahead in 1983 after a change of government in West Germany that brought the Christian Democrats back to power.

At this point it is worth mentioning another aspect of the Madrid conference. It was very much in the minds of Western participants, particularly the Americans, that the meeting could help educate West Europeans in the iniquities of the Soviet system and thereby stiffen their support for NATO's two-track decision. The negotiations in Madrid were thus also a battle for the hearts and minds of West Europeans, a battle that was largely won in so far as many became more critical of the Soviet Union as they heard more from Soviet and East European dissidents.

Rethinking in left-wing circles had been under way for some time, especially since the Soviet-led invasion of Czechoslovakia in 1968 and the publication in the West in 1973 of Aleksandr Solzhenitsyn's *Gulag Archipelago*, followed by the author's expulsion from the Soviet Union. Madrid contributed by intensifying publicity for persecuted dissidents in the Soviet bloc, thanks partly to the tireless work of transnational networks (see Chapter 16). Repression under Soviet rule had, in fact, increased as détente broke down. Most of the individuals who had been trying to monitor compliance with the Helsinki Final Act had been imprisoned or were under investigation, or in a few cases had been allowed to emigrate. Nor did the persecution stop with the opening of the Madrid conference. By September 1982 pressure had become so great that the Moscow Helsinki Watch group reluctantly closed down. Madrid, however, continued to sustain the hopes of the persecuted.

The key figure in Madrid was Max Kampelman.[3] Initially appointed by President Carter as co-chair of the US delegation, Reagan retained his services and promoted him to head of the US delegation. The US State Department had opposed Kampelman's appointment and struggled to exclude or downgrade the Helsinki Commission, which had played such an important role in raising human rights issues at Belgrade. The career diplomats hoped that the US delegation to Madrid would be made up mainly of their own people, who would ensure a moderate tone and leave the more controversial initiatives to the West Europeans. Ambassador Albert Sherer, who, as we have seen, was displaced at Belgrade by Arthur Goldberg, published an article in *Foreign Policy* criticising the confrontational stance of the American delegation at Belgrade.[4] When the National Security Council asked the State Department to assess the results of Belgrade and make proposals for the future, the State Department did not even inform the Helsinki Commission. Its staff director, Spencer Oliver, learnt about the request only by accident at a White House ceremony honouring Ambassador Goldberg. Thus provoked, the commission produced its own rival assessment urging the White House to take a leading role on human rights at Madrid. The State Department lost the argument and Kampelman, a political appointee, took over.

He was another late convert to the Helsinki Process. A lawyer, like Goldberg, and a vigorous anti-Communist and advocate of human rights, he had been among the Democrats around Senator Henry Jackson who opposed signing the Helsinki Final Act. Goldberg advised him not to take the Madrid job, and so did Henry Kissinger, but he turned out to be extraordinarily successful. He was, in fact, the only high-level Democrat from the Carter administration to be retained by President Reagan.

He had an unusual background. After obtaining a law degree, he became a conscientious objector during World War II and volunteered for a starvation experiment at the University of Minnesota. After that he renounced pacifism, studied political science and embarked on an academic career. He was soon recruited by Senator Hubert Humphrey, who later became a presidential candidate and vice-president to Lyndon Johnson. He worked on Humphrey's staff for six years before moving to a Washington law firm, although he continued to advise Humphrey.

Before taking up his post in Madrid he toured European capitals in a largely successful effort to gather the support that had eluded Goldberg in an admittedly different context. Once in Madrid, he managed to combine vigorous support for human rights with a remarkable ability to negotiate not only with Soviet representatives but also, and most importantly, with his allies. Like Goldberg at Belgrade, he arrived with massive documentation of human rights abuses. Unlike Goldberg, he did not hesitate, even in the early stages, to mention cases by name. Whereas Goldberg had been relatively cautious and named only seven cases, Kampelman had already referred to 65 by December 1980.

Despite this provocative stance, Kampelman managed to develop a valuable channel of communication with the Soviet Union. This proved useful when so many other channels had fallen victim to the collapse of détente. Altogether he spent more than 400 hours in private conversations with Soviet representatives.[5] He also took trouble to brief his European allies on these talks. This was much appreciated as they had become very anxious about the breakdown of relations between Washington and Moscow.

The embattled Soviet delegates at Madrid tried at first to limit the review of implementation to a few days, or at most one or two weeks. When this effort failed they challenged the so-called Yellow Book, which contained the guidelines agreed at Belgrade. This stipulated seven weeks for review of implementation but with no definite cut-off date and no date for concluding the meeting. It set various target dates but laid down that the meeting would end by adopting a concluding document and by fixing the date and place for the next follow-up meeting. This meant that the conference could—and did—continue until everyone agreed on a concluding document.

The Soviet delegation tried to use procedural issues to get their way. On the eve of the opening meeting it refused to agree to drawing lots to decide the order of speakers. When midnight approached with no decision on this and other procedural issues, the clock was stopped at two minutes before midnight so that technically the pre-meeting continued into what was supposed to be the opening day, with the Hungarian ambassador still in the chair. The United States objected as the meeting was supposed to start with the host country, Spain, in the chair. Eventually, the Spanish and Soviet delegations reached a compromise. The Hungarian was allowed to remain in the chair while the Spanish Foreign Minister formally opened the proceedings.

But there was still no agenda or order of speakers until the issue was resolved after midnight.

During one of the more critical moments, when it seemed that the conference might break down irrevocably, a morose Hungarian journalist who was drowning his sorrows at the bar told this author that people in the West did not realise how détente shaped the dynamics of domestic politics in the Soviet sphere. If the whole Helsinki Process came to grief, he said, it would drastically alter the political situation in his country. Liberals like himself would be pushed out in favour of hard-line communists who would take the country back to grimmer times. His fears were certainly shared by many members of the intelligentsia in the Soviet Union and Eastern Europe.

During this very ifficult opening stage the Soviet delegate hinted more than once that if he did not get his way the Soviet Union would withdraw altogether. This turned out to be a bluff, as at Belgrade, so eventually the meeting got underway on roughly Western terms, allowing flexible time for the review of implementation, which was the West's principal priority. Moscow appeared to have hoped that it could exploit divisions in the NATO camp as it had done at Belgrade, but this time NATO stuck together. Indeed, Soviet tactics irritated Western and neutral delegations so much that solidarity actually increased, along with negative publicity for the Soviet Union.

In the end, two considerations kept the Soviet Union in the meeting. The first was the prestige that Brezhnev had invested in the whole Helsinki Process. To bring it to an end would involve a severe loss of face, even if it could be blamed on the West. The second was the Soviet hope that Madrid would agree to a separate conference on military détente and disarmament. This, it believed, would distract attention from human rights and provide a platform for the Soviet Union to present itself as an advocate of peace. It might also bring some reduction of military costs.

The idea of a separate conference on military détente had been put forward by the French in May 1978. It envisaged two stages. The first would extend the confidence-building measures (CBMs) in the Final Act that provided for prior notification of military manoeuvres and the exchange of observers. The second stage would aim to reduce conventional forces. The US feared that bringing arms control into the CSCE would distract from human rights and thereby upset the careful balance achieved in the Final Act. Moreover, neutral and non-aligned members of the CSCE were not members of the military alliances, so they were felt to have no standing in talks on arms control. However, the French proposal was eventually accepted by NATO as a useful concept provided it was part of a balanced outcome of the CSCE talks. Thus, agreement on an arms control meeting would require Soviet concessions on human rights. This gave the West some valuable leverage.

Just as the Madrid meeting seemed to be approaching a conclusion on 13 December 1981, martial law was declared in Poland as the regime tried to crush Solidarity.[6] The Polish leadership claimed that martial law had averted a Soviet invasion. Subsequent evidence revealed that the Soviet leaders never had any intention of invading,[7] but the fear in Poland was real, given memories of Soviet tanks suppressing revolts in East Germany, Hungary and Czechoslovakia. Under martial law Solidarity was banned after 15 months of legal activity. Some of its leaders went into hiding just in time, but most were arrested and imprisoned.

This was a clear violation of the Final Act, so it could not be ignored by the Madrid meeting. An adjournment for the holiday season had been scheduled for 18 December, but before it started all the Western ambassadors rose to denounce the Polish regime. Then, during the holiday, divisions began to emerge. The Americans felt it would be wrong to continue normal business after such a gross breach of the Final Act. The West Germans, by contrast, argued that the crisis made it all the more important to continue so as to retain a forum in which to discuss this and other breaches elsewhere.

Eventually a compromise was reached. When the conference resumed, foreign ministers would speak out and then call for a quick adjournment, conveying the message that there could be no substantive progress while a CSCE member was under military rule. On 9 February 1982 US Secretary of State Alexander Haig told the meeting that "we are at a critical crossroads in the post-war history of Europe". He called for the release from prison of "those trade union leaders and others who seek to realise the objectives of the Helsinki Final Act for their people". He concluded that no new undertakings were possible while existing obligations were being so blatantly ignored.[8]

The Polish ambassador, who was in the chair, then tried to close the session, but there were still eight foreign ministers from Western countries to speak, the first of whom should have been the now very angry French foreign minister, Claude Cheysson. When Ireland called for all speakers to be given the floor the Soviet Union and Czechoslovakia refused consensus. The Polish ambassador remained determined to end the meeting but the West then deployed the consensus rule to prevent adjournment. Arguments raged for seven hours until Austria appealed to both sides for a night adjournment. Cheysson stormed out of the meeting while the Norwegian Foreign Minister, Sven Stray, delivered a sharp rebuke to the Polish chairman: "If you believe that you can stop people from the free West using their right to speak you are mistaken, sir!"[9]

Next day, with Portugal in the chair, the rest of the Western foreign ministers were able to speak. The Swiss foreign minister then called for an adjournment, stating that a continuation of the meeting could only damage the Helsinki Process. The Soviet Union, however, did not want to see the Helsinki Process closed down, particularly as it was near to agreeing on disarmament talks. Under the consensus rule, it could keep the meeting in continuous session.

Procedural wrangles continued. On 5 March 1982 NATO refused to take part in preparing the work schedule for the coming weeks. It would schedule only plenary meetings, which would be confined to discussing the situation in Poland or Soviet violations of the Final Act. When the Czechoslovak chairman asked for proposals the Western delegations remained silent. This was the famous "night of silences", interrupted only by coffee breaks. When midnight came it should have been the turn of Turkey to take the chair but the Soviet Union argued that the meeting was still continuing, so the Czechoslovak chairman refused to leave. Eventually, at 5.30 a.m., it was decided that the coffee break would extend to Monday morning. Over the weekend the neutrals suggested a compromise under which the drafting committee would have three meetings in one week and the conference would then go into recess until November. During the three working sessions, the West and some neutrals remained silent.

In November, the situation in Poland remained unchanged. The US hesitated to return to Madrid but its allies pressed for a resumption. Eventually a compromise permitted a return to Madrid on condition that NATO would press for inclusion in the concluding document of 14 amendments on human rights tabled by Denmark, including recognition of trade unions, the right to strike and an end to jamming of Western broadcasts, which had intensified under martial law in Poland.

When the meetings resumed the Soviet delegation continued to press for the security conference on military aspects of détente (as the French had proposed in 1978) but it was noticeable that their enthusiasm for the Helsinki Process had cooled. Previously, Helsinki had featured prominently in the list of key slogans issued annually by the Communist Party on the anniversary of the Bolshevik revolution. Now these slogans disappeared. Brezhnev's influence was waning. He had been sickening for some time and eventually died on 10 November 1982. His successor, Yuri Andropov, who, as former head of the KGB, had been acutely aware of the trouble that Helsinki was causing among dissidents, spoke about détente without mentioning Helsinki. But he did not withdraw his delegation from Madrid, and he even sent his son as a member.[10]

A fundamental disagreement between East and West was, as we have seen, that the West wanted these follow-up meetings to focus on reviewing implementation of the Final Act while the Soviet Union wanted to curtail reviews and concentrate on the mandate to consider new proposals. At Belgrade their new proposals had been largely propagandistic. At Madrid they pressed hard for the proposed meeting on military CBMs to be followed by arms control, partly in the hope of stopping NATO's deployment of new missiles in Europe. They were too late. By the time the arms control conference had been agreed and the starting date set for January 1984 in Stockholm, roughly a month had passed since the NATO deployments were due to start.

After much discussion, in return for Western approval of the Stockholm conference, the Soviet Union agreed to a six-week meeting of human rights experts in Ottawa in May 1985. Another Western proposal was for a meeting of experts to discuss family reunions under the heading of "human contacts". There had been much criticism of the Soviet Union for placing obstacles in the way of families, particularly Jewish families, wanting to emigrate to join relatives abroad. The Soviet representative at first called the proposal totally unacceptable, but, after a dramatic personal intervention by the Spanish Prime Minister, Felipe González, the Soviet official flew to Moscow for consultations. When he returned he gave way, accepting a Swiss invitation to Bern in April 1986 to discuss how best to achieve the provisions of the Final Act on "human contacts". The West eased his path a little by dropping its demand for an end to radio jamming, but the main reason for Soviet agreement was that Moscow feared losing the Stockholm arms control conference.

The West also won some further concessions. Exit visas would be decided within six months, or even faster in emergency cases. Applicants for emigration would not be penalised by loss of jobs, social benefits or housing rights, as had happened frequently to Soviet Jews. Fees for visas and passports were also reduced and freedom of religion reaffirmed. The right of workers to establish trade unions was affirmed, with an eye on the Polish Solidarity movement, but qualified by a statement that these rights would be exercised "in compliance with the law of the state and in conformity with the state's obligations under international law". Thus, the concluding document of Madrid registered modest progress, and the mere fact of agreeing on a document of substance was in contrast to the failure to do so at Belgrade.

The Reagan administration was now fully supportive. Indeed, the closing session on 9 September 1983 heard a remarkable speech by US Secretary of State George Shultz in which he set out for the first time a bold American view of the long-term aim of the Helsinki Process. The division of Europe, he said, was "unnatural and inhuman" and could be maintained only by "raw power" that must be a source of instability. Lasting security or cooperation could not be achieved so long as "one government is afraid of its own people" and its next-door neighbours. He went on: "In the most profound sense the Helsinki process represents an historic effort to erode the cruel divisions between East and West in Europe".[11] Shultz thus took a major step beyond previous American statements, which had envisaged little more than improving cooperation. He now adopted the European view that the Helsinki Process should aim to overcome the division of Europe.

Finally, the meeting ensured continuation of the Helsinki Process by fixing the next follow-up meeting for November 1986 in Vienna, though not without accepting a Bulgarian condition that it also set the time and place of the disarmament conference: Stockholm, January 1984.

Not everyone was happy. Arthur Goldberg chimed in with objections to separate meetings in Ottawa and Bern, arguing that they separated the security aspects of the Final Act from the human rights and humanitarian provisions, thereby unbalancing the document and weakening the West's leverage on human rights. Stockholm, he feared, would be a propaganda platform for the Soviet Union, especially as it was being allowed a run of nearly three years while the human rights meetings were scheduled to last only a few weeks. Moreover, he pointed out, the human rights meetings had been downgraded by being included in the chairman's statement instead of in the body of the document.

However, it was clear that up to this point Western leverage had been reasonably successful in achieving some advances on the Final Act, although very little progress had been made in improving respect for human rights in the Soviet sphere, or on the broader issues of détente. In November 1983, following West Germany's approval of the deployment of the new missiles on its territory, the Soviet Union broke off negotiations on strategic arms and intermediate-range nuclear weapons and withdrew from the long-running and largely fruitless Vienna negotiations on mutual and balanced force reductions (MBFR).

At the same time, although some Eastern European countries agreed to ease travel restrictions and access to information, repression in the Soviet Union increased. Many dissidents were imprisoned. Exit visas were denied, foreign journalists harassed and dissidents punished for contacts with foreigners. More than half the Jewish requests for emigration were refused on grounds that were arbitrary and unpredictable. Moscow was clearly determined to dampen any hopes that had been raised by its concessions on human rights, particularly at a time when its leadership was in a state of unstable transition.

This in itself was enough to inhibit progress. After Brezhnev died, he was followed in quick succession by Yuri Andropov, who died in February 1984, and then by Konstantin Chernenko, who died in March 1985, prompting President Reagan to complain that he could not negotiate with Soviet leaders because "they keep dying on me".[12] During this difficult period, the fragile threads of agreement at Madrid helped to prevent a complete rupture, while Western Europeans remained determined to preserve détente on their continent, even when it broke down between the superpowers.

This period of repression is often forgotten by those who chart a straight line from Helsinki to the end of the Cold War. It is entirely possible that the whole Helsinki Process would have been crushed if it had not been rescued by Mikhail Gorbachev after he was elected Soviet leader on 11 March 1985. A different leader without the personal commitment of Brezhnev or the reforming ambitions of Gorbachev might have clamped down even more harshly on dissent and eventually abandoned the CSCE as being more trouble that it was worth. The Cold War would then have continued for many years, leaving the agreements at Madrid an empty shell.

Even if that had happened, the Helsinki Process would have maintained some life outside official structures. The ferment to which it contributed would have continued to erode Soviet power and credibility. Underground activity, particularly in Poland and Czechoslovakia, would have continued. Nor would Moscow have remained unaffected. Helsinki had engendered more hopes of change among the restless intelligentsia than were obvious at the time. These hopes had been crushed when Soviet tanks invaded Czechoslovakia in 1968, but Helsinki had revived them, and this time dissent reached more deeply into the party apparatus.[13] At the same time Helsinki helped to illuminate and accelerate the crisis into which Eastern Europe was sliding as a result of political and economic stagnation. Thus, even if a repressive regime had prevailed in Moscow for a time, it would have been unable to kill the spirit of Helsinki entirely. At some point the ice would have cracked again.

As it turned out, the Helsinki Process was called into new life when Mikhail Gorbachev realised that if he wanted to end the Cold War in Europe he would have to accept virtually the entire Helsinki agenda. This his delegation eventually did at the next follow-up meeting in Vienna.

Notes

1 Korey, *The Promises We Keep*, 123–4.
2 Snyder, *Human Rights*, 148.
3 See Kampelman's fascinating memoir *Entering New Worlds: the Memoirs of a Private Man in Public Life*.
4 Sherer 'Goldberg Variations' in *Foreign Policy* 39, Summer 1980.
5 Kampelman, 239.
6 For a vivid account see Garton Ash, *The Polish Revolution*.
7 Garton Ash, 360–1.
8 Korey, 152.
9 Korey, 153.
10 Korey, 156
11 Korey, 160.
12 Quoted in Matlock, *Reagan and Gorbachev*, 36.
13 See English, *Russia and the Idea of the West*.

18 1985–6: Four meetings and the first breakthrough

The dramatic changes wrought by Mikhail Gorbachev were slow to filter down to the CSCE. They did not arrive until well into the transformational follow-up meeting that began in Vienna in November 1986 (see Chapter 19). Hopes were raised in July 1985, when Gorbachev appointed Eduard Shevardnadze, party leader in Georgia, to replace Andrei Gromyko, who had been the dour face of Soviet foreign policy since 1957. Yet even Shevardnadze stuck carefully to the orthodox line when CSCE foreign ministers met in Helsinki in July–August 1985 to mark the tenth anniversary of the signing of the Final Act.[1] Nor was there at first any sign of movement in four smaller meetings of experts mandated by the Madrid meeting:

- Ottawa (May–June 1985): Experts' Meeting on Human Rights and Fundamental Freedoms.
- Budapest (October–November 1985): Cultural Forum.
- Bern (April–May 1986): Experts' Meeting on Human Contacts.
- Stockholm (January 1984–September1986): Conference on Confidence- and Security-Building Measures in Europe (CSBMs).

Only in the latter phase of the Stockholm meeting did progress start to appear, when the other three were already over. We shall therefore deal with Stockholm last of the four because, although it started first, it ended last and helped open the way to Vienna.

Ottawa

The Ottawa meeting remained stuck in the now-familiar confrontation over human rights, except in one small respect. Hitherto the Soviet Union had consistently denounced Western criticism of its human rights record as illegitimate interference in its internal affairs, citing its own patently false interpretations of the Final Act. At Madrid, its delegates had sometimes tried to hit back with criticism of human rights abuses in the West but they usually drew back when they found that their move was welcomed by Western delegates as vindicating the right of mutual criticism. In the opening phase of the Ottawa meeting the Soviet representatives continued with their familiar

DOI: 10.4324/9781003146124-23

misquoting of the Final Act on non-intervention, claiming that it ruled out criticism of their internal affairs. They also misquoted the Madrid document by translating it into Russian to mean that states could review only their own implementation of human rights.

However, as the Western delegations continued to produce copious evidence of worsening violations of human rights in the Soviet sphere, the Soviet delegation retaliated with massive, well-prepared attacks on what they denounced as Western violations of economic, social and cultural rights, citing the right to work in the Universal Declaration of Human Rights and the Covenant on Economic, Social and Cultural Rights. A three-hour argument between the British and Soviet delegates ranged over social problems in Britain, Irish terrorists, the use of Yiddish in the Soviet Union and Gaelic in Scotland, maternity leave in both countries, unemployment and illiteracy in Britain and numerous violations of human rights in the Soviet Union. West Germany was also criticised for its treatment of Turkish workers. The United States came under attack for racism, anti-Semitism, lack of free health care and "genocide" against Native Americans.[2] Soviet delegates also claimed that the "right to life" meant "the right to live in peace", which, they argued, imposed on the participants the obligation to strive for disarmament, as if disarmament would necessarily lead to peace.[3]

Western delegates replied robustly, but also welcomed Soviet criticism. As the British delegate Sir Anthony Williams said in his closing speech, "We have finally exploded the groundless contention that such discussion constitutes interference in the internal affairs of others".[4] The US delegate, Richard Schifter, responded to Soviet attacks with a measured discussion of the difference between political and civil rights on the one hand, and economic and social rights on the other. He said he had not intended to engage in a debate on the respective advantages of the US and Soviet models but as the Soviet Union had initiated this discussion he would join in the debate. After a detailed examination of social problems and unemployment in the United States, the rights of trade unions, and the status of Native Americans, he continued with comparative statistics on health care, life expectancy, infant mortality and other related matters. He pointed out that the Soviet standard of living remained barely one-third of the US level and much lower than in any developed country. "The average Soviet citizen, in fact, lives less well than someone living at the official US poverty line". Soviet growth rates had plummeted, and the Soviet Union was no longer closing the gap between itself and the developed West. Life expectancy of males in the Soviet Union had declined over the previous 20 years from 66 to just under 62 years while that of males in the United States had risen from 66 to 71. He continued with a devastating indictment of severe shortages in the Soviet Union, gross inequalities, increasing infant mortality, and per capita spending on defence at least as twice as high as in any developed Western country.[5]

Visiting Congressman Sandor Levin was struck by the fact that Soviet delegates seemed genuinely ignorant about the United States: "They went into wild flights of fiction about what is happening in the United States and showed an ignorance that was truly shocking".[6] A better argument for the Final Act's commitment to freer movement of people and information could hardly be found.

Predictably, it proved impossible to agree on a concluding document. The Soviet draft, which contained 18 proposals, asserted that the main human right was "the right to be permitted to live under conditions of peace and freedom [and] the prevention of nuclear war". Its definition of "freedom" was obviously not shared by the West. It reiterated the familiar demand for "non-intervention in internal affairs" (ignoring their own criticism of the United States) and called for future meetings to exclude the use of human rights as "a weapon for inciting enmity and hatred between peoples [and] for exacerbating international tensions". The Western draft contained 15 proposals calling for freedom of movement, frank discussion of violations of human rights and protection of minorities.[7]

Back home in the United States, critics, including Arthur Goldberg, blamed the lack of progress on the separation of human rights from security issues, thereby denying the West the leverage it had enjoyed in negotiating the Final Act.[8]

At this time, too, a debate built up in the United States over whether to remain in the Helsinki Process. Commentators who had always been against it spoke up, claiming vindication. Professor Richard Pipes wrote that the West, by crediting the Soviet Union with willingness to abide by human rights commitments, "effectively implied that at bottom there is no difference between democracy and communism".[9] George Will, who much later admitted that he had been wrong, wrote that talking earnestly and for so long with communist diplomats gave the public the impression that they shared a political vocabulary and frame of reference, "so the Helsinki process spreads a fog of false but soothing assumptions".[10] Some prominent dissidents in exile, such as Vladimir Bukovsky, also urged withdrawal. However, Ludmilla Alexeyeva, former spokesperson of the Moscow Helsinki Watch Group, and now resident in the United States, wrote that no-one among the Soviet human rights activists in the Soviet Union wanted the West to abandon Helsinki "because, through these accords, human rights has ceased to be a purely internal affair for the Soviet leadership".[11] In March 1985 the US Helsinki Commission countered critics with a long and closely argued report working through the arguments for and against remaining in the Helsinki Process and concluding strongly in favour of remaining.[12]

Budapest

A particularly gloomy picture emerged at the Budapest Cultural Forum (October to November 1985). It was supposed to discuss widening cultural cooperation between East and West but there was an unbridgeable gap between Western and Soviet notions of the role of culture. For the Western delegations it meant freedom of creative activity, including freer contacts among cultural figures, so the American delegate called for the release of some 20 writers in Soviet prisons.

For the Soviet Union, culture had to serve the party and be controlled by it. The secretary of the Soviet Writers' Union, Nikolai Federenko, insisted that the writer's duty was to work for peace. "Nothing", he said, "is worth writing about except peace".[13] This had been the standard line since the start of the Dipoli negotiations in 1972 and indeed since the days of Josef Stalin, who called writers "engineers of the human soul". Their job, he said, was to engineer the new Soviet man. Under his successors their job was to promote peace on Soviet terms. Whereas the West regarded the freer movement of information and ideas as a good in itself, a road to mutual understanding and thereby conducive to peace, the Soviet Union saw it as good only if it directly served Soviet interests (which is why the freer movement of "ideas" did not make it into the Final Act—see Chapter 11). In the end, and not unexpectedly, the Budapest meeting proved unable to agree on a concluding document. There was, however, some gain in that the meeting provoked discussion and encouraged dissidents in Poland, Czechoslovakia and Hungary to produce voluminous dossiers on cultural repression in their countries. Also, the Hungarian government, which was slightly more relaxed than others in Eastern Europe, allowed the International Helsinki Federation to hold seminars and meetings in the private apartments of Budapest residents.[14]

Bern[15]

The Bern meeting on human contacts (15 April to 27 May 1986) was scarcely more encouraging. The Soviet delegation at Madrid had resisted agreeing to this meeting but eventually gave way after intervention by the Spanish prime minister. Naturally, it would involve discussing emigration from the Soviet Union, particularly Jewish emigration, as well as general questions of travel and family reunions. Appeals flooded in from Soviet Jews and from the International Society for Human Rights. Many individuals and groups also came to Bern to protest personally.

The chief Soviet delegate, Yuri Kashlev, began by trying to insist that there were neither social nor national reasons to emigrate from the Soviet Union, but it was quickly pointed out that the Universal Declaration of Human Rights treated emigration as a right in itself, unrelated to the reasons for it. The next Soviet tactic was an attempt to limit visas for family visits to "participating states", which would have meant excluding emigration to Israel. The chief US delegate, Dr Michael Novak, had previously travelled to Moscow to explain to officials that he would be raising many cases of divided families. In Bern he was true to his word and pointed out that around one in ten Americans had at least one family root in Central and Eastern Europe. The Americans, he said, were family people so "our hearts are drawn to the divided spouses, separated from each other's arms for so many years". Then, referring back to the speech of Sir Alec Douglas-Home, British Foreign Secretary, at the founding meeting of the CSCE in Helsinki in 1973, he added that if the Helsinki Process did not improve the lives of ordinary people its words would be empty.[16]

Kashlev had wanted to keep the sessions closed to the public, arguing that the West would use them to bring in anti-Soviet agitators. He also objected to a Western proposal that three weeks should be devoted to discussing violations of the Final Act. The bitter arguments lasted almost a week, culminating in a nearly all-night session the day before the opening. Kashlev eventually accepted three weeks for a review of implementation but gained Western agreement that only the first session would be open. This made little difference to later closed sessions because Western delegates took care to give detailed briefings to the press after the meetings, as Goldberg had done at Belgrade.

Once under way, the meetings became increasingly acrimonious but they eventually came close to agreeing on a compromise document proposed by the neutrals and non-aligned. This document was unsatisfactory for the Western side because it contained phrases that could be used as loopholes to prevent travel. For instance, it said that governments would grant exit permits "when personal and professional circumstances permit". It also said that travel for medical reasons required a medical certificate issued by the country of residence. However, European delegates gave it their reluctant agreement.

Dr Novak therefore shocked delegates when, at the last moment, and under pressure from the Helsinki Commission and others in Washington, he withheld his consent.[17] The State Department had left him to make the lonely decision on his own. This caused consternation among Western delegates as it was the first time the United States had openly broken with the NATO consensus. Criticism was intense and widespread from East and West, particularly as it was said that Novak might have gained NATO support if he had signalled his doubts earlier and subjected them to negotiation. But in the end his veto turned out to be quite useful because it denied the Soviet Union the escape clauses that it might otherwise have been able to cite. Also, a relatively large number of the cases raised by the Western countries were, in fact, settled after the conference, among them about a thousand cases of bi-national marriages or family reunions that had previously been rejected.[18] So, in the end, the Bern meeting, even without a concluding document, appeared to have achieved mildly encouraging results in the field of human contacts.

In the meantime, however, signs of change had started to emerge from Gorbachev himself at his summit meeting with President Reagan in Geneva in November 1985. There the two leaders agreed to cooperate on a resolution of humanitarian issues. Gradually the Soviet leader also became more flexible on issues of arms control. Then, at the 27th Communist Party Congress in February–March 1986, he said that a fundamental principle of international security would be "a resolution in a humanitarian and positive spirit of questions related to the reuniting of families, marriage, and the promotion of contacts between people and between organisations". This was the first time a Soviet representative had openly accepted the Final Act's link between security and humanitarian issues. None of this, however, appeared to filter down to the Soviet delegation in Bern. As we shall see in Vienna, the Soviet bureaucracy took time to respond to new ideas at the top, probably trying to protect their careers in case Gorbachev fell.

In July 1986, after the Bern meeting had closed, Gorbachev took another step away from old positions by specifically mentioning human rights. During a visit by President Mitterrand of France, he said that "the theme of human rights becomes even more acute on the threshold of the twenty-first century..., [they are] one of the components of the all-embracing system of security".[19]

Nevertheless, in November 1986 the Helsinki Commission listed many continuing abuses of human rights in the Soviet Union, Czechoslovakia, Romania, Poland and East Germany, all of which countries still held political prisoners. In addition, the Soviet Union still retained the particularly nasty policy of incarcerating dissidents in psychiatric institutions. On the other hand, Anatoly Shcharansky, a prominent dissident, had been released in February, and by December Gorbachev had personally telephoned Andrei Sakharov to inform him that his exile was over.

The stage was thus set for the much more dramatic changes that slowly shaped the Vienna meeting (see Chapter 19).

Stockholm Conference on Disarmament in Europe (CDE)

This meeting, as we have seen in the previous chapter, emerged from a controversial French proposal in 1978. But the Soviet Union was also anxious for what it called a disarmament conference. By 1980 it had become increasingly worried by US defence spending on new weaponry and particularly by the NATO decision of 1979 to deploy Pershing II and cruise missiles in Europe in response to the Soviet deployment of SS-20s. Détente, it insisted, depended on halting the arms race, although it was still racing quite hard. It also wanted to shift the focus away from human rights, complaining regularly that the Helsinki Process should be about "security", rather than human rights, rejecting the Western thesis that there could be no true security while human rights were denied in Eastern Europe.

The French proposed moving forward in two stages. The first would attempt to improve on the Confidence-Building Measures (CBMs) contained in the Final Act. These were designed to provide some reassurance against surprise attack. They obliged participating states to give at least 21 days' notice of military manoeuvres in Europe involving more than 25,000 troops within 250 kilometres of frontiers facing or shared with any other European participating state. Members were also to be obliged to invite observers from other participating states. A recommendation urged members voluntarily to report on smaller manoeuvres and military movements but compliance on the Soviet side had turned out to be very limited. Since 1975, the Warsaw Pact had given notice of only three smaller manoeuvres while NATO had notified them of 20.[20]

If "substantial results" were achieved in the first stage, according to the French, a second stage would seek agreement on actual reductions in conventional weapons and forces.

President Carter had been against the proposal, as was the Helsinki Commission. Some NATO members also had doubts. There were three main objections. First, by allowing security issues to be treated separately from human rights the West would lose the leverage that it had enjoyed so far. Second, the conference would be exploited purely for propaganda purposes by the Soviet Union. Third, arms reductions (as distinct from CBMs) belonged with the MBFR talks, where only members of the military alliances were represented, not neutrals and non-aligned.

To meet the first of these objections, in December 1979 NATO ministers specified that the conference must be "part of a balanced outcome", meaning that agreement to hold it would depend on Soviet concessions on other parts of the Final Act, notably with regard to human rights and other humanitarian issues. Secondly, to reduce the scope for propaganda, the conference would discuss measures that were militarily significant, verifiable and "applicable to the entire continent of Europe"—defined later as including the whole of the European part of the Soviet Union up to the Ural mountains. This reflected not only strategic realities but also a long-time dream of General de Gaulle, that Europe from the Atlantic to the Urals should be treated as a whole. In other words, the measures would have to go well beyond the 250 kilometres specified in the Final Act.

At first the Soviet Union strongly resisted the extension of CBMs to the Urals but then, in February 1981, Brezhnev, addressing the 26th Congress of the Soviet Communist Party, suddenly conceded the point, while demanding concessions in return, initially that manoeuvres in the eastern United States should be included. However, he subsequently settled for including air, naval and military manoeuvres in European waters.

Thus agreement was eventually reached at Madrid to hold what was now to be called the Conference on Confidence- and Security-Building Measures and Disarmament in Europe (normally abbreviated to CSBMs) in Stockholm, starting on 17 January 1984. As required by NATO, it was agreed that the measures discussed would "cover the whole of Europe as well as the adjoining sea area and air space. They will be of military significance and politically binding and will be provided with adequate forms of verification which correspond to their content". The second stage would then depend on evaluation of the first.

The essential link between Stockholm and the rest of the CSCE was tested on 18 September 1984, when the US representative at the Stockholm conference, James Goodby, brought up the case of the distinguished Soviet scientist Andrei Sakharov, who had been on hunger strike in exile in Gorky (now Nizhny Novgorod) to protest against the conditions under which he was held. The US scientific community had been campaigning on his behalf; in May 1984 the US Congress had adopted a resolution demanding that the Soviet Union should adhere to the terms of the Final Act in its treatment of

Sakharov. By the autumn of that year Sakharov's life appeared to be in danger, so Goodby boldly raised his case at Stockholm, telling the conference that the United States "holds that human rights, peace and security are inseparable and that it is only on this basis that the spirit of the Helsinki accords truly can be realised".[21] The Soviet response was relatively mild, reflecting Moscow's desire to keep the talks on track, but Sakharov had to wait for Gorbachev to assume the leadership of the Soviet Union in 1985 before he was allowed to return to Moscow.

On matters of substance Soviet stonewalling largely continued until the spring of 1986, when Gorbachev told an East German audience that he was ready to move forward on conventional arms control.[22] A significant breakthrough came in July, when the Soviet delegation began to drop its objections to verification procedures, including especially on-site inspections. These had been strongly resisted by the Soviet military but they were essential if the CSBMs were to contribute effectively to reducing the danger of surprise attack. As the closing date of 19 September drew closer, negotiations intensified. Unable to meet the deadline, delegates stopped the clock until they eventually reached agreement two days late, on 21 September.

The agreement moved considerably beyond the CBMs of the Final Act. Advance notification would now have to be given for smaller land exercises, and troop concentrations involving 13,000 or more soldiers or 300 tanks (where the previous threshold had been 25,000 troops). Furthermore, the area on the Soviet side would extend to the Urals instead of the mere 250 kilometres specified in the Final Act. There was also provision not only for observers but also for snap inspections on land or from the air where a signatory suspected that military activity had not been properly notified. Gorbachev welcomed the agreement as representing "shoots of new thinking in world politics that are germinating on European soil".[23]

The Western side was mostly pleased but now emphasised the need for balanced progress on humanitarian issues. Worries about shifting the emphasis from human rights to military security also occupied the Helsinki Commission in Washington, particularly when the Warsaw Pact proposed abandoning the moribund MBFR talks in Vienna and replacing them with new talks on conventional arms in the CSCE.

These worries were put aside when the CSCE follow-up meeting in Vienna began to make dramatic progress on all fronts. To this we shall now turn.

Notes

1 Shevardnadze, E. 1985, *Address on the tenth anniversary of the signing of the Helsinki Final Act*, OSCE viewed 30 December 2021, https://www.osce.org/files/f/documents/a/e/16138.pdf

2 Radio Free Europe report in Mastny, *Helsinki, Human Rights and European Security*, 2.

3 Korey, *The Promises We Keep*, 172.

4 Korey, 172.

5 Text in Mastny, 289–303.

6 Mastny, 332 and Korey 177.
7 Korey 176–7, and Mastny, Appendix D.
8 Quoted in Korey, 178, from Dorothy Goldberg's *A Personal Journey*.
9 Quoted in Korey, 180.
10 Quoted in Korey, 180.
11 Quoted in Korey, 181.
12 Korey, 214–17 and Mastny, *The Helsinki Process*, 53.
13 Radio Free Europe report quoted in Mastny, 319.
14 Korey, 187.
15 This section draws a lot on Korey's detailed and illuminating account of the meeting so individual references have been kept to a minimum.
16 Korey, 199–200.
17 For a detailed account of this episode see Korey, 202–12. See also Novak's account in Mastny, 67.
18 Korey, 211–12.
19 Korey, 190.
20 Korey, 147.
21 Korey, 168.
22 Korey, 222.
23 Korey, 224.

19 Vienna 1986–9: The ice cracks[1]

The third follow-up meeting, from 4 November 1986 to 19 January 1989, took place amid the imperial grandeur of the Hofburg Palace in Vienna. The outlook at the start was much more promising than in the past but there were still struggles ahead before the meeting could end with a final transformative breakthrough that brought an end to the ideological dimension of the Cold War.

Mikhail Gorbachev had come to power in Moscow the previous year, but he had not yet established his authority. His new Foreign Minister, Eduard Shevardnadze, had no foreign experience but as party leader in Georgia he had pushed through reforms that had caught Gorbachev's eye. He had even told Gorbachev in 1984: "Everything is rotten. It has to be changed".[2] So the two men shared a common outlook and were able to move together to transform Soviet foreign policy.

Gorbachev had been doing some deep thinking about Europe ever since his private travels in Western Europe in the 1970s, when, as he wrote later, "my previous belief in the superiority of socialist democracy over the bourgeois system was shaken".[3] Although he presented himself as a reforming communist, he was gradually becoming a social democrat, much influenced by Willy Brandt (Chancellor of West Germany 1969–74) and especially by long discussions on socialism with Felipe González (Prime Minister of Spain 1982–96). He saw Europe not only as a source of modernisation for the Soviet economy but also as an example of democratic socialism that he hoped to emulate.

After meeting Margaret Thatcher in 1987 he had told the Politburo: "We cannot do without such a partner as Western Europe… Europe is our business. Our interests there are enormous… The Helsinki process offers new opportunities, and we have to enter a new phase, step by step".[4] His great hope was that the CSCE would provide a framework for a new European security system. In this he was eventually disappointed (see Chapter 22).

In his *Memoirs* he wrote of his vision for Europe: "Reflecting on the goals to set for our new foreign policy, I found it increasingly difficult to see the multi-coloured patchwork of Europe's political map as I used to see it before [rigidly divided between East and West]. I was thinking about the common roots of this multiform and yet fundamentally indivisible European

DOI: 10.4324/9781003146124-24

civilisation".[5] Soon he was talking about Europe as a "common home". This was, he writes in his *Memoirs*, "a spontaneous thought" that came to him on his visit to France in 1985, "but the symbolic image eventually acquired an existence of its own".[6] He later elaborated on the theme of the common home in a speech in Prague in 1987 and most notably when addressing the Council of Europe in Strasbourg in July 1989: "Our idea of a common European home… was born out of our realisation of new realities, of our realisation of the fact that the linear continuation of the path, along which intra-European relations have developed until the last quarter of the twentieth century, is no longer consonant with these realities…; what we have in mind is a restructuring of the international order existing in Europe that would put European common values in the forefront and make it possible to replace the traditional balance of forces with a balance of interests".[7]

At the same time his broader foreign policy was developing along similar lines through a series of speeches culminating in his dramatic speech to the United Nations on 7 December 1988, where he announced large unilateral cuts in his military forces and dropped an ideological bombshell by dumping a central axiom of Marxist-Leninist foreign policy. This held that the world was divided between two hostile camps, socialism and capitalism, which would engage in intense ideological struggle (preferably peaceful) until the inevitable victory of socialism. Gorbachev offered a sharply different view: "Today we have entered an era when progress will be shaped by universal human values…; world politics, too, should be guided by the primacy of universal human values… The use or threat of force no longer can or must be an instrument of foreign policy".

More shock waves reached Eastern Europe when he went on to say that "the principle of freedom of choice is mandatory… Denying that right to the peoples under whatever pretext or rhetorical guise means jeopardizing even the fragile balance that has been attained. Freedom of choice is a universal principle that should allow for no exceptions… The new phase also requires de-ideologizing relations among states".[8] In other words, the Brezhnev Doctrine was dead. Ever since he had taken office in 1985 Gorbachev had been privately warning the leaders of Eastern Europe that they were on their own, but "I had the feeling that they were not taking it altogether seriously".[9] Now he went public on freedom of choice. He believed that the East Europeans would choose a reformed version of socialism but he was disappointed. Within two years they had thrown off Soviet control and headed towards the European Community and NATO.

Robert Kaiser wrote in *The Washington Post*: "In a speech as remarkable as any ever delivered at the United Nations, Mikhail Gorbachev proposed to change the rules the world has lived by for four decades". *The New York Times* called the speech "Breathtaking. Risky. Bold. Naive. Diversionary. Heroic".[10]

The first impact of this new thinking hit the astonished delegates in the Hofburg Palace when Shevardnadze spoke in terms that had never before been heard from a Soviet official: "We see the goals of the CSCE process as promoting more democratic relations between States and greater democracy in public life within each country".[11] In other words, the CSCE was to help promote change within the Soviet Union, an idea that had been privately held by many in Moscow (see Chapter 12) but which had never been admitted as official policy. Soviet regimes had always strenuously rejected any discussion of its internal affairs.

Then Shevardnadze produced another surprise. He offered to host a conference on humanitarian cooperation in Moscow.[12] The crusty Soviet delegation was dumbfounded, as were other members of the Warsaw Pact. The Western delegations also took time to adjust. A Vienna newspaper likened the proposal to holding a meeting of chickens in a fox's den.[13]

Once the statesmen had left Vienna, the conference reverted to Cold War habits and familiar accusations flew to and fro. Gorbachev was having trouble getting his new ideas accepted by his officials, some of whom were doubtless trying to protect their careers in case he was overthrown.[14] Resistance continued for a long time. As late as 21 April 1988, Shevardnadze found himself apologising to US Secretary of State George Shultz for the recalcitrant attitude of the Soviet delegation in Vienna: "We have a hard delegation… in Vienna… We tell them one thing, they do something different".[15]

As at previous follow-up meetings, the Western nations and the neutrals and non-aligned saw the main purpose of the Vienna meeting as monitoring compliance with Principle VII on human rights and Basket III on humanitarian issues, these two being often lumped together as "the human dimension". They took the position that normalising relations with the Soviet Union and Eastern Europe depended on more respect for human rights, including better treatment of activists who were trying to monitor compliance with the Final Act.

Thus initial debates were as stormy as they had been at Belgrade and Madrid. Warsaw Pact speakers accused the West of "political hooliganism" and "psychological warfare" while the British delegate complained about the "bullying and browbeating" tactics of the Eastern delegates and their refusal to answer questions.[16] The Canadian ambassador said: "The Soviet human rights record remains deplorable. The new wind which we are told blows from Moscow brings no refreshing change".[17] The US ambassador argued that "there is a vital connection between a state's approach toward human rights domestically and its conduct internationally".[18]

The problem was that progress on human rights in the Soviet Union still lagged far behind Gorbachev's words. Two prominent dissidents, Yuri Orlov and Anatoly Shcharansky (who changed his name to Natan Sharansky on getting an Israeli passport), both of whom had been founders of the Moscow Helsinki Watch Group, were released before the conference in response to persistent pressure from the West, but 41 members of Helsinki monitoring groups remained in prison. One of them, Anatoly Marchenko, died in particularly brutal circumstances just a month after the opening of the meeting, provoking vigorous protests in Vienna. The record in Czechoslovakia was no better. Jamming of Western radio still continued, as did many restrictions on travel. Romania was particularly resistant to change right up to the end of the conference, when its representative made clear that it would ignore parts of the final document that it regarded as interfering in its internal affairs.[19] So there was still a hill to climb.

Gorbachev was, however, making progress. He realised that he had to improve on human rights if he was to make diplomatic progress. After Marchenko's death he faced down angry objections in his own Politburo and personally phoned the distinguished dissident nuclear scientist Andrei Sakharov to tell him he could return from exile in Gorky.[20] Gradually more and more political prisoners were released: more than 600 during 1987–88.[21]

Western governments were anxious not to let up on criticism too soon. They were uncertain about Gorbachev's new policies. Were they genuine? And, even if they were, would they last? While waiting for answers, it seemed important to prevent public opinion becoming too enamoured of the new face that Moscow was now presenting to the world.

Junior members of the Warsaw Pact reinforced Western caution by sticking to their standard responses to criticism. At first they tried to shift the focus to military security, arguing once again, as at previous meetings, that the right to life was the most fundamental of human rights. Then they accused the West of trying to wreck the conference with destructive criticisms of their internal affairs. They also counter-attacked with dossiers of complaints about Western abuses of human rights, citing poverty, unemployment, homelessness, inadequate health services and so on. All this was a repeat of previous meetings, such as that in Ottawa (see Chapter 18).

Western officials responded by admitting shortcomings and welcoming the fact that Warsaw Pact States now appeared to accept the principle that the conference could examine the internal affairs of other countries. They pointed out that some civil rights could be granted in the socialist countries simply by removing restrictions on speech and travel, for instance, whereas in a free market system full employment and other "economic rights" required long-term government policies. However, there were signs of increasing divergence in a bloc that had hitherto been tightly disciplined. It soon became clear that Poland and Hungary were willing to accept most Western demands, while the Soviet Union initially resisted, together with East Germany, Czechoslovakia and Bulgaria. Romania remained a total outlier in its rigid objection to change. A certain fatalism had, however, begun to creep into ruling circles in Czechoslovakia. Border controls became laxer than usual, as this author discovered in late 1987, when he passed easily through customs with a bag of taped interviews, evoking only a helpless shrug from the officer. Privately, he was told: "They know the game's up but they don't know what to do so they just hang on".

Meanwhile, the opening of the Vienna meeting had encouraged a revival of dissident activity throughout the Soviet bloc. New groups sprang up in many places demanding multi-party systems, free trade unions, a free press and national rights to self-determination.[22] According to Shevardnadze, sober recognition reached the Kremlin that the division of Europe could not continue.[23] Already at the tenth anniversary of the signing of the Final Act he had listened patiently to the list of complaints instead of angrily dismissing them, as his predecessor had done.[24]

At the start of the Vienna meeting there had been divisions on the Western side over whether to draft new provisions or merely monitor compliance within the existing terms of the Final Act. Denmark proposed that new provisions would strengthen and complement existing commitments and thereby encourage improved compliance, while the United States argued, in the words of George Shultz, that "escape from the violation of existing commitments cannot be found in the flight to new commitments".[25] Gradually, however, the rapid progress of Soviet compliance raised hopes that new commitments would help close loopholes in the Final Act and promote more progress. Thus, new proposals started flooding in from Western nations aimed at, for instance, more religious freedom, the right to leave one's country, protection for dissidents, and reunification of families. Many of these eventually found a place in the concluding document.

At the same time the West became more interested in trying to set up permanent machinery for monitoring human rights rather than relying on follow-up meetings every two years. The idea was to oblige states to submit information on human rights and human contacts on demand, and to attend meetings on these questions without waiting for the next follow-up meeting. These ideas bore fruit at the Paris meeting in 1990 (see Chapter 20).

Eventually Gorbachev's new thinking reached Vienna. To the surprise of Western delegates, and to the consternation of rigid communist officials, the Soviet team accepted virtually the entire Western agenda, including human rights, freer movement of people and information, intrusive monitoring of arms control, and the right of citizens to leave their country and return (the first time this right had been explicitly contained in a CSCE document).[26] The Soviet Union also ceased jamming Western broadcasts and dropped its long-standing opposition to the discussion of its internal affairs. It had released hundreds of political prisoners, and—perhaps the greatest concession of all—had allowed dissident groups to monitor implementation of the Final Act. The rest of the Warsaw Pact, with the exception of Romania, felt obliged to go along with these dramatic new policies, willingly in the case of Poland and Hungary, and more reluctantly in the case of Czechoslovakia, Bulgaria and East Germany. Romania signed the concluding document but announced that it would not comply.[27] As Lehne observes, "the Vienna meeting confirmed that these regimes were obsolete, highlighted their isolation, and in so doing speeded along their departure".[28] A year later Romania withdrew its reservations.[29]

By the time the Vienna meeting ended on 19 January 1989 the scenery of East–West relations was changing dramatically. To the extent that the Cold War was about ideology and values it was now over, but change still had to come on the ground. This it did very quickly in just over one tumultuous year. Once the people of Eastern Europe became confident that Gorbachev would not use force his empire crumbled, and once the communist leaders, except in Romania, were assured a safe exit they left the stage, a remarkably peaceful end to an empire that had been maintained by force.

On 4 June 1989 the Solidarity movement in Poland won an overwhelming victory in a partially free election, causing consternation not only within the party that had ruled Poland for more than 40 years but among the other communist leaders in Eastern Europe, who expressed themselves in a stormy closed meeting in Bucharest on 7–8 July. Gorbachev reported that "we are receiving letters of panic from everywhere" but he remained firm in Bucharest, forcing through a communiqué that bore little or no resemblance to the proceedings or to the views of many of those present. It said, among other things: "One of the basic conditions for assuring peace and cooperation in Europe is the application, in every country, of the entire gamut of freedoms and fundamental human rights, as they were formulated in the Universal Declaration of Human Rights and the international accords on human rights in the Final Act of Helsinki".[30]

- On 27 June the foreign ministers of Hungary and Austria met on their frontier with bolt cutters to breach the barbed wire, ceremonially opening a hole in the Iron Curtain that allowed East Germans to cross through Hungary into Austria, greatly annoying the East German regime. By August some 1,600 East Germans had used this route to reach the West.[31]
- In October demonstrations started to build in East Germany.
- On 7 October Hungary's ruling Socialist Workers' Party voted for its own dissolution.
- On 9 November, a hasty announcement by a confused official caused East German border guards to open a crossing point in the Berlin Wall, allowing thousands of their citizens to stream into West Berlin.
- On 10 December, after massive demonstrations, a non-communist government took over in Prague, bringing the prominent dissident playwright Vaclav Havel almost straight from prison to the presidency, which he assumed just three weeks later.
- On 22 December the brutal government of Nicolae Ceaușescu in Romania was overthrown, and he and his wife were shot. Unfortunately, he was not replaced by democrats.
- The following year, on 18 March, the East Germans voted to unite with West Germany.
- On 3 October 1990 Germany was reunited.[32]

At this point states of the CSCE might have declared their work done. Germany and Europe were reunited and human rights had been granted. Mission accomplished, they might have said. Instead, the Helsinki Process entered an entirely new phase, celebrated by the Paris Declaration of November 1990 (see Chapter 20), and then continued to evolve up to the present day.

Military détente

Meanwhile the Warsaw Pact had been wanting to shift attention away from human rights to focus on military matters, moving on from Stockholm I to Stockholm II to look for "real disarmament in Europe", in Shevardnadze's words. He was echoing the Madrid mandate that instructed members to "continue their efforts for security and disarmament in Europe".

The West remained interested primarily in continuing to monitor implementation of the human dimension of the Final Act but both sides shared an interest in reducing the enormous concentration of armed forces in Europe. In 1988 there were more than 4.5 million active troops stationed between the Atlantic and the Urals, with about 75,000 battle tanks.[33]

Very little progress had been made at the MBFR talks in Vienna (as noted above). NATO had wanted asymmetric cuts to reach a common ceiling while the Warsaw Pact demanded equal cuts that would have left in place the huge imbalance in its favour. Eventually agreement was reached on a common ceiling of 700,000 troops on each side but there was no agreement on how many troops were actually on the ground.

In truth, there had been little will on either side for progress in these talks. The Soviet Union had been steadily building up its superiority in conventional forces and was reluctant to change course, while the United States wanted to prolong the negotiations in order to hold off Congressional pressure to bring US forces home. At the same time a certain unreality prevailed because the area under negotiation was confined to the central sector, leaving the Soviet Union free to amass as many forces as it wished behind its own frontier while the Americans would have had to take many of its troops back across the Atlantic, since France refused to have American troops on its soil.

Could more progress be made in another forum? This idea came to seem more realistic after April 1986, when Gorbachev proposed force reductions from the Atlantic to the Urals. His acceptance of a wider area marked a major change in Soviet policy, although he still spoke of equal cuts that he must have known would be unacceptable to NATO. Two months later, the Warsaw Pact's "Budapest appeal" of June supported and developed Gorbachev's idea, showing remarkable flexibility by including, among other things, short-range nuclear weapons and extensive provisions for verification. Three possible forums were suggested: the second stage of the Stockholm CDE conference; a new forum; or an expanded mandate for the MBFR negotiations. Soon, however, it narrowed its proposal down to the CDE, so that steps to reduce armed forces would move in parallel with continued negotiations on CSBMs.[34]

NATO remained opposed to equal cuts because they would leave the asymmetry in place. It also hesitated to include nuclear weapons because it relied on the threat of their use to compensate for its inferiority in conventional forces. However, it was encouraged by the offers on verification and exchanges of information, and particularly by the inclusion of the whole area from the Atlantic to the Urals. Experts were also coming to accept that Gorbachev's new thinking on Soviet security, emphasising sufficiency for defence rather than superiority, was genuine and backed by the urgent need to transfer Soviet resources to the civilian economy.

Faced with this new situation, NATO foreign ministers meeting in Halifax in May 1986 set up a task force to work on new proposals. These emerged in December of the same year, when NATO adopted the "Brussels Declaration on Conventional Arms Control", which proposed building on the results of the Stockholm conference to "eliminate existing disparities, from the Atlantic to the Urals, and to establish conventional stability at lower levels".[35]

A compromise was needed between the French view that arms talks should be conducted within the CSCE and the US view that they should be limited to the 23 members of the two alliances outside the CSCE framework. The US believed that including the neutrals and non-aligned would overcomplicate matters. Eventually a compromise was reached by which there would be a single mandate from the Vienna meeting for talks in two forums, one of 23 members and the other of 35. Given the complexities of the various views on each side, the meeting simply reaffirmed the Madrid mandate and left progress to future talks. In the meantime, the Vienna meeting of the CSCE proved helpful in monitoring compliance with the measures agreed at Stockholm.

Notes

1 For an excellent full account of the Vienna meeting see Stefan Lehne, *The Vienna Meeting of the Conference on Security and Cooperation in Europe, 1986–1989*.
2 Shevardnadze, *The Future Belongs To Freedom*, 37.
3 Gorbachev, *Memoirs*, 130.
4 Chernyaev, *My Six Years with Gorbachev*, 105.
5 Gorbachev, 553.
6 Gorbachev, 552.
7 Gorbachev, 6 July 1989, *Speech to the Council of Europe*, CVCE, viewed 30 December 2021, https://www.cvce.eu/content/publication/2002/9/20/4c021687-98f9-4727-9e8b-836e0bc1f6fb/publishable_en.pdf
8 Gorbachev, 7 December 1988, *Speech to the United Nations* [English translation], AP News, viewed 30 December 2021, https://apnews.com/article/1abea48aacda1a9dd520c380a8bc6be6
9 Gorbachev, 465.
10 Both quoted in Gorbachev's *Memoirs*. For a fuller look at Gorbachev's new thinking on foreign policy see Archie Brown, *The Gorbachev Factor*, 212–51.
11 Lehne, 56–7.
12 Lehne, 73.
13 Quoted by Thomas in *The Helsinki Effect*, 238, and by Mastny in *The Helsinki Process and the Reintegration of Europe*, 11.
14 Ligachev, *Inside Gorbachev's Kremlin*, 105–7.
15 National Security Archive Electronic Briefing Book No. 481. DOCUMENT 5: Record of Shultz-Shevardnadze Conversation in Moscow, April 21, 1988. Source: FOIA request to the Department of State. See https://nsarchive2.gwu.edu/NSAEBB/NSAEBB481/docs/Document%205.pdf, viewed 14 February 2022.
16 Lehne, 89.
17 Lehne, 89.

18 Lehne, 91.
19 Lehne, 132.
20 Thomas, 238.
21 Thomas, 242.
22 Thomas, 239.
23 Thomas, 230.
24 Thomas, 230.
25 Lehne, 56.
26 For a guide to the Vienna document see Appendix II.
27 For Romania's explanation, see Mastny, *The Helsinki Process*, 141.
28 Lehne, 14.
29 Mastny, 192.
30 Lévesque, *The Enigma of 1989*, 120–1.
31 Spohr, *Post Wall, Post Square*, 76–7.
32 For brilliant accounts of the extraordinary events of 1989 see Lévesque, *The Enigma of 1989*; Garton Ash, *The Magic Lantern: the Revolutions of '89*; Sarotte, *1989*; Spohr, *Post Wall, Post Square*.
33 Lehne, 58–60, quoting International Institute for Strategic Studies, *The Military Balance, 1988–1989*.
34 Mastny and Byrne, *A Cardboard Castle?*, 531.
35 North Atlantic Council, 11 December 1986, *Brussels Declaration On Conventional Arms Control*, NATO, viewed 30 December 2021, https://www.nato.int/cps/en/natohq/official_texts_23337.htm

20 Paris 1990: Euphoria

The euphoria that greeted the end of the Cold War found full expression in the *Charter of Paris for a New Europe*, a document of soaring ideals that seemed to presage a new era of democracy, peace and prosperity in the troubled continent.[1] It was signed by 34 heads of state or government meeting in Paris 19–21 November 1990. There was one signature fewer than at the Helsinki Summit of 1975 because Germany had become one country, the Federal Republic having swallowed up its communist counterpart.

Among the delegations were new faces from Eastern Europe including former opposition figures who had come to power from the ruins of the communist system, notably President Václav Havel of Czechoslovakia, fairly recently out of prison, and the new Polish Prime Minister, Tadeusz Mazowiecki, a distinguished writer and adviser to the Solidarity movement. Then there were the astonished facilitators of German reunification, Chancellor Helmut Kohl of Germany and President George Bush of the United States, together with a more reluctant President François Mitterrand of France, who had not entirely welcomed German reunification but had come to terms with its inevitability, insisting on a currency union (the Euro) as the price of his support in order to bind united Germany safely into the European Community.[2]

One who had not come to terms with German unity was Prime Minister Margaret Thatcher of Great Britain, who had tried to enlist Gorbachev's support to keep Germany divided, disgracing herself by failing to understand the historic moment. Nor had she grasped the transformation that West Germany had undergone since the war, building itself into one of the most stable, prosperous and reliable liberal democracies in Europe. She arrived late at Versailles, having been preoccupied with threats to her leadership in London. Her downfall followed soon after.

The star of the show was Mikhail Gorbachev, President of the Soviet Union, who had released his European empire from Soviet control and abandoned the ideology that had fuelled the Cold War for 45 years and gripped his country since the 1917 revolution. Yet even he had not yet come fully to terms with the new world that he had brought into being. He still could not bring himself to accept the imminent loss of the three Baltic states: Estonia, Latvia and Lithuania. They had been forcibly absorbed into the

DOI: 10.4324/9781003146124-25

Soviet Union in 1940, then occupied by the Nazis, and then taken back into the Soviet Union in 1944, each time suffering horrendous brutality. The United States had continued to recognise them as independent states with diplomatic missions in Washington throughout the Cold War. Their representatives, who had been pressing for independence, were invited to Paris under a special arrangement negotiated with the French and accepted unofficially by the Soviet delegation in Vienna, apparently without Gorbachev's knowledge. Under this arrangement they were admitted to the public spaces of the conference centre using name cards on which their countries were not specified, but they could not attend the sessions because they were not recognised by the Soviet Union. In fact, Gorbachev was still clinging to the hope that they would remain within the Soviet Union, so when he spotted Lennart Meri from Estonia he asked Mitterrand to have him and all three Baltic delegations removed. Meri was a very distinguished multilingual writer and film-maker whose family had suffered under Stalin. He and the other Baltic delegations were taken away to the French Foreign Ministry for an apologetic explanation. Gorbachev also angrily cancelled a meeting with Václav Havel, who had met with the Baltic representatives. Yet less than a year later all the Baltic states were admitted to the United Nations and the CSCE, such was the speed at which the Soviet Union unravelled. Meri himself became president of Estonia in 1992.[3]

The euphoria of Paris did not last long. For domestic reasons, Margaret Thatcher was out of office within a week. Mazowiecki was gone within a few weeks, and Gorbachev in just over a year. The Soviet Union broke up amid chaos and hardship under Boris Yeltsin as democracy failed to take root, opening the way for Vladimir Putin. Yugoslavia fell into a long and bitter war.

Yet the Paris document registered a transformational moment in European history, even if its results fell very far short of the hopes it raised. Much of the groundwork had been done at a meeting in Copenhagen from 5 to 19 June 1990. The concluding document of that meeting[4] reaffirmed the Final Act's link between human rights and security and went further by asserting that "pluralistic democracy and the rule of law are prerequisites for progress in setting up the lasting order of peace, security, justice and cooperation that they seek to establish in Europe". It set out rights in detail and standards for a free press and democratic elections, obliging states to invite observers. It also tightened up the Vienna procedure for requesting information from states on questions relating to the human dimension, setting a limit of four weeks for a response. This was later reduced to ten days, following the Moscow Meeting of 1991.

The Paris summit built on this foundation. Its *Charter of Paris for a New Europe* started by declaring: "The era of confrontation and division of Europe has ended…; henceforth our relations will be founded on respect and cooperation. Europe is liberating itself from the legacy of the past". Citing the Helsinki Final Act as both an inspiration and the foundation of a new order, it reiterated that document's commitment to the full range of human rights, and added a ringing endorsement of political pluralism, market economics and private property as aims for all members: "We undertake to build, consolidate and strengthen democracy as the only system of government of our nations".

Paris thus took a big step beyond the Vienna conclusions (see Chapter 19), which still acknowledged the communist system by referring only to "increased autonomy for enterprises". Communist rule was now dead in Europe.

It also moved beyond the Final Act by stressing the importance of "free movement" (not "freer" movement, as in the Final Act) and the "free" (not "freer") flow of information, adding a reference to "ideas", which had been excluded from the Final Act on Soviet insistence.

The leaders then set about arranging for the good work to continue. Follow-up meetings were to take place every two years, starting with a summit in Helsinki in 1992. Ministers of foreign affairs would meet regularly as a Council at least once a year, starting in Berlin. A committee of senior officials would meet to prepare Council meetings. Other ministerial meetings could also be agreed by participating states. Representatives could also meet when necessary to discuss questions of urgent concern.

Then came further innovations. Up to this point the CSCE had consisted—as its name indicated—of a series of conferences with monitoring continuing between them. Now it started moves towards becoming an institution by setting up three bodies:

- A permanent secretariat in Prague.
- A Conflict Prevention Centre in Vienna to provide a mechanism for consultation and cooperation on unusual military activities, annual exchanges of military information, a communications network, annual assessment meetings, and procedures for conciliation of disputes.
- An Office for Free Elections in Warsaw, soon to widen its remit as the Office for Democratic Institutions and Human Rights (ODIHR), often referred to as "Oh Dear" when states all too frequently fell short of the democratic standards to which they had signed up.

(see Chapter 24)

The Paris document also called for a CSCE parliamentary assembly consisting of representatives from the parliaments of member countries. This eventually came into being in April 1991. Later it ran into trouble when parliamentarians on brief visits to observe elections clashed with trained observers.

The Paris summit also adopted three other documents:

- An agreement on Confidence- and Security-Building Measures (CSBMs), signed by all 34 members.
- A treaty on Conventional Armed Forces in Europe (CFE), signed by the 22 members of NATO and the Warsaw Pact.[5] The CFE treaty not only

required substantial cuts in Soviet weaponry (including 40,000 tanks) but, together with further CBMs, greatly extended the basic CSCE principle of transparency to include military budgets, new weapons, and procedures for questioning unusual military activities. However, it was soon found that the Soviet Union had removed beyond the Urals much of the equipment it was supposed to destroy and re-classified some army units as part of the navy to prevent them being counted.[6]

- A Joint Declaration by the same 22, declaring that they were no longer adversaries.

For the next two years, the CSCE continued to expand and evolve. In June 1991 Albania joined after being refused until it could demonstrate progress towards democracy. In September 1991 came the three Baltic republics, Estonia, Lithuania and Latvia, which had just emerged as independent states from the Soviet Union. Then, in January 1992, the CSCE decided to admit Armenia, Azerbaijan, Belarus, Ukraine, Moldova, and the five "stans"—Kazakhstan, Kyrgyzstan, Tajikistan, Turkmenistan and Uzbekistan.

The CSCE had to bend its principles for some of the new members, particularly the "stans", which were neither European nor democratic. The hope was that within the warm embrace of the CSCE they would be more likely to evolve in a democratic direction than if they had been excluded. They had, after all, been part of the Soviet Union and therefore by proxy signatories of the Final Act, but each one now had to renew its vows individually to respect human rights and all the other obligations contained in the Final Act and the documents of Vienna and Paris. Some of them showed a marked lack of enthusiasm but signed up anyway. To encourage their adherence to the values of the CSCE they had to accept missions charged with helping them to comply and reporting on their progress—or lack of it.

After the "stans", in March 1992, came Georgia, Croatia and Slovenia, and then in April Bosnia-Herzegovina. In January 1993 the Czech Republic and Slovakia joined as separate states after Czechoslovakia divided into two states.

This brought the number of participating countries to 53, creating a body very different from the relatively intimate assembly of 35 that had come together in Helsinki in 1975.

Meanwhile meetings and agreements proliferated:[7]

- Valletta (15 January to 8 February 1991) produced an agreement on the peaceful settlement of disputes, known as the Valletta mechanism, useful but somewhat weakened by various "safety" clauses allowing members to withdraw. Modified later in Stockholm 1992.
- Berlin (19–26 June 1991) produced the "Berlin mechanism", an emergency procedure intended develop further "the CSCE's capability to safeguard human rights, democracy and the rule of law through peaceful means". It could be activated by one state, if backed by 12 other participating states, making a request to the Chairman-in-Office

following "a violation of one of the Principles of the Final Act or as the result of major disruptions endangering peace, security or stability".

- Geneva (July 1991) considered measures for protecting the rights of persons belonging to minorities.
- Moscow (10 September–4 October 1991) reinforced commitments to human rights with arrangements for missions of experts. It introduced a compulsory procedures for rapporteurs linked to the Vienna mechanism[8] plus a compulsory rapporteur system not related to the Vienna Mechanism to respond to "serious threats". The procedure was activated in 1992 in response to the conflict in Bosnia-Herzegovina and Croatia. A mission was able to visit only Croatia but reported "gross violations" in both Croatia and Serbian-held territory. In December 1992, the procedure was activated in Estonia in response to Russian concerns for the rights and language of the Russian minority, which it deemed insufficiently protected by Estonia's citizenship laws. A mission of two experts was also sent to Moldova in January 1993.
- Prague (30–31 January 1992). The main purpose of this meeting was to draw up guidelines for negotiating the Helsinki II summit due in July.
- An important modification was made to the consensus rule: "consensus minus one" allowed the Council or the Committee of Senior Officials to "take appropriate action… if necessary in the absence of the consent of the State concerned, in cases of clear, gross and uncorrected violations of relevant CSCE commitments. Such actions would consist of political declarations or other political steps to apply outside the territory of the State concerned. This decision is without prejudice to existing CSCE mechanisms".

This procedure was used for the first time on 12 May 1992 to overcome Yugoslav objections to a declaration blaming Belgrade and the Yugoslav National Army for the conflict in Bosnia-Herzegovina, where the Yugoslav National Army was accused of "clear, gross and uncorrected violations of CSCE commitments". It was used again on 8 July to ban Yugoslavia from attending the CSCE summit in Helsinki or any subsequent meetings of the CSCE until 14 October 1992.[9]

In December the same year the Council, meeting in Geneva, went further and introduced a system of consensus minus two—that is, minus the two disputants—for the peaceful settlement of disputes.[10]

All this activity was working up to the summit known as Helsinki II, which is the subject of the next chapter.

Notes

1 *Charter of Paris for a New Europe*, OSCE, viewed 28 January 2022, https://www.osce.org/files/f/documents/0/6/39516.pdf
2 Bozo, *Mitterrand, the End of the Cold War and German Unification.*
3 Maresca, *Helsinki Revisited*,132–6.
4 https://www.osce.org/gsearch?qr=osce%20copenhagen%20document%20

5 https://www.osce.org/files/f/documents/4/9/14087.pdf
6 Mastny, *The Helsinki Process*, 36.
7 Reports on all these meetings are to be found by searching on www.osce.org
8 The Vienna Mechanism of 1989 laid down procedures for requesting and supplying information relating to the human dimension of the CSCE. It was strengthened in 1990 by the Copenhagen Mechanism, which set a time limit of four weeks for responding to requests and three weeks for holding a bilateral meeting.
9 Heraclides, *Helsinki-II and its aftermath*, 84.
10 CVCE, 'The procedures and mechanisms of the OSCE', viewed 7 January 2022, https://www.cvce.eu/obj/the_procedures_and_mechanisms_of_the_osce-en-32a78695-6b86-46d0-98cc-e6db63fd4037.htm

21 Helsinki II 1992: Gloom[1]

The euphoria of Paris wore off very quickly. By July 1992, when leaders of 52 CSCE states gathered in Helsinki for a grand two-day summit, the political skies had darkened. There were wars in Yugoslavia, conflicts in Nagorno-Karabakh and Georgia, and simmering disputes elsewhere. The idea had been to renew the vows of 1975 and set an optimistic course for the future but the Declaration that emerged from the summit observed sadly: "This is a time of promise but also a time of instability and insecurity. Economic decline, social tension, aggressive nationalism, intolerance, xenophobia and ethnic conflicts threaten stability in the CSCE area. Gross violations of CSCE commitments in the field of human rights and fundamental freedoms, including those related to national minorities, pose a special threat to the peaceful development of society, in particular in new democracies. There is still much work to be done… For the first time in decades we are facing warfare in the CSCE region".[2]

Like its predecessor in 1975, Helsinki II was preceded by difficult negotiations, now made more difficult by the expansion of its membership to 52, with many new members lacking CSCE experience. A preparatory meeting started on 10 March and ended with opening speeches by foreign ministers from 24–26 March. More negotiations then followed until consensus was reached on 8 July 1992, permitting the summit to take place on 9–10 July.

The aim was to complete the CSCE's transformation from a process to an organisation by creating permanent bodies and giving some of them operational powers that would take them beyond the declarations, exhortations and resolutions that had been the main product of Helsinki I. There were disagreements about how far this process should go. For instance, on the thorny issue of peacekeeping, should the CSCE have its own military capabilities or rely on NATO? Should it have enforcement powers or be confined to monitoring? Should minority rights focus on individual rights or group rights? Should the CSCE become a legal entity?

Out of these negotiations came two documents to be signed at the summit under the heading *The Challenges of Change*: a Declaration and a list of Decisions.[3]

Here are a few points from the two long documents.

DOI: 10.4324/9781003146124-26

Declaration

"The CSCE has been instrumental in promoting changes; now it must adapt to the task of managing them. Our decisions in Helsinki are making the CSCE more operational and effective". (para. 18)

"We... have returned to the birthplace of the Helsinki process, to give new impetus to our common endeavour". (para. 1) "The Charter of Paris... set forth guidelines for... a community of free and democratic States from Vancouver to Vladivostok". (para. 2.) "We reaffirm the... guiding principles and common values of the Helsinki Final Act and the Charter of Paris". (para. 7.)

The Declaration then made a special point of endorsing the right to monitor the internal affairs of participating States. This had been implicit in the Final Act and explicit in the follow-up meetings in Belgrade, Madrid and Vienna, but was consistently disputed by the Soviet Union. It continued to be disputed or ignored by successive Russian governments complaining about "interference" in their internal affairs.

To make it clear above all doubt that this was out of order, the Declaration stated:

> We reaffirm the validity of the guiding principles and common values of the Helsinki Final Act and the Charter of Paris, embodying responsibilities of States towards each other and of governments towards their people. These are the collective conscience of our community. We recognize our accountability to each other for complying with them. We underline the democratic rights of citizens to demand from their governments respect for these values and standards.
>
> (para. 7)

> We emphasize that the commitments undertaken in the field of the human dimension of the CSCE are matters of direct and legitimate concern to all participating States and do not belong exclusively to the internal affairs of the State concerned. The protection and promotion of human rights and fundamental freedoms and the strengthening of democratic institutions continue to be a vital basis for our comprehensive security.
>
> (para. 8)

Decisions

- Meetings of heads of state or government are to take place every two years to coincide with review conferences, which are to be managed by the Committee of Senior Officials (CSO). The review conferences will cover the entire range of activities. In between these meetings, the CSO will act as the Council's agent.

- "Ad hoc steering groups may be established on a case-by-case basis in order to... assist the Chairman-in-Office, in particular in the field of conflict prevention, crisis management and dispute resolution".
- Minorities: The Council will appoint a High Commissioner on National Minorities who will be an "eminent international personality with long-standing relevant experience", mandated to provide early warning and appropriate action to avert conflict.
- Early Warning, Conflict Prevention and Crisis Management: States will "strengthen the structure of their political consultations and increase their frequency..., to provide for...better early warning and dispute settlement", and to "enhance their capability to identify the root causes of tension through a more rigorous review of implementation... Fact-finding and rapporteur missions can be used as an instrument (*sic*) of conflict prevention and crisis management".
- Peacekeeping to complement the political process of dispute resolution may involve civilian and/or military personnel in monitoring ceasefires, troop withdrawals, maintenance of law and order, and providing humanitarian aid, but will not engage in enforcement action and will require the consent of the parties directly concerned. The CSCE can request the help of the EC, NATO and the WEU in peacekeeping activities.
- Peaceful settlement of disputes is a "cornerstone of the CSCE process". A meeting of experts is to be held in Geneva in October 1992 to negotiate a coherent set of measures that will "take into account the ideas expressed regarding procedures for a compulsory element in conciliation, setting up a court of conciliation and arbitration within the CSCE". (The Geneva results were then integrated into the Stockholm Ministerial Council Document in December 14–15 (q.v.).)
- "The CSCE is a regional arrangement in the sense of Chapter VIII of the Charter of the United Nations [about the peaceful settlement of local disputes] and as such provides an important link between European and global security".
- Arms control: Start new negotiations on arms control, disarmament and Confidence- and Security-Building Measures. Establish a new CSCE Forum for Security Cooperation. Aim at "new security relations based upon co-operative and common approaches to security". A global exchange of military information.
- The Human Dimension: "Broaden the operational framework of the CSCE, including by further enhancing the ODIHR [Office for Democratic Institutions and Human Rights] so that information, ideas and concerns can be exchanged in a more concrete and meaningful way, including as an early warning of tension and potential conflict... Keep the strengthening of the Human Dimension under constant consideration". Meetings at expert level to review implementation.
- Seminars on free media.
- Intensify economic cooperation. Support for states making the transition to market economics. Economic Forum to be created.

- Intensify environmental cooperation.
- Support recently admitted states with diplomatic, legal and administrative advice.

Despite all this activity and a plenitude of good intentions over two years, the CSCE failed to fulfil the hopes of Gorbachev and many others that it could replace NATO and the Warsaw Pact as a pan-European security organisation including Russia. Instead, the Warsaw Pact collapsed, Russia fell into disorder, and NATO gradually filled the void by taking in the states of Eastern Europe, leaving Russia to nurse a lasting sense of grievance that developed into open hostility. Debates continue to this day on whether an opportunity was missed to include Russia in a new pan-European security system. We address this debate in the next chapter.

Notes

1 For a very detailed account of these negotiations see Heraclides, *Helsinki-II and its Aftermath*.
2 CSCE, *Helsinki Document 1992: the Challenges of Change*, OSCE, viewed 28 January 2022, https://www.osce.org/files/f/documents/7/c/39530.pdf. Also in Heraclides, Appendix.
3 See Note 2.

Part V

Where to now?

22 Was an Opportunity Missed?

Was an Opportunity Missed?

President Putin's savage attack on Ukraine in February 2022 reignited debates over two related questions: was it wrong to expand NATO into Eastern Europe and the Baltic states after the Cold War, thereby, it is sometimes argued, provoking Putin? And was an opportunity missed to set up a new pan-European security system that would have included Russia, enabling it to feel less isolated and threatened? If the answer to both questions is yes, then a case can be made for loading some of the blame for Putin's war on misjudgements by the West.[1] The following is an attempt to assess that case.

There were certainly plenty of warnings at the time. In June 1997 50 former US senators, cabinet secretaries, ambassadors, and arms control and foreign specialists wrote an open letter to President Clinton saying that "the current US-led effort to expand NATO is a policy error of historic importance". They gave a series of reasons, among them that it would be deeply resented in Russia, galvanise resistance in the Russian parliament and be opposed across the whole political spectrum in Russia.[2]

In the same year, George Kennan, the veteran US diplomat who is credited with shaping US policy in the Cold War with his famous "long telegram" from Moscow in 1946, wrote in the *New York Times*: "Expanding NATO would be the most fateful error of American policy in the entire post-cold war era. Such a decision may be expected to inflame the nationalist, anti-Western and militaristic tendencies in Russian opinion; to have an adverse effect on the development of Russian democracy; to restore the atmosphere of the cold war in East–West relations and to impel Russian policy in directions decidedly not to our liking".[3] He died in 2005 but one can imagine his ghost now muttering "I told you so, I did warn you".

The first question, then, is how and why did NATO expand? We have to go back a bit. When the Cold War ended and the Soviet empire collapsed it left both sides floundering in search of ways to cope with the newly liberated states of Eastern Europe and, in particular, newly united Germany, which aroused anxiety on all sides. Ideas proliferated. In those euphoric days Russia seemed to be heading towards joining Europe as a liberal democracy. If that had happened, NATO might have become irrelevant or been transformed

DOI: 10.4324/9781003146124-28

into a pan-European security alliance. Mikhail Gorbachev, who led the Soviet Union from 1985, was clear that he wanted the Soviet Union to join what he called the "common European home".[4] This had been the dream of Russian Westernisers since far back in Russian history, especially since the nineteenth century, when Slavophiles and Westernisers argued over whether Russia was a European or Asiatic country. Gorbachev was a frank Westerniser. His spokesman, Andrei Grachev, described him as inspired by an almost religious faith in the feasibility of finally bridging the "chasm that separated… the 'lost world' of the USSR from the rest of civilisation".[5]

In his vision the two military and economic blocs would first cooperate and then gradually dissolve, giving way to a new but as yet ill-defined European security structure, including Russia and the United States. He and West German Chancellor Helmut Kohl agreed on 13 June 1989 "to build a Europe of peace and cooperation…, a European order, the Common European Home, where the United States and Canada will have their place".[6] President Mitterrand of France pressed for a revised version of the old Gaullist idea of a united Europe from the Atlantic to the Urals without the United States, but that was killed by the new leaders of Eastern Europe, who did not want any new system that left them exposed to Russian influence without the counterbalance of an American presence in Europe.

East German dissidents, who entered the government of East Germany shortly before it disappeared, wanted a neutral Germany in a nuclear-free zone in central Europe, as did many Social Democrats and others in East and West.[7] Neutrality for Germany was indeed much discussed, as it had been after World War II, but there were fears that such a large and powerful country would become a contested space and eventually chafe at the restrictions and throw them off, as Hitler had done. No matter how peaceful and democratic West Germany had become, memories of two world wars were still raw.

All these ideas for the future of Europe were overtaken by the rush of events in 1989–91, three of the most astonishing years in European history, when all the communist regimes of Eastern Europe collapsed after Gorbachev withdrew Soviet protection.[8] As his colleague and diarist Anatoly Chernyaev recalled, "Gorbachev thought that bringing freedom to our Eastern [European] satellites would lead them to adopt a socialism with a human face. He made an enormous mistake because these countries brutally turned their back on us".[9] Which was really not surprising after what they had suffered for 45 years under Russian rule.

Crucial was East Germany's first free election in March 1990, which gave a large majority to parties that promised rapid merger with West Germany. Reunification of Germany became unstoppable and duly took place on 3 October 1990 after Kohl, pressed by Mitterrand, agreed to the Euro as a single European currency to bind Germany into a more integrated Europe. (Margaret Thatcher, Prime Minister of Great Britain, disgraced herself by trying to stop reunification, even appealing to Gorbachev to support her.[10] He had a better sense of history, accepting that reunification was inevitable.)

The final blow to Gorbachev's vision of a twin-pillar security system came on 31 March 1991, when the Warsaw Pact dissolved itself, leaving NATO as the sole pillar. History then lurched forward again when the Soviet Union also fell apart. Gorbachev was elbowed aside by Boris Yeltsin, who became President of Russia, leaving Gorbachev as President of the Soviet Union. At first Yeltsin thought he could create a new form of union with the 15 republics of the Soviet Union. President George H.W. Bush also hoped Ukraine would remain in the union as he feared wars would break out like those in Yugoslavia. In August 1991 he went to Kiev and gave his famous (or infamous, in the opinion of some) "Chicken Kiev" speech in which he tried to persuade the Ukrainians to stay in the union. "Freedom is not the same as independence", he told the Ukrainian Parliament, thereby giving the lie to later accusations that Washington had tried to break up the Soviet Union.[11]

A few months later Ukraine ignored his advice and declared independence after 92 per cent voted for it, even in Russian-speaking areas that Putin later claimed should belong to Russia. Merely being a Russian speaker in Ukraine did not mean wanting to live under Russian rule.

Yeltsin accepted the inevitable. On 8 December 1991 he met the leaders of Ukraine and Belarus at a hunting lodge in Belarus, where the three of them decided to break from the Soviet Union. They phoned Gorbachev afterwards to let him know, having already told Bush. Gorbachev's power drained away rapidly until 25 December, when he announced his resignation, effectively ending the existence of the Soviet Union.

Thus, in just a few short years of turmoil, the vast edifice of the Soviet Union and its empire had fallen apart, leaving everyone scrambling to adjust.

It was in this period that the seeds of today's disputes were sown. Gorbachev's agreement was needed for Germany to reunite. As one of the four occupying powers after the war the Soviet Union still had a huge military presence in East Germany and residual powers over the whole of Germany pending a peace treaty. No treaty had been signed because there was no all-German government with which to sign it. In fact, a peace treaty was not signed until 1990. Gorbachev was persuaded to agree by two inducements: lots of money, mainly from West Germany, plus what he believed were promises that NATO would not expand eastwards. He was also reminded that the Helsinki Final Act of 1975 gave signatories the right to choose their alliances. The money largely disappeared. In 1991 Gorbachev complained to James Baker, US Secretary of State: "Things disappear around here. We got a lot of money for German reunification, and when I called our people I was told they didn't know where it was..., nobody knows".[12]

As for the alleged promises that NATO would not expand, they too dissolved, spawning a story of betrayal that Putin vigorously exploited. Yet Gorbachev never received a formal written promise, nor any agreement in writing. Mary Sarotte, who has written two brilliant books on the subject, has looked closely at the records and found a story of muddle, misunderstandings and divided opinions in Washington, Moscow, Bonn and East Berlin.[13]

Baker and Chancellor Kohl were desperate for Gorbachev's agreement to German reunification, so they gave him verbal assurances that NATO would not expand eastwards. As Baker put the now much-quoted question to Gorbachev: "Would you prefer to see a unified Germany outside of NATO, independent and with no US forces, or would you prefer a unified Germany to be tied to NATO with assurances that NATO's jurisdiction would not shift one inch eastward from its present position?".[14]

To such a loaded question Gorbachev could give only one answer, especially as Baker added that Germany unbound might acquire its own nuclear weapons. Gorbachev also received what has been described as a "cascade of assurances" from other European leaders.[15] But back in Washington the National Security staff objected that Germany could not be half in and half out of NATO, so President Bush overruled Baker and insisted that a unified Germany must remain within NATO for the sake of European stability. This also left the door open to further enlargement into Eastern Europe.

The Americans could later claim that they had made no written promises on NATO expansion, and none with the authority of the President, while Gorbachev remained convinced that he had, in fact, received binding verbal assurances. Unsurprisingly, the issue continues to rankle with Russians.

When Bill Clinton became president of the United States in January 1993 the situation had changed. Russia no longer seemed set on a steady course to democracy. Gorbachev's "new thinking" had always had shallow roots in the Russian apparatus. He had now been replaced by Boris Yeltsin, who tried to follow in Gorbachev's footsteps by promoting democracy and market reforms but mismanaged the process so badly that the result was chaos, suffering, and public disillusion with democracy. Out of this emerged the "kleptocracy" run largely by former members of the KGB and very rich oligarchs. They had acquired state assets, particularly in oil and gas, at ridiculously low prices, paving the way for Vladimir Putin to become President in 2000 with a promise not to prosecute the Yeltsin family.[16]

Clinton saw no reason to be bound by verbal assurances given under very different circumstances. However, he wavered, caught in a difficult dilemma. On the one hand he did not want to weaken Yeltsin by pushing NATO enlargement and thereby enraging Yeltsin's opponents. He was fully aware of mounting opposition to Yeltsin, whom he described as "up to his ass in alligators" and badly in need of support.[17] On the other hand, he was under pressure from the Eastern Europeans, initially mainly Poland, the Czech Republic and Hungary, to join NATO as soon as possible. They had been under Soviet rule for 45 years and saw the alliance not only as a guarantor against a future resurgent Russia but also as one of their tickets to rejoining democratic Europe, from which they had been separated for too long.

Clinton did not see expanding NATO as an anti-Russian move but as contributing to European security by avoiding a grey area in which nationalist conflicts could break out. Europe's long history of wars was seen as a warning. Madeleine Albright, Clinton's Secretary of State, told her counterpart in

Moscow, Yevgeny Primakov: "You should regard NATO enlargement as a way to assure stability in Central Europe. That is in Russia's interest".[18] Primakov was not impressed. The mental adjustment required to see the old enemy as a friend was just too much for him and many Russians.

Clinton made a series of efforts to reassure the Russians. In January 1994, he set up the Partnership for Peace (PfP). This was intended to avoid drawing a sharp line across Europe by allowing potential members of NATO to gain experience of working with the West and building Western institutions before earning the full protection of NATO. It was open to all post-Soviet states, including Russia and Ukraine. Clinton enthused to Yeltsin: "We have the first chance ever since the rise of the nation state to have the entire continent of Europe live in peace".[19]

However, the PfP was allowed to lapse after Yeltsin launched a brutal war against separatists in Chechnya in 1994, leading East European states to argue that they could be next, and should therefore become full members quickly. Clinton also came under pressure after Republicans took the Senate and House of Representatives in the mid-term elections of 1994. They urged rapid NATO enlargement, driven partly by the electoral power of the large diaspora of East Europeans in the United States. There were 20 million Americans of Eastern European descent living in 14 states that accounted for close to 40 per cent of the Electoral College.[20]

Long discussions in Washington and among allies meant that it was not until March 1999 that the Czech Republic, Hungary and Poland joined NATO. They were quickly followed by Estonia, Latvia and Lithuania. The Russians had made their objections clear but Yeltsin was in too weak a position to do anything, so resentment simmered on.

Meanwhile a further attempt to draw Russia into European security had been made in December 1994, when the "Budapest Memorandum on Security Assurances" was signed by Ukraine, Russia, the United States and Britain. It gave Ukraine "assurances" (but no guarantees) of territorial integrity in return for giving up the vast nuclear arsenal it had inherited from the Soviet Union.[21] The Ukrainians had no illusions that the Russians would live up to the agreement.[22] They were proved tragically right in 2014, when Putin seized Crimea and invaded eastern Ukraine, and again when he attacked Ukraine in 2022.

As Russian complaints mounted, so did worries in Western capitals, so another attempt to meet Russian concerns was made on 27 May 1997, when NATO and Russia signed the NATO–Russia Founding Act.[23] This remarkable document was supposed to open a wholly new chapter in Russia's relations with the West. The two former adversaries undertook to "build together a lasting and inclusive peace in the Euro-Atlantic area on the principles of democracy and cooperative security. NATO and Russia do not consider each other as adversaries. They share the goal of overcoming the vestiges of earlier confrontation and competition and of strengthening mutual trust and cooperation… to build a stable, peaceful and undivided Europe, whole and free, to the benefit of all its peoples".

This document also contained a clause respecting the right of all states to "choose the means to ensure their own security", so the door was left open to further NATO enlargement. Yeltsin had to be bribed with the promise of a substantial aid package to agree to those terms. Clinton marveled that he did so "into the teeth of ferocious opposition from Russian authoritarians back home".[24]

In the same document NATO stated that it had "undertaken a historic transformation", revising its strategic doctrine and radically reducing its conventional and nuclear forces, emphasising its role as a political alliance open to cooperation with Russia. To help put all this into effect the two sides set up the NATO–Russia Permanent Joint Council "to build trust and habits of consultation and cooperation". Russia was invited to maintain a permanent mission in NATO headquarters in Brussels headed by a person of ambassadorial rank.

The signatories also promised to strengthen the OSCE and enhance its operational capabilities "as a primary instrument in conflict prevention, crisis management, post-conflict rehabilitation and regional security cooperation… The OSCE, as the only pan-European security organization, has a key role in European peace and stability". At its Istanbul Summit in November 1999 all participants signed the OSCE's Charter for European Security, in which they solemnly pledged to "contribute to the formation of a common and indivisible security space".[25]

Nevertheless, relations with Russia soon began to deteriorate. Already the wars in Yugoslavia, which started in 1991, had been a source of tension because Russia chose to support the murderous regime of Slobodan Milošević out of misplaced loyalty to the Serbs, who had started a vicious war and committed numerous atrocities.

In 1999 the Serbs were slaughtering Albanians, so NATO bombed Serbia, including Belgrade, without UN approval or Russian consent, which would certainly have been refused: "Russia will never agree to air strikes against the Serbs", said the Russian Foreign Minister.[26] Russia was affronted by this attack on its Serbian brothers, whose atrocities it seemed to consider irrelevant, but it eventually pressed Milošević to withdraw his forces. It was left, however, with a sense of humiliation at NATO's failure to respect its views, despite the promises of cooperation in the NATO–Russia Founding Act.

At the end of 1999 Putin became acting President of Russia, and then, in May 2000, president. He did not mourn the failure of communism but felt deeply about the loss of great power status. Nevertheless, he was initially friendly to the West as he cleared up the mess left by Yeltsin. In an interview with the BBC in March 2000 he said: "Russia is part of the European culture. And I cannot imagine my own country in isolation from Europe and what we often call the civilised world. So it is hard for me to visualise NATO as an enemy… We are open to equitable cooperation, to partnership. We believe we can talk about more profound integration with NATO but only if Russia is regarded as an equal partner". Asked if Russia might join NATO, Putin replied: "I don't see why not. I would not rule out such a possibility, but I repeat: if and when Russia's views are taken into account as those of an equal partner".[27]

Putin's demand for equality was his constant theme, and a measure of the humiliation he felt at Russia's loss of status as a great power. At that time Russian membership of NATO was not considered out of the question. Gorbachev and Yeltsin had suggested it, as had Malcolm Rifkind, the British Defence Secretary, in 1995, though only with associated status,[28] and US Secretary of State James Baker in 2002, provided Russia first embrace democracy and free markets.[29] It never did embrace democracy so that ruled it out of membership.

Even so, relations between Russia and the United States took an upward turn under the presidency of George W. Bush, who took office in January 2001. Putin rushed to his support when terrorists attacked the World Trade Center in New York and the Pentagon in Washington in September 2001. He approved US military bases in Central Asia and overflights to supply them, and helped in other ways to support the war against the Taliban. Visiting Bush's ranch in Texas in November he said "Today we are already prepared to seek solutions in all areas of our joint activities. We are willing to dismantle, once and for all, the legacy of the Cold War and begin fashioning a strategic partnership for the long term".[30]

Still hoping for an equal partnership with the United States, Putin went along with yet another attempt to improve relations in May 2002, when a new version of the NATO–Russia Council was announced by their foreign ministers in Reykjavik, leading to a lavish NATO–Russia summit in Rome. It was to move beyond consultation and actually take decisions: "It is not a consultative body, it's an executive body", said Igor Ivanov, Russia's Foreign Minister. "It will develop and make decisions and jointly fulfil them". Jack Straw, Britain's Foreign Secretary, was ecstatic: "There could be no bigger change… This is the last rites, the funeral of the Cold War… Fifteen years ago, Russia was the enemy, now Russia becomes our friend and ally".[31] In 2003 Putin was accorded a state visit to Britain, a major acknowledgement of his importance and a huge boost to his ego. In December 2004 Putin even declared that "if Ukraine wants to join the EU and if the EU accepts Ukraine as a member, Russia, I think, would welcome this because we have a special relationship with Ukraine".[32]

Yet clouds had already been gathering.

Putin deeply resented the American invasion of Iraq in March 2003, seeing it as evidence that the US was willing to do anything it liked without consultation or UN approval. Obviously, he concluded, rules were for little people. Then came the "colour revolutions" in Georgia in 2003, Ukraine in 2004 and Kyrgyzstan in 2005, all of which brought Western-oriented leaders to power and were seen in Moscow as fomented by the West.

Putin's pent-up frustration with being sidelined eventually exploded. In 2007 he gave vent to his deep feelings of resentment and humiliation in a bitter speech at the Munich security conference. He complained that his once-great country was not being treated with sufficient respect. He attacked the hegemony of the United States, its triumphalism, its attack on Iraq and other breaches of international law.[33]

He was also turning against the OSCE, complaining that "people are trying to transform the OSCE into a vulgar instrument designed to promote the foreign policy interests of one or a group of countries... The OSCE is designed to assist country members in observing international human rights norms at their request... This does not mean interfering in the internal affairs of other countries, and especially not imposing a regime that determines how these states should live and develop". This complaint about "interference" echoed the Soviet Union's unremitting complaints about "interference" after the signing of the Helsinki Final Act in 1975.

A critical point was reached at the NATO summit in Bucharest in April 2008. George W. Bush wanted to admit Georgia and Ukraine while France and Germany did not. The summit took no action but issued a statement that "these countries will become members of NATO".[34] Putin was furious. He warned that this would represent a direct threat to Russia. He began to act. In August 2008, after months of increasing tension, his troops invaded Georgia and set up two of its regions as separate entities.

In 2011 the "Arab Spring" broke out, sparking waves of demonstrations against corrupt and oppressive Arab regimes. Putin saw behind them the sinister influence of Western money ostensibly promoting democracy but in fact producing chaos. Next stop Moscow, he feared. His fears seemed vindicated in 2011–12, when demonstrators took to the streets in Moscow and elsewhere to protest against rigged parliamentary elections and then his own rigged return to the presidency in 2012. At one point he specifically blamed Hillary Clinton, then US Secretary of State, provoking some demonstrators to hold up mocking signs saying "Hillary, I am still waiting for my money".[35] To add to Putin's problems, the Russian economy was feeling the effects of falling oil prices and Western sanctions. Growth slowed, shortages appeared, and millions were living below the poverty line. An external enemy became increasingly useful.

Relations with the West then plunged further in 2013–14, when Putin persuaded Viktor Yanukovych, President of Ukraine, to renege on a trade association negotiated with the European Union. This sparked huge pro-European demonstrations which eventually drove Yanukovych to flee to Russia. Putin took the fall of his protégé personally. (He was particularly affronted when Ukrainians flooded into Yanukovych's monstrous luxurious palace and bought up toilet rolls and doormats carrying Yanukovych's portrait.) He responded by seizing Crimea and sending special troops without uniforms as "volunteers" to support pro-Russian secessionists in eastern Ukraine, starting a long-running conflict that cost at least 14,000 lives and exacerbated Ukrainian fears of Russia, thereby setting back any remaining hopes that Russia could be a constructive partner in finding a new status for Ukraine.

As Putin saw it, the West was trying to drag Ukraine into its orbit by luring it into the EU and NATO and giving financial and political support to street demonstrations. As the West saw it, the vast majority of Ukrainians wanted democracy and a close association with the EU, so it was legitimately supporting the will of the people against an extremely corrupt Ukrainian government that was pillaging the country.

There was also another factor at work. As Russia sank deeper into corrupt kleptocracy it became obvious that it could not meet the democratic norms required by the West for membership of NATO, nor the standards set by the Helsinki Final Act of 1975 and the Paris Charter of 1990. Putin found he needed a different set of values and an ideology to replace communism, consumerism and liberal democracy. Various Russian thinkers were invoked, notably Ivan Ilyin, a Russian émigré philosopher who had propagated the Russian school of thought known as "Eurasianism". He was born in 1883 and died in Switzerland in 1953 after being expelled by the Bolsheviks. Putin told his inner circle to read his books and had his remains brought back to Russia and reburied with full religious ceremony. While supporting Hitler and Mussolini, Ilyin opposed both Soviet communism and Western democracy, envisaging a special path for Russia based on the Orthodox Church and traditional values that would rescue Russia from the decadent influence of the West.

In a far-sighted essay in 1950 Ilyin predicted the fall of the Soviet Union and gave instructions on how to save Russia from the evils of the Western world. He became convinced that the West wanted to destroy Russia. Once it had annexed Ukraine, he wrote, it would use the territory to undermine the Russian state. Ukrainians had no right to any form of statehood. While trying to destroy Russia, the West would use the ideas of "democratisation", "federalisation" and "triumph of freedom" against Russia in order to weaken it and rob it. Democracy, he argued, was impossible in such a huge country. It needed a "national dictatorship" to unite its geographic, ethnic, and cultural diversity. The alternative was chaos.[36]

Putin often echoes those words almost exactly. Over time he established a clear narrative pumped out continuously by the Russian media at home and abroad. According to this, the Russian people were deceived by Western promises of democracy, which had brought only poverty and humiliation (unfortunately true). The West, he said, took advantage of Russia's weakness at the end of the Cold War to expand NATO and break up the Soviet Union. Its support for democracy was merely a cover for attempts to subvert Russia, detach Ukraine, and undermine many other countries, including some in the Middle East. What the United States claimed as universal values were, in fact, American values that it tried to foist on others. Russia had different values and should be proud of them. Russia stood for a strong state, patriotism, family, community and religious faith, in contrast to Western individualism, inequality, decadence and homosexuality. His familiar theme is the arrogance of America, its claim to exceptionalism and its misguided support for "so-called democracy". For him, demonstrations are not valid expressions of popular will but threats to legitimate authority financed by Western powers under the guise of promoting democracy. The West in all its forms—military, economic, political—must therefore be regarded as hostile to Russia.

So, is the West to blame for Putin's war?

The essence of the case against the West is that, after the break-up of the Soviet empire, it failed to appreciate the need to bring Russia into a new European security structure. It should have had a better understanding of Russian history, Russian fears, and the deep humiliation that Russians felt after seeing more than 70 years of communism discredited and their East European empire, for which so many of their soldiers had died, abandoned.

There are two main replies to that case. First, as we have seen, President Clinton and others made very strenuous efforts to bring Russia into a close and more trusting relationship with NATO. Secondly, when the Cold War ended it was difficult to see a safe, viable alternative to expanding NATO beyond extending the Partnership for Peace, which was explicitly intended to be temporary. It was a time of great hope but also great anxiety. Two world wars and the Cold War within the space of 75 years had left Europe with deep scars and fears and many open questions. Would the oppressed states of Eastern Europe opt for nationalism or even fight each other when released from Soviet captivity? Would the model democracy built up by West Germany survive unification with East Germany, which had had no experience of democracy since 1933? Would Russia itself remain benign? In 1991, even under nice Mr Gorbachev, though not on his orders, Soviet troops killed a number of people seeking independence for Lithuania. Later that same year the old guard in Moscow tried to remove him. What if another attempt succeeded? In 1993 Boris Yeltsin faced a crisis that ended with him shelling his own parliament. His position remained fragile as his drinking increased and his health deteriorated. In 1998 Russia defaulted on its debt. Could it ever be a reliable partner in any sort of a new European security system? Conflicts simmered or broke out not only in Yugoslavia but also in Moldova, Azerbaijan, Georgia, Tajikistan and Nagorno Karabakh.

Not surprisingly, it did not seem to many Western leaders an appropriate time to experiment with some undefined new security system or neutral zones or even temporary solutions. Much safer, surely, to lock in the gains to democracy while the chance was there by expanding the tried and tested institutions of NATO and adapting them to the new situation. After all, NATO's purpose had always been not only to defend Europe against the Soviet Union but also to establish democracy in its area and prevent members fighting each other. Those latter reasons seemed more valid than ever. In due course, said the optimists, Russia would surely come to recognise that NATO was no longer a hostile military alliance but a potential partner in creating a new and more secure Europe. That turned out to be a miscalculation.

Clearly the West could have assessed Putin better. After a good beginning it had to deal with an angry and humiliated former member of the KGB, not the wise statesman it would have preferred. Putin had grown up and been trained at a time when the Soviet Union was treated as a great power with an empire stretching from central Europe to the Pacific, from the Baltic to the Black Sea. Before that the Tsars had ruled a large empire that earned Russia recognition as a major power in Europe. Under Stalin the Soviet Union, after first being allied with Hitler, had won a devastating war against Germany in which it lost some 27 million of its citizens. At the same time it gained an empire in Eastern Europe to protect it against any new Napoleons or Hitlers who might wish to invade. It had then joined the other victorious powers in controlling occupied Germany. Under Brezhnev, it had achieved nuclear parity with the United States and found itself at the top table negotiating on seemingly equal terms, a matter of huge pride to the Russians. At the same time it was the leading centre of an ideology that promised to prevail around the world in accordance with the supposedly scientific laws of history.

Now Putin found himself in charge of a greatly shrunken realm, its armed forces reduced and demoralised, its economy in a mess, its empire gone, and its ideology discredited. This hurt his pride. If he had been a more mature statesman, he might have accepted the reality of Russia's reduced status for the time being and worked to build respect as a constructive partner in the new Europe while improving the lot of his people. He could have recognised NATO's positive role in European security and seen that it was in Russia's interest for the alliance to contain a reunified Germany. He could have grasped the hand that the West reached out by building on the Partnership for Peace and the NATO–Russia Founding Act to develop a more trusting relationship.

Instead, his personal feelings of anger and humiliation took over, and he found that confrontation won him support at home. It was much easier for him to tap into popular feelings of humiliation, resentment and traditional suspicion of the West than to persuade Russians to see themselves as a defeated nation taking lessons in democracy from the victors. Thus NATO became once again the useful enemy against which he could rally support. He had grown up with it and been trained to defend the Soviet Union against the threat that it allegedly posed. He was returning to his comfort zone.

He also came to believe that Russia was not ready for democracy, which was anyway obsolete in his view. As he told the *Financial Times* in 2019, "liberal democracy has outlived its purpose".[37] While neglecting reform at home he embarked on a massive military build-up, repeating the mistakes of the Soviet Union by attempting to "make Russia great again" by means of military strength.[38] Instead of earning him respect, this scared the people of Eastern Europe and provoked the West to rearm: a major tragedy for Europe. His attack on Ukraine in 2022 even caused Germany to increase its defence budget and abandon the semi-pacifist stance it had adopted since 1945, thereby bringing about exactly what Russia had most feared and what all post-war arrangements had been designed to avoid. At the same time neutral Finland and Sweden began seriously planning to join NATO.

Would different policies by the West have avoided this? It is certainly true that NATO's declaration in 2008 of future membership for Ukraine and Georgia was a step too far at that moment, a provocative move pushed by President George W. Bush. A fuzzier stance would have been wiser. Bush failed to appreciate the deep historical and religious roots of Russia's relationship with Ukraine and its strategic importance on the invasion route from the West. Russians trace the origins of their state and religion back to the ancient kingdom of Kievan Rus', founded in 882, which in 988 converted to the Christianity of the Eastern Orthodox Church under the authority of Byzantium.

Yet few Ukrainians share Moscow's view that they belong together. Although they share this common ancestry with Russia and Belarus, Ukraine developed its own language and identity through the subsequent centuries of its complex history under a variety of empires and rulers, even after it was taken into the Soviet Union in 1922. Stalin was always afraid of Ukrainian nationalism. In the 1930s he devastated Ukraine, killing three to four million by deliberate starvation and deporting 76,000 of its people to prison camps.[39] That left a legacy of strong anti-Russian feeling that was reflected in the 92 per cent vote for independence in 1991. Putin's attempt to brand Ukrainians as Nazis goes back to World War II, when a Ukrainian insurgent army under Stephan Bandera collaborated with the Nazis. Bandera is still revered by right-wing groups, but in the 2019 parliamentary election these groups failed to win even one seat, while in the presidential election Volodymyr Zelensky, a Russian-speaking Jew, was elected with 73 per cent of the vote.

Yet Putin persisted in denying Ukraine's right to a separate identity. "We are one people", he repeated constantly, referring also to "spiritual unity". His war took on the nature of a holy war to reunite old Russia. It was blessed by the Russian Orthodox Church, from which the Ukrainian Orthodox Church had split in 2018. One can assume that Putin's views were accurately reflected in a chilling article in RIA Novosti, the Russian state news agency, in April 2022: "Ukrainians are an artificial anti-Russian construct. They should no longer have a national identity. Denazification of Ukraine also means its inevitable de-Europeanization… Ukraine's political elite must be eliminated as it cannot be re-educated".[40]

That mention of "Europeanization" highlights another aspect of Putin's thinking. It was not only NATO that worried him. Indeed, NATO may have been partly an excuse to conceal his fear of Ukraine becoming a prosperous Western democracy, no matter how distant that prospect might seem, because Russians would then start asking for the same future. That is why, instead of putting forward constructive proposals for Ukraine, his response to the massive demonstrations in Kyiv in 2013–14 was to support the extremely corrupt and unpopular regime of Viktor Yanukovych, which only exacerbated the situation and strengthened anti-Russian feeling.

Where does that leave the arguments over NATO expansion? Mary Sarotte makes a strong point when she argues that it was a reasonable policy but the problem was how it happened. In her view Clinton should have made more effort to maintain the Partnership for Peace because that would have avoided drawing a line across Europe too quickly and provided a "grey space" for Ukraine and a role for Russia while the habit of cooperation with NATO developed.[41]

The counter-argument is that Russian resentment and fear of NATO enlargement would have grown anyway as Gorbachev's pro-Western legacy was abandoned. For how long would Putin have been comfortable with the uncertainties of a grey area on his borders, especially as Ukraine was straining to turn westwards? Even if the PfP solution had proved durable, decisions would have had to be made at some point.

If NATO had not expanded, was an opportunity missed to construct a new pan-European security system? At the start of the transition in 1989–1991 great hopes were placed on the CSCE as the potential basis for such a system. It had proved itself over 15 years as a valuable forum for negotiating through difficult times across the divide between East and West. When it transformed itself into the OSCE (see Chapter 23), it seemed uniquely placed to knit the old continent together again as the only pan-European body that also included the United States and Russia. Membership increased from the original 35 to 57 as it took in the liberated states of Eastern Europe and reconstituted states that had been within the Soviet Union itself.[42] All signed up with very varying levels of conviction to the commitments of the Final Act of 1975, the Paris Declaration of 1990 (see Chapter 20), and the "Helsinki-II" declaration of 1992 (see Chapter 21), so its mission remained essentially the same: to work for a just and stable order in Europe by promoting security and cooperation in the broadest sense across all three baskets of the Final Act: political/military, economic, and humanitarian. That meant—and still means—promoting human rights, reinforcing democratic institutions and market economies, observing elections, developing Confidence-Building Measures, and establishing procedures for settling or monitoring disputes.

Yet its potential for a new role gradually dwindled. James Baker had already dismissed it at a meeting in Moscow on 18 May 1990, when he told Gorbachev: "It's nice to talk about pan-European security structures, the role of the CSCE. It's a wonderful dream, but just a dream. In the meantime, NATO exists and participation in NATO will mean that Germany will continue to rely on this alliance to ensure its security".[43] Then, as we have seen, Putin gradually turned against the OSCE. By 2022 he presumably no longer cared that his attack on Ukraine delivered a shocking blow to the organisation, challenging its most basic principles and possibly threatening its very future, though not immediately destroying its future potential as a negotiating forum, mediator, monitor and supplier of field missions.

Whether, at some point along the line, it missed an opportunity to replace NATO remains an open question, but the evidence suggests that it did not. At no point did anyone on either side describe a system that would have worked, given the gulf between the perceptions of the two sides, the still vivid memories of war, the lingering suspicions of the Cold War, and the profound reluctance of the East Europeans to allow Russia a say in their affairs, especially as Russia retreated from democracy. Even in retrospect it is difficult to envisage such a system functioning in the prevailing conditions of the time. As Robert Legvold has written: "Neither side ever truly tried to build the comprehensive, integrated European security system that their vaulted rhetoric promised at the end of the Cold War… Russia bears equal responsibility for the failure of what could and should have been. No version of Europe whole and secure was or is possible unless Russia's neighbours are comfortable in its shadow… Had Russia from the beginning invested heavily in softening the hardened views of Eastern Europeans and the new post-Soviet states and laboured earlier to build a constructive, respectful relationship with them, the pressure to enlarge NATO would have been less".[44]

Let us not forget, too, that during the long transition from communism the West was responding to public opinion. In Ukraine, there was strong pressure to join or become associated with the EU, and warm popular support for the West's efforts to assist it towards democracy. In Eastern Europe, too, most people, after a brief period of being attracted by neutrality, also wanted to join both NATO and the EU. They did not trust Russia and did not want to belong to any organisation that appeared to give it a say in their affairs. For how long could the West have ignored the wishes of the people of Eastern Europe, betraying its own values and losing their confidence? Realpolitik may sometimes demand that public opinion be ignored but the Cold War showed that a security system built on that basis was neither just nor stable.

Looking back, the West could certainly have moved more slowly, but in the end Putin made choices. He chose to declare NATO a threat although it was not, to break numerous agreements, to violate most of the Helsinki principles, to attack Georgia, to spend vast sums on rebuilding Russia's military strength against an imaginary threat, to defy the wishes of the Ukrainian people and invade their country at the cost of many thousands of lives, to attempt subversion of the Baltic states, to murder or attempt to murder "traitors" abroad, to support war criminals in former Yugoslavia and Syria, to seek to influence American elections and to flood the world with misinformation. Those were his choices. They were not forced on him by the West. Nor can they be excused by reference to Western mistakes. He could have made wiser choices that would have served Russia better in the long run. He is not the first politician to put his own power ahead of statesmanship, but there is no reason for the West to take all the blame.

Notes

1 Cogently argued by, among others, Michael McGuire, 'Nato expansion: a policy error of historic importance' in *Review of International Studies* 24, 1998, reprinted in *International Affairs* (Chatham House) 84/6 November 2008, p.1282 with introduction by Michael Clarke, p. 1281; Laurien Crump, 'A Missed Opportunity for a New Europe?' in Braat and Corduwener eds., *1989 and the West: Western Europe Since the End of the Cold War*; John Mearsheimer 'Why the Ukrainian Crisis is the West's Fault' in *Foreign Affairs* September/October 2014, 77–89. For a balanced assessment apportioning blame to both sides see Robert Legvold's extended essay *Return to the Cold War*. See also Richard Sakwa, *The Putin Paradox*.

2 Open letter to President Clinton in 1977 by 55 former officials, diplomats and other experts, quoted by Michael McGuire (see Note 1 above).

3 George Kennan, "A Fateful Error". *New York Times*, 5 February 1997.

4 Most fully expressed in his address to the Council of Europe on 6 July 1989. https://www.cvce.eu › publication › publishable_en.

5 Grachev, *Final Days*, 25.

6 Rey, '"Europe is our Common Home": A study of Gorbachev's diplomatic concept', in *Cold War History*, 4/2 (2004), 34.
7 Sarotte, *1989*, 198.
8 See Chapter 19 and a brilliant account of that year by Levésque, *The Enigma of 1989*. See also Garton Ash, *The Magic Lantern: The Revolution of '89*, and Spohr, *Post Wall, Post Square*.
9 Quoted by Rey in Bozo et al., *Europe and the end of the Cold War*, 32. Chernyaev was principal foreign policy adviser to Gorbachev. He kept a diary that became a valuable resource for historians.
10 https://www.margaretthatcher.org/document/112005
11 Plokhy and Sarotte 'The shoals of Ukraine' in *Foreign Affairs*, January/February 2020, 81.
12 Sarotte, *1989*, 212.
13 Sarotte, *1989* and *Not One Inch*.
14 Sarotte, *1989*,111, and *Not One Inch, 1*, and in *Foreign Affairs*, September/October 2014, 92. For a graphic insiders' account of decision-making in that period see also Zelikow and Rice, *To Build a Better World*.
15 Savranskaya and Blanton, 'Nato Expansion: What Gorbachev Heard'. National Security Archive 12 December 2017, viewed 28 January 2022, https://nsarchive.gwu.edu/briefing-book/russia-programs/2017-12-12/nato-expansion-what-gorbachev-heard-western-leaders-early
16 Belton, *Putin's people*, passim.
17 Legvold, 98.
18 Albright, *Madam Secretary*, 255. See also Legvold, 99.
19 Plokhy and Sarotte, 'The Shoals of Ukraine', 87.
20 Sarotte, *Not One Inch*, 227 quoting Steil, 389.
21 United Nations, 'Memorandum on Security Assurances', 19 December 1994, viewed 28 January 2022, https://www.securitycouncilreport.org/atf/cf/%7B65BFCF9B-6D27-4E9C-8CD3-CF6E4FF96FF9%7D/s_1994_1399.pdf
22 Plokhy and Sarotte, see Note 19.
23 'Founding Act on Mutual Relations, Cooperation and Security between NATO and the Russian Federation', 27 May 1997, viewed 28 January 2022, https://www.nato.int/cps/en/natohq/official_texts_25468.htm
24 Sarotte, *Not One Inch*, 270.
25 OSCE, 1999, *Istanbul Summit* (2000), viewed 13 January 2022, https://www.osce.org/files/f/documents/6/5/39569.pdf, §1.
26 Albright, 309.
27 Vladimir Putin, in 'BBC Breakfast with Frost', 5 March 2000, viewed 28 January 2022, http://en.kremlin.ru/events/president/transcripts/24194
28 *The Times* (London) 31 December 2019, quoting British National Archives.
29 *Washington Quarterly*, Winter 2002, 95–103, quoted in Sarotte, *1989*, 205.
30 Quoted in Legvold, 103, from joint press conference with Bush, 13 November.
31 *The Guardian* (London), 15 May 2002.
32 Vladimir Putin, Press Conference following talks with Spanish Prime Minister Jose Luis Rodriguez Zapatero, 10 December 2004, viewed 28 January 2022, http://en.kremlin.ru/events/president/transcripts/22742
33 Vladimir Putin, 'Speech and the Following Discussion at the Munich Conference on Security Policy', 10 February 2007, viewed 12 February 2022, http://en.kremlin.ru/events/president/transcripts/24034
34 Bucharest Summit Declaration', para. 23, NATO, 3 April 2008, viewed 28 January 2022, https://www.nato.int/cps/en/natohq/official_texts_8443.htm?selectedLocale=en
35 Observed on television.
36 Barbashin and Thoburn 'Ivan Ilyin and the ideology of Moscow's rule' in *Foreign Affairs*, September 2015. See also T Snyder, *The Road to Unfreedom*.
37 *The Financial Times*, 27 June 2019.

38 Sam Perlo-Freeman, 21 November 2016, '65 Years of Military Spending', SIPRI, viewed 28 January 2022, https://www.sipri.org/commentary/blog/2016/65-years-military-spending. Russian spending on defence rose by 175 per cent between 2000 and 2019; see Siemon T. Wezeman, 27 April 2020, 'Russia's Military Spending: frequently asked questions', https://www.sipri.org/commentary/topical-backgrounder/2020/russias-military-spending-frequently-asked-questions, viewed 27 February 2022.

39 Applebaum, *Red Famine*, passim. See also Snyder, *The Road to Unfreedom*, 111–112.

40 Quoted by Roger Boyes in *The Times* (London), 6 April 2022, page 28.

41 Sarotte, 'Containment beyond the Cold War', *Foreign Affairs*, November/December 2021. Her argument is developed in detail in her very impressive more recent book, *Not One Inch*.

42 Among them the three Baltic states (Latvia, Estonia and Lithuania), the five former Soviet republics in Central Asia (Kazakhstan, Kyrgyzstan, Tajikistan and Uzbekistan), and Georgia and Armenia.

43 US National Security Archive. Record of conversation between Mikhail Gorbachev and James Baker in Moscow. Document 18 published 11 December 2017. See https://nsarchive.gwu.edu/document/16132-document-18-record-conversation-between, viewed 12 February 2022.

44 Legvold, 99–100.

23 The OSCE

More members, same tasks, rough road

When the Cold War ended the CSCE could have dwindled into irrelevance or closed down. Its original missions appeared to have been largely accomplished in so far as its values and principles had been accepted by the former Soviet bloc, at least on paper, and Eastern Europe had been liberated. Yet, instead of packing its bags, it reinvented itself to become the largest regional security organisation in the world. With 57 members,[1] it covers an area from the western edge of Alaska around the globe to the eastern edge of Russia, nearly meeting across the Bering Sea, taking in all the original European members plus the Baltic states[2] as well as the five Central Asian Republics[3] that were part of the Soviet Union, plus even Mongolia as the latest addition. (Its extent is normally but slightly inaccurately described as "Vancouver to Vladivostok".) It is unique in bringing together Russia and the United States in a pan-European framework.[4] True to the original purpose of the Final Act of 1975, it aims to promote cooperative security in the broadest sense, including democracy, human rights and the rule of law.

The CSCE/OSCE's vast range of activities has spread out like a giant delta from the small uncertain stream that Molotov started, with very different aims, forty years earlier. Its website[5] lists a breath-taking range of tasks under the general heading of security, its three main components being political/military, economic and humanitarian, as in the Baskets of the Helsinki Final Act. These include arms control, border management, combating human trafficking, countering terrorism, conflict prevention and resolution, cyber security, democratisation, economic activities, education, observing elections, environmental activities, gender equality, good governance, human rights, media freedom, migration, minority rights, policing, reform and cooperation in the security sector, Roma and Sinti, rule of law, tolerance, non-discrimination, and the interests of youth.

To further these aims it runs a proliferation of observation missions, practical assistance programmes, training programmes and workshops, particularly for new democracies emerging from the ruins of the Soviet empire. These produce copious reports that can be found on its website. Much of the value of the OSCE today lies in this fieldwork, which is often out of sight and unrecognised beyond those involved. In 2021 it had field missions in 15 states in South-Eastern Europe, Eastern Europe and Central Asia.

DOI: 10.4324/9781003146124-29

All participating states remain committed on paper, though not always in practice, to the principle that lasting security cannot be achieved without respect for human rights, as agreed in Principle VII of the Final Act of 1975 and reinforced by the Paris Charter of 1990 and the Helsinki-II Declaration of 1992, the last two of which also committed signatories to democracy and market economics. In both Paris and Helsinki II they also recognised the principle that the affairs of one are the affairs of all (see Chapters 20 and 21). In other words, signatories are entitled to monitor the extent to which others are implementing the accords. This essential right has come to be increasingly resented by Russia and many of the post-Soviet states that signed up in the heady days of post-Soviet optimism. They have reverted to old complaints from the time of the Cold War about "interference" in their internal affairs, mostly to hide their retreat from their commitments.

The CSCE functioned reasonably well as it entered the post-Soviet world in the 1990s. It declared itself a regional arrangement under Chapter VIII of the United Nations, which provides for member states to make regional arrangements for settling disputes. It had many missions in the field and enjoyed widespread support for its work on elections, arms control, and the removal of nuclear weapons from the post-Soviet space, notably Belarus, Kazakhstan and Ukraine.

At the 1994 summit in Budapest it changed its name to the Organization for Security and Co-operation in Europe (OSCE) to reflect its transformation from a series of conferences to a standing organisation. Demonstrating that it could now produce action as well as words, it agreed on procedures to send a multinational peace-keeping force to Nagorno-Karabakh to oversee a cease-fire, which unfortunately did not last.

However, clouds gathered early. The Budapest meeting produced 58 pages of declarations and decisions mixing optimism and pessimism.[6] To start with the optimistic part of the document: "We believe in the central role of the CSCE in building a secure and stable CSCE [now OSCE] community, whole and free. We reaffirm the principles of the Helsinki Final Act and subsequent CSCE documents. They reflect shared values which will guide our policies, individually and collectively, in all organizations and institutions to which we belong… We are determined to give a new political impetus to the CSCE, thus enabling it to play a cardinal role in meeting the challenges of the twenty-first century. The CSCE has been instrumental in overcoming barriers and in managing change throughout our region. Since we last met, there have been further encouraging developments. Most vestiges of the Cold War have disappeared. Free elections have been held and the roots of democracy have spread and struck deeper".

But now the skies darken: "Yet the path to stable democracy, efficient market economy and social justice is a hard one. The spread of freedoms has been accompanied by new conflicts and the revival of old ones. Warfare in the CSCE region to achieve hegemony and territorial expansion continues to occur. Human rights and fundamental freedoms are still flouted, intolerance persists and discrimination against minorities is practised. The plagues of aggressive nationalism, racism, chauvinism, xenophobia, anti-semitism and ethnic tension are still widespread. Along with social and economic instability, they are among the main sources of crisis, loss of life and human misery. They reflect failure to apply the CSCE principles and commitments".

As the organisation set about trying to face these challenges it clarified and strengthened its structure, which, with some modifications, has continued to this day. This is how it works:

Summit meetings of heads of state or government form the top decision-making body, although they meet very rarely. The only one since Istanbul has been in Astana in 2010. Another has been suggested for Helsinki in 2025 to mark the 50th anniversary of the signing of the Final Act.

The Chairperson-in-Office[7] is the foreign minister of one of the participating States. He or she is chosen by the Ministerial Council and holds office for one year.

Independent bodies. Five are autonomous in their operations, and therefore not subject to the consensus rule for their daily functioning. The first three, however, are dependent for their budgets on the Permanent Council, which does require consensus:

- The Office for Democratic Institutions and Human Rights (ODIHR – see Chapter 24).
- A High Commissioner on National Minorities.
- A Representative on Freedom of the Media.
- A Parliamentary Assembly.
- A Court of Conciliation and Arbitration.

The **Ministerial Council** is the central governing body. It consists of the foreign ministers of participating States and meets normally once a year towards the end of the Chairperson's term of office.

The **Permanent Council** (initially Committee) was created by the Rome Ministerial Council in 1993. It took over the residual functions of the Senior Council by a decision of the Ministerial Council in Brussels in 2006. It is the principal decision-making body for regular political consultations and for governing the day-to-day operational work of the OSCE between the meetings of the Ministerial Council. It is composed of delegates from the participating States accredited to the OSCE in Vienna on a full-time basis. The heads of these delegations have ambassadorial rank. It meets every week chaired by an ambassador designated by the Chairperson-in-Office from his or her own diplomatic service. Its main functions are to discuss topical events happening within the OSCE's region, to hear and respond to guest speakers invited by the Chair (such as high-level officials from participating States and other international organisations, institutions and initiatives), and to take decisions required for running the organisation, such as adopting and renewing mission mandates, approving budgets, adopting agendas, and setting organisational modalities for OSCE meetings.

The OSCE Secretariat in Vienna is under the direction of the **Secretary General**, whose role was strengthened in 2004. It provides operational support and assists the Chairperson by offering expertise and analysis and by drafting decisions.

There was criticism at the time that the Budapest summit did not agree a common position on the conflict in Bosnia-Herzegovina. Even if it had done so, it would not have changed the situation because it lacked instruments to enforce its will. This failure highlighted the paralysis that would have afflicted any version of the pan-European security system regularly proposed by Russia (see Chapter 22). It also showed up the importance of maintaining the operational autonomy of bodies such as the ODIHR, which would have been paralysed if the Russians had managed to bring it under the control of the Permanent Council.

By the time of the Istanbul summit in November 1999 the OSCE could still present an optimistic face, describing itself "as a primary organization for the peaceful settlement of disputes within its region and as a key instrument for early warning, conflict prevention, crisis management and post conflict rehabilitation".[8] It adopted a Charter for European Security, which set up new machinery to strengthen its ability to prevent or settle conflicts and rehabilitate societies ravaged by war. It also updated the 1990 Treaty on Conventional Forces in Europe (CFE) to move it from bloc-to-bloc limits to individual national commitments.[9] At the same time Russia agreed to withdraw its troops from Georgia and Moldova, but did not do so. NATO then refused to ratify the treaty. Russia suspended its participation in 2007 and withdrew altogether in 2015.

This was part of a general crumbling of the arms control regime in Europe, not directly linked to the OSCE but symptomatic of the deterioration of relations with Russia that also impacted on the work of the OSCE. For instance, the Open Skies Treaty exemplified the Helsinki principle of transparency. It permitted each state to conduct short-notice, unarmed reconnaissance flights over the others' entire territories to collect data on military forces and activities. It was signed in March 1992 and came into force on 1 January 2002. The United States withdrew in November 2020, and Russia withdrew in December 2021, blaming the United States. The anti-ballistic missile treaty of 1972 (ABM) barred the United States and the Soviet Union from deploying nationwide anti-missile systems, allowing just limited protection of a few sites. The idea was to stop each side building ever more missiles to overwhelm defences, leaving each so vulnerable to counter-attack that neither would risk a first strike. In other words, rely on the fear of mutual assured destruction (MAD) to avert nuclear war. The United States closed even its permitted sites in 1975 as not being worth the expense, while the Soviet Union kept its sites around Moscow. The United States withdrew from the ABM treaty in 2002.

The leaders at the Istanbul summit could not avoid qualifying their optimism, as they had done in Budapest: "Since we signed the Charter of Paris it has become more obvious that threats to our security can stem from conflicts within States as well as from conflicts between States. We have experienced conflicts which have often resulted from flagrant violations of OSCE norms and principles. We have witnessed atrocities of a kind we had thought were relegated to the past. In this decade it has become clear that all such conflicts can represent a threat to the security of all OSCE participating States".[10]

Worries increased as more and more states began to retreat from the commitments to which they signed up after the collapse of the Soviet empire. Basic principles of democracy, such as equal rights for opposition parties, free media and independence of the judiciary, were being gradually eroded.

In 2015 the OSCE Parliamentary Assembly[11] held a big conference in Helsinki for the 40th anniversary of the Final Act. It presented a melancholy report called *Helsinki+40*: "Unfortunately, the entire Decalogue of Principles has been broken during the Ukraine crisis. The damage that has been done may be irreparable and the OSCE, even if it does survive, will emerge in a greatly diminished form unless all participating States reconfirm the relevance of, and their respect for, the Helsinki Commitments and recommit to follow it not only in words but also in action". It identified "a dire need for structural reform of the OSCE" and called for more transparency, including opening the Permanent Council to press and public.[12]

Doubts about the ability of the OSCE to survive turned out to be unjustified, but five years later gloom still pervaded the 2019 annual report[13] by Thomas Greminger, Secretary-General of the OSCE, delivered in March 2020: "Last year, many complex and interrelated security challenges continued to beset our region: growing divisions within and between states; armed conflict; terrorism; violent extremism and trafficking of drugs, arms and people; as well as heightened risks related to climate change… Civil society and independent media continued to experience severe restrictions in a number of participating States, and manifestations of intolerance, xenophobia, hate speech and hate crime continued to spread in the OSCE area".

Greminger was nevertheless able to find successes in military transparency, risk reduction, incident prevention, greater openness in Central Asia and "new dynamics in and around Ukraine", where he found new hope (later disappointed) for conflict resolution. He also welcomed an agreement in the long-running dispute between Skopje and Athens on a name for the former Yugoslav Republic of Macedonia, now to be called North Macedonia.

Although the OSCE remains an important actor in the continuing search for a just and stable order in Europe, it is squeezed by the competing functions of bodies such as NATO and the United Nations for security, the EU for economic and political development, the Council of Europe for human rights, and maybe to some extent the Commonwealth of Independent States (CIS) (a body created in 1991 as an association of Central Asian states that had been part of the Soviet Union, to provide a Russia-led counter to Western intergovernmental organisations). This problem derives partly from the fact that the OSCE, unlike other international organisations, does not have a legal personality.

Another problem is that the OSCE can apply no serious sanctions to states that violate its principles. It did not even try to impose conditions when it eagerly gathered in the post-Soviet states of Central Asia, hoping they would learn to love democracy and human rights. Most of them did not. Further west, Yugoslavia was suspended in 1992 because of its internal wars, but this was an exception, and the only time the OSCE had employed the "consensus minus one" mechanism (see Chapter 20). In contrast, when NATO and the European Union expanded they were able to make membership conditional on achieving certain standards, including commitments to human rights and democracy. They could do this because they offered tangible benefits, including military security and economic assistance. Those levers diminished once membership had been achieved, but some remain, although members have been reluctant to apply them. The Council of Europe also proclaims standards that must be upheld, though it has been relatively tolerant of deviations. Its Parliamentary Assembly suspended Russia's voting rights after Russia annexed Crimea in 2014, but eventually restored them in June 2019 after acrimonious exchanges, with a split of 118 to 62 in favour of Russia's return and 10 abstaining. Since then, the Council of Europe has adopted a new procedure for responding to violations by member states of their statutory obligations to respect human rights and adhere to the other obligations of membership.[14]

Even where the OSCE has contributed to arms control and Confidence-Building Measures or economic cooperation it has done so primarily as a negotiating forum, not as an organ of enforcement. For the most part it is a voluntary organisation based on a commitment to values. When these are challenged or simply abandoned by participating States it can impose no sanctions. Nor does it have legal powers. It relies only on promises, exhortations and the intangible benefits of "respectability", or the equally intangible penalties of being named and shamed. When participating states fall short of their declared principles, the Ministerial Council is hampered by the consensus rule. Only the ODIHR (of which more in the next chapter) and the other semi-autonomous bodies can speak and act more freely because they are not subject to veto, which is why Russia has consistently tried to curb them.

A tempting chance to impose conditions arose when Kazakhstan, strongly supported by Russia, applied in 2003 for the annual Chairperson-in-Office (CiO) of the OSCE. The story is interesting because it reveals the limits of the OSCE's powers to enforce its values. Kazakhstan had not fulfilled its most basic commitments to democracy and human rights. Nor had it ever held an election that met OSCE standards. Indeed, President Nursultan Nazarbayev had joined in Russian attacks on the OSCE for interfering in its internal affairs. Its democratic deficit was judged so great that in 1999 the ODIHR decided not to mount a full observation mission for the presidential election of that year.[15] In September 2004 Kazakhstan joined Armenia, Belarus, Kyrgyzstan, Russia, Tajikistan, Uzbekistan and Ukraine (later also

Turkmenistan) in the "Astana Appeal" urging the OSCE to downgrade the human dimension of its activities and stop monitoring the internal political affairs of participating states.[16] This directly challenged the most fundamental principles of the Helsinki Process.

Now it was applying to run the organisation for a year. Western opinion divided. Some argued that a country with such an abysmal human rights record had no claim to the chairmanship until it introduced substantial reforms, prospects for which seemed negligible. In the words of Colin Powell, then US Secretary of State: "Any state wishing to assume the chairmanship must demonstrate it can conduct free and fair elections".[17] Human Rights Watch expressed similar objections, as did NGOs on the spot, one member of which called the idea "insane".[18] There were also fears that Moscow was hoping to use a Kazakh chairmanship as a "Trojan Horse" to promote Russian interests in the organisation.[19]

The opposing view was that the chairmanship might encourage Kazakhstan and other Central Asian states to pursue domestic political reforms. Maybe the OSCE could gain some leverage from President Nazarbayev's apparent desire for international visibility and respectability. The more Nazarbayev pressed his case the more likely it seemed that a price could be exacted. Support even came from Yevgeny Zhovtis, a leading opposition figure and human rights advocate, who hoped that the regime would be obliged to make changes.[20]

The more realistic view was that no changes could be expected, but Western states had been under increasing pressure to agree to a chairman from the eastern regions. Had they continued to refuse, Russia, Kazakhstan and others could have blocked the appointment of another Western chairman, inflicting paralysis on the organisation.

In 2006 the OSCE delayed a decision in the hope of pushing Kazakhstan to meet its OSCE commitments. The government seemed to comply in so far as it promised at a ministerial meeting in Madrid in November 2007 that it would embark on a range of domestic reforms in cooperation with the OSCE and the ODIHR. These "Madrid commitments" were accepted by the United States and others, so it was agreed that Kazakhstan would assume the chairmanship in 2010. It would then become the first post-Soviet country, the first predominantly Muslim country, and the first Central Asian country to be entrusted with such a responsibility. But it would do so under new conditions. Instead of the customary "troika" of previous, current, and incoming chairmen working together, four states would join Kazakhstan: Spain (2007), Finland (2008), Greece (2009) and Lithuania, which was to take over in 2011.

Once Kazakhstan had won the chairmanship its interest in reform dwindled. A few small gains for the OSCE were noticed after it took the chair in January 2010. For a while it refrained from joining Russia in attacking the OSCE, and it managed to organise the Astana summit in 2010 at which participating states once more pledged themselves to respect democracy, human rights and fundamental freedoms.[21] It also helped to get through a budget that Russia was trying to obstruct, while the mere fact of its being in the chair made it no longer possible for Russia to accuse the OSCE of favouring only Western appointments. But few, if any reforms were actually introduced. As soon as its year in the chair was over it reverted to its old habits, and even regressed. The attempt to impose conditionality had failed.[22]

The OSCE in conflict zones

As we have seen above, the OSCE still claims a primary role in preventing or resolving conflicts, but it has had only limited success in these efforts. It has no military forces of its own but Chapter 3 of the Helsinki-II Decisions of 1992 authorises it to conduct non-coercive peace-keeping operations and to call on NATO to protect its missions. We look at four examples of its peace-making efforts.

Chechnya

In 1995 Russia agreed to an OSCE presence in Chechnya, where Russia was engaged in a brutal war against rebels. The OSCE was initially successful in bringing the two sides together to sign an agreement but then made what many critics regarded as a mistake by concentrating on arranging elections before conditions were ripe. Russia then accused it of legitimising separatism. The mission withdrew from Grozny at the end of 1998 as fighting continued, then closed altogether in 2003 after Russia, which was crushing the rebels with extreme cruelty, refused to extend its mandate. It was allowed in again to monitor a referendum in the same year but refused to observe the presidential election, citing security fears.

Nagorno-Karabakh

This has been among the most difficult and disappointing of the OSCE's efforts. Under the Soviet Union Nagorno-Karabakh had been an ethnically Armenian autonomous region within Azerbaijan. When the Soviet Union broke up it voted to secede and join Armenia. More than 30 years of conflict followed involving mainly Armenia, Azerbaijan, Russia and Turkey. The OSCE set up the "Minsk Group" to find a solution but its efforts were largely in vain.[23] Conflict flared again in 2020 and has continued.

Kosovo

The OSCE could do little to stop savage fighting in the wars that followed the break-up of Yugoslavia in 1992. Huge numbers were killed or displaced, leaving deep chasms of bitterness that persist to the present day. There was a brief period of hopeful military cooperation in 1995, when Russia (and others) joined the NATO-led multinational peace-keeping force (IFOR) to implement the Dayton Peace Accords that were supposed to end the fighting. Conflict later broke out again. In 1998 the OSCE launched a verification mission to monitor and investigate violations of human rights committed during the war, and to monitor Kosovo's border with Albania. In October of that year it helped broker a cease-fire, but was powerless when this broke down the following year. As Serbian atrocities against Kosovan Albanians mounted, NATO stepped in to stop a massacre by bombing the Serbs, including their capital, Belgrade. Russia, which had seemed indifferent to the atrocities, eventually induced the Serbs to withdraw their forces from Kosovo, but it remained furious at this attack on its Serbian "brothers". Its chief complaint was that the attack was launched without the approval of the United Nations Security Council, where Russia could have used its veto. Russia then refused to recognise Kosovo as an independent state. Recognition came, however, from 98 of the 193 members of the United Nations and 22 of the 27 members of the European Union. A number of Serbian leaders were later indicted and convicted for war crimes, including Slobodan Milošević, the Serbian leader, who died in prison in the Netherlands in 2006.

After the bombing an OSCE mission was established in Kosovo to promote human and community rights (especially the rights of the Serbian minority), democratisation, and public safety. It worked within the United Nations mission as part of a wider international package of support for Kosovo. In 2001 it organised Kosovo's first election. In 2021 it was still at work, with five regional centres, 30 field teams, 117 international staff and 380 local staff. This work remains an example of the detailed, dedicated work on the ground, mostly unnoticed by the outside world, which often achieves more verifiable results than the resolutions passed at top levels. Many people with direct knowledge of such missions regard them as providing a large measure of justification for the existence of the OSCE.

Georgia

The CSCE/OSCE also had little success preventing conflict in Georgia. Its mission was active there from 1992 doing valuable work encouraging democratisation, respect for human rights and the rule of law during the painful transition from communism, which was causing a lot of hardship. The ODIHR's scathing report on the election of 2003 brought to a head rising public frustration with the government, which then fell in the "Rose Revolution" that brought Mikheil Saakashvili to power. He turned the country westward, aiming for membership of NATO and the European Union, much to the annoyance of the Russians, who began to exert pressure, for instance by refusing to buy Georgia's excellent wine.

In Georgia, the OSCE mission had also been tasked with managing the chronic conflict with the two separatist territories of South Ossetia and Abkhazia, both bordering on Russia and supported by it. Here the OSCE largely failed. In the course of years of conflict and negotiation South Ossetia was offered a high degree of autonomy within Georgia but rejected the terms in a referendum in 2006. In 2008 President Saakashvili sent in armed forces to assert control and occupy the region's capital, Tskhinvali. Russia responded by invading Georgia, claiming to be conducting a "peace enforcement" mission, a category used by the United Nations Secretary General Boutros Boutros-Ghali in his 1992 report *Agenda for Peace* but inappropriately applied by Russia to its actions in Georgia. (Russia similarly misappropriated the UN concept of "Responsibility to Protect" to justify its actions in Ukraine in 2014.) It then recognised the disputed territories as independent states, causing the displacement of nearly 200,000 Georgians who fled or were driven out.

The origins of this small war are disputed. A strong case is made for showing that the Russians encouraged the South Ossetian separatists to provoke a Georgian attack on their capital in order to provide an excuse for Russian forces to intervene. In other words, President Saakashvili fell into a trap laid by the Russians. Certainly the Russian forces were very well prepared. They quickly poured across the frontier and occupied not only South Ossetia and Abkhazia but far wider areas of Georgia, at one point seeming to threaten the capital.

This assault on Georgian sovereignty was a clear breach of the Helsinki principles. It provoked alarm in the West, which feared more armed Russian interventions in post-Soviet states. The Russians countered criticism of their invasion and their recognition of the breakaway provinces by citing NATO's attack on Serbia and its recognition of Kosovan statehood, a typical example of Russia's addiction to "whataboutism".[24] The Russians were, however, relatively unsuccessful in gaining international recognition for their protégé, winning over only Venezuela, Syria, Nauru, Abkhazia, and Transnistria. Russia then refused to allow an OSCE mission to monitor the cease-fire and Georgia turned instead to the EU.[25] Russia could not veto the EU deploying a mission inside Georgia's borders, whereas it could and did veto the continuation of the OSCE mission.

The OSCE continued to operate in areas close to South Ossetia until June 2009, when Russia vetoed the extension of its mandate.[26] Although its mission to Georgia remained closed, it continued to send observers to Georgian elections. Their verdict on the parliamentary elections in 2020 was not favourable.

Ukraine

In March 2014 Russia seized Crimea, where it already had a naval base and many soldiers. It then sent unidentified "volunteers" (in fact soldiers) into parts of eastern Ukraine to help separatists set up local regimes.

The OSCE's response was to set up a Special Monitoring Mission (SMM) to monitor and, if possible, resolve the conflict. Later, it received a mandate from the Minsk Agreements. These were meant to end the war in the Donbas region. The first was drafted by the Trilateral Contact Group (TCG) consisting of Ukraine, Russia and the OSCE, with mediation by France and Germany. It was signed on 5 September 2014 by the TCG and, without recognition, by the leaders of self-proclaimed republics of Donetsk and Luhansk. The fighting continued so another attempt was made with Minsk II, signed on 12 February 2015. Its provisions included a cease-fire, withdrawal of heavy weapons, release of prisoners of war and self-government for certain areas of Donbas while granting the Ukraine government (nominal) control of its state border. Fighting still continued. In February 2022 Putin recognised the Donetsk and Luhansk republics, declared the Minsk Agreements dead, and invaded Ukraine.

Also set up were much smaller Observer Missions at the Russian Checkpoints Gukovo and Donetsk. A typical weekly report in March 2019 complains that some individuals crossing the border use private vehicles or buses with tinted windows or drawn curtains so they can't be checked. "On some occasions, the OTs [Observer Teams] noticed the bus drivers removing the itinerary signs from the windshields of their buses, while some buses do not display their route at all… All trucks undergo systematic inspection by Russian Federation officials, which may include an X-ray check. Due to the unfavourable observation position at the Gukovo crossing the OTs continued to be unable to observe any X-ray checks".[27] And so on. Reports in January 2021 continued to describe vehicles failing to display their route, the inability to use X-ray checks, and trains obscured by trees.[28]

The work can be dangerous. For example, in June 2014 eight OSCE monitors were captured by the rebels and held for some months, released only after appeals by the Patriarch of the Russian Orthodox Church.[29] In April 2017 one of its paramedics was killed and two monitors taken to hospital after their vehicle was heavily damaged by an explosion in the Luhansk region. Again, some of its monitors were detained by rebel forces and released only after lengthy negotiations.

The Austrian Foreign Minister, Sebastian Kurz, who was OSCE Chairperson-in-Office at the time, commented: "The SMM is doing an outstanding job, day by day, to stabilize the crisis in and around Ukraine. But the mission is too often hampered by threats, by access restrictions, by disinformation or the destruction of its technical means. This is simply unacceptable".[30] His remarks were aimed primarily at Russia, which was supposed to be an objective monitor but was in fact backing one side. There were even unconfirmed reports of Russian monitors passing military information from the Ukrainian side to the rebels.

In spite of these problems and dangers, the OSCE monitors kept up a steady stream of daily reports. They were heavily redacted but still registered every relevant incident and breach of the cease-fire, creating an invaluable archive. For instance, between the evenings of 16 and 18 July 2021 it recorded 608 cease-fire violations, including 64 explosions. In the previous reporting period it recorded 286 cease-fire violations in the region. In 2019 it recorded 299,633 such breaches, in 2020 134,783, many involving deaths of troops and civilians. The fact that the drop in these grim numbers was hailed as a success is a measure of the scale of the problem and its intractability. It has also reported signal interference with its drones. The only glimmer of light was provided by occasional local cease-fires to allow work on infrastructure, such as the Donetsk filtration plant.[31]

In the spring of 2022, when the SMM's mandate came up for renewal, the Russians refused consensus so the mission had to close, ending the OSCE's monitoring activity in Ukraine.[32]

Despite this setback, the OSCE has generally done better at monitoring conflict situations than solving or preventing them. Increasingly, it has found itself operating in adverse circumstances, its work either hampered or prevented altogether. At the same time it is accused of fomenting instability by trying to impose alien values on participating states. In other words, an organisation dedicated to working for a just and stable order in Europe now finds itself frequently accused of achieving the opposite by supporting human rights, minorities, free media and other challenges to authority.

Russia and the OSCE

Many of the problems derive from the fact that Russia's attitude to the CSCE/OSCE changed over the years. For many years it pressed for reform of the OSCE in various versions. From 1993 onwards its aim was to give the organisation a central role in peace-keeping by turning it into a fully-fledged treaty-based regional organisation with an Executive Committee resembling the United Nations Security Council. This would have a maximum of 10 members and take binding decisions by consensus. It bore some resemblance to Molotov's 1954 proposal for a European security treaty (see Chapter 2) in so far as it reflected Russia's continuous desire since World War II to control its environment from a seat at the table of a pan-European security structure.

Like Molotov's proposal, the new idea never took off because NATO members would never agree to being subordinate to such a body, and nor would smaller states, because they feared losing their voice in the full organisation. Similar proposals continued to be put forward up to the mid-2000s but, as they failed to find consensus, Russia turned increasingly to weakening OSCE activities in the field by, for instance, blocking budgets, expelling missions, withholding mandate renewals, and refusing to grant privileges and immunities to OSCE personnel.

When Putin became President in 2000 his view of the OSCE remained relatively positive at first as he continued to see it as a potential pan-European security organisation in which Russia could play an active part while working to diminish the role of NATO, particularly if he could achieve the reforms mentioned above, promoted in the form of a "Draft Charter" in 2007 (see below).[33] He was also enthusiastic about cooperation with the United States. After the terrorist attack on the World Trade Center on 11 September 2001 he told the Washington press in November: "Today we are already prepared to seek solutions in all areas of our joint activities. We are willing to dismantle, once and for all, the legacy of the Cold War and begin fashioning a strategic partnership for the long term".[34] This was the sort of cooperation between supposedly equal great powers for which he hankered. In 2002 he joined the

United States in signing the Strategic Offensive Reductions Treaty (SORT), which reduced the number of deployed nuclear warheads. In the same year he joined the NATO–Russia Council (see Chapter 22) giving Russia a voice in joint deliberations.

He was, however, disappointed that the United States refused to join him in labelling the rebels in Chechnya terrorists. Then, when the United States attacked Iraq in 2003 without United Nations approval, the Russian leadership came to see it as a rogue country intervening with military force wherever it wanted, paying no heed to the United Nations or international law while lecturing Russia on values and ignoring its views—probably its worse offence in Russian eyes. This view had already been reinforced when NATO bombed Serbia in 1999 (see above) and became even stronger after NATO's intervention in Libya in 2011. Obviously, concluded Putin, rules were not for great powers, so why should he observe them?

In September 2004 terrorists attacked a school in the Russian town of Beslan, which provided Putin with a reason or an excuse to tighten political controls severely at home. In the same period came the "colour revolutions" in Georgia in 2003, Ukraine in 2004 and Kyrgyzstan in 2005. All of them removed regimes close to Moscow, which blamed Western machinations and in particular its "democracy projects", alleging that the OSCE/ODIHR were directly involved.[35]

By the time Putin returned for his second term in 2004 his frustration had been growing, exacerbated by the ODIHR's very critical report on his presidential election on 14 March 2004.[36] For a while Russia banned further election observations by the ODIHR and complained with increasing vigour about what it perceived as a bias in favour of Basket III of the Final Act (the human dimension) at the expense of Baskets I (security) and II (economic cooperation), just as the Soviet Union had done while negotiating the Final Act of 1975. ODIHR observers were, however, allowed in again later for a number of parliamentary and presidential elections up to 2021.

In 2005 the Russian delegation told the Permanent Council of the OSCE that the human dimension of the OSCE's work was characterised by "double standards, politically motivated and biased assessments… and the use of human rights issues for exerting political pressure".[37] At the Munich security conference in 2007 (see Chapter 22), Putin accused Western states of trying to transform the OSCE into a 'vulgar' instrument to ensure the foreign policy interests of one or a group of countries.[38]

The theme was repeated by Sergei Lavrov, Russian Foreign Minister, at the 15th meeting of the OSCE Ministerial Council on 29 November 2007. Echoing Putin's speech in Munich, Lavrov said: "I should like to reiterate the absolute unacceptability of attempts by some countries or groups of countries to claim 'absolute knowledge' with regard to the nature and principles of democracy and to use the OSCE for 'lessons in democratisation'. No one has a monopoly on the truth. Dialogue on the humanitarian agenda can be only equal and mutually respectful".[39] In other words, there was to be no more talk of shared values, only equal rights and mutual respect.

Russia called repeatedly for all the work of the OSCE to be brought under the control of participating States. As mentioned above, in 2007 a draft charter for the OSCE was presented by the states of the Collective Security Treaty Organisation (CSTO), a Eurasian military alliance created in 1992 and led by Russia. Echoing many Russian speeches, it proposed that the OSCE should be put on a legal basis with a legally binding charter that would end the semi-autonomy of the ODIHR, the High Commissioner on National Minorities and the Representative on Freedom of the Media. They would become accountable to the Ministerial Council, where every participating state, including, of course, Russia, has a veto.

According to the draft charter, their mandates would have to be agreed with the authorities of the states in which they operated. Questions relating to their functioning and format would be resolved exclusively at the request of the host country and on the basis of national requirements and priorities. This would, of course, render impossible much of the ODIHR's work. At one point the ODIHR was told it should report only on how far a state conformed to its own electoral laws, a truly absurd suggestion.

As this idea was pressed, the tone of Russian statements became sharper. At the 20th Council meeting on 5 December 2013 Mr Lavrov said that "attempts to adapt the OSCE area to the interests of a single group of countries through the aggressive imposition of neoliberal interpretations of human rights will ruin European civilisation. An arrogant disregard for traditional values and moral norms—common to all of us and characteristic of every nation—is unacceptable".[40]

Russia's attitude to the OSCE is a throwback to the Soviet Union's original positions during negotiation of the Final Act from 1972 to 1975. Then, as now, it wanted to give priority to Baskets I and II of the Final Act while downgrading or separating Basket III on humanitarian issues (see Chapters 11 and 13). At that time it seldom overtly contested the validity of Western values because it wanted to be seen as part of Europe. Sometimes it claimed to be observing the Principles of the Final Act when it was not, or it attacked the West for being equally guilty, or simply claimed that the "right to peace" or social rights, such as the right to work, were superior to the civil rights propagated by the West. That was one of its main themes. Even at that time, however, it made some efforts to assert cultural relativity. After reluctantly accepting a raft of measures on freer movement of people and information in Basket III, it tried to neutralise them by inserting preambles requiring respect for the "laws and customs" or "cultural foundations" of participating states. These flexible formulae would have allowed it to ban almost anything it did not like. It failed in most of those efforts.

Forty years later, it was trying again, using very similar language as it pressed for a "proper balance among the baskets", making it clear that this would mean downgrading Basket III, acknowledging different values and subjecting the troublesome ODIHR to government controls. As Mr Lavrov told the Ministerial Council in Sofia on 7 December 2004, "It is important to understand that real unity in the pan-European process can be ensured only through recognition of and respect for diversity and due regard for the cultural, historical, national and other differences between our countries".[41] At the same time Russia has tried to block or restrict the regular Human Dimension meetings in terms of topics, dates, agendas and budgets. All these meetings were often used by the US and countries west of Vienna to criticise Russia's conduct in the humanitarian dimension.

Eventually Putin ceased to pay even lip service to Western values, asserting that they were inappropriate in current circumstances, or culturally alien, or simply no longer relevant because liberal democracy had become an outmoded concept.[42] Instead he promoted a version of Eurasianism that rejected both communism and liberal democracy and endorsed a specifically Russian set of values (see Chapter 22). He still hoped he could re-shape the OSCE to serve Russian interests by shifting its emphasis from human rights to security issues, such as terrorism and drug trafficking. He also wanted it to become a partner of his Eurasian Economic Union (EAEU). After signing the EAEU treaty in May 2014, he suggested that the OSCE should "harmonize and couple integration processes in Europe and Eurasia".[43] He seemed to envisage three centres of power, the United States, the European Union and the EAEU, cooperating on an equal basis as a sort of security council. This fitted with his broader vision of a European security system based on multipolarity in which Russia would be acknowledged as one of the dominant centres of power, equal to the United States, promoting mutual respect and the absolute sovereignty of states. This partly explains why Putin has remained in the OSCE despite his severe criticisms. It is the only pan-European structure in which he can still hope to have some influence, whether constructive or negative, by deploying the veto.

Essential to his vision would be putting the ODIHR under the control of participating States,[44] rendering it unable to make independent assessments of elections and other aspects of the humanitarian elements of security.

That is the subject of the next chapter.

Notes

1 See https://www.osce.org/participating-states for the full list, viewed 28 February 2022.
2 Latvia, Estonia and Lithuania.
3 Kazakhstan, Turkmenistan, Tajikistan, Uzbekistan and Kyrgyzstan.
4 For a long analysis of European security architecture in 2020 covering the overlapping functions of the OSCE, NATO and the European Union, and including maps, see a useful EU publication: www.case-study-of-the-european-security-architecture-nato-and-osce.11317.pdf, viewed 23 April 2022.
5 OSCE, viewed 13 January 2022, www.osce.org
6 CSCE, 1994, *Budapest Summit Declaration: Towards a Genuine Partnership in a New Era*, viewed 13 January 2022, https://www.osce.org/files/f/documents/5/1/39554.pdf
7 Still often referred to as Chairman or Chair.
8 OSCE, 1999, *Istanbul Summit* (2000), viewed 13 January 2022, https://www.osce.org/files/f/documents/6/5/39569.pdf, §7.

9 OSCE, 1999, *Istanbul Summit* (2000), viewed 13 January 2022, https://www.osce.org/files/f/documents/6/5/39569.pdf, §29.
10 OSCE, 1999, *Istanbul Summit* (2000), viewed 13 January 2022, https://www.osce.org/files/f/documents/6/5/39569.pdf, §2.
11 The OSCEPA is not an official OSCE institution. It is closely associated but is an independent body governed by separate rules.
12 OSCEPA, July 2015, *Helsinki +40: building the OSCE of the future*, viewed 13 January 2022, https://www.oscepa.org/en/documents/all-documents/helsinki-40/final-report/2949-helsinki-40-final-report/file
13 Thomas Greminger, 2020, 'The OSCE Annual Report 2019', OSCE, viewed 21 March 2022, https://www.osce.org/files/f/documents/0/9/449104_0.pdf, pp 4–5.
14 2020, Council of Europe, *Serious violation by a member State of its statutory obligations*, viewed 13 January 2022, https://www.coe.int/en/web/portal/-/serious-violation-by-a-member-state-of-its-statutory-obligations-committee-of-ministers-adopts-a-new-complementary-procedure
15 Fawn, *International Organizations and Internal Conditionality*, 200.
16 Fawn, 67.
17 Fawn, 197.
18 Fawn, 197.
19 Fawn, 204.
20 Fawn, 198.
21 OSCE, 2010, 'Astana Commemorative Declaration: Towards a Security Community', viewed 21 March 2022, https://www.osce.org/files/f/documents/b/6/74985.pdf
22 Fawn, 229.
23 A lively description of these efforts is to be found in *Helsinki Revisited* by John Maresca, who was personally involved.
24 "Yes, we did this, but what about when you did that?".
25 For a brilliant analysis of the Georgian war and its implications see Roy Allison, 'Russia resurgent? Moscow's Campaign to "Coerce Georgia to peace"' in *International Affairs* 84/6, November 2008.
26 OSCE, 2006, 'The Georgian-Ossetian Conflict', viewed 13 January 2022, https://www.osce.org/georgia-closed/44630
27 OSCE, 2019, 'Weekly Update from the OSCE Observer Mission at Russian Checkpoints Gukovo and Donetsk based on information as of 5 March 2019', viewed 20 January 2022, https://www.osce.org/observer-mission-at-russian-checkpoints-gukovo-and-donetsk/413183
28 OSCE, 2021, 'Weekly Update from the OSCE Observer Mission at Russian Checkpoints Gukovo and Donetsk based on information as of 05 January 2021', viewed 20 January 2022, https://www.osce.org/observer-mission-at-russian-checkpoints-gukovo-and-donetsk/475310
29 For press releases 26, 28, 30 June 2014 see https://www.osce.org/press-releases/weekly%20update?filters=+ds_date:([2014-06-01T00:00:00Z%20TO%202014-07-01T00:00:00Z])&solrsort=score%20desc&rows=10&category=News, viewed 13 January 2022.
30 OSCE, 2017, 'OSCE Special Monitoring Mission to Ukraine patrol member killed in explosion near Luhansk', viewed 13 January 2022, https://www.osce.org/special-monitoring-mission-to-ukraine/312951
31 For full daily and weekly reports see https://www.osce.org/press-releases, viewed 13 January 2022.
32 https://www.osce.org/chairmanship/516933
33 2012, 'Report to the Ministerial Council on Strengthening the Legal Framework of the OSCE in 2012', OSCE, viewed 20 January 2022, https://www.osce.org/files/f/documents/8/c/97950.pdf

34 Quoted by Legvold in *Return to the Cold War*, 103. This quotation is also in Chapter 22 but the repetition has been included because that chapter is intended to stand alone if desired.
35 See the references to these events in Chapter 22.
36 OSCE, 2004, *Russia, Presidential Election, 14 March 2004: Final Report*, viewed 13 January 2022, https://www.osce.org/odihr/elections/russia/33101
37 Statement at the 540th meeting of the OSCE Permanent Council, PC.DEL/3/05 (13 January 2005).
38 Speech and discussion at the Munich Conference on Security Policy, 10 February 2007, viewed 13 January 2022, http://kremlin.ru/events/president/transcripts/24034
39 OSCE, 2007, 'Statement by the Minister for Foreign Affairs of the Russian Federation at the 15th OSCE Ministerial Council meeting', viewed 13 January 2022, https://www.osce.org/files/f/documents/8/a/29330.pdf
40 OSCE, 5 December 2013, 'Statement by Mr. Sergey Lavrov, Minister for Foreign Affairs of the Russian Federation, at the 20th Meeting of the OSCE Ministerial Council', viewed 19 February 2022, https://www.osce.org/files/f/documents/7/f/109306.pdf
41 OSCE, 2004 'Statement by the Minister for Foreign Affairs of the Russian Federation at the 12th OSCE Ministerial Council meeting', viewed 13 January 2022, https://www.osce.org/files/f/documents/1/3/38796.pdf
42 See Chapter 22, note 46.
43 Statement at the 1089th meeting of the OSCE Permanent Council, PC.DEL/161/16, 12 February 2016.
44 Statement at the 1156th meeting of the OSCE Permanent Council, 31 August 2017.

24 ODIHR

Human rights and dodgy elections

"The OSCE is good for nothing anymore. The OSCE must be destroyed". Those angry words exemplify the hostility that the OSCE has encountered among some of its participating states. They came from a journalist on a state-owned newspaper in Azerbaijan at a press conference given by Tana de Zulueta, head of the election observation team from the OSCE's Office for Democratic Institutions and Human Rights (ODIHR). The press conference had to be abandoned amid shouting and booing and accusations that the observers had prepared their report before the election.

The team had been observing the presidential election of 9 October 2013 in which President Aliyev claimed to have won 85 per cent of the vote for a third consecutive term. His government had committed itself to democracy by signing up to the OSCE after emerging from the Soviet Union but it had no experience of democracy and showed little interest in learning. The ODIHR team found the election seriously flawed, but neither the government nor its tame journalists wanted to hear the verdict:

"The 9 October election was undermined by limitations on the freedoms of expression, assembly and association… Continued allegations of candidate and voter intimidation and a restrictive media environment… Detentions, criminal prosecutions, testimony of physical attacks and other forms of pressure on journalists… Clear indications of ballot box stuffing in 37 polling stations… A number of other procedural violations. The counting was assessed in overwhelmingly negative terms, with 58 per cent of observed polling stations assessed as bad or very bad…, manipulation of voter list entries, results or protocols, including cases of votes being reassigned to a different candidate".[1] And so on. It was also reported that local observers had posted videos showing the same group of women voting at six different polling stations.

Two years later, the government of Azerbaijan had not forgotten. In June 2015, in response to persistent criticism of its poor record on civil liberties and media freedoms, it gave the OSCE a month in which to close its mission in Baku.

This is just one example of the troubled world in which the ODIHR struggles to promote democracy and human rights. It was set up by the CSCE (as it then was) in Warsaw in 1991. Originally called the Office for Free

DOI: 10.4324/9781003146124-30

Elections, its mandate was soon broadened and its name changed. In the noble words of the Helsinki Document of 1992 (see Chapter 21), its job is to assist participating states to "ensure full respect for human rights and fundamental freedoms, to abide by the rule of law, to promote principles of democracy and... to build, strengthen and protect democratic institutions, as well as promote tolerance throughout society". In pursuit of those aims it not only observes elections but runs hundreds of meetings, workshops, training programmes and events to promote democracy and help states and civil societies to bring laws and institutions into line with the requirements of the OSCE.[2] Unsurprisingly, given the amount of resistance it encounters, ODIHR is often pronounced as "Oh dear!". Nevertheless, by the end of 2021 it had observed more than 400 elections since its creation.

Being autonomous in its operations, it is free to criticise states that fall short of its standards but it still depends for its budget on the Council, where each member has a veto, To take two random examples that did not involve elections: in April 2017 the ODIHR expressed "grave concern" over new laws in Hungary that threatened the autonomy of the Central European University;[3] in the same month it called on the Russian authorities to investigate reports of shocking human rights violations against gay men in Chechnya.[4] No improvements followed in either case. The ODIHR may be free to criticise but the Russians, Hungarians and others are free to ignore its criticism—and to complain about interference in their internal affairs, just as the Soviet Union did in the Cold War.

Yet the opinions and reports of the ODIHR are not necessarily wasted. They provide an invaluable archive, and, as in the Cold War, they may help to sustain democratic forces under oppressive governments, so they can have results over time. They also inform the outside world which then feeds the information back through radio broadcasts or social media to people in the countries concerned, who may otherwise be dependent on government-controlled media. Thus the "boomerang effect" that was a feature of human rights work in the Cold War can still operate to some extent (see Chapter 15).

Much of the work of the ODIHR on behalf of democracy and human rights remains largely unnoticed beyond the country concerned, but sometimes its reports on elections contribute to the fall of governments. For instance:

Georgia

Georgia's "Rose Revolution" immediately followed the parliamentary elections of 2 November 2003 (see also Chapter 23). The leader of Georgia at the time was Eduard Shevardnadze, who had been in that role from 1972 to 1985 before being spotted by Mikhail Gorbachev as a fellow reformer and whisked up to Moscow to become Foreign Minister. He then played a key role in ending the Cold War. Disillusioned with Gorbachev, he resigned in 1990 but returned briefly until the Soviet Union was abolished in 1991, after which he went back to lead Georgia. There he allowed corruption to flourish while at the same time making enemies by adopting a strongly pro-Western policy, even accepting US military aid and announcing his intention to join NATO and the European Union. By the time the 2003 elections came along public anger with corruption was bubbling. The ODIHR sent in a big team of long-term observers from 16 of its states. On election day they were joined by hundreds of short-term observers and parliamentarians from the OSCE's Parliamentary Assembly, the Council of Europe and the European Parliament.

The ODIHR report was devastating. It found that Georgia "fell short of a number of OSCE commitments and other international standards for democratic elections. Inaccuracies in the voter list seriously challenged the fundamental guarantee of universal and equal suffrage". After acknowledging some progress since previous elections, the report went on to say that "confidence in the election administration remains low…; the authorities did not provide equal conditions for all election contestants…; the election preparations were characterized by persistent delays…, a climate of uncertainty and mistrust…, questions about the willingness and capacity of the Georgian governmental and parliamentary authorities to conduct a credible election process… On election day observers reported relatively large numbers of voters being turned away…, serious acts of violence during campaign events…, ballot stuffing, use of pre-marked ballots, multiple voting, and destruction of ballot boxes…, presence of large numbers of unauthorised persons inside polling stations, including police and local government officials, some of whom interfered in or directed the process…, instances of intimidation",[5] and so on.

When the ODIHR's preliminary report was made public on 3 November, public anger boiled over. The opposition organised massive demonstrations that eventually drove Shevardnadze to resign on 23 November. The Supreme Court annulled the election. New ones were held, bringing Mikheil Saakashvili to power. He served two separate terms, mostly successful, and was then invited to be governor of Ukraine's Odessa province. He resigned from that post in 2016, went to the United States and returned to Georgia, where he was arrested on what he said were political charges, finding himself among prisoners who had been his political enemies. In December 2021 he was in a prison hospital in Georgia.

Ukraine

In 2004 the "Orange Revolution" in Ukraine followed a damning ODIHR report on the rigged presidential elections of 31 October and 21 November that gave victory to pro-Russian Viktor Yanukovych.[6] Huge crowds gathered in Kyiv to protest. The Supreme Court annulled the results and new elections were held in December which gave victory to Viktor Yushchenko, who leaned to the West. Unsurprisingly, Russia praised the first round of elections and condemned the second, while the ODIHR did the opposite.

In the presidential election of April 2019 Volodymyr Zelensky was elected by a vote of 73 per cent against the incumbent, Petro Poroshenko, who gained only 24 per cent. The ODIHR mission found that, despite some shortcomings, the election "was competitive, voters had a broad choice and turned out in high numbers... Fundamental freedoms were generally respected. Candidates could campaign freely".[7] So much for Putin's claim, as he attacked Ukraine in 2022, that the government was illegitimate.

Kyrgyzstan

In 2005 the "Tulip Revolution" in that country also followed a critical ODIHR report on the parliamentary elections of February and March.[8] Thousands took to the streets and ended 14 years of rule by President Askar Akaev, who fled to Russia. The Russian foreign ministry called the ODIHR mission "intrusive" (what else was it supposed to be?) and said that its "premature" statements risked destabilising the region.

Kyrgyzstan's revolution did indeed send shock waves around the area. The anxiety it provoked was exemplified by the reaction of an adviser to Akaev, who complained that "a single process is unfolding...; Kyrgyzstan is a kind of trigger that will spread this unrest to our neighbours and beyond. We are witnessing the second breakup of the Soviet Union".[9]

The new regime in Kyrgyzstan was more amenable to ODIHR advice. After the presidential election in July, the ODIHR reported "'tangible progress' towards meeting OSCE commitments... Fundamental civil and political rights, such as freedom of expression and freedom of assembly, were generally respected throughout the election process". Progress continued. According to the ODIHR, the presidential election in October 2017 "contributed to the strengthening of democratic institutions by providing for an orderly transfer of power from one elected president to another".[10]

Obviously the ODIHR was not solely responsible for bringing down these governments. Frustration with corruption and other problems had been growing among the populations, but in each case an objective outside report by the ODIHR confirmed widely suspected corruption in the electoral system and put wind in the sails of protesters. As Christopher H. Smith, chairman of the Helsinki Commission, said in January 2005: "Peaceful popular protests backed by OSCE standards on elections can bring down entrenched corrupt regimes that rely on fraud to remain in power".[11]

Even where they do not bring down governments, critical reports by the ODIHR can provoke repercussions.

Russia

In December 2003 the ODIHR delivered a negative report on Russia's parliamentary (Duma) elections.[12] The Russian government protested. In July of the following year it gathered other aggrieved states to present the OSCE Permanent Council with a protest known as the Astana Appeal (mentioned in Chapter 23), which urged the downgrading of Basket III of the Final Act (the humanitarian section most relevant to the work of the ODIHR) in favour of the first two Baskets on security and economic cooperation. Sergei Lavrov, Russian's Foreign Minister, followed up with a speech to the Ministerial Council of the OSCE in Sofia on 7 December 2004 calling for "objective criteria to be applied throughout the OSCE area". In the absence of such criteria, he said, "election monitoring is not only ceasing to make sense but is also becoming an instrument of political manipulation and a destabilizing factor".[13]

Russia gradually shifted its tactics. It had been trying to work through OSCE headquarters in Vienna to shackle or dismantle the election activities of the ODIHR. Now it shifted the focus to putting local restrictions on ODIHR missions. In October 2007, for instance, it specified that only a short-term mission of 70 people would be allowed to the Duma elections on 2 December, compared with the normal 400 allowed on a long-term mission of several weeks that had been permitted for the parliamentary vote in 2003. On 16 November the ODIHR informed Russia that it would be unable to observe the 2007 election.

Thus, we find the paradox of an organisation dedicated to promoting a just and stable order in Europe now accused of fomenting instability. Putin had come to see the ODIHR as an arm of the broader Western "democracy project" that, in his view, aimed to subvert and replace undemocratic regimes, including his own. When the "Arab Spring" broke out in Tunisia in late 2010, spread to Libya and Egypt, and infected areas beyond, he alleged that the West's subversive hand was behind it, heading for Moscow. He claimed vindication when unrest broke out in Russia itself. Mass demonstrations spread across the country after the ODIHR criticised the Duma elections of 4 December 2011. The government blamed Hillary Clinton, then US Secretary of State, for deliberately encouraging the demonstrators.

Putin either believed, or found it convenient to proclaim, that he was under direct threat from Western powers intent on removing him. Even if there was a little bit of truth in that, the demonstrators were fired up by genuine grievances. The critical ODIHR report merely strengthened their case. "The elections", it found, "were marked by the convergence of the state and the governing party…, also slanted in favour of the ruling party…, evidenced by the lack of independence of the election administration, the partiality of most media, and the undue interference of state authorities at different levels… The count… was characterised by frequent procedural violations, and… serious indications of ballot box stuffing". And so on in devastating detail".[14]

The Russian government's reaction was not to reform but to attack outside "interference". In 2012 it passed a law making NGOs register as "foreign agents", a term usually applied to spies. The move was strongly condemned by the OSCE.[15] Later, the law was extended to include foreign media and then foreign journalists.

Five years later, the verdict of the ODIHR on the Duma election of 18 September 2016 was little better:[16] In August 2021 the ODIHR announced that it would not send observers for the Duma elections in September because of limitations imposed by Russian authorities.[17]

Hungary

The Hungarian government was also defiant when the ODIHR reported negatively on the parliamentary elections of 6 April 2014: "The main governing party enjoyed an undue advantage because of restrictive campaign regulations, biased media coverage and campaign activities that blurred the separation between political party and the State".[18] In 2018 the ODIHR reported that the parliamentary elections of that year were "were characterized by a pervasive overlap between state and ruling party resources, undermining contestants' ability to compete on an equal basis. Voters had a wide range of political options but intimidating and xenophobic rhetoric, media bias and opaque campaign financing constricted the space for genuine political debate, hindering voters' ability to make a fully-informed choice".[19]

Hungary has been the greatest disappointment to the European project. Having been among the first to throw off communism, it has steadily retreated from the norms and values of the European Union and the OSCE. Freedom House puts it in the category of "partly free". An ODIHR Needs Assessment Mission sent in to report in advance on the conditions in which the parliamentary election of 3 April 2022 would be held, found itself listening to numerous complaints about the deterioration of conditions for democratic elections, the politicisation of the judiciary, curbs on media freedom and manipulation of electoral law to favour the ruling party. Some hope of change was found in the fact that six opposition parties had managed to unite for the first time in a bid to overthrow the government of Viktor Orbán but he nevertheless won by a large margin.

Turkey

President Recep Tayyip Erdogan reacted angrily when his constitutional referendum of April 2017 was severely criticised by the ODIHR for lack of equal opportunities, one-sided media coverage and limitations on fundamental freedoms.[20]

Turkey has also been active in trying to restrict access of NGOs to the annual Human Dimension Implementation Meetings (HDIM), Europe's largest annual human rights and democracy conference, organised by the ODIHR to take stock of the implementation of OSCE human dimension commitments and make recommendations for further improvement. Turkey has tried to insist on each participating state's right to block attendance by any particular NGO, with Gülenist organisations particularly in mind.

Belarus

A more recent example of hostility to the OSCE was provided by Belarus in 2020. President Lukashenko presumably thought he could avoid trouble by not having an ODIHR mission to observe his shamelessly rigged presidential election of 9 August, which supposedly gave him a landslide victory. He sent out the invitation to the ODIHR too late, which was generally assumed to be deliberate. He miscalculated. Even without an ODIHR report—or maybe partly because of its absence—the people were not convinced by the election result. They came out in massive and prolonged demonstrations that were brutally put down.

United States

The ODIHR was set up largely to help struggling new democracies emerging from Soviet rule, so its work in established democracies is often seen as undertaken merely to demonstrate balance rather than to encourage substantial change, but the fact remains that its strictures deserve more attention. Few established democracies have remained totally unscathed by its reports. Nor have the ODIHR teams always been warmly welcomed in the West. For the 2012 presidential election in the United States nine out of fifty states banned the OSCE observers altogether, either not knowing or not caring that the United States was a member. In Texas, the mission was even threatened with criminal proceedings by the Attorney General. As for the election itself, the mission called for further steps "to improve the electoral process in areas such as voting rights, the accuracy of voter lists, campaign finance transparency, recount procedures, and access of international election observers".[21] In 2016 an ODIHR team also found the presidential election seriously flawed, noting, for instance, that an estimated 35 million eligible voters were not registered to vote.[22] In neither case did the ODIHR challenge the result.

In the turbulent presidential election of 2020 the ODIHR found itself in an unfamiliar situation in which the usual pattern was reversed. Although its observers offered many criticisms of the American electoral system it pronounced the result valid, while President Trump, who had lost, issued furious claims of fraud. The ODIHR scornfully dismissed his "baseless allegations of systematic deficiencies".[23] Unfortunately, its verdict attracted little attention in the heated atmosphere that followed.

Internal problems

As well as struggling with recalcitrant and hostile governments, the ODIHR has had internal problems. For many years there were disagreements between its teams of trained election observers and the parliamentarians who turn up shortly before polling day. Sometimes the parliamentarians are members of its own Parliamentary Assembly (OSCEPA), drawn from national parliaments. Others may be members of the European Parliament (EP) or the Parliamentary Assembly of the Council of Europe (PACE).

The anger generated by the Azerbaijani election described at the start of this chapter was exacerbated by the fact that the verdict of the ODIHR contrasted strongly with the largely favourable verdicts of several teams of parliamentary observers. There had been big international interest, so observers piled in from about 50 different organisations. Forty-nine of them praised the elections as free and fair while the ODHIR team disagreed strongly. When Pino Arlacchi, head of the European Parliament delegation, was asked why his members had reached an assessment so different from that of the ODIHR, he launched into a savage attack on that body: "The ODIHR consists of so-called experts with no political responsibilities, who were not elected by anybody. So it is easy to manipulate them". Later the Italian magazine *Panorama* alleged that Arlacchi had explained to other members of the European Parliament that in Azerbaijan he had "defended the interests of Italy in the region". *Panorama* then referred to Italian investments in the energy sector.[24] The row was described in detail in a report by the European Stability Initiative called *Caviar Diplomacy*.[25]

How can there be such widely differing verdicts on an election? The question goes to the heart of the ODIHR's work. Its substantial teams of trained long-term observers go into a country six to eight weeks before polling day. They report in depth on the context in which the election is held, including voter registration, media coverage, women's rights and treatment of opposition candidates. They are then joined before polling day by short-term observers who fan out to polling stations across the country to watch voting and counting. The procedures for both teams are set out in an impressively detailed 120-page handbook that draws on the accumulated wisdom of many years of observing elections and has been through many editions. There are also additional handbooks on specific issues, such as voter registration, media balance and the role of women.

In contrast, most parliamentarians arrive shortly before polling day, visit only a few polling stations and are in some cases, as in the case of Azerbaijan above, allegedly compromised by being involved in commercial or political relations with the host country.

Some people with experience of observation missions will admit that in its early days the ODIHR may have been too absolute in its standards, lacking understanding for the difficulties facing post-Soviet countries trying to adapt their long traditions and habits to the requirements of the new democratic order. At the same time, ODIHR observers could hardly be expected to depart from their rule book and ignore cases where standards agreed by all participating states were not met.

In practice, this dilemma was often fudged by the absence of machinery for monitoring compliance with the post-election recommendations of the ODIHR. Electoral sins remained unaddressed until mentioned again after the next elections, with no action taken in the meantime. Yet, even when ignored at the time, the efforts of the observer teams are not wholly wasted.

Their mere presence in conflicted states can sometimes help local NGOs, while their detailed reports remain on public record, immune to efforts by governments to conceal sins or re-write history, so they provide a valuable resource for reference today and for future historians.

The standard defence of the parliamentarians' often more tolerant approach was that as politicians they could understand and assess democratic procedures better than unelected observers. Some also claimed that their networks of trans-European political parties gave them long-term insights denied to visiting observers. This view was propagated most vigorously by Spencer Oliver, Secretary General of the OSCEPA from 1993 to 2015. He came to be much resented by ODIHR observers. He had done splendid work as Chief of Staff of the Helsinki Commission in Washington from 1976 to 1985 (see Chapter 15) but after his appointment to the OSCEPA he was accused of being too ready to condone elections in which human rights were conspicuously flouted.

He defended his record vigorously, regularly attacking ODIHR observers. As might be expected, ODIHR observers argued back, claiming that their teams provide deeper and more objective verdicts on elections than parliamentarians on relatively brief visits. In recent years relations have improved.

Among the reasons for these difficulties is the fact that the ODIHR is committed by paragraph 8 of the Copenhagen Document of 1990 to encouraging practically anyone to observe elections, not just its own teams. A result is that it is all too easy for corrupt regimes to select from different verdicts on their elections, or to play off one against another.

At the same time the ODIHR has not been immune to the worries experienced by the OSCE and described in the previous chapter. When Michael Georg Link, outgoing Director of ODIHR, reported on election work to the OSCE Permanent Council in Vienna on 6 April 2017 he was deeply troubled:

"Through our missions and our broader monitoring work, we observe a growing number of challenges with the implementation of numerous election-related OSCE commitments, such as unreasonable and disproportional limitations of suffrage rights, lack of the necessary conditions to allow parties and candidates to compete on a level playing field, and a shrinking space for civil society, including citizen observer organizations. We also note that well established principles such as the division of powers and the rule of law are increasingly questioned, both East and West of Vienna, and that the use of intolerant rhetoric in election campaigns is on the rise…

> We are witnessing attempts in different countries to alter the balance of democratic powers, and to ultimately favour the establishment of a dominant executive power at the expense of effective legislature and judiciary. It is our duty to state that no majority government is above the law. Let me go further: 'No one is above the law, not even an elected government.'… The cascading effects of all these challenges are coming

> at a time of growing public mistrust, rising populism, nationalism as well as increasing polarization, intolerance, and xenophobia. These are matters of direct and legitimate concern to all of us and these challenges, as it has been restated in the OSCE numerous times, do not belong exclusively to the internal affairs of any state.[26]

The verdict was no better in 2020. The Director for that year, Matteo Mecacci, wrote in his report: "2020 was a difficult year for democracy and human rights across the OSCE region in many ways beyond the pandemic. Conflicts returned and democratic development stalled or went into reverse, in some cases together with a serious deterioration in the human rights situation".[27]

These gloomy words should not obscure all the good work still done by the ODIHR. Banned in some states and obstructed in others, it has persevered where it can operate and shone light where it cannot. This chapter has focussed perhaps too much on observing elections because that is the most visible and controversial part of the ODIHR's work. Just as important but less visible are the numerous field missions in which dedicated people work very hard to strengthen the rule of law, battle against intolerance, collect data for the largest hate crime database in the world, increase gender equality, fight for the safety of human rights defenders, and strive for the participation of Roma in communities from which they have been excluded. They help develop civil societies, modernise legislations and in general do all the groundwork that is essential for democracy to work.

Not to be forgotten, too, are the annual meetings of the Human Dimension Implementation Meetings (HDIMs) organised by the ODIHR. This is Europe's largest annual human rights conference, bringing together hundreds of government officials, international experts, civil society representatives and human rights activists to take stock of how states are implementing their commitments to the core values that promote respect for human rights and fundamental freedoms.[28] It has, however, been hampered by Russia's negative attitude. For instance, in August 2021, Courtney Austrian, Deputy Chief of Mission at the US Mission to the OSCE, complained that Russia was the only participating state obstructing the will of all the other 56 and blocking a thorough review of participating states' implementation of OSCE commitments on human rights, democracy and the rule of law: This "is not how a responsible participating State behaves".[29] The HDIM did not meet in 2020 because of the pandemic, and it failed to meet in 2021 because of lack of agreement. However, some Supplementary Human Dimension Meetings (SHDMs) continued, for instance on violence against women in November 2021[30] and scheduled for March 2022 to address violations of international humanitarian law and international human rights law.[31]

All these activities have continued despite frequent organisational and other problems at the Vienna headquarters of the OSCE, including attempts by Russia and others to restrict budgets, difficulty finding the right candidates for short-term contracts, or reluctance of governments to pay them. At the same time it has successfully resisted Russian attempts to bring it under the control of national governments. All in all, with major and minor projects, the ODIHR has done more than most people realise to improve the quality of life in those states that have allowed it to operate. Add up everything and the balance is certainly positive. As clouds gather over liberal democracy its work becomes more important than ever.

Notes

1 OSCE/ODIHR, 2013, 'Azerbaijan, Presidential Election, Final Report', OSCE, viewed 14 January 2022, https://www.osce.org/institutions/110015
2 See its annual reports on the OSCE website, https://www.osce.org/annual-reports, viewed 17 February 2022.
3 OSCE, 2017, 'Press release, 5 April', viewed 14 January 2022, https://www.osce.org/chairmanship/309976
4 OSCE, 2017, 'Press release, 13 April', viewed 17 January 2022, https://www.osce.org/odihr/311611
5 OSCE/ODIHR, 2004, 'Georgia, Parliamentary Elections, Final Report, 2 November 2003', OSCE, viewed 14 January 2022, https://www.osce.org/odihr/elections/georgia/22206
6 OSCE/ODIHR, 2005, 'Presidential Election, 31 October, 21 November and 26 December 2004', OSCE, viewed 14 January 2022, https://www.osce.org/odihr/elections/ukraine/eoms/presidential_2004
7 OSCE, 20 November 2019 'Ukraine, Presidential Election, 31 March and 21 April 2019: Final Report', viewed on 20 March 2022, https://www.osce.org/odihr/elections/ukraine/439631
8 OSCE/ODIHR, 2005, 'Parliamentary Elections, 27 February and 13 March 2005', viewed 14 January 2022, https://www.osce.org/node/57850
9 Fawn *International Organizations and Internal Conditionality*, 72–3.
10 OSCE/ODIHR, 2018, 'Kyrgyz Republic, Presidential Elections, Final Report, 15 October 2017', OSCE, viewed 14 January 2022, https://www.osce.org/odihr/elections/kyrgyzstan/374740
11 Quoted in Fawn, 72.
12 OSCE/ODIHR, 2003, 'Parliamentary Elections, 7 December 2003', OSCE, viewed 14 January 2022, https://www.osce.org/odihr/elections/57864
13 OSCE, 2004, 'Statement by the Minister for Foreign Affairs of the Russian Federation, at the 12th meeting of the OSCE Ministerial Council', viewed 14 January 2022, https://www.osce.org/files/f/documents/1/3/38796.pdf
14 OSCE/ODIHR, 2012, 'Russian Federation, State Duma Elections, Final Report, 4 December 2011', OSCE, viewed 14 January 2022, https://www.osce.org/odihr/86959
15 OSCEPA, 2021, 'Russia's "Foreign Agent" Legislation Detrimental to Civil Society', viewed 14 January 2022, https://www.oscepa.org/en/news-a-media/press-releases/2021/russia-s-foreign-agent-legislation-detrimental-to-civil-society-osce-pa-s-kauma-says
16 OSCE/ODIHR, 2016, 'Russia, State Duma Elections, Final Report, 18 December', OSCE, viewed 14 January 2022, https://www.osce.org/odihr/elections/russia/290861
17 OSCE, 4 August 2021, Press Release 'No OSCE observers for Russian parliamentary elections following major limitations', viewed 19 March 2022, https://www.osce.org/odihr/elections/russia/494488
18 OSCE/ODIHR, 2014, 'Hungary, Parliamentary Elections, Final Report, 6 April' OSCE, viewed 14 January 2022, https://www.osce.org/odihr/elections/hungary/121098

19 OSCE/ODIHR, 27 June 2018, 'Hungary Parliamentary Elections 8 April 2018: ODIHR Limited Election Observation Mission Final Report' viewed 14 March 2022, https://www.osce.org/files/f/documents/0/9/385959.pdf

20 OSCE/ODIHR, 2017, 'Turkey, Constitutional Referendum, Final Report, 16 April', OSCE, viewed 14 January 2022, https://www.osce.org/odihr/elections/turkey/324816

21 OSCE/ODIHR, 2013, 'United States of America, General Elections, Final Report', OSCE, viewed 14 January 2022, https://www.osce.org/files/f/documents/a/a/99573.pdf

22 OSCE/ODIHR, 2016,'United States of America, General Elections, Final Report', OSCE, viewed 14 January 2022, https://www.osce.org/files/f/documents/d/9/294196.pdf

23 OSCEPA, 2020, 'United States of America, General Elections, 3 November 2020: Statement of Preliminary Findings and Conclusions', viewed 14 January 2022, https://www.osce.org/files/f/documents/9/6/469437.pdf

24 *Panorama* (Italy), 28 October 2013.

25 European Stability Initiative, 2013, *Disgraced: Azerbaijan and the end of election monitoring as we know it*, viewed 14 January 2022, https://www.esiweb.org/publications/disgraced-azerbaijan-and-end-election-monitoring-we-know-it. "The full video of the stormy press conference can be found on YouTube: "Pro-government reporters turn the OSCE/ODIHR news conference into chaos", Obyektiv TV Channel, uploaded 12 October 2013, https://www.youtube.com/watch?v=yLFvVza0558

26 Michael G Link, 2017, *Report to the OSCE Permanent Council*, OSCE, viewed 17 January 2022, https://www.osce.org/files/f/documents/5/c/310046.pdf

27 OSCE/ODIHR, 2020, *Democracy and Human Rights in the OSCE*, viewed 14 January 2022, https://www.osce.org/files/f/documents/e/1/483026_1.pdf

28 Reports of the annual Human Dimension Implementation Meetings can be accessed at https://www.osce.org/odihr/hdim, viewed 13 March 2022.

29 Courtney Austrian, 'Russia's Continued Obstruction of the 2021 Human Dimension Implementation Meeting', August 2021,US Mission to The OSCE, viewed 19 March 2022, https://osce.usmission.gov/russias-continued-obstruction-of-the-2021-human-dimension-implementation-meeting/

30 OSCE, 16–17 November 2021, 'Preventing and Combating Violence Against Women and Girls: Human Dimension Seminar', OSCE Office for Democratic Institutions and Human Rights, viewed 19 March 2022, https://www.osce.org/odihr/hds_2021

31 OSCE/ODIHR, 28–29 March 2022, 'International co-operation to address violations of international humanitarian law and international human rights law: Supplementary Human Dimension Meeting I', viewed 19 March 2022, https://www.osce.org/odihr/shdm_1_2022

25 Conclusions, achievements, legacy

This book has tracked the Helsinki Process from its origins to the present day, demonstrating its remarkable resilience and longevity. It has survived the confrontations of the Cold War, the euphoria of the Paris summit of 1990, the disappointments that followed, the return of confrontation with Russia, and the sad discovery that the world is not on a one-way road to liberal democracy. In a darkening political climate, made darker by Russia's invasion of Ukraine in February 2022, it continues to do valuable work, not only in public but also in many local missions that are largely invisible to those not directly involved. Its aims and values, as embodied in the Final Act of 1975 and the Paris Declaration of 1990, have remained constant throughout: to promote democracy,[1] human rights, the rule of law, economic cooperation, arms control and other elements of cooperative security in Europe. Only its environment has changed. This can be divided into two phases:

The Cold War

The Helsinki summit of 1975 was a major diplomatic success for the Western alliance, dramatically confounding its many critics and demonstrating the value of slow, patient diplomacy conducted largely out of the limelight. The nine members of the European Union, supported by neutrals and the non-aligned, and alternately helped and hindered by the United States, transformed a Soviet attempt to freeze the status quo into a compromise strongly weighted in favour of change. While acknowledging the realities of the time (which the Soviet Union deliberately misinterpreted as endorsing its empire), it committed its signatories to changing their behaviour in ways that constituted a profound challenge to the political systems of the Soviet Union and Eastern Europe, while also usefully reminding Western states to live up to their own rhetoric.[2] By committing all to a series of follow-up meetings, it maintained the pressure for change until change arrived, largely as a result of the accession of Mikhail Gorbachev to the leadership of the Soviet Union.

Just how much the Helsinki Process contributed to the end of communism in Eastern Europe is open to debate. In the broader context of European détente it certainly weakened Soviet control by mobilising dissent and exposing the area to more outside influence, even despite the clampdown

DOI: 10.4324/9781003146124-31

in the 1980s. It also encouraged reformers within the Soviet apparatus. Its norms and institutions helped shape the transition to democracy and prepare future leaders to take over peacefully. But the unravelling of the Soviet empire did not follow the trajectory envisaged by early supporters of the Helsinki Process. Most expected a gradual process of liberalisation in Eastern Europe and Moscow that would slowly build bridges across divided Germany and Europe until, in the distant future, both could be reunited. Instead, the communist systems and the Warsaw Pact collapsed much faster than expected, obliging the CSCE/OSCE to shift from promoting change to managing it.

Thus, the CSCE did not cause the collapse. Nor, incidentally, did Ronald Reagan, as some mythologists still maintain, by threatening and outspending the "evil empire". If he had continued with that confrontational approach he would merely have stiffened Soviet resistance. Instead, he switched from hawk to dove, although Jack Matlock, former US ambassador to Moscow, has argued convincingly that Reagan was always partly dove at heart, anxious to negotiate with the Russian leaders but foiled by their frequent deaths ("They keep dying on me", he complained) until Gorbachev arrived.[3] In any case, by removing the perceived threat to the Soviet Union, he gave Gorbachev the space to pursue his "new thinking" and negotiate constructively to bring the confrontation to an end. As Vladislav Zubok has written, "It was Reagan the peacemaker, negotiator, and supporter of nuclear disarmament, not the cold warrior, who made the greatest contribution to international history".[4] One sign of this was that he dropped his vociferous opposition to the CSCE and allowed his diplomats to work constructively at the Madrid follow-up meeting and beyond.

Change would have been much delayed if Mikhail Gorbachev had not come to power in 1985, or if he had been overthrown in the attempted coup of 1991, or if the coup had come earlier, when it might have succeeded. Not until he publicly renounced the use of force in Eastern Europe in his speech to the United Nations in 1988, after many private warnings to the regimes of that area, could the peaceful revolutions succeed there; and not until he abandoned most of Soviet ideology could the Cold War end. Even Lech Walesa, Poland's first democratically elected president since the war, who liked to boast that Poland destroyed communism, admitted that "we could not have done it without him".[5]

If power had remained in the hands of more orthodox leaders they could have maintained control for many more years in the Soviet Union and, with sufficient force or threats of force, in Eastern Europe. The suppression of dissent would have intensified, as it did in the early 1980s in the Soviet Union and, with the imposition of martial law, in Poland in 1981. The visible role of the Helsinki Process would then have ground to a halt. Thus, there is no straight line from 1975 to the collapse of communism.

Yet the ferment encouraged by the Helsinki Process would surely have continued beneath the surface of the decaying systems and brought them down eventually. Belief in communism had drained away, and the multiple failures of its promises were increasingly obvious to populations and to their rulers in Moscow and Eastern Europe as they watched the Western democracies surge ahead. Even in the Third World, countries that adopted free enterprise were demonstrating the irrelevance of the Soviet model. As better educated generations rose in the Soviet Union the pressure for change would have grown, as it was already growing behind the scenes before Gorbachev came to power.[6] He was not alone in questioning the stultifying system of central planning, the suppression of freedoms, the mounting costs of the arms race and the growing burden of subsidising Eastern Europe and clients in the Third World. So change would surely have come anyway at some point, whether gradually or suddenly, but without Gorbachev, and without Helsinki, it would have come later, differently, and perhaps more violently.

It is sometimes argued that without the CSCE Gorbachev would have missed one of the many sources of inspiration for his new thinking, his dedication to democratic values and the idea of a common European home.[7] He certainly referred frequently to the Final Act, and invoked it against his numerous reactionary colleagues when he needed to remind them of the norms to which the Soviet Union had signed up, but for him the CSCE was primarily a useful instrument to deploy against his opponents and a framework to structure and validate his beliefs, not a cause of change. His beliefs came from deeper sources and experiences within the Soviet Union and from social democrats in Western Europe.[8]

After the Cold War

The second phase of the Helsinki Process came after the end of the Cold War, when the CSCE transformed itself into the OSCE and participating states signed up in Paris in 1990 to democracy and market economies. This gave the Process new impetus and a new role in helping the often wobbly efforts of the Soviet Union and its empire to build democracy. Here it had only limited success and faced many setbacks. As we have seen, it failed to create a new European security system that included Russia, leaving open the question whether that was ever possible. Some of the Western experts who rushed in to give their advice on the transition showed insufficient appreciation of how slow and difficult that would be in countries with no democratic traditions, weak civil societies, and often regimes that did not even want to learn new systems and values. Nor was there enough awareness of the difficulty of turning a state-run planned economy into a market economy, particularly in Russia, where the transition was largely mishandled. Corruption ran wild, oligarchs pillaged assets and the people of Russia suffered years of hardship, rendering them as sceptical of capitalism as they had been of communism—and ready to welcome Putin when he became President in 2000.[9]

Nevertheless, the immediate post-communist years in the Soviet Union and Eastern Europe would have been even more difficult and possibly more violent without the work of the OSCE: its field missions, its election observers, its engagement in conflict zones, and its dedication to standards, values and cooperative procedures. That work continues against increasing resistance and in the context of a wider weakening of belief in the liberal democratic order.

Is the OSCE doomed?

Some gloom is clearly justified. As we have seen, many participating states are simply ignoring their obligations while some have turned actively hostile. A recent lengthy OSCE report by Bernhard Knoll-Tudor and others[10] asks whether the OSCE is sliding into irrelevance. It points out that the situation of human rights defenders in a growing number of OSCE participating states is becoming increasingly difficult, not only in Poland and Hungary but also in Bulgaria, Greece, Malta, Croatia and Slovenia. Missions in some states have been subject to restrictive laws, bureaucratic burdens and verbal and physical assaults.

Thus the compromises reached with the Soviet Union at Helsinki in 1975 are no longer being honoured by Russia and many others. Russia's seizure of Crimea and parts of eastern Ukraine in 2014 and its savage attack on Ukraine in 2022 were particularly blatant violations of the Final Act. Nor are the additional commitments undertaken in Paris in 1990 being honoured. Instead, Russia is leading some states into a Eurasian alliance that overtly rejects Western values. Hungary and Poland have also been curtailing media freedoms, politicising the judiciary and restricting electoral choices.

Yet the OSCE survives and its work continues. Members remain members, even those that have been most heavily criticised or have themselves criticised the organisation. The OSCE's norms remain valid and its institutions, though battered and often demoralised, remain functional. Many of its missions still operate. In some places its mere presence can contribute to the visibility of local problems and the work of local bodies. Its voluminous records remain a hugely valuable resource for current policy-makers and future historians. For as long as it remains reasonably intact and operational there must be some hope that it will revive and receive the recognition it deserves. Meanwhile, in the words of the British poet Arthur Hugh Clough (1819–1861), "Say not the struggle nought availeth".

Notes

1 Democracy is not specifically mentioned in the Final Act but it is in the Paris Declaration.
2 Morgan, *The Final Act*, 140, with references to British documents urging caution in pressing too hard for certain rights.
3 Matlock, *Reagan and Gorbachev*, 36, Kindle edition Location 759; see also Matlock, *Autopsy on an Empire*, James Mann, *The Rebellion of Ronald Reagan*, and Service, *The End of the Cold War*, 20.
4 Zubok, *A Failed Empire*, 343. For a longer discussion of this issue see Archie Brown, *The Gorbachev Factor*, 226–30.

5 Remarks at a Solidarity conference, Warsaw, May 2014.
6 "The number of Soviet citizens with higher education increased from 8.3 million in 1959 to 18.5 million in 1984". Archie Brown, *The Gorbachev Factor*, 18. See also English, *Russia and the Idea of the West*.
7 "The Final Act exerted a powerful influence on Gorbachev's views and on those of his advisors and supporters", Morgan, 235.
8 See Gorbachev, *Memoirs*. See also Brown, *The Gorbachev Factor*, 98.
9 See Catherine Belton, *Putin's People*.
10 Bernhard Knoll-Tudor, Márta Pardavi, and Marta Achler. 2022, *Is the OSCE Sliding into Irrelevance? Engaging with human rights defenders to address the rollback of the rule of law in the European Union*. Vienna: OSCE Network of Think Tanks and Academic Institutions. Available with other recent reports at: https://osce-network.net/publications, viewed 19 March 2022.

26 Can Helsinki be a model for other trouble spots?

Many people have suggested deploying the Helsinki model in other troubled parts of the world. There have been calls for a "Middle East Helsinki", a "Korean Helsinki", an "Asian Helsinki" and even a re-run of the original Helsinki.[1] This is not surprising. The Helsinki Final Act was an extraordinary achievement by 35 nations with conflicting aims and interests. After struggling through nearly three years of complex negotiations they produced a single document with far-reaching effects. Could that process—that near-miracle—be replicated elsewhere?

The short answer is no. Helsinki was specific to its time and place in Cold War Europe. It came at a moment when both sides were committed to détente and had achieved a certain level of mutual trust. Although they were still adversaries they could seek compromises and areas of cooperation in order to reduce the costs and risks of confrontation.

As we have seen, they had different ideas on how to proceed. The Soviet Union hoped to finalise the division of Europe whereas the Western side hoped to make the division more permeable and, in the long run, to overcome it. The negotiations gained impetus from Brezhnev's strong desire for a summit conference, which drove his side to accept the larger share of compromise. In addition, both sides had by that time come to see that new approaches were needed to the unsatisfactory legacy of World War II in Europe. Once talks started they were shaped by the two superpowers, the European Union, and the grouping of the neutrals and non-aligned, while all sides had simultaneously to negotiate multiple disagreements among themselves.

Any attempt to redeploy the Helsinki model in other areas would face very different motives, groupings and constellations of power. Nevertheless, it can still be mined for ideas, principles and procedures to be used selectively and adapted for other contexts. For that, it is necessary to have a clear view of the Helsinki Process, which this book has tried to provide. It should be seen not just as a simple process by which the West forced the Soviet Union to accept obligations on human rights, which then contributed to its downfall, but as a much more complex phenomenon. There was certainly a strong adversarial element in the negotiations but they are better seen as aimed at "cooperative security", a much-discussed concept that describes a security system based

DOI: 10.4324/9781003146124-32

on reassurance and engagement rather than deterrence and containment (see Lesson 12 below).

The process also needs to be examined over a long period. As we have seen in previous chapters, agreement on the Final Act was preceded by much diplomatic clearing of the decks. In 1967 NATO adopted the Harmel Report, with its specific commitment to détente. In 1969 came the *Ostpolitik* of Willy Brandt, Chancellor of West Germany, who (provisionally, pending a peace treaty) accepted the loss of pre-war German territories to Poland, recognised (with reservations) the state of East Germany and reached agreements with the Soviet Union and Czechoslovakia. In 1970 the Warsaw Pact eventually accepted US participation in a security conference. In the same period the four powers responsible for Germany achieved an agreement that helped to stabilise the situation in divided Berlin. They also agreed on the start of talks on mutual and balanced force reductions (MBFR). All these developments were necessary preconditions for embarking on the security conference for which the Soviet Union had been pressing over many years.

Then came nearly seven months of preparatory talks in Dipoli. These were initially intended merely to decide if a full-scale conference had a chance of success but turned out to involve substantial pre-negotiation of the Final Act in order to find the answer. There followed nearly two years of intense committee work in Geneva before agreement was reached on a document that could be signed by all 35 participating states.

The process continued with follow-up meetings, first in Belgrade in 1977, where it nearly broke down amid stormy debates on human rights, then in Madrid, where, again, breakdown came close, and then in Vienna, where Mikhail Gorbachev's team eventually accepted almost the entire Western agenda, effectively ending the Cold War. Confirmation was then sealed at the euphoric Paris summit of 1990.

That was still not the end. The Helsinki Process continued with the institutionalisation of the CSCE as the OSCE,[2] which grew to include 57 members. This new organisation failed to provide a new security system in Europe to replace NATO and the Warsaw Pact (see Chapter 22). Further disappointments followed as some new and old states challenged the values to which they had signed up. Russia committed particularly blatant breaches of the Final Act when it invaded Georgia, Crimea and Eastern Ukraine. Nevertheless, despite these and other setbacks, the OSCE has persisted in its struggle to fulfil the original aims of the Final Act: mutual security, respect for human rights, transparency, military confidence-building, economic cooperation, and the freer movement of people and information. Its survival through so many vicissitudes has shown that the process can be as important as the substance in so far as it provides a continuous forum for dialogue, adaptation, and monitoring of performance. For instance, although OSCE missions to eastern Ukraine had only limited influence on the fighting, they supplied a mass of detailed information for reference today and for future research until their mandate expired in March 2022. Moreover, it is not unreasonable to suggest that the situation might have been even worse if all parties to the conflict had not known themselves to be under constant observation (see Chapter 23).

From that long arc of experience, what procedures can be copied and what lessons can be learned? Attention usually focuses on the negotiation of the Final Act and then on the text itself, a masterpiece of comprehensive diplomatic compromise in which single words and their translations and even single commas carry the weight of long struggles. But the process should be seen as a whole over its long life through the Cold War and up to the present, including follow-up, institutionalisation, and continuing work. Any attempt to replicate it elsewhere would need to bear that in mind, even while trying to use only parts of the Helsinki model.

An example of how not to export the Helsinki model came when foreign ministers from Europe and the southern Mediterranean agreed on the Barcelona Declaration of 1995. Their declared aim was to create a common area of peace, stability and prosperity through dialogue, exchange and cooperation by means of three partnerships resembling Helsinki baskets: political/security, economic/financial, and a "partnership in social, cultural and human affairs". All three largely failed because they did not emerge from years of negotiation and mutual learning, as the Helsinki Final Act had. Instead, they were an attempt to impose European liberal-democratic norms on an area that was not ready for them. It was a perfect lesson in getting Helsinki wrong.[3]

The most frequently suggested candidates for regional negotiations along the lines of Helsinki are the Mediterranean, Asia and the Middle East. None is ripe for such a venture at the time of writing, but discussions on the subject can have some influence in preparing the ground for when substantive negotiations might have a chance.

In Asia various regional groupings contain elements of the Helsinki Process. ASEAN (Association of Southeast Asian Nations), founded in 1967 by Indonesia, Malaysia, the Philippines, Singapore and Thailand, grew to ten members after the Vietnam War. In 2007 they adopted the ASEAN Charter giving the group legal status and establishing three "communities" resembling the Helsinki baskets: political/security, economic, and socio-cultural. ASEAN+3 then brought in China, Japan and South Korea. The ASEAN Regional Forum (ARF) of 27 members, including the United States, Russia, India and the European Union, aims to foster dialogue contributing to confidence-building and preventive diplomacy in the region. The Asia-Pacific Economic Cooperation forum (APEC), with 21 members, discusses security cooperation, energy, North Korea, air defence and trade. The Shanghai Cooperation Organization (SCO), which includes China, Russia, and four Central Asian countries, initially discussed mostly security (terrorism, separatism, and extremism) but then expanded its agenda to include two more baskets: social and economic.

So they all share with Helsinki the idea of multiple baskets contributing to cooperation and wide definitions of security. They have had some success in promoting freer trade and regional talks but less in finding a common approach to issues such as human rights and maritime disputes. Gathering them all into a single Helsinki-type conference would be a huge and probably impossible task without a lot of prior groundwork, but the Helsinki model remains a source of ideas.

On the potential for an Asian Helsinki, Wenger and Möckli have commented: "Against the background of East Asia's strategic asymmetries, ongoing conflicts, and border disputes, the record of regional cooperation is not negligible. Principles like informality, an emphasis on process and dialogue, consensus-building, reassurance, incrementalism, and voluntary rather than legal commitment that are the hallmarks of multilateral security cooperation in East Asia may well be representative of the art of the possible in the region today. Instead of groping for an overly ambitious new security architecture there, the best way forward may then be that of building on the existing frameworks".[4]

The big prize would be a Middle East conference bringing together the regional actors with the United States, Russia and some Europeans. In principle, it would make a lot of sense. Like Helsinki, it would try to build a settlement around the contents of all four baskets, therefore including political relations, frontiers, human rights, CBMs, economic relations, freer movement, cultural and humanitarian issues and follow-up. It would be a huge undertaking, infinitely more complex than Helsinki, and almost certainly impossible without a prior trend towards détente and a lot of pre-negotiation, but if the context became more favourable the Helsinki model would certainly be helpful.

In the meantime the best way of approaching the transferability of the Helsinki process is to see it as a toolbox from which to borrow principles and instruments appropriate to different situations and as a series of lessons to be learned for the future.

Here are 12 possible lessons in no particular order. Some are specific to the Helsinki Process, others generic and thus applicable to many types of negotiation, but both categories belong in the Helsinki package:

1 **Diplomacy**. The CSCE/OSCE provides an almost perfect lesson in the value of patient, skilful diplomacy. Much doubted and derided at the start, the diplomats struggled on doggedly over many years until they reached agreement. It took 21 years to get from Molotov's initial proposal to the Helsinki summit; five years from the Warsaw Pact's acceptance of US participation; and nearly three years from the start of negotiations in Dipoli in 1972. The Helsinki model does not offer quick fixes but it does offer a lesson in multilateral diplomacy.
2 **Prior agreement on key issues**. It is important to remember that the Final Act did not resolve any substantive disputes over matters such as frontiers. Apart from very specific agreement on prior notification of military manoeuvres exceeding 25,000 troops, it conferred political endorsement on agreements already reached and provided a framework of principles and promises to promote a lengthy agenda for peaceful

change. There would have been no road to Helsinki without NATO's commitment to détente in 1967, Willy Brandt's *Ostpolitik*, US participation, and agreements on Berlin and the start of talks on MBFR. Only prior agreements on these issues made fruitful negotiation possible. The same would doubtless apply to any attempt to emulate Helsinki in the Middle East or, for instance, in maritime disputes involving China.

3 **Transparency**. The value of transparency runs right through the Final Act. Basket I contains the important measures on military transparency, mentioned above, to reduce the danger of surprise attack or miscalculation. Basket II calls for the publication and dissemination of economic and commercial information. In Basket III signatories undertake "to facilitate freer movement and contacts... [and] the freer and wider dissemination of information of all kinds". Basket IV contains provision for follow-up meetings to review implementation. In other words, openness and freer movement of people and information were seen as basic to security and cooperation. As an ideal, if not always immediately achievable, this would apply anywhere in the world.

4 **Compromise**. The Final Act achieved a delicate balance between stability and change. Respect for frontiers was balanced against agreement on peaceful change. Respect for sovereignty was balanced against the right to monitor the internal behaviour of participating states on humanitarian issues. While the ten principles in Basket I are absolutes, the commitments in Basket III are relative, providing no rigid benchmarks. They depend on political will to implement them over time. For instance, the signatories merely "make it their aim" to facilitate freer movement and contacts. They do not commit themselves to more than doing their best, still less to numbers. Nor do they promise an absolute such as "free" movement, which was originally in the Western agenda but had to be abandoned in favour of "freer". Thus the Final Act allows the signatories some flexibility and breathing space in the matter of implementation within a framework of clear principles.

5 **Follow-up**. Without the follow-up meetings the Final Act would probably have drifted into irrelevance as nothing more than a set of pious intentions that could be safely ignored. Although the meetings were sometimes stormy and plagued by conflicting views on what they were supposed to be about (monitoring compliance, according to the West; cooperation, according to the East), they kept the process alive and maintained pressure on the Warsaw Pact to fulfil their obligations under the Final Act. Some kind of regular follow-up would probably be essential if the Helsinki model were to be tried in another context.

6 **Baskets**. Helsinki's basket structure has proved the most useful transferable experience for complex multilateral negotiations. It allowed simultaneous discussion of multiple aspects of security, all treated as inter-related and balanced or traded against each other. This experience was, for instance, formative for Jonathan Powell, who served as a young diplomat on the British delegations to the CDE in Stockholm and the

CSCE in Vienna. He later became Chief of Staff to Prime Minister Tony Blair in 1997 and chief negotiator in the successful Irish peace talks that produced the Good Friday agreement of 1998. Since then he has written books on resolving conflicts[5] and co-founded Inter-Mediate, a charity that helps with conflicts around the world.

He has found the basket structure particularly helpful: "I quote it a lot when I do negotiations around the world because the danger is that otherwise you end up with a sequential negotiation, and then you can never get past item one to make trade-offs between the different items. We had a three-basket structure at the end of the FARC negotiations in Colombia, and we had three 'strands' in Northern Ireland, although these were not quite the same as the Helsinki baskets.[6] It is really the framework in almost all multinational negotiations, so the CSCE model has been quite influential". He also points out that many of the issues contained in the Helsinki baskets, such as individual and minority rights, remain very much alive in conflicts today.[7]

7 **Consensus**. During the Helsinki talks the consensus rule sometimes caused delays and intense irritation, as when Malta tried to hold up the signing of the Final Act at the last moment and Romania briefly blocked the final document of the Vienna meeting in 1989. But the consensus rule was not the same as unanimity. It was defined in the rules of procedure as "the absence of any objection expressed by a representative and submitted by him as constituting an obstacle to the taking of the decision in question".[8] In other words, a participating state could withhold consent without actually voting against a measure, thereby allowing it to go forward. At Vienna in 1989 Romania went so far as to announce that it would not be bound by the decisions of the meeting, but it did not cast its veto. In this form the consensus rule was immensely valuable in ensuring that small states could not be ignored or easily bullied into agreements they did not like. It gave all participants a stake in the outcome. The rule has since been diluted by the OSCE (see Chapter 20).

8 **Regional**. Helsinki showed that in the right circumstances a regional approach can prove more fruitful than leaving matters to the parties directly concerned. Granted that some negotiations are best conducted privately in back rooms (there was some of that in the Helsinki Process), there is no doubt that a regional approach has the potential to bring great benefits. Had the Helsinki talks been left to the two superpowers they would have endorsed the status quo. Had they been left to the Europeans, neither side could have mustered the weight to reach a significant agreement. Had the neutrals and non-aligned been excluded, many good ideas and pressures would have been missing. The key to success was involving 35 nations, including outside powers with vital security interests in the region (the United States and Canada), in a broad four-basket agenda covering multiple aspects of security.

9 **Mindset**. Negotiations must be approached with the right mindset and sound background knowledge. Critics of the Helsinki talks seemed

largely unaware of the potential for change that had been developing behind the Iron Curtain since the 1960s. Economic and political stresses were building up in Eastern Europe,[9] while in Moscow new thinking was struggling for expression behind the façade of ideology.[10] As we have seen, Moscow's pressure for agreement at Helsinki came not only from the vanity of Mr Brezhnev but also from enlightened members of the Soviet elite who hoped it would induce change within their own country. Western sceptics such as Henry Kissinger ignored the evidence and dismissed the notion that the conference could promote internal changes within the Soviet bloc. To them the communist system seemed so deeply rooted and tightly controlled that no change was conceivable. Even when human rights and other humanitarian issues were included in the Final Act they saw no potential for internal change.

That rigid and uncomprehending mindset persisted to the end of the Cold War. As late as 1988, when Mikhail Gorbachev was already bringing fundamental change to the Soviet Union, Caspar Weinberger, Ronald Reagan's Defense Secretary until 1987, could write in *Foreign Affairs* that "no General Secretary [of the Soviet Union] will be allowed to alter in any fundamental way the never changing Soviet goal of world domination".[11] Closed minds of that type would rule out any attempt to replicate Helsinki in any context. A similar mindset is to be found among those who routinely oppose talking to terrorists.[12]

10 **Appeasement?** The process showed that engaging with hostile regimes should not be equated with appeasement, as it too often was, and still is, by confrontational critics. During the Cold War those critics saw the Soviet Union and its allies as implacable adversaries with whom negotiation could only be a zero-sum game. Anything to which the Soviet Union agreed was bound to be to the disadvantage of the West. The notion that there could be areas of cooperation within an adversarial relationship was largely alien to them, as was the idea of making any concessions. As some of them used to say, "compromise is for wimps". Still more difficult did they find it to believe that a conference proposed by the Soviet Union could be turned to the West's advantage by skilful diplomacy. They also displayed a remarkable lack of confidence in the fundamental political strengths of Western democracies, arguing that they were too weak, gullible and divided to stand up to the ruthless machinations of the Soviet Union. Many predicted that the Helsinki Process would strengthen the Soviet Union and weaken the West (see Chapter 7). As we have seen, it achieved the opposite.

11 **Soft power**. Helsinki showed that soft power—the power of ideas, culture, information, trade and travel—is real power that tends to undermine totalitarian systems when they depend for their survival on a siege mentality.[13] That remains one of the stronger general arguments for engaging carefully with undemocratic regimes. Awareness of the importance of soft power has grown among historians of the Cold War, as mentioned in Chapter 7. In other words, engagement in this context

can be seen not only as contributing to security but also as a form of peaceful subversion pursued, one might say, by "hawks in doves' feathers". In fact, each side was hoping to subvert the other. The Soviet Union financed communist parties and publications in the West, while the West financed broadcasts in local languages to the East, smuggled in forbidden literature, and gave some cautious help to dissidents who were judged to have peaceful aims. In the end the soft power of the Western side proved more effective, as the Soviet leaders had always feared. Thus, to a significant extent the Cold War was won by the power of example because the Western model proved so much more successful than that of the Soviet Union. But for the example to work, it had to become known on the other side of the Iron Curtain by penetrating the barrier of censorship and encouraging easier travel, which did indeed increase greatly during the period of détente, particularly between East and West Germany but also, with considerable effect, among influential elites in Moscow, Washington and Western Europe, who learned much from each other.

Mutual subversion sounds on the face of it incompatible with fostering peace and cooperation, but its aim, when responsibly pursued by both sides, was to promote gradual, peaceful internal change, not revolution. Given that the Cold War was, in part, a contest between two sets of ideas about society, government and human nature, competition was inevitable, even healthy, but it needed to be pursued within mutually agreed rules. These were to some extent provided by the Helsinki Final Act. Competition of this sort could make sense elsewhere in so far as more open relations between states and peoples can help to reduce the mental isolation and mutual ignorance that often contribute to hostility.

12 **Security**. What is it? In traditional power politics security for one state normally means insecurity for another. The cooperative security pursued at the Helsinki talks aimed to improve relations between antagonists across a broad range of issues in ways that promoted change at the same time as enhancing the security of both sides, even while both continued the arms race in pursuit of traditional concepts of security. As part of this process, Helsinki introduced the concept of "human security", meaning that the rights, welfare and consent of the people involved should be fundamental elements of a security system. The Soviet Union rejected the concept but still signed up to the principle. Since then the concept has been broadened and developed, defined by the UN Commission on Human Security as "moving away from traditional, state-centric conceptions of security that focused primarily on the safety of states from military aggression to one that concentrates on the security of the individuals, their protection and empowerment… creating political, social, environmental, economic, military and cultural systems that together give people the building blocks of survival, livelihood and dignity".[14]

In recognising the need for human security, the Helsinki process showed that the distinction often drawn between the cold calculations of

> Realpolitik and the idealism of Moralpolitik was false in this case. European idealists turned out to be more realistic than the "realists" in Washington. They understood that the post-war security system in Europe was potentially unstable and ultimately unsustainable by force, so they pressed hard for an agenda to promote peaceful change and establish the principle that human rights are a legitimate concern of international relations, not just for moral reasons, nor only to win propaganda points, but because lasting security in Europe, as they saw it then, required the consent of the governed. That was the essential link between human rights and security.

Unfortunately, this lesson has not proved universally applicable. There have been too many examples, especially in the Middle East, of authoritarian regimes being succeeded by chaos. Many manifestly lacked the consent of the governed but uprisings by the governed, or well-intentioned interventions from outside, have not always produced better situations. So context is all. But these failures do not entirely invalidate the view that a system resting on the suppression of human rights is likely to contain weaknesses that can prove destabilising in the long run, quite apart from the moral issues. Nor do they invalidate the central Helsinki principle that the internal affairs of a nation are the legitimate concern of other nations when discussing security.

Thus, if we are to learn from the Helsinki model, before selecting from its toolbox we must see it whole in its historical context as a long arc running right through the Cold War and up to the present. Like a rainbow, it contains many layers of the political spectrum that illuminate different aspects of security. As with rainbows, too, the mythical pot of gold that would represent fulfilment of its aims remains always out of reach. Yet the values to which it has been committed since 1975, augmented by the Paris Declaration of 1990, remain constant, and the institutions that were formed to further those values have survived many setbacks, so disappointment in adversity should be tempered by hope for a better future. Its work has become if anything more important now that its values are facing greater challenge.

Notes

1 Among many examples:

- Prince El Hassan Bin Talal of Jordan in a lecture at St Antony's College, Oxford, 26 November 2010, and on other occasions.
- Ki-Joon Hong, *The CSCE Security Regime Formation: An Asian Perspective*.
- Andreas Marchetti (ed.), 'The CSCE as a Model to Transform Western Relations with the Greater Middle East', Discussion Paper C137, Zentrum für Europäische Integrationsforschung, Bonn, 2004.
- Frank Schimmelfennig, 'The CSCE as a Model for the Third World? The Middle East and African Cases', in Michael R. Lucas (ed.), *The CSCE in the 1990s: The Helsinki Meeting and the Evolution of a Pan-European Order of Security and Cooperation*.

- Margret Johannsen, 'The "Helsinki-Coup": A Model for American Democratization Efforts in the Middle East?', *OSCE Yearbook*, 2004. www.osce.org
- Ray Takeyh, "'Beware of Iranians Bearing Talks', *Washington Post*, 27 September 2009.
- Mohamed Kadry Said, 'Potential Egyptian Contribution to a Security Framework in the Gulf', *Middle East Policy*, 11/3 (2004). See https://onlinelibrary.wiley.com/doi/10.1111/j.1061-1924.2004.00166.x, viewed 26 February 2022.
- Dmitry Medvedev speech in Berlin 5 June 2008, rather surprising in view of how badly the original went for the Soviet Union.

2 Organization for Security and Cooperation in Europe.
3 Andreas Wenger and Daniel Möckli, 'The Conference on Security and Cooperation in Europe as a Regional Model' in Mastny and Zhu Liqun, *The Legacy of the Cold War*, 222.
4 Wenger and Möckli, 224.
5 For instance, Powell, *Great Hatred, Little Room: Making Peace in Northern Ireland.*
6 The three strands were: relations within Northern Ireland, relations between Northern Ireland and the Republic of Ireland, and relations between Great Britain and the Republic of Ireland.
7 Conversation with the author, 9 November 2017.
8 Paragraph 69 of the Rules of Procedure.
9 Davy, in *The Washington Quarterly* 7/2, Spring 1984.
10 See English, *Russia and the Idea of the West.*
11 *Foreign Affairs* 66/4, Spring 1988.
12 Powell, *Talking to Terrorists.*
13 Nye, *Soft Power.*
14 UN Commission on Human Security, 2003, 'Human Security Now', UN, viewed 10 February 2022, https://reliefweb.int/sites/reliefweb.int/files/resources/91BAEEDBA50C6907C1256D19006A9353-chs-security-may03.pdf, listed at https://www.un.org/humansecurity/reports-resolutions/

Appendix A
A guide to the Helsinki Final Act

The Final Act is not a treaty. It is a very long political declaration signed by 35 states in Helsinki on 1 August 1975 after nearly three years of negotiation. Its full title is the Final Act of the Conference on Security and Co-operation in Europe (CSCE).[1]

It emerged from a series of Soviet proposals for a European security conference going back to 1954. The Soviet aim was to obtain multilateral endorsement of the political and territorial arrangements that followed World War II, including the new Polish frontier, the division of Germany, and Soviet control of Eastern Europe. The result fell far short of Soviet hopes and contained much that Moscow had tried to exclude, notably on human rights and freer movement of people and information. In no way was it a substitute peace treaty. Nor did it change the status of frontiers. Despite some compromises, it avoided endorsing the status quo and instead set an ambitious agenda for change in Europe.

The Final Act consists of four sections that came to be called Baskets as negotiators deposited their proposals under four headings. This convenient unofficial terminology has since entered general use and will be adopted here.

Basket I—Questions relating to security in Europe

This contains a preamble and ten "Principles Guiding Relations between Participating States" plus a section on military Confidence-Building Measures (CBMs).

The **Preamble** contains three important points:

1 Affirming the need to make détente "*a continuing process*", the signatories declare that implementation of the Final Act "*will be a major contribution to this process*". This makes it clear that détente is conditional, depending on continuing implementation of the Final Act, a point resisted by the Soviet Union, which had wanted the conference to endorse a more static view of European security in which détente had allegedly been achieved and was to be declared irreversible.

2 The Principles apply to "*relations with all other participating States, irrespective of their political, economic or social systems*".
This important point makes it clear that the Principles are not about East–West relations but apply equally to Soviet relations with the states of Eastern Europe that were then under its control. The Western aim in pushing for this phrase was to exclude the so-called "Brezhnev Doctrine" (see Appendix III), which had been invented by the Soviet leader to justify his invasion of Czechoslovakia in 1968 on the grounds that the defence of socialism took precedence over respect for sovereignty. The Final Act was thus trying to impose some inhibitions on the Soviet habit of invading its East European allies. It carefully excluded Soviet claims to special rights in Eastern Europe, making nonsense of accusations by some Western critics that it endorsed the Soviet sphere of influence or sanctified the political division of Europe.
3 All the Principles "*are of primary significance*".

This was to prevent any state trying to claim, for instance, that a state's right to determine its own laws (Principle I) should take precedence over its obligation to respect human rights (Principle VII). The point is repeated in Principle X below.

....

The Ten Principles. These are essentially a code of conduct applying to relations between all participating states.

I "*The participating States will respect each other's sovereign equality and individuality as well as all the rights inherent in and encompassed by its sovereignty… They will also respect each other's right freely to choose and develop its political, social, economic and cultural systems as well as its right to determine its laws and regulations*".

These rights are not absolute. Conditions and limitations are imposed in Principle X below.

States also have "*the right to belong or not to belong to international organizations, to be or not to be a party to bilateral or multilateral treaties including the right to be or not to be a party to treaties of alliance; they also have the right to neutrality*".

Note that these rights are held by states, not peoples. Since the member states of the Warsaw Pact were wholly under Soviet control at the time, these rights seemed theoretical but became relevant when the Soviet empire collapsed. The right to neutrality, however, was important from the start for neutral and non-aligned participants in the CSCE.

In the midst of this Principle is the important phrase: "*They consider that their frontiers can be changed, in accordance with international law, by peaceful means and by agreement*".

This was strongly resisted by East Germany, which wanted its frontier with West Germany to be declared immutable. After lengthy wrangles it had to give way under Soviet pressure because the West Germans would not sign the Final Act unless it kept open the door to the reunification of Germany. Eventually the phrase was pushed through by Dr Kissinger in bilateral negotiations with Moscow.

II "*The participating States will refrain in their mutual relations, as well as in their international relations in general, from the threat or use of force against the territorial integrity or political independence of any State*".

Here again, the Soviet Union is bound to respect the sovereignty of its allies, as it noticeably failed to do in Hungary in 1956 and Czechoslovakia in 1968.

III "*... regard as inviolable all one another's frontiers as well as the frontiers of all States in Europe and therefore they will refrain now and in the future from assaulting these frontiers*".

The clear sense of this Principle in English is that frontiers should not be physically assaulted. The Soviet Union tried, as in Principle I above, to introduce the principle of immutability by using the Russian word *nerushimost*, meaning indissolubility. It continued to claim that the Final Act had made frontiers permanent but the important commitment to peaceful change is clear enough in Principle I.

IV "*... will respect the territorial integrity of each of the participating States... [and] will likewise refrain from making each other's territory the object of military occupation... No such occupation or acquisition will be recognized as legal*".

This phrase was intended by the West to deter future Soviet invasions of its allies and, in particular, to deny recognition of the Soviet Union's incorporation of the pre-war Baltic States in 1939–40, a particularly important political issue in the United States, where there was a large diaspora from these states.

V "*... will settle disputes among them by peaceful means*".

The Swiss had proposed an elaborate system for peaceful settlement of disputes in Europe but failed to get sufficient support. They settled for a commitment in the final section of Basket I to pursue the subject later in a meeting of experts.

VI "*... will refrain from any intervention, direct or indirect, individual or collective, in the internal or external affairs falling within the domestic jurisdiction of another participating State... They will accordingly* *refrain from any form of armed intervention or threat of such intervention against another participating State… [and] from any other act of military or of political, economic or other coercion… [and] refrain from direct or indirect assistance to terrorist activities, or to subversive or other activities directed towards the violent overthrow of the regime of another participating State*".

This Principle gave rise to much argument. The wording in English clearly refers to physical intervention but the Soviets regularly (and wrongly) invoked it to claim that Western criticism of their violations of human rights constituted "interference" in their internal affairs. They revealed themselves as acutely afraid of Western influence within their empire, while they, of course, had no hesitation in trying to influence the internal affairs of Western countries by financing communist parties, trade unions, newspapers, demonstrations and propaganda. Double standards never bothered them.

VII "… *will respect human rights and fundamental freedoms, including the freedom of thought, conscience, religion or belief… They will promote and encourage the effective exercise of civil, political, economic, social, cultural and other rights and freedoms all of which derive from the inherent dignity of the human person and are essential for his (sic) free and full development*".

This remarkable text, resisted by the Soviet Union, required a record 56 negotiating sessions.[2] It provided a text that citizens in the Soviet bloc grasped eagerly to invoke against their governments. It is particularly important in stating that human rights are not just privileges granted by governments but inherent to the dignity of the human person.

"*The participating States recognise the universal significance of human rights and fundamental freedoms, respect for which is an essential factor for the peace, justice and well-being necessary to ensure the development of friendly relations and cooperation among themselves as among all States*".

This passage makes the essential link between respect for human rights and peace in Europe. It says, in effect, that there can be no lasting peace in Europe until the rights of its citizens are respected. To put it another way, any settlement in Europe requires the consent of its people, which was manifestly lacking in Eastern Europe at the time. This placed human rights on the diplomatic agenda and made them legitimate objects of Western interest, invalidating Soviet objections that criticism of another state's record on human rights constituted impermissible "interference".

"*They confirm the right of the individual to know and act upon his rights and duties in this field*".

Here is the licence for citizens under Soviet rule to demand information about their rights and then to assert them, which they did.

VIII *"... will respect the equal rights of peoples and their right to self-determination... All peoples always have the right, in full freedom, to determine, when and as they wish, their internal and external political status, without external interference".*

Unlike in Principle I, here the people have the right to self-determination. The Soviet Union objected that self-determination applied only in colonial situations, not under socialism. Other European states with restless minorities were also uneasy about this text but the West Germans were particularly anxious to establish the principle of self-determination for the future reunification of their country. This Principle was also invoked in later disputes over enlarging NATO.

IX *"... will develop their cooperation with one another and with all States in all fields in accordance with the purposes and principles of the Charter of the United Nations... They confirm that governments, institutions, organizations and persons have a relevant and positive role to play".*

Note the inclusion of "persons", resisted by the Soviet Union, which did not want individuals playing any role outside official bodies.

X *"In exercising their sovereign rights, including the right to determine their laws and regulations, they will conform with their legal obligations under international law; they will furthermore pay due regard to and implement the provisions in the Final Act of the Conference on Security and Cooperation in Europe".*

This puts conditions on the right of states, granted in Principle I, to determine their laws and regulations by stating that such laws and regulations must not violate international law or the provisions of the Final Act. Thus, for instance, laws should not deny human rights.

> *"The participating States, paying due regard to the principles above and, in particular, to the first sentence of the tenth principle,... note that the present Declaration does not affect their rights and obligations, nor the corresponding treaties and other agreements and arrangements".*

This somewhat obscure phrase, agreed with great difficulty, was designed to protect the Quadripartite Agreement of 3 September 1971 on Berlin, where the four wartime allies (the United States, the Soviet Union, Britain and France) retained occupation rights deriving from their victory in World War II. The problem had been to find a formula that would protect these rights without condoning the Brezhnev Doctrine of limited sovereignty (see above).[3]

Confidence-Building Measures (CBMs)

The main aim of the CBMs was to lower tension and reduce the danger of surprise attack by introducing elements of transparency.

Since several members of the CSCE were neutral or non-aligned, the Final Act could not deal with force levels in Europe, which were the subject of separate negotiations on Mutual and Balanced Force Reductions (MBFR) held in Vienna by the two military alliances, NATO and the Warsaw Pact. These opened in Vienna in 1973 but made almost no progress.

The United States was sceptical of CBMs but went along with the talks out of alliance solidarity. The Soviet Union struggled to protect its deep tradition of secrecy. It hoped to avoid any detailed commitments, merely suggesting generalities. In contrast, the neutrals and non-aligned, plus Romania and Spain, saw the CBMs as their opportunity to inject some military security into the CSCE.

The initial NATO position was that all members should give all other members 60 days' notice of any manoeuvres involving more than about 10,000 men. They should also include full details of the type and duration of the manoeuvres and the area involved. The Russians countered by proposing five days' notice of larger manoeuvres (30,000 to 50,000 men) within border zones. Complex negotiations followed involving the relevant areas, the size of forces and periods of notice.

Here are the main points of the final compromise:

> *Participating States… will notify their major military manoeuvres to all other participating States…* [when] *exceeding a total of 25,000 troops, independently or combined with any possible air or naval components… on the territory, in Europe, of any participating State as well as, if applicable, in the adjoining sea area and air space.*
>
> *In the case of a participating State whose territory extends beyond Europe,* [notably the Soviet Union, the United States and Canada] *prior notification need be given only of manoeuvres which take place in an area within 250 kilometres from its frontier facing or shared with any other European participating State.*
>
> *Participating States… may also notify smaller-scale military manoeuvres.* [Note that this is voluntary.]
>
> [They]… *will invite other participating States… to send observers to attend military manoeuvres.* [Obligatory.]
>
> [They]… *may, at their own discretion…, notify their major military movements.* [Voluntary.]

Note the difference between movements and manoeuvres.

Basket II—Cooperation in the field of economics, of science and technology and of the environment.

This basket was the longest but "the most meagre in terms of actual impact and substance". [4]

It should have been the easiest basket if only because both sides had a growing interest in economic relations and industrial cooperation—although there were disagreements within the Warsaw Pact on whether it was desirable to become too dependent on the West. Total East–West trade turnover had risen from $6 billion in 1960 to $44 billion by 1974.[5] The CSCE could do little to influence this trend, nor prevent its later decline.

These matters were dealt with largely in bilateral agreements between participating states, or by the European Community or the Economic Commission for Europe (ECE) in Geneva, which had almost the same membership as the CSCE and whose officials took part in the CSCE negotiations.

However, problems arose in trying to bridge the gulf between centrally planned economies and the free markets of the West. The East wanted to reduce tariff barriers and gain Most Favoured Nation status while the West saw the main obstacles to trade as deriving from state control of trade (which could impose tariff barriers whenever it chose) and the deeply ingrained habits of secrecy in the Warsaw Pact. This, combined with bureaucratic inertia or outright obstruction, made it difficult to obtain reliable statistics and commercial information and often prevented contacts with end users. Many obstacles also stood in the way of contacts between scientists despite strong pressure from East European scientists for more contacts with the West. Thus the commitments in Basket III (see below) to "*freer movement and contacts…* [and] *freer and wider dissemination of information*" were also relevant to Basket II.

Here are the main points in Basket II.

> *The participating States… will take measures further to improve conditions for the expansion of contacts between representatives of official bodies,… in particular… between sellers and users of products and services.*
>
> [They]… *will promote the publication and dissemination of economic and commercial information at regular intervals and as quickly as possible, in particular statistics concerning production, national income, budget, consumption and productivity* [and] *foreign trade statistics drawn up on the basis of comparable classification.*
>
> [They will]… *encourage the development of industrial cooperation…* [and] *improve the quality and the quantity of information relevant to industrial cooperation.*
>
> [Possibilities exist]… *to remove obstacles to such cooperation, in particular through the improvement of opportunities for the exchange and dissemination of scientific and technological information,*
>
> [and]… *to expand cooperation within… agriculture… energy… new technologies… transport technology… physics* [and many other areas including the environment and tourism].

Basket III—Cooperation in humanitarian and other fields

This was the most hotly contested section of the Final Act. Often referred to as the human rights basket, it does not mention human rights as such (those are in Principle VII of Basket I) but it sets out a long catalogue of practical measures that can be seen as implementing human rights by promoting, among other things, freer movement of people and information. The Soviet side made strenuous efforts to dilute it or remove it to a separate document or nullify it with impossible conditions, such as respect for the "laws and customs" of participating states, or confining information to the promotion of "peace". Western states, with support from neutrals and non-aligned, stood firm because it contained the only real gains they could expect from the Final Act in return for granting the Soviet Union limited and conditional endorsement of the post-war frontiers. It represented the Western view that détente meant nothing if it did not ease life for ordinary people. It also emphasised the essential point (already made in Basket I) that détente depended on progress in these areas, which were therefore a legitimate area of Western interest. As the Eastern bloc was well aware, the ultimate Western aim was to penetrate Eastern Europe and weaken Soviet control. Unsurprisingly, the Soviet Union gave in late and unwillingly only when faced with the failure of the conference.

Main points:

> *The participating States… make it their aim to facilitate freer movement and contacts, individually and collectively, whether privately or officially, among persons, institutions and organizations.*

The Soviet side wanted all contacts to be under official control so they were particularly unhappy with the mention of individual and private contacts.

> *… will favourably consider applications for travel with the purpose of allowing persons to enter or leave their territory temporarily, and on a regular basis if desired, in order to visit members of their families…* [They] *intend to facilitate wider travel by their citizens for personal or professional reasons,… to ease regulations…* [and] *to lower, where necessary, the fees for visas and official travel documents.*

Foreign travel was seen by the Eastern regimes as a privilege to be granted in return for good behaviour, so the power to issue or refuse travel documents was a jealously guarded aspect of state control. It was also among the most resented aspects of the system among ordinary people.

> *They… confirm that religious faiths, institutions and organizations, practising within the constitutional framework of the participating States, and their representatives can, in the field of their activities, have contacts and meetings among themselves and exchange information.*

A significant concession by the Eastern regimes—on paper, at least—after years obstructing contacts with Western churches.

> *Make it their aim to facilitate the freer and wider dissemination of information of all kinds.*

Strongly resisted by the Eastern bloc, particularly the reference to "all kinds" of information. Control over information was seen as vital to regime security. Note, by the way, that there is no mention of disseminating "ideas", which was on the original NATO agenda but was reluctantly dropped during the preparatory talks at Dipoli in the face of adamant resistance from regimes that nevertheless had no hesitation in promoting their own ideas in the West.

Basket IV—Follow-up to the conference

Initially, the Soviet Union had wanted the CSCE to give birth to a new security structure that would gain it a role in European affairs and exclude the United States. When it became clear that this was unobtainable, and that the Western powers would use follow-up meetings to monitor implementation of the Final Act, its enthusiasm cooled, though it eventually signed up for the meetings. These turned out to be very uncomfortable as the whole Soviet bloc was hauled over the coals for multiple violations of the Final Act.

> *The participating States… Declare their resolve, in the period following the Conference, to pay due regard to and implement the provisions of the Final Act… [and] to continue the multilateral process… by proceeding to a thorough exchange of views both on the implementation of the provisions of the Final Act and of the tasks defined by the Conference…, [and] by organizing to these ends meetings among their representatives…, The first of the meetings indicated above will be held at Belgrade in 1977.*

A very stormy meeting duly followed in Belgrade, with the American delegation under Arthur Goldberg taking the lead in raising human rights issues, instructed by the new American President, Jimmy Carter.

> *The text of this Final Act will be published in each participating State, which will disseminate it and make it known as widely as possible.*

A big mistake from the Soviet point of view. After hesitating and publishing distorted accounts, the Soviet bloc regimes did indeed publish the full text, provoking astonishment among their readers, who now saw just what their leaders had signed up to. The result was to give huge encouragement to human rights activists and provoke many ordinary people, especially in East Germany, to apply for exit visas. The texts found their way into many opposition documents and manifestos, particularly in Poland and Czechoslovakia.

Notes

1 For the full text in eight languages see https://www.osce.org/helsinki-final-act, viewed 23 February 2022.
2 Maresca, *To Helsinki*, 129.
3 Maresca, *To Helsinki*, 80–87.
4 Juhana Aunesluoma, 'Finlandisation in Reverse: the CSCE and the Rise and Fall of Economic Détente, 1968–1975' in Bange and Niedhart, *Helsinki 1975 and the Transformation of Europe*.
5 Aunesluoma, 'Finlandisation in Reverse'.

Appendix B
The Vienna concluding document, 1989

Key points from the Vienna Concluding Document, signed on 15 January 1989.

The document starts by reporting "intensive and controversial discussion" on implementation of the Final Act, which "had not been sufficiently realised". This confirms that there had been acrimonious clashes before the conclusions below were reached, partly reflecting the time it took Gorbachev to establish his authority. Romania explicitly rejected the conclusions.[1]

Questions relating to security in Europe

Principles

11. They [the participating States] *confirm that they will respect human rights and fundamental freedoms, including the freedom of thought, conscience, religion or belief.*

13.5 [They] will respect the right of their citizens to contribute actively, individually or in association with others, to the promotion and protection of human rights and fundamental freedoms.

13.8 [They will] ensure that no individual exercising, expressing the intention to exercise or seeking to exercise these rights and freedoms or any member of his family, will as a consequence be discriminated against in any manner.

This was intended to protect people pressing for implementation of the Final Act, many of whom had been persecuted.

13.9 [They will] ensure that effective remedies as well as full information about them are available to those who claim that their human rights and fundamental freedoms have been violated.

These remedies to include the right of appeal to a fair and public hearing, to present legal arguments and to be represented by legal counsel of one's choice.

14. The participating States recognize that the promotion of economic, social, cultural rights as well as of civil and political rights is of paramount importance for human dignity… They will therefore continue their efforts with a view to achieving progressively the full realization of economic, social and cultural rights.

This was a Western concession to the constant efforts by Eastern states to equate economic rights with political rights.

16.4[They will] ...respect the right of these religious communities to establish and maintain freely accessible places of worship or assembly, organize themselves according to their own hierarchical and institutional structure, select, appoint and replace their personnel..., solicit and receive voluntary financial and other contributions.

These and other rights of religious believers had been constantly violated in the past.

20. The participating States will respect fully the right of everyone to freedom of movement and residence within the borders of each State, and to leave any country, including his own, and to return to his country.

This was an astonishing departure from the tight control that communist states had maintained over foreign travel by their citizens, for whom it was a special privilege to be granted sparingly under strict conditions to those who showed sufficient loyalty to the regime. It was thus an important element of political control. Relinquishing that control (if carried out in practice) was therefore a major step. This basic right to travel is reinforced later in the Vienna document (see *Human Contacts 1*).

23. The participating States will ensure that no one will be subjected to arbitrary arrest, detention or exile,... [and] *that all individuals in detention or incarceration will be treated with humanity and with respect for the inherent dignity of the human person,... [will] prohibit torture,...* [and] *protect individuals from any psychiatric or other medical practices that violate human rights.*

An important attempt to establish the rule of law in countries where the law had been regarded as the servant of the ruling party. The last point was a response to the common Soviet practice of treating dissidents as psychiatric cases and subjecting them to cruel "treatments".

26. They confirm that governments, institutions, organizations and persons have a relevant and positive role to play in contributing to the achievement of the aims of their co-operation and to the full realization of the Final Act. To that end they will respect the right of persons to observe and promote the implementation of CSCE provisions and to associate with others for this purpose. They will facilitate direct contacts and communication among these persons, organizations and institutions within and between participating States and remove, where they exist, legal and administrative impediments inconsistent with the CSCE provisions. They will also take effective measures to facilitate access to information on the implementation of CSCE provisions and the free expression of views on these matters.

All this amounted to a fundamental departure from the basic principles of the Soviet and East European systems hitherto, which had denied any rights to civic organisations independent of state control. In addition, it gives specific support to individuals and non-governmental organisations monitoring implementation of the Final Act, a major concession in view of the harassment to which monitors had been subjected. Not surprisingly, the Eastern delegations resisted at first but in the end had to be content with merely removing a Western draft that endorsed the right to form and join independent organisations, leaving that right implicit in the reference to "association with others". This breakthrough came in July 1988, when independent organisations had already been sprouting in the Soviet Union and, from an earlier date, in Eastern Europe.

Confidence- and security-building measures and certain aspects of security and disarmament in Europe

The meeting welcomed the adoption at Stockholm of a set of mutually complementary Confidence- and Security-Building Measures (CSBMs).

Agreed that Negotiations [on CSBMs] will take place in order to build upon and expand the results already achieved at the Stockholm Conference... in Vienna, commencing in the week beginning on 6 March 1989.

Also agreed was that negotiations on Conventional Armed Forces in Europe [CFE] would start in Vienna in the same week, replacing MBFR, which had made little progress. These talks were important for both sides. Gorbachev's need for arms reductions was one of several factors that encouraged him to remain with the CSCE process. At the UN in December 1988 he had announced unilateral cuts of 500,000 men by 1991 plus reductions in equipment and tanks. The West was more cautious about reductions because its conventional forces were already inferior to those of the Warsaw Pact. It hoped for a better balance, however, and needed to ensure that the CFE was linked to progress on the human dimension in the CSCE.

Annex III: Chairman's statement on CFE—included here although it is actually placed after the main text.

The participants in this [CFE] negotiation shall be the 23 above-listed States [members of NATO and the Warsaw Pact].

The participants decided to take part in meetings of the States signatories of the Helsinki Final Act to be held at least twice during each round of the Negotiation [on CFE] in order to exchange views and substantive information concerning the course of the Negotiation.

This was primarily in deference to French insistence that the CFE talks should remain within the framework of the CSCE.

The objectives of the negotiation shall be to strengthen stability and security in Europe through the establishment of a stable and secure balance of conventional armed forces... at lower levels... and the elimination, as a matter of priority, of the capability for launching surprise attack and for initiating large-scale offensive action.

Here the Warsaw Pact states admit for the first time that there is a conventional imbalance in Europe that needs correcting.

The area of application shall be the entire land territory of the participants in Europe from the Atlantic to the Urals, which includes all the European island territories of the participants. In the case of the Soviet Union the area of application includes all the territory lying west of the Ural River and the Caspian Sea. In the case of Turkey the area of application includes the territory of Turkey north and west of the following fine: the point of intersection of the border with the 39th parallel, Muradiye, Patnos, Karayazi, Tekman, Kemaliye, Feke, Ceyhan, Dogankent, Gozne and thence to the sea.

As already noted, this represents a major change from the limited area covered by the MBFR talks.

Compliance... shall be verified through an effective and strict verification regime which, among other things, will include on-site inspections as a matter of right and exchanges of information.

The right to on-site inspections represented another major advance.

End of Annex III.

The provisions of the CFE mandate in the Vienna document "bear a striking resemblance to the draft proposal submitted by NATO in July 1987, but hardly reflect any of the elements of the original Warsaw Pact position of June 1987".[2]

....

Cooperation in the field of economics, of science and technology and of the environment

Trade and industrial cooperation

5. *The participating States recognize that, within their respective economies, increased autonomy for enterprises can help achieve a better response to market needs and thus contribute to the development of trade and co-operation among them.*

A somewhat cautious endorsement of reforms envisaged by Gorbachev and already being introduced slowly in Poland and Hungary, still accepting the basics of the socialist economies but pointing towards the free market endorsed at the Paris summit the following year.

This section also contains many other detailed provisions to facilitate freer trade and cooperation on science, transport, technology and protection of the environment.

6. *[They]... will further promote the publication and availability of comprehensive, comparable and timely economic and commercial information.*

Lack of reliable information (often withheld as "secret" or merely reflecting inefficiency) made life difficult for western businessmen as well as hindering economic development within the countries themselves.

7. *[They]... will examine... prospects for improved access to the services market.*

Co-operation in humanitarian and other fields

Human contacts

1. *Everyone shall be free to leave any country, including his own, and to return to his country.*

Reinforces **Principle 20** above.

5. [The participating States] *will decide upon applications relating to family meetings in accordance with the Final Act and the other aforementioned CSCE documents in as short a time as possible and in normal practice within one month.*

12. [The participating States] *will decide within three working days upon applications relating to visits to a seriously ill or dying family member.*

Another humanitarian concession, followed by more detailed provisions for easier travel.

Information

34. [The participating States] *will make further efforts to facilitate the freer and wider dissemination of information of all kinds* [as promised in the Final Act]*... They will ensure that radio services operating in accordance with the ITU Radio Regulations can be directly and normally received in their States.*

This was a highly significant undertaking to stop jamming Western radio stations. It was in fact honoured, thereby formally abandoning the socialist states' attempts to monopolise information. Their extreme sensitivity to broadcasts in local languages by Radio Free Europe, Radio Liberty, the BBC, Deutsche Welle and others was always a sign of their profound insecurity. They saw control over information as essential for political control. It never inhibited their own broadcasts in local languages to the West.

39. Recalling that the legitimate pursuit of journalists' professional activity will neither render them liable to expulsion nor otherwise penalise them, they [the participating States] *will refrain from taking restrictive measures such as withdrawing a journalist's accreditation or expelling him because of the content of the reporting of the journalist or of his information media.*

This was to counter the common habit of expelling Western journalists or denying them visas when their coverage displeased the authorities.

40. [The participating States] *will ensure that... journalists... are free to seek access to and maintain contacts with public and private sources of information.*

46. [The participating States] *agree to convene an Information Forum to discuss improvement of the circulation of, access to, and exchange of information... in London from 18 April to 12 May 1989.*

The human dimension of the CSCE

The participating States... have... decided... to exchange information and respond to requests for information and to representations made to them by other participating States on questions relating to the human dimension of the CSCE... [and] to hold bilateral meetings with other participating States that so request, in order to examine questions relating to the human dimension of the CSCE, including situations and specific cases, with a view to resolving them... Any participating State which deems it necessary may bring situations and cases in the human dimension of the CSCE... to the attention of other participating States through diplomatic channels.

The aim here was to establish procedures for continuous monitoring of implementation rather than relying on periodic follow-up meetings.

Finally, it was decided to hold the fourth main follow-up meeting in Helsinki commencing on 24 March 1992.

Notes

1 Lehne, *The Vienna Meeting of the Conference on Security and Cooperation in Europe, 1986–1989*, 131–2. Or https://www.osce.org/files/f/documents/a/7/40881.pdf

2 Lehne 141.

Appendix C
The Brezhnev doctrine

The Brezhnev Doctrine was invented by Leonid Brezhnev to justify his invasion of Czechoslovakia in August 1968. It became a landmark in East-West diplomacy because it asserted a Soviet claim to special rights in its East European empire, overriding national sovereignty and international law. It played a central role in the negotiation of the Final Act because the Western negotiators were determined to exclude it from the text in order to establish a code of conduct applying everyone, clearly rendering any future Soviet invasions of Eastern Europe illegitimate. The Soviet negotiators made many attempts to include the Brezhnev Doctrine in various forms but finally failed, ensuring that the ten Principles of behaviour in Basket I apply to relations between all participating states "irrespective of their political, economic or social systems…".

The task of justifying the invasion fell first to S. Kovalev (not to be confused with Anatoly Kovalev, who later led the Soviet delegation to the CSCE). In the party newspaper *Pravda* on 26 September, 1968, Kovalev published an article called "Sovereignty and the International Obligations of Socialist Countries".

Brezhnev then weighed in with a rambling speech to the Polish Workers' Party on 13 November in which he quite wrongly accused the Czechoslovak leadership of wanting to introduce capitalism and enable NATO forces to come to the border of the Soviet Union. The clumsy Soviet translation conveys the full flavour of his convoluted argument and its relevance to the Helsinki process:[1]

"The measures taken by the Soviet Union jointly with other socialist countries in defending the socialist gains of the Czechoslovak people are of great significance for strengthening the socialist community, which is the main achievement of the international working class. We cannot ignore the assertions, held in some places, that the actions of the five socialist countries [which took part in the invasion] run counter to the Marxist-Leninist principle of sovereignty and the rights of nations to self-determination. The groundlessness of such reasoning consists primarily in that it is based on an abstract, non-class approach to the question of sovereignty and the rights of nations to self-determination. The peoples of the socialist countries and

Communist parties certainly do have and should have freedom for determining the ways of advance of their respective countries. However, none of their decisions should damage either socialism in their country or the fundamental interests of other socialist countries, and the whole working class movement, which is working for socialism.

"This means that each Communist party is responsible not only to its own people, but also to all the socialist countries, to the entire Communist movement. Whoever forgets this, in stressing only the independence of the Communist party, becomes one-sided. He deviates from his international duty. Marxist dialectics are opposed to one-sidedness. They demand that each phenomenon be examined concretely, in general connection with other phenomena, with other processes. Just as, in Lenin's words, a man living in a society cannot be free from the society [in which he lives], one or another socialist state, staying in a system of other states composing the socialist community, cannot be free from the common interests of that community. The sovereignty of each socialist country cannot be opposed to the interests of the world of socialism, of the world revolutionary movement. Lenin demanded that all Communists fight against small-nation narrow-mindedness, seclusion and isolation, consider the whole and the general, subordinate the particular to the general interest.

"The socialist states respect the democratic norms of international law. They have proved this more than once in practice, by coming out resolutely against the attempts of imperialism to violate the sovereignty and independence of nations... However, from a Marxist point of view, the norms of law, including the norms of mutual relations of the socialist countries, cannot be interpreted narrowly, formally, and in isolation from the general context of class struggle in the modern world... Each Communist party is free to apply the basic principles of Marxism Leninism and of socialism in its country, but it cannot depart from these principles... Concretely, this means, first of all, that, in its activity, each Communist party cannot but take into account such a decisive fact of our time as the struggle between two opposing social systems—capitalism and socialism. This is an objective struggle, a fact not depending on the will of the people, and stipulated by the world's being split into two opposite social systems. Lenin said: "Each man must choose between joining our side or the other side. Any attempt to avoid taking sides in this issue must end in fiasco".

"It has got to be emphasized that when a socialist country seems to adopt a 'non-affiliated' stand, it retains its national independence, in effect, precisely because of the might of the socialist community, and above all the Soviet Union as a central force, which also includes the might of its armed forces. The weakening of any of the links in the world system of socialism directly affects all the socialist countries, which cannot look indifferently upon this. The anti-socialist elements in Czechoslovakia actually covered up the demand for so-called neutrality and Czechoslovakia's withdrawal from the socialist community with talking about the right of nations to self-determination.

However, the implementation of such 'self-determination', in other words, Czechoslovakia's detachment from the socialist community, would have come into conflict with its own vital interests and would have been detrimental to the other socialist states. Such 'self-determination', as a result of which NATO troops would have been able to come up to the Soviet border, while the community of European socialist countries would have been split, in effect encroaches upon the vital interests of the peoples of these countries and conflicts, as the very root of it, with the right of these people to socialist self-determination. Discharging their internationalist duty toward the fraternal peoples of Czechoslovakia and defending their own socialist gains, the USSR and the other socialist states had to act decisively and they did act against the antisocialist forces in Czechoslovakia".

Note

1 This text from *Pravda*, translated by Novosti, the Soviet press agency, is to be found in the Fordham University Internet Modern History Sourcebook: https://sourcebooks.fordham.edu/mod/1968brezhnev.asp

Bibliography

Albright, Madeleine. *Madam Secretary*. New York: Miramax Books, 2003.

Alexander, Michael. *Managing the Cold War: A View from the Front Line*. London: Royal United Services Institute for Defence and Security Studies, 2005.

Alexander, Michael. *British Diplomatic Oral History Programme*, interview 34. https://www.chu.cam.ac.uk/media/uploads/files/Alexander.pdf

Allison, Roy. 'Russia resurgent? Moscow's campaign to "coerce Georgia to peace"', in *International Affairs* 84/6, November 2008.

Andréani, Jacques. *Le Piège: Helsinki et la Chute du Communisme*. Paris: Odile Jacob, 2005.

Andréani also contributes to *CSCE Testimonies*.

Andrén, Nils; Birnbaum, Karl, eds. *Belgrade and Beyond: The CSCE Process in Perspective. East-West Perspectives 5*. Alphen aan den Rijn: Sijthoff and Noordhoff, 1980a.

Andrén, Nils; Birnbaum, Karl, eds. *Beyond Détente: Prospects for East-West Co-operation and Security in Europe. East-West Perspectives 3*. Leyden: A. W. Sijthoff, 1980b.

Applebaum, Anne. *Iron Curtain: The Crushing of Eastern Europe: 1944–1956*. London: Allen Lane, 2012.

Applebaum, Anne. *Red Famine: Stalin's War on Ukraine*. London: Allen Lane 2017.

Armstrong, David; Goldstein, Erik, eds. *Special Issue on The End of the Cold War. Diplomacy and Statecraft* 1, no. 3. London: Frank Cass, 1990.

Ash, Timothy Garton, see Garton Ash.

Aunesluoma, Juhana. 'Finlandisation in Reverse. The CSCE and the Rise and Fall of Economic Détente, 1968–1975' in Bange and Niedhart, *Helsinki 1975 and the Transformation of Europe*. New York and Oxford: Berghahn Books, 2008.

Badalassi, Nicolas; Snyder, Sarah B. eds. *CSCE and the End of the Cold War: Diplomacy, Societies and Human Rights, 1972–1990*. New York, Oxford: Berghahn Books, 2018.

Badalassi, Nicolas et al. *Reconstructing Europe 45 years after Yalta: The Charter of Paris (1990)*. Aubervilliers: CTHS, 2021.

Bange, Oliver; Niedhart, Gottfried, eds. *Helsinki 1975 and the Transformation of Europe*. New York and Oxford: Berghahn Books, 2008.

Baudet, Floribert. 'It was Cold War and we wanted to win', in *Origins of the European Security System: the Helsinki Process Revisited, 1965–75*, eds Andreas Wenger, Vojtech Mastny and Christian Nuenlist. London and New York: Routledge, 2008.

Belton, Catherine. *Putin's People: How the KGB Took Back Russia and then Took on the West*. London: William Collins, 2020.

Bialer, Seweryn. 'The Political System', in *After Brezhnev: Sources of Soviet Conduct in the 1980s*, ed. R. F. Byrnes. London: Pinter in association with the Center for Strategic and International Studies, Georgetown University, 1983.

Bobbitt, Philip. *The Shield of Achilles: War, Peace and the Course of History*. London: Penguin Books, 2002.

Bock, Siegfried. Interview with the author, Berlin, 11 June 2008.

Bozo, Frédéric; Rey, Marie-Pierre; Ludlow, N. Piers, Nuti, Leopoldo, eds. *Europe and the End of the Cold War: A Reappraisal*. Abingdon: Routledge, 2008.

Bozo, Frédéric. *Mitterrand, the End of the Cold War, and German Unification*. New York and Oxford: Berghahn Books, 2009.

Bozo, Frédéric; Rey, Marie-Pierre; Ludlow, N. Piers; Rother, Bernd, eds. *Visions of the End of the Cold War in Europe, 1945–1990*. New York and Oxford: Berghahn Books, 2012.

Braat, Eleni; Corduwener, Pepijn, eds. *1989 and the West: Western Europe since the end of the Cold War*. London: Routledge, 2019.

Braithwaite, Rodric. *Afgantsy, the Russians in Afghanistan 1979–89*. London: Profile Books, 2011.

Brandt, Willy. *My Life in Politics*. London: Penguin Books, 1993 (paperback).

British Diplomatic Oral History Programme. https://www.chu.cam.ac.uk/archives/collections/bdohp/

Brown, Archie. *The Gorbachev Factor*. Oxford: Oxford University Press, 1996.

Brown, Archie. *Seven Years that Changed the World*. Oxford: Oxford University Press, 2007.

Brown, Archie. *The Rise and Fall of Communism*. London: The Bodley Head, 2009.

Brown, Archie. *The Human Factor: Gorbachev, Reagan and Thatcher, and the end of the Cold War*. Oxford: Oxford University Press, 2020.

Brzezinski, Zbigniew. *The Grand Failure: The Birth and Death of Communism in the Twentieth Century*. New York: Collier Books, 1990.

Brzezinski, Zbigniew. 'Human rights in foreign policy', in *25 Years, From Solidarnosc to Freedom, International Conference Warsaw-Gdansk August 29–31, 2005*. Warsaw: The Solidarity Center Foundation, 2005.

Buckley, William F. 'Human rights and foreign policy: a Proposal', in *Foreign Affairs*, Spring, 1980.

Byrnes, Robert F. ed. *After Brezhnev: Sources of Soviet Conduct in the 1980s*. London: Pinter in association with the Center for Strategic and International Studies, Georgetown University, 1983.

Cambridge History of the Cold War, The, see Leffler, Melvyn P.

Ceska, Franz. Oral history conference on the historical experience of the neutral and non-aligned states in the CSCE. *Austrian Institute for International Affairs and the Parallel History Project on Cooperative Security*, Swiss Federal Institute of Technology. Vienna, 22–23 February 2007.

Chernyaev, Anatoly. Translated and edited by Robert English and Elizabeth Tucker. *My Six Years with Gorbachev*. Pennsylvania: Pennsylvania State University Press, 2000.

Cox, Michael, Kennedy-Pipe, Caroline. 'The Tragedy of American Diplomacy? Rethinking the Marshall Plan' in *Journal of Cold War Studies* 7/1, (Winter 2005).

Crump, Laurien. *The Warsaw Pact Reconsidered: Inquiries into the Evolution of an Underestimated Alliance: 1960–1969*. Abingdon: Routledge, 2015.

Crump, Laurien. 'A missed opportunity for a new Europe' in *1989 and the West: Western Europe since the end of the Cold War*, eds Eleni Braat and Pepijn Corduwener. London: Routledge, 2019.

CSCE Testimonies, see Nemcova, Alice.

Dahrendorf, Ralf. *Reflections on the Revolution in Europe*. London: Chatto and Windus, 1990.

Dassu, Marta. 'An Italian View' in Davy, *European Détente: a Reappraisal*.

Davy, Richard. 'The CSCE Summit', in *The World Today*, September 1975. London: The Royal Institute of International Affairs.

Davy, Richard. 'Helsinki Scoreboard' in *The World Today*, August 1976, 32/8. London: The Royal Institute of International Affairs.

Davy, Richard. 'The United States' in Nils Andrén and Karl E. Birnbaum eds, *Belgrade and Beyond: The CSCE Process in Perspective*. Alphen aan den Rijn, Netherlands: Sijthoff and Noordhoff, 1980.

Davy, Richard. 'Policies for Eastern Europe' in Robert E. Hunter, ed. *NATO, the Next Generation*. Boulder: Westview Press, for the CSIS, 1984a.

Davy, Richard. 'Eastern Europe: New Policies for Old' in *Washington Quarterly*, Spring 1984b.

Davy, Richard. 'Helsinki Myths: Setting the record straight on the Final Act of the CSCE, 1975', in *Cold War History* 9/1, (February 2009). Abingdon: Routledge, 2009.

Davy, Richard, ed. *European Détente: A Reappraisal*. London: Sage Publications for the Royal Institute of International Affairs, 1992. Reprint by Fast-Print Publishing, Peterborough, 2014.

DBPO – Documents on British Policy Overseas, Series III, Vol. II: The Conference on Security and Cooperation in Europe, 1972–75, eds G. Bennett and K. A. Hamilton. London: The Stationery Office, 1997.

DBPO – Documents on British Policy Overseas, Series III, Vol. III: Détente in Europe, 1972–76, eds G. Bennett and K. A. Hamilton. London: Frank Cass, 2001.

DBPO – Documents on British Policy Overseas Series III, Vol. IV: The Year of Europe: America, Europe and the Energy Crisis: 1972–1974, eds Keith Hamilton and Patrick Salmon. Abingdon: Routledge, 2006.

Djilas, Milovan. *Conversations with Stalin*. New York: Harcourt, Brace and World, Inc., 1962.

Dobbs, Michael, *Six Months in 1945: from World War to Cold War*. London: Hutchinson, 2012.

Dobrynin, Anatoly. *In Confidence: Moscow's Ambassador to America's Six Cold War Presidents* (1962–1986). New York: Times Books, 1995.

Ellsberg, Daniel. *The Doomsday Machine: Confessions of a Nuclear War Planner*. New York: Bloomsbury, 2017; London: 2018.

English, Robert D. *Russia and the Idea of the West: Gorbachev, Intellectuals, and the End of the Cold War*. New York: Columbia University Press, 2000.

Fawn, Rick. *International Organizations and Internal Conditionality: Making Norms Matter*. Basingstoke: Palgrave Macmillan, 2013.

Ferraris, Luigi Vittorio, ed. Translated by Marie-Claire Barber. *Report on a Negotiation: Helsinki-Geneva-Helsinki 1972–1975*. Alphen aan den Rijn: Sijthoff and Noordhoff, 1979.

Final Act of the Conference on Security and Cooperation in Europe. Available in eight languages at https://www.osce.org/helsinki-final-act

Fischer, Thomas. *Neutral Power in the CSCE: The N+N States and the Making of the Helsinki Accords 1975*. Baden-Baden: Nomos, 2009.

Ford, Gerald. *A Time to Heal*. New York: Berkley Books, 1980 (paperback).

Foreign Relations of the United States (FRUS). Individual volumes for 1969–1976 are listed at https://history.state.gov/historicaldocuments/nixon-ford, n.d.

Foreign Relations of the United States (FRUS), Volume XXXIX: European Security 1969–1976. Department of State, Washington DC: Government Printing Office, 2007. https://history.state.gov/historicaldocuments/frus1969-76v39

Gaddis, John Lewis. *We Now Know: Rethinking Cold War History*. Oxford: Oxford University Press, 1997.

Gaddis, John Lewis. *The Cold War*. London: Allen Lane, 2006.

Garthoff, Raymond L. *Détente and Confrontation: American–Soviet Relations from Nixon to Reagan*. Revised Edition. Washington D.C.: The Brookings Institution, 1994.

Garton Ash, Timothy, *The Uses of Adversity: Essays on the Fate of Central Europe*. Cambridge: Granta Books, 1989.

Garton Ash, Timothy, *In Europe's Name: Germany and the Divided Continent*. London: Jonathan Cape, 1993.

Garton Ash, Timothy. *The Magic Lantern: the Revolution of '89*. London: Atlantic, 2019 (paperback).

Garton Ash, Timothy. *The Polish Revolution: Solidarity*. New Haven and London: Yale University Press, 2002 (third edition). Also Granta Books 1991.

Gates, Robert M. *From the Shadows*. New York: Simon and Schuster, 1996.

Gati, Charles. *Failed Illusions: Moscow, Washington, Budapest and the 1956 Hungarian Revolt*. Stanford: Stanford University Press, 2006.

Goldberg, Dorothy K. *A Private View of a Public Life*. New York: Charterhouse, 1975.

Gorbachev, Mikhail. *Memoirs*. London: Doubleday, 1996.

Gorbachev, Mikhail; Mlynář, Zdeněk. *Conversations with Gorbachev on Perestroika, the Prague Spring and the Crossroads of Socialism*. New York and Chichester: Columbia University Press, 2002.

Grachev, Andrei S. *Final Days: The Inside Story of the Collapse of the Soviet Union*. Translated by Margo Milne. New York: Routledge, 1995.

Griffith, William, ed. *Central and Eastern Europe: The Opening Curtain?*. Boulder, Colorado: Westview Press, 1989.

Grimm, Kevin E. *America Enters the Cold War: the Road to Global Commitment 1945–1950*. New York and Abingdon: Routledge, 2018.

Grinevsky, Oleg A. *Tauwetter: Entspannung, Krisen Und Neue Eiszeit*. Berlin: Siedler, 1996.

Hakkarainen, Petri. 'From linkage to freer movement: the Federal Republic of Germany and the nexus between Western CSCE preparations and Deutschland-politik', in Wenger et al., *Origins of the European Security System: the Helsinki Process Revisited, 1965–75*. London and New York: Routledge, 2008.

Hakkarainen, Petri. *A State of Peace in Europe: West Germany and the CSCE, 1966–1975*. Oxford: Berghahn Books, 2011.

Hamilton, Daniel S.; Spohr, Kristina; *Open door: NATO and Euro-Atlantic security after the Cold War*. Washington, D.C.: Paul H. Nitze School of Advanced International Studies, Johns Hopkins University, 2019.

Hanhimäki, Jussi M., Westad, Odd Arne, eds. *The Cold War: A History in Documents and Eyewitness Accounts*. Oxford: Oxford University Press, 2003.

Harpprecht, Klaus. *Willy Brandt: Portrait and Self Portrait*. London: Abelard-Schuman, 1972.

Havel, Vaclav. *Disturbing the Peace*. London: Faber and Faber, 1990.

Hebel, Kai. 'Propaganda Tools and Idealistic Goals: Britain and the Cold War Politics of Human Rights in the CSCE, 1972–1973', in Mariager et al., *Human Rights during the Cold War*. London: Routledge, 2014.

Hebel, Kai. *Fathers of the Final Act: Britain, Détente and the CSCE, 1954–1975*. Abingdon: Routledge (forthcoming).

Heraclides, Alexis. *Helsinki-II and its aftermath*. London and New York: Pinter Publishers, 1993.

Hofmann, Arne, *The Emergence of Détente in Europe: Brandt, Kennedy and the formation of Ostpolitik*. Abingdon and New York: Routledge, 2007.

Hong, Ki-Joon. *The CSCE Security Regime Formation: An Asian Perspective*. Basingstoke: Macmillan, 1997.

Hunter, Robert E. *NATO, The next generation*. Boulder, Colorado: Westview Press in collaboration with the Centre for Strategic and International Studies, Washington DC., 1984. Also: Routledge 2019.

Ignatieff, Michael. *Isaiah Berlin, A Life*. London: Chatto and Windus, 1998.

Institute of Contemporary British History (ICBH), Oral History Programme. https://www.kcl.ac.uk/sspp/departments/politicaleconomy/research/british-politics-and-government/witness-seminars/witsemscomplete, and see Kandiah and Staerck.

International Institute for Strategic Studies. The Military Balance, 1988–1989, London, Eastern Press Ltd., 1988.

Johannsen, Margret. 'The "Helsinki-Coup": A Model for American Democratization Efforts in the Middle East?', *OSCE Yearbook*, 2004.

Judt, Tony. *Postwar*. London: William Heinemann, 2005.

Kampelman, Max. *Entering New Worlds: the Memoirs of a Private Man in Public Life*. New York: HarperCollins, 1991.

Kandiah, Michael D.; Staerck, Gillian, eds. 'The Helsinki Negotiations: The Accords and Their Impact', 19 February, 2002. London: Institute of Contemporary British History (ICBH), 2006. https://www.kcl.ac.uk/sspp/assets/icbh-witness/helsinki.pdf

Kashlev, Yuri. 'The CSCE in the Soviet Union's Politics' in *International Affairs* (Moscow), 11–12 (1995).

Khrushchev, Nikita S. *Memoirs of Nikita Khrushchev: Volume 3: Statesman, 1953–1964*. Pennsylvania State University Press, 2007.

Kieninger, Stephan. *Dynamic Détente: The United States and Europe, 1964–1975*. London: Lexington Books, 2016.

Kieninger, Stephan. *The Diplomacy of Détente: Cooperative Security Policies from Helmut Schmidt to George Shultz*. London and New York: Routledge, 2018.

Kissinger, Henry. *The White House Years*. London: Weidenfeld and Nicolson,1979.

Kissinger, Henry. *Years of Renewal*. London: Simon & Schuster, 2012.

Korey, William. *The Promises We Keep: human rights, the Helsinki process, and American foreign policy*. New York: St. Martin's Press in association with the Institute for East–West Studies, 1994.

Kovalev, Anatoly. *Azbuka diplomatii*, Mezhdunar Otnosheniia: Moscow, 1993.

Kramer, Mark; Makko, Aryo; Ruggenthaler, Peter, eds. *The Soviet Union and Cold War Neutrality and Nonalignment in Europe*. The Harvard Cold War Studies Book Series. Lexington: Lexington Books, 2021.

Kultura (Paris), June 1971. Translation in *Survey* (London), Summer 1971.

Leffler, Melvyn P. 'Bringing it together: the parts and the whole' in Westad, ed., *Reviewing the Cold War*, 46.

Leffler, Melvyn P. *For the Soul of Mankind: The United States, the Soviet Union and the Cold War*. New York: Hill and Wang, 2007.

Leffler, Melvyn P., Westad, Odd Arne, eds. *The Cambridge History of the Cold War*, Vols I–III. Cambridge: Cambridge University Press, 2010.

Legvold, Robert. *Return to the Cold War*. Cambridge, UK and Malden, MA: Polity Press, 2016.
Lehne, Stefan. *The Vienna Meeting of the Conference on Security and Cooperation in Europe, 1986–1989*. Boulder: Westview Press, 1991a.
Lehne, Stefan. *The CSCE in the 1990s: Common European House or Potemkin Village?*. Vienna: Braumüller, 1991b.
Lévesque, Jacques. *The Enigma of 1989: the USSR and the Liberation of Eastern Europe*. Berkeley, Los Angeles and London: University of California Press, 1997.
Ligachev, Yegor. *Inside Gorbachev's Kremlin*. New York: Pantheon, 1993.
Littell, Robert, ed. *The Czech Black Book*. London: Pall Mall Press, 1969.
Lucas, Michael R., ed. *The CSCE in the 1990s: The Helsinki Meeting and the Evolution of a Pan-European Order of Security and Cooperation*. Baden-Baden: Nomos, 1993.
Lundestad, Geir. 'Empire by Invitation? The United States and Western Europe, 1945–1952' in *Journal of Peace Research*, 23/3 (Sept. 1986), 263–277.
Macmillan, Margaret, *The War that Ended Peace*. London: Profile Books, 2013.
Mann, James. *The Rebellion of Ronald Reagan: a History of the End of the Cold War*. New York: Viking, 2009.
Marchetti, Andreas, ed. 'The CSCE as a Model to Transform Western Relations with the Greater Middle East', Discussion Paper C137, Zentrum für Europäische Integrationsforschung, Bonn, 2004.
Marer, Paul. 'Economies and trade of Eastern Europe' in Griffith ed., *Central and Eastern Europe: The Opening Curtain?*. Boulder Colorado: Westview Press, 1989.
Maresca, John J. *To Helsinki: The Conference on Security and Cooperation in Europe 1973–1975*. Durham and London: Duke University Press, 1987.
Maresca, John J. *Helsinki Revisited*. Stuttgart: ibidem-Verlag, 2016.
Mariager, Rasmus; Molin, Karl; Brathagen, Kjersti eds. *Human Rights during the Cold War*. London: Routledge, 2014.
Mastny, Vojtech. *Helsinki, Human Rights, and European Security: Analysis and Documentation*. Durham, N.C.: Duke University Press, 1986.
Mastny, Vojtech. *The Helsinki Process and the Reintegration of Europe, 1986–1991: analysis and documentation*. New York: New York University Press (Institute for East–West Security Studies), 1992.
Mastny, Vojtech, *The Cold War and Soviet Insecurity: The Stalin Years*. Oxford: Oxford University Press, 1996.
Mastny, Vojtech, *The Warsaw Pact: An Inside History 1955–1991*. CSS Studies in Security and International Relations, 2008.
Mastny, Vojtech; Byrne, Malcolm. *A Cardboard Castle? An Inside History of the Warsaw Pact 1955–1991*. Budapest: Central European University Press, 2005.
Mastny, Vojtech; Zhu Liqun, eds. *The Legacy of the Cold War: Perspectives on Security, Cooperation, and Conflict*. Lanham: Lexington Books, 2014.
Matlock, Jack F. Jr. *Autopsy on an Empire*. New York: Random House, 1995.
Matlock, Jack F., Jr. *Reagan and Gorbachev: How the Cold War Ended*. New York: Random House, 2004.
Mearsheimer, John J. 'Why the Ukraine Crisis Is the West's Fault' in *Foreign Affairs* September/October 2014.
Milward, Alan S. *The Reconstruction of Western Europe 1945–1951*. London: Methuen, 1984.
Möckli, Daniel. 'The EC Nine, the CSCE, and the changing pattern of European security', in Wenger, et al., *Origins of the European Security System: The Helsinki Process Revisited 1965–75*. Abingdon and New York: Routledge, 2008.

Möckli, Daniel. *European Foreign Policy during the Cold War: Heath, Brandt, Pompidou and the Dream of Political Unity*. London and New York: I.B. Tauris, 2009.

Morgan, Michael Cotey. *The Final Act: the Helsinki Accords and the Transformation of the Cold War*. Princeton: Princeton University Press, 2018.

Naimark, Norman M. *The Russians in Germany: a History of the Soviet Zone of Occupation 1945–1949*. Cambridge MA: Harvard University Press, 1995.

Nemcova, Alice. *CSCE Testimonies: Causes and Consequences of the Helsinki Final Act 1972–1989*. Prague: OSCE Secretariat, 2013.

Nye, Joseph S. Jr. *Soft Power: The Means to Success in World Politics*. New York: Public Affairs, 2004.

Ouimet, Matthew J. *The Rise and Fall of the Brezhnev Doctrine in Soviet Foreign Policy*. Chapel Hill and London: The University of North Carolina Press, 2003.

Oxley, Andrew; Pravda, Alex; Ritchie, Andrew, eds. *Czechoslovakia, the Party and the People*. London: Allen Lane The Penguin Press, 1973.

Pelikán, Jiří, ed. *The Secret Vysočany Congress; proceedings and documents of the Extraordinary Fourteenth Congress of the Communist Party of Czechoslovakia, 22 August 1968*; translated by George Theiner and Deryck Viney. London: Allen Lane, The Penguin Press, 1971.

Pipes, Richard. *Soviet Strategy in Europe*. London: Macdonald and Jane's for the Stanford Research Institute, 1976.

Portes, Richard. 'Debt and the Banks: East Europe's Debt to the West: Interdependence is a Two-Way Street', in *Foreign Affairs* 22/4 (July 1977).

Powell, Jonathan. *Great Hatred, Little Room: Making Peace in Northern Ireland*. London: The Bodley Head, 2009.

Powell, Jonathan. *Talking to Terrorists*. London: Vintage 2014.

Puddington, Arch. *Broadcasting Freedom: The Cold War Triumph of Radio Free Europe and Radio Liberty*. Kentucky: University Press of Kentucky, 2000.

Rey, Marie-Pierre. 'The USSR and the Helsinki Process, 1969–75: Optimism, Doubt, or Defiance?' in Wenger et al.. *Origins of the European Security System: The Helsinki process revisited, 1965–75*. Abingdon: Routledge 2008.

Roberts, Adam with Philip Windsor. *Czechoslovakia 1968: Reform, Repression and Resistance*. London: Chatto & Windus for Institute for Strategic Studies, London, 1969.

Roberts, Geoffrey. *Stalin's Wars: from World War to Cold War, 1939–1953*. New Haven, London: Yale University Press, 2006.

Roberts, Geoffrey. *Molotov: Stalin's Cold Warrior*. Washington, D.C.: Potomac Books, 2011.

Romano, Angela. *From Détente in Europe to European Détente: How the West Shaped the Helsinki CSCE*. Brussels: Peter Lang, 2009.

Rostagni, Carla Meneguzzi, ed. *The Helsinki Process: A Historical Reappraisal: Proceedings of the workshop held in Padua, June 7, 2004*. Padova: CEDAM, 2005.

Ruggenthaler, Peter. 'The 1952 Stalin Note on German Unification: The Ongoing Debate' in *Journal of Cold War Studies*, 13/4 (2011).

Rupnik, Jacques. *The Other Europe*. London: Weidenfeld and Nicolson, 1988.

Russell, Harold S. 'The Helsinki Declaration: Brobdingnag or Lilliput?', in *American Journal of International Law*, 70, no. 3 (1976).

Said, Mohamed Kadry. 'Potential Egyptian Contribution to a Security Framework in the Gulf', in *Middle East Policy*, 11/3 (2004).

Sakwa, Richard. *The Putin Paradox*. London, New York: I.B. Tauris, 2020.

Sarotte, Mary Elise. *1989: The Struggle to Create Post-Cold War Europe*. Princeton Studies in International History and Politics. Princeton: Princeton University Press, 2009.

Sarotte, Mary Elise. *Not one Inch: America, Russia, and the Making of Post-Cold War Stalemate*. New Haven: Yale University Press, 2022.

Savranskaya, Svetlana. 'Unintended consequences: Soviet interests, expectations and reactions to the Helsinki Final Act', in *Helsinki 1975 and the Transformation of Europe*, Oliver Bange and Gottfried Niedhart eds. Oxford and New York: Berghahn Books, 2008.

Schaefer, Bernd. 'Europe must not become Greater Finland' in Wenger et al., *Origins of the European Security System*. Abingdon: Routledge 2008.

Schimmelfennig, Frank. 'The CSCE as a Model for the Third World? The Middle East and African Cases', in Michael R. Lucas (ed.), *The CSCE in the 1990s: The Helsinki Meeting and the Evolution of a Pan-European Order of Security and Cooperation*. Baden-Baden: Nomos, 1993.

Selvage, Douglas. 'The Warsaw Pact and Nuclear Nonproliferation, 1963–1965'. Cold War International History Project, 2001. At https://www.wilsoncenter.org/publication/the-warsaw-pact-and-nuclear-nonproliferation-1963-1965

Selvage, Douglas. 'The Warsaw Pact and the European security conference, 1964–69: Sovereignty, hegemony, and the German question', in Wenger et al., *Origins of the European Security System*. Abingdon: Routledge 2008.

Service, Robert. *Comrades: Communism, a World History*. London and Basingstoke: Macmillan, 2007.

Service, Robert. *Stalin, a Biography*. London and Basingstoke: Macmillan, 2004, and Pan Books, 2010 (paperback).

Service, Robert, *The End of the Cold War: 1985–1991*. London: Macmillan, 2015.

Shawcross, William, *Dubček and Czechoslovakia 1918–1990*. London: The Hogarth Press, 1990 (paperback).

Sherer, Albert W Jr. 'Goldberg Variations', in *Foreign Policy*, 39, Summer 1980.

Shevardnadze, Edvard. *The Future Belongs to Freedom*, translated by Catherine A. Fitzpatrick. New York: The Free Press, 1991.

Skilling, Gordon. *Czechoslovakia's Interrupted Revolution*. Princeton: Princeton UP, 1976.

Smith, Richard, ed. *Preparing for Helsinki: The CSCE Multilateral Preparatory Talks* (Documents from the British Archives No.2). London: Foreign and Commonwealth Office, ed. 2, 2020.

Snyder, Sarah, *Human Rights Activism and the end of the Cold War*. Cambridge: Cambridge University Press, 2011.

Snyder, Timothy. *The Road to Unfreedom*. London: Vintage, 2019.

Spohr, Kristina, *Post Wall Post Square: Rebuilding the World after 1989*. London: William Collins, 2019.

Steglich, Peter; Leuschner, Günther. *KSZE: Fossil oder Hoffnung?* Berlin: Edition Ost, 1996.

Steil, Benn, *The Marshall Plan: Dawn of the Cold War*. New York: Simon and Schuster, 2018.

Suri, Jeremi. 'Henry Kissinger and the Reconceptualization of European Security, 1969–75' in Wenger et al., *Origins of the European Security System*. Abingdon and New York: Routledge, 2008.

Takeyh, Ray. 'Beware of Iranians Bearing Talks', *Washington Post*, 27 September 2009.

Taubman, William. *Khrushchev*. London: Simon and Schuster, 2005.
Thomas, Daniel C. *The Helsinki Effect: International Norms, Human Rights, and the Demise of Communism*. Princeton and Oxford: Princeton University Press, 2001.
Tigrid, Pavel, *Why Dubcek Fell*. Translated from French. London: Macdonald and Co., 1971.
Urban, G. R., ed. *Détente*. London: Maurice Temple Smith Ltd, 1976.
Walker, Martin. *The Cold War*. London: Vintage, 1994.
Wenger, Andreas, Mastny, Vojtech, Nuenlist, Christian, eds. *Origins of the European Security System. The Helsinki process revisited, 1965–75*. Abingdon and New York: Routledge 2008. Also available at https://epdf.pub/origins-of-the-european-security-system-the-helsinki-process-revisited-1965-75-c.html
Wenger, Andreas; Möckli, Daniel. 'The Conference on Security and Cooperation in Europe as a Regional Model' in Mastny and Zhu Liqun, *The Legacy of the Cold War*. Lanham: Lexington Books, 2014.
Westad, Odd Arne, ed. *Reviewing the Cold War: Approaches, Interpretations, Theory*. London and New York: Frank Cass, 2000.
Williams, Kieran, *The Prague Spring and its aftermath: Czechoslovak politics 1968–1970*. Cambridge: Cambridge University Press, 1997.
Williams, Philip, 'Britain, Détente and the Conference on Security and Cooperation in Europe', in Kenneth H. F. Dyson, *European Détente: Case Studies of the Politics of East-West Relations*. London: Frances Pinter, 1986.
Windsor, Philip; Roberts, Adam. *Czechoslovakia 1968: Reform, Repression and Resistance*. London: Chatto and Windus for the Institute of Strategic Studies, 1969.
Wolf, Markus. *Man Without a Face*. New York: Public Affairs, 2007.
Zelikow, Philip; Rice, Condoleezza, *To Build a Better World*. New York and Boston: Twelve, 2019.
Zubok, Vladislav; Pleshakov, Constantine. *Inside the Kremlin's Cold War: from Stalin to Khrushchev*. Cambridge: Harvard University Press, 1996.
Zubok, Vladislav, *A Failed Empire: The Soviet Union in the Cold War from Stalin to Gorbachev*. Chapel Hill: University of North Carolina Press, 2007.
Zubok, Vladislav. *Collapse: The Fall of the Soviet Union*. London: Yale University Press, 2021.

Index

Pages followed by n refer notes.

For Product Safety Concerns and Information please contact our EU representative GPSR@taylorandfrancis.com Taylor & Francis Verlag GmbH, Kaufingerstraße 24, 80331 München, Germany